14.56

ZP 3/94

Thinking, Feeling, and Being

The New Library of Psychoanalysis is published in association with the Institute of Psycho-Analysis. The New Library has been launched to facilitate a greater and more widespread appreciation of what psychoanalysis is really about and to provide a forum for increasing mutual understanding between psychoanalysts and those working in other disciplines such as history, linguistics, literature, medicine, philosophy, psychology, and the social sciences. It is planned to publish a limited number of books each year in an accessible form and to select those contributions which deepen and develop psychoanalytic thinking and technique, contribute to psychoanalysis from outside, or contribute to other disciplines from a psychoanalytical perspective.

The Institute, together with the British Psycho-Analytical Society, runs a low-fee psychoanalytic clinic, organizes lectures and scientific events concerned with psychoanalysis, publishes the *International Journal of Psycho-Analysis* and the *International Review of Psycho-Analysis* and runs the only training course in the UK in psychoanalysis leading to membership of the International Psychoanalytical Association – the body which preserves internationally agreed standards of training, of professional entry, and of professional ethics and practice for psychoanalysis as initiated and developed by Sigmund Freud. Distinguished members of the Institute have included Wilfred Bion, Anna Freud, Ernest Jones, Melanie Klein, John Rickman, and Donald Winnicott.

The New Library is under the general editorship of David Tuckett; Eglé Laufer and Ronald Britton are associate editors.

IN THE SAME SERIES

NEW LIBRARY OF PSYCHOANALYSIS

5

General editor: David Tuckett

Thinking, Feeling, and Being

CLINICAL REFLECTIONS ON THE FUNDAMENTAL ANTINOMY OF HUMAN BEINGS AND WORLD

IGNACIO MATTE-BLANCO

A TAVISTOCK PROFESSIONAL BOOK

ROUTLEDGE · LONDON AND NEW YORK

First published in 1988 by
Routledge
a division of Routledge, Chapman and Hall
11 New Fetter Lane, London EC4P 4EE

Published in the USA by
Routledge
a division of Routledge, Chapman and Hall, Inc.
29 West 35th Street, New York, NY 10001

Set by Hope Services, Abingdon
Printed in Great Britain by Richard Clay
(The Chaucer Press) Ltd
Bungay, Suffolk

British Library Cataloguing in Publication Data
Matte-Blanco, Ignacio
Thinking, feeling, and being: clinical
reflections on the fundamental antinomy
of human beings and world.——(New library
of psychoanalysis).
1. Thought and thinking
I. Title II. Series
153.4'2 BF455
ISBN 0–415–00677–5
ISBN 0–415–00678–3 Pbk

Library of Congress Cataloging in Publication Data
Matte-Blanco, Ignacio.
Thinking, feeling, and being : clinical reflections on the
fundamental antinomy of human beings and world /
Ignacio Matte-Blanco.
p. cm. — (New library of psychoanalysis : 5)
Bibliography: p.
Includes indexes.
ISBN 0–415–00677–5
ISBN 0–415–00678–3 (pbk.)
1. Subconsciousness. 2. Freud, Sigmund, 1856–1939. 3. Logic,
Symbolic and mathematical. 4. Psychoanalysis. I. Title. II. Series.
BF315.M34 1988 154 — dc19 87–33517

This book is lovingly dedicated to my family: from my past, my father, Enrique, my mother, Trinidad, and my seven brothers and sisters; my present and their future: Luciana, my wife, my seven sons and daughters, and their beloved ones.

Contents

Contents

Contents

Acknowledgements

I am deeply grateful to Eric Rayner and David Tuckett for their unbounded generosity towards me, shown in numerous ways, and for writing an introductory chapter to this book to which they devoted much of their valuable time carefully revising its text and making it more acceptable to the English reader.

I thank Luciana, my wife, for her permission to include her paper on projective identification in this book. This paper has been very stimulating and has enabled me to base many of my comments about Melanie Klein on the quotations from her contained in it.

I.M.B.

PART ONE

The subject

An introduction to Matte-Blanco's reformulation of the Freudian unconscious and his conceptualization of the internal world
by Eric Rayner and David Tuckett

1 The Freudian unconscious

Over the past thirty years Ignacio Matte-Blanco has been developing a fundamentally new way of conceiving conscious and unconscious processes which we believe is of enormous importance to the practising psychoanalyst and to the more academic scholar of the mind and its processes. However, the particular discipline of his arguments may be strange to the psychoanalyst, just as his psychoanalysis may be new to the more academically minded. He works with one arm, as it were, in psychoanalysis and the other in the concepts of basic mathematical logic and he is definitely not an easy read. In helping him to prepare his manuscript for publication we had the opportunity to read this book in draft and to talk to him a good deal. So in this chapter we are aiming not to give a critical survey but to help the reader unfamiliar with his thinking to appreciate his more central and elementary ideas. Most of these were addressed by Matte-Blanco in his first volume in English, *The Unconscious as Infinite Sets* (1975a). Other concepts appear for the first time in English later in this book. Our brief notes are of course no substitute for a grasp of these works.[1]

Matte-Blanco's starting point is the way Freud conceived unconscious thought. That Freud's conception of the unconscious was a momentous step is widely accepted, at least among those who value the study of humanity's subjective world. But Matte-Blanco believes that both psychoanalysts and those interested in applying psychoanalysis to other aspects of thought have never truly and fully made use of its revolutionary impact. His main purpose has been to show, by reformulating some of Freud's ideas about unconscious processes by the use of quite simple mathematical logic, just how revolutionary and valuable psychoanalytic insights are.

The idea of an unconscious side to human life was not, of course, unique to Freud.[2] Freud's special contribution was to formulate how unconscious thinking worked and also to draw attention to the implications that it operated with a systematic structure of its own. He argued, for example, that 'The governing rules of logic carry no weight in the unconscious; it might be called the Realm of the Illogical' (SE 23: 168-9) and that 'We have found that processes in the unconscious or in the Id obey different laws from those in the preconscious ego. We name these laws in their totality the primary process, in contrast to the secondary process which governs the course of events in the preconscious in the ego' (1940 [1938a], SE 23: 164).

Freud clearly drew attention to the importance he attached to his recognition of the different logic of the unconscious. He formulated this in detail in *The Interpretation of Dreams*. Of this work he wrote that it 'contains, even according to my present-day judgement, the most valuable of all the discoveries it has been my good fortune to make. Insight such as this falls to one's lot but once in a lifetime' (SE 4: xxxii). Here, it is most likely that he was referring to his ideas about the logical characteristics of the unconscious as they emerged from his formulation of the language of the dream thoughts. He wrote that

'The dream-thoughts and the dream-content are presented to us like two versions of the same subject-matter in two different languages. Or, more properly, the dream-content seems like a transcript of the dream-thoughts into another mode of expression, whose characters and syntactic laws it is our business to discover by comparing the original and the translation. The dream-thoughts are immediately comprehensible, as soon as we have learnt them. The dream-content, on the other hand, is expressed as it were in a pictographic script, the characters of which have to be transposed individually into the language of the dream-thoughts.' (SE 4: 277)

The unconscious domain, which Freud formulated, is accessible through the world of our dreams and of childhood thinking. It is a world in which the ordinary concepts of cause and effect, time, and space, to mention but a few of its characteristics, are turned on their head. In our dreams, when being highly emotional, or as children, we think what is unthinkable or nonsensical in other waking or conscious life. Inconvenient as it may be, the relationship between the events and experiences of psychic reality and the material world is not that of ordinary science and logic. It is here that psychoanalysis makes a unique contribution to human understanding.

In Matte-Blanco's view neither psychoanalysts nor others that use it have really pursued Freud's fundamental discovery about the unconscious and its logic. Instead, attention has been directed too exclusively to debating or modifying Freud's 'strange' ideas about sexuality, the death instinct, or similar subjects. Or it has gone into formulating psychoanalysis in ways which tame the revolutionary characteristics of the Freudian unconscious. Many analysts have not taken seriously enough the idea that the mind works within a framework of timelessness and spacelessness. Nor have they investigated the fundamental properties which permit the processes of condensation, displacement, projection, introjection, and so on. As a result, they have not understood what the consequences of these must be for thinking processes. Analysts have tended not to consider the matter or have moved their discipline towards conventional psychology and conventional logic.

Although the logic of the unconscious is used intuitively in daily clinical work, we do not often stop to consider the fundamental and disturbing implications of the concepts employed. Timelessness, for instance, is implied in clinical work when the co-presence of adulthood and infancy in the same person is taken for granted. But the wider implications of such an idea, as to what it might mean for a patient's thought processes in general, for instance, are not pursued.

Matte-Blanco feels that theoreticians have often moved psycho-analysis away from the unconscious. For example, the American psychoanalyst H. Hartmann did much to gain psychoanalysis a more respectable place in scientific psychology. But Freud's revolutionary discoveries about the nature of the unconscious played no real part in Hartmann's systematization of psychoanalysis as a science. He argues much the same about a recent attempt to systematize the theories of Melanie Klein. De Bianchedi *et al.* (1984), for example, discuss Klein's work in terms of positional, economic, spatial, and dramatic points of reference but in doing so seem to lose the impact of what she was saying. In their formulation Klein's work becomes too tidy, ever so rational – the same effect, some feel, Hartmann had on Freud. Matte-Blanco could find only one sentence in which the irrational Freudian unconscious is implied, and even there rather timidly and ambiguously. In it the authors say: 'Both the ego and its objects can be alternately or simultaneously spectators or protagonists of the drama' (De Bianchedi *et al.* 1984: 396). He points out that if instead of writing 'or' they had put 'and' things would have been different. They would have been doing justice to the idea of the coexistence of incompatibles in the unconscious. In other ways the authors' ideas are serious and valuable, but their use of 'or' renders ordinary something which is extraordinary to conscious thought. It is in subtle ways like this that psychoanalysis loses the Freudian unconscious. In some ways it thus loses an essence of psychoanalysis itself.

Klein never says so explicitly but only a brief acquaintance with *The Psycho-Analysis of Children* (1932) makes one aware that the ideas in her book are inconceivable without Freud's conception of the unconscious. Almost every page is filled with observations about children and their thought processes which are a living testimony to this. The thoughts of the children observed by Melanie Klein are replete with the logic of the unconscious and cannot be understood without it. Matte-Blanco suggests that although she did not pay that much attention to the abstract formulation of her theories she was the most creative and original of all those who have drawn inspiration from Freud. Her famous concept of projective identification, for example, which he deals with later in this book, is inconceivable without the framework of Freud's characteristics of the unconscious.

The rationalizing process is encountered very frequently in psychoanalytical literature. It is as apparent in the 'object-relations school' as in the more traditional classical metapsychology. For these reasons Matte-Blanco believes he has been right to say that 'psychoanalysis has wandered away from itself' (Matte-Blanco 1975a: 10). He remembers that there is a story of a man who entered a bar and began to walk up the vertical wall, arriving at the ceiling. He walked along it, head down, then went down the opposite wall. He sat down and asked for a whisky mixed with beer. People were astonished. When he finished drinking, he paid, and repeated the same journey in the opposite direction. When he closed the door somebody observed: 'What a strange man: to drink whisky mixed with beer!' Matte-Blanco feels that his purpose is to try to recover the essentials of Freud's contribution.

Two-valued or bivalent logic

To show just how revolutionary and important Freud's formulation of the unconscious was, Matte-Blanco has examined some very obvious everyday propositions of the kind that are fundamental to ordinary, contemporary, logical, and scientific thought. He does this in order to demonstrate the existence of some hidden assumptions in ordinary thought which are often ignored.

He takes a physical proposition, Archimedes' Principle, as an example. This principle, which led him to cry out his famous 'Eureka', states that 'a body immersed in a liquid loses as much of its weight as the weight of the liquid which it has displaced' (Nelkon 1981: 106). What concepts and processes are employed in order to state this principle? Archimedes certainly had to draw on those of solid body, liquid, immersion, weight, volume, and difference of weight. He then established the various very definite relations between these concepts. It would take too long a time here to isolate and describe in a precise way all the concepts implied in the principle. For our purposes you need only reflect about a few of them and verify that the following underlying concepts are all, among others, essential to the principle:

(a) *the principle of identity* — A is identical to A;
(b) *the concept of two-valued or bivalent logic* – either A or not A (either proposition A is true or it is not true);
(c) *the principle of formal contradiction* – two contradictory assertions cannot both be true at the same time;
(d) *the principle of incompatibility* – A cannot be different from and totally equal to B; for example, A cannot be liquid and solid at the same time and under the same conditions;
(e) *the operation of subtraction* – if a part is subtracted from a given, positive quantity, the result is a smaller quantity.

These are selected because they will be referred to, one way or another, later. Research findings in the natural sciences normally respect these and other related rules. Put briefly, scientific knowledge is expressed in language submitting to the laws of bivalent or two-valued logic.

Likewise, psychoanalytical research and formulation have also developed largely in conformity with two-valued logic. Thus Freud's writing and argument are quite clearly structured with respect for the principles and rules of bivalent logic. This is emphasized by the construction of such a work as his *Introductory Lectures* (1916–17). In his editorial introduction to this work, Strachey (SE 15: 6) makes the following comments about all of Freud's lectures: 'they almost always had a definite form – a head, body and tail – and might often give the hearer the impression of possessing an aesthetic unity'. Each subject Freud tackles in the lectures is organized in a systematic way. Concepts such as trauma, resistance, repression, development of the libido, regression, formation of symptoms, and transference are all formulated with full respect to the laws of this bivalent logic. These laws furnish the framework where the concepts develop, and without them no understanding of the concepts is possible.

However, it is not only the structure of Freud's argument which respects bivalent logic. The concepts themselves are permeated by the same approach. Take, for instance, the concept of repression. This entails an opposition, in the mind, between two incompatibles: a tendency to satisfy a wish and a psychical organization which tends to block the realization of this satisfaction. In the case of a trauma the struggle again would be between two incompatibles: between the tendency to remember the traumatic event, face it, and bring it to full light, and a tendency to keep the peace by preventing access to consciousness. This is described and formulated by Freud in terms of two-valued logic.

Matte-Blanco is thus stressing that psychoanalysis, like philosophy and the natural sciences, has been conceived and developed in the territory where respect for the principles and rules of bivalent logic is essential. But at the same time psychoanalysis can usefully be conceived as a unique undertaking. As we have mentioned, it sets out to study the special characteristics of unconscious ideas, and in doing so makes a radically new addition to scientific and logical thinking. To unfold his argument, Matte-Blanco starts by considering Freud's ideas about the characteristics of the unconscious to draw out their radical nature. We will now turn to this.

The characteristics of the unconscious

Let us begin by listing the unconscious processes Freud identified when trying to understand the language of the unconscious. In his paper 'The Unconscious' (SE 14) he sums up what he considers to be its nature in five characteristics. In *The Interpretation of Dreams* Matte-Blanco has found eight others. A more thorough survey of Freud's writings and those of other psychoanalysts might reveal still more. However, the thirteen characteristics of unconscious functioning that have been found in this way are as follows.

In 'The Unconscious':
  (1) The absence of mutual contradiction and negation (SE 14: 186).
  (2) Displacement (SE 14: 186).
  (3) Condensation (SE 14: 186).

(4) Timelessness (SE 14: 187).
(5) The replacement of external by internal reality (SE 14: 187).

In *The Interpretation of Dreams*:
(6) The co-presence of contradictories (SE 4: 312).
(7) The alternation between absence and presence of temporal succession (SE 4: 314).
(8) Logical connection reproduced as simultaneity in time (SE 4: 314).
(9) Causality as succession (SE 4: 314–16).
(10) Equivalence-identity and conjunction of alternatives (SE 4: 316, 318).
(11) Similarity (SE 4: 319–20).
(12) The co-presence in dreams of thinking and not-thinking (SE 4: 313).
(13) The profound disorganization of the structure of thinking (SE 4: 312).

Matte-Blanco uses Freud's own writing to describe what he had in mind by each of these processes; he then makes some general remarks.

By the *absence of mutual contradiction and negation* Freud refers to a mode of thinking which is quite foreign to what has been termed bivalent logic. He argues that 'There are in this system [the unconscious] no negation, no doubt, no degrees of certainty' (SE 14: 186) and that 'The logical laws of thought do not apply in the id, and this is true above all of the law of contradiction' (SE 22: 73). Elsewhere, the same point is made in the language of the drives; instinctual impulses are said to exist side by side and to be exempt from mutual contradiction.[3] The revolutionary implications of such thinking are apparent when one realizes that if there is no mutual contradiction or negation one cannot distinguish, for instance, '*A* is white' from '*A* is not white', or from 'I am not sure whether *A* is white or not'. If there are no degrees of certainty, all shades of meaning disappear. Under such circumstances, perhaps all one could know is something like 'there is an idea about whiteness'.

The notions of *displacement* and *condensation* also refer to a mode of thinking quite foreign to bivalent logic. They imply an unusual spatial geometry. By *displacement* Freud refers to the way an idea's emphasis, interest, or intensity is liable to be detached from it and to become superimposed on to other ideas. By *condensation* he refers to the way several chains of association, several ideas, may be expressed through a single idea. As he himself put it: 'By the process of displacement one idea may surrender to another its whole quota of cathexis; by the process of condensation it may appropriate the whole cathexis of several other ideas' (SE 14: 186).

Freud illustrates this process of condensation in *The Interpretation of Dreams*:

'They were concealed behind the dream figure of 'Irma', which was thus turned into a collective image with, it must be admitted, a number of contradictory characteristics. Irma became the representative of all these other figures which had been sacrificed to the work of condensation, since I passed over to *her*, point by point, everything that reminded me of *them*. There is another way in which a "collective figure" can be produced for purposes of dream-condensation, namely by uniting the actual features of two or more people into a single dream-image. . . . Dr R. in my dream about my uncle with the yellow beard . . . was a similar composite figure. But in his case the dream-image was constructed in yet another way. I did not combine the features of one person with those of another and in the process omit from the memory-picture certain features of each of them. What I did was to adopt the procedure by means of which Galton produced family portraits: namely by projecting two images on to a single plate, so that certain features common to both are emphasized, while those which fail to fit in with one another cancel one another out and are indistinct in the picture. In my dream about my uncle the fair beard emerged prominently from a face which belonged to two people and which was consequently blurred; incidentally, the beard further involved an allusion to my father and myself through the intermediate idea of growing grey.'

(SE 4: 293)

Freud's descriptions of condensation and displacement are interesting particularly for the implications they evoke for the spatial geometry lived in the unconscious. The collective figure of Irma and that of a Galton portrait involve several different people who naturally invoke contradictory ideas but are put in the same place (space) occupied by one person. At the same time it is interesting to note that Freud reports that the result of such projection is naturally to create a contradiction which is represented by the blurring in the dream, as in the case of the face behind the fair beard. This seems to imply that some elements of two-valued logic remain in the unconscious.

The characteristic of *timelessness* in the unconscious also violates ordinary thinking. Freud insists that 'The processes of the system Ucs are timeless, i.e. they are not ordered temporally, are not altered by the passage of time; they have no reference to time at all' (SE 14: 187). But, of course, by definition a process is something which normally develops in time. Yet Freud speaks of timeless processes in the unconscious. This is not, Matte-Blanco thinks, careless imprecision. As in the case of the face behind the fair beard, he is juxtaposing what he observed, in unconscious processes – both ideas which conform with two-valued logic and those that do not. His adherence to his initial observation leads him to open the door to an entirely new mental world ruled by two sets of behaviour: two-valued logic and something else. Freud was quite aware of the momentousness of his idea about timelessness in the unconscious. Only a few years before his death he wrote: 'Again and again I have had the impression that we have made too little theoretical use of this fact, established beyond any doubt, of the unalterability by time of the repressed. This seems to offer an approach to the most profound discoveries. Nor, unfortunately, have I myself made any progress here' (SE 22: 74).

The idea that, in the unconscious, there is a *replacement of external by psychical reality* is equally extraordinary. It would seem that as far as the unconscious is concerned they are known only as one and the same. Freud wrote that 'The Ucs processes pay just as little regard to reality. They are subject to the pleasure principle; their fate depends only on how strong they are and on whether they fulfil the demands of the pleasure–unpleasure regulation' (SE 14: 187). Again, 'Real and imaginary events appear at first sight in dreams as having equal validity; and this is so not only in dreams but also in the production of more important psychical structures.'

The next characteristic of the Freudian unconscious, that there is a *co-presence of contradictories*, is of course also a direct violation of two-valued logic. Although linked to the first characteristic of the unconscious (absence of mutual contradiction), Matte-Blanco does not think they are quite the same. Absence of mutual contradiction treats an idea and its negation as being identical. But Freud put the co-presence characteristic as follows: 'Each train of thought is almost invariably accompanied by its contradictory counterpart, linked with it by antithetical association' (SE 4: 312). Matte-Blanco thinks there are a number of ways of understanding this formulation. The fact that the two contradictory ideas both appear together stresses their difference: presence of contradiction. On the other hand, it serves to stress their identity so that, when one is presented with an assertion, it is the same as being presented with its negation; there is thus also an *absence* of contradiction. What is more, it serves to show that one can be presented both with a contradiction *and* with an absence of

11

contradiction, at the same time. This emphasizes, as it were, the difference between the two ideas. It will be from the context in which this curious fact appears in each case that one can decide which of the three alternatives holds. The basic point is that the very existence of alternatives does not have the same meaning in the unconscious as it does in bivalent logic. In summary, this characteristic seems to be an interesting mixture in the unconscious of two-valued logic and its negation. We will return to this again in a moment.

The next characteristic, the *alternation between the absence and presence of temporal succession*, also involves a curious mixture of two-valued logic and its negation. Freud wrote:

> 'While some dreams completely disregard the logical sequence of their material, others attempt to give as full an indication of it as possible. In doing so dreams depart sometimes more and sometimes less widely from the text that is at their disposal for manipulation. Incidentally dreams vary similarly in their treatment of the chronological sequence of dream-thoughts, if such a sequence has been established in the unconscious.'
>
> (SE 4: 314)

Here there seems to be a mixture of atemporality (a fundamental characteristic of the unconscious) and temporality (that is, respect for the logic of moral thinking).

As a further characteristic Freud has argued that in dreams *logical connections are reproduced as simultaneity in time*.

> 'Here they are acting like the painter who, in a picture of the School of Athens or of Parnassus, represents in one group all the philosophers or all the poets. It is true that they were never in fact assembled in a single hall or on a single mountain-top; but they certainly form a group in the conceptual sense.'
>
> (SE 4: 314)

A logical connection between two thoughts or events is, therefore, expressed in dreams by putting them next to one another (a spatial relation) and in their occurring at the same time. In this characteristic spatial separation is retained, but temporal succession disappears.

Next, *causal relations are represented by putting two thoughts in succession*, i.e. as a sequence. The order (cause first, effect afterwards) is reversible. In the end, therefore, the relation cause–effect is represented in terms of contiguity in space or time, without respecting the notion of temporality which would be essential in two-valued logic. Once again the unconscious thought process respects some aspects of two-valued logic but is transformed so that it does not necessarily entail precedence in time; it is atemporalized.[4]

Summarizing this characteristic and some of the earlier ones we may say that in dreams we witness various mixtures of presence of time, space, and causal relations with a disappearance of them. There is respect for bivalent logic and its negation.

Another characteristic Freud observed, *equivalence-identity and conjunction of alternatives*, also involves a complex admixture and negation of two-valued logic. Freud observed: 'The alternative "either-or" cannot be expressed in dreams in any way whatever. Both of the alternatives are usually inserted in the text of the dream as though they were equally valid' (SE 4: 316). 'If, however, in reproducing a dream, its narrator feels inclined to make use of an "either-or", e.g. "it was either a garden or a sitting-room", what was present in the dream-thoughts was not an alternative but an "and", a simple addition' (SE 4: 317). Like the identity of psychical and external reality, this is a characteristic which indicates that the unconscious treats as equal two things which for bivalent thinking are not identical. One may say that the identity of psychical and external reality is an example of 'either/or'. Indeed we are accustomed to think ordinarily of either external (material) reality or psychical reality. As Freud put it:

> 'The way in which dreams treat the category of the contraries and contradictories is highly remarkable. It is simply disregarded. . . . They show a particular preference for combining contraries into a unity or for representing them as one and the same thing. Dreams feel themselves at liberty, moreover, to represent any element by its wishful contrary; so that there is no way of deciding at a first glance whether any element that admits of a contrary is present in the dream-thoughts as a positive or as a negative.'
>
> (SE 4: 318)

In these words Freud provides another example of what Matte-Blanco stresses; an assertion and its negation can be treated in the unconscious as identical. This corresponds exactly to the absence of contradiction and negation, violating the bivalent principle of contradiction. Indeed we can now recognize a consequence of the absence of contradiction; if two things cannot be distinguished in any way from one another, then they are normally treated as though they were identical. This is Leibniz's *identitas indiscernibilium*.

One characteristic of the unconscious, *similarity*, enjoyed, in Freud's view, a privileged relation in the process of dream formation. Similarity, consonance, or approximation – the relation of 'just as' – unlike any other characteristic, is capable of being represented in dreams in a variety of ways. Parallels or instances of 'just as' are inherent in the material of the dream thoughts. They constitute the first foundations for the construction of a dream, and no inconsiderable part of the dream work consists in creating fresh parallels where those which are already present cannot find their way into the dream owing to the censorship imposed by resistance. The representation of the relation of similarity is assisted by the tendency of the dream work towards condensation. Similarity, consonance, the possession of common attributes – all these are represented in dreams by unification, which may either be present already in the material of the dream thoughts or be freshly constructed. The first of these possibilities may be described as 'identification' and the second as 'composition'. Identification is employed where persons are concerned; composition where things are the material of the unification. Nevertheless composition may also be applied to persons; localities are often treated like persons (SE 4: 319–20).

Freud's proposal that there is the *co-presence in dreams of thinking and 'not-thinking'* once again raises complex questions. On the one hand, he himself says that 'What is reproduced by the ostensible thinking in the dream is the subject-matter of the dream-thoughts and not the mutual relations between them, the assertion of which constitutes thinking' (SE 4: 313). On the other, he argues: 'Nevertheless, I will not deny that critical thought-activity which is not a mere repetition of material in the dream-thoughts does have a share in the formation of dreams' (SE 4: 313). In the first quotation Freud asserts that thinking involves an establishment of relations and adds that such relations are absent in dreams. At the same time he does not deny that thinking does participate in dreams. In other words, he affirms the co-presence of 'not-thinking' and thinking.

Matte-Blanco suggests that 'thinking', as Freud has been using it, corresponds to the use of ordinary two-valued logic. The presence of 'not-thinking' corresponds to some unconscious process. So what can he have meant by 'not-thinking': which aspect of the unconscious is the problem? Recalling the principles of bivalent logic, is it absence of contradiction which defines not-thinking? Matte-Blanco thinks not, because certain relations (and, therefore, thinking) can both exist and have nothing to do with the absence of contradiction; for example: my house is white.

Is it then displacement or condensation? Again, he thinks not. Both characteristics introduce identities that are not acceptable in thinking. None the less, it is possible in many cases to be able to think without touching the question of displacement.

Is it the problem of timelessness? The question becomes more serious here. Take any relation – for instance, 'John is the father of Peter.' The relation goes from John (first or to the left) to Peter (afterwards or to the right). If you put Peter first then you change the relation: Peter is the son of John. In other words, the concept of relation has a structure similar to that of the concepts of time and place (or space); it is, one may say, isomorphic to them.

And what of the equation of psychical and external reality? If this is the only characteristic present, then thinking is likely to be restricted. But it can take place. The point is that each of the original five characteristics of the Freudian unconscious (absence of contradiction, displacement, condensation, timelessness, and the equation of psychical and external reality) can exert some influence on the possibility of being able to think in bivalent logical terms. But only timelessness by itself appears likely to be a decisive factor.

The *profound disorganization of the structure of thinking* which takes place in the unconscious, the thirteenth characteristic Matte-Blanco has recognized, has been described very clearly by Freud.

'The different portions of this complicated structure stand, of course, in the most manifold logical relations to one another. They can represent foreground and background, digressions and illustrations, conditions, chains of evidence and counter-arguments. When the whole mass of these dream-thoughts is brought under the pressure of the dream-work, and its elements are turned about, broken into fragments and jammed together – almost like pack-ice – the question arises of what happens to the logical connections which have hitherto formed its framework. What representation do dreams provide for "if", "because", "just as", "although", "either-or", and all the other conjunctions without which we cannot understand sentences or speeches?

'In the first resort our answer must be that dreams have no means at their disposal for representing these logical relations between the dream-thoughts. For the most part dreams disregard all these conjunctions, and it is only the substantive content of the dream-thoughts that they take over and manipulate. The restoration of the connections which the dream-work has destroyed is a task which has to be performed by the interrelative process.'

(SE 4: 312)

Discussion of these characteristics of the unconscious

You will be now getting the idea that Matte-Blanco is painstakingly arguing that the unconscious described by Freud is a mixture of normal thinking and what he called the characteristics of the unconscious. Primarily Matte-Blanco thinks these are the first five characteristics. These appear in various ways in the remaining eight characteristics (which are mixtures of the five) and in each other.

One trait does, however, appear to be common to all thirteen characteristics; this is that they *unite* or unify things which for ordinary thinking are distinct and separated. The *absence of contradiction* unites things which are quite distinct in ordinary thinking – when something is affirmed and something is denied. *Displacement* and *condensation* do the same in regard to spatial aspects which do not deal with contradiction. This identification–union, as we have seen, leads to blurring. *Timelessness* removes the distinction between instants. The lack of a division between *psychic and external reality* means that material reality and psychical reality become the same.

The *co-presence of contradictories* has the same effect, while the *alternation between absence and presence of temporal succession* leads to an association of temporality and timelessness. The characteristic in which *logical connections are reproduced as simultaneity in time* links the concept of time with that of logical connection. *Causality as succession* joins and identifies alternatives. *Equivalence-identity and the conjunction of alternatives* disregard the differences between contraries and those between contradictories. *Similarity* also joins things. *The co-presence in dreams of thinking and not-thinking* approaches the inconceivable. Here thinking and not-thinking would become the same. Finally, *the profound disorganization of the structure of thinking* leads, sooner or later, to the confusion of everything with everything else.

To conclude, one might say that, while thinking usually works within a framework of distinguishing things, the unconscious that Freud investigates tends to unite and fuse everything. Herein lies the radical nature of this different mode, a subject to which we shall return.

The characteristics of the unconscious and their contribution to human thought

Historically most of humanity's formal efforts to think about, understand, and know the world have relied on the acquisition and development of what has come to be called reason. Over the years certain laws or rules of reasoning have been laboriously devised and codified in a system (which is based on propositions that are conceived as either true or not true) which Matte-Blanco has roughly subsumed under the term 'bivalent logic'. This was the first logic at humanity's disposal for understanding the world. It has helped to unravel innumerable enigmas.

Yet, Matte-Blanco points out, it has always been evident to many that bivalent logic is necessary but not sufficient. In spite of the fact that much research showed that the world could often be illuminated by principles conforming to its rules – the principle of contradiction, for instance – few thinkers have considered (bivalent) logical 'reason' sufficient to understand everything. This conviction is eloquently expressed in Pascal's *pensées* (1670): 'Le coeur a ses raisons que la raison ne connaît point.'

We have just been following Freud's argument that the unconscious does not conform to the known logical rules, notably the principle of contradiction. This unconscious mind must have its own system of rules; otherwise dreams, for instance, could never be meaningful. It must have its own mode of 'thinking'. Throughout the twentieth century psychoanalysis has worked within this frame given by Freud. But, as we have seen, Matte-Blanco thinks it has not explored it sufficiently nor discovered its enormous potentialities.

Matte-Blanco argues that it is interesting that, roughly at the time when Freud was thinking about the unconscious, eminent mathematicians were scrutinizing the concepts of infinity and of the set. Not surprisingly neither Freud nor the mathematicians knew of each other's work and it has taken Matte-Blanco to see possible connections. By using some elementary mathematical logical notions, which have become common knowledge since Freud's day, he puts forward a radical reformulation of the characteristics of the system unconscious.

2 A reformulation of the Freudian unconscious

Symmetry and asymmetry

We hope you will have got some flavour, by now, of how Matte-Blanco thinks about Freud. He goes into very careful details, particularly about what he thinks most important, Freud's ideas about the nature of unconscious processes. At the same time he delights in searching out the implications of an idea to its conclusion, no matter how odd it may sound. He tells us that his father nicknamed him 'Hair-splitter' by the age of five or so! This characteristic is certainly what makes him often difficult to read but, coupled with his imaginative courage, it is his great strength.

Let us turn now from his consideration of Freud to the main thrust of Matte-Blanco's own ideas. In starting out on this it is most important to remember one thing: Matte-Blanco begins his task by using a very different conceptual framework from Freud. Freud developed his ideas, among other things, around the basic idea of the mind as *dynamic* – having impulses, instincts, drives, wishes, or desires, which could, of course, be in conflict with each other. Matte-Blanco does not in any way contradict this, but he starts, quite intentionally, from a different conceptual frame. He views the mind not only as dynamic but also as a *discriminator* and *classifier*. Mathematical *set theory* is his basic conceptual background. Now the idea of a set is very simple. *A set is a collection of any sort*; it can contain any item or an infinite number. When we have a set of things that have an attribute or characteristic in common, we have what is called a *class* by most people. Matte-Blanco makes it plain that the human mind is, every second, carrying out classificatory activity; it forms, using the mathematical term, sets. This must go on for *recognition*, a vital activity, to occur.

So we advise you, whilst you go on reading this book: let yourself think in terms of classification and sets. It is different from the usual psychoanalytic mode of conceptualizing, but this is the very point of Matte-Blanco's task.

Matte-Blanco starts by arguing that all ordinary or 'logical' (i.e. bivalent) thinking activity is constantly dealing instantaneously with combinations of triads. The mind is always recognizing or making propositions to itself about one thing, another thing, and the *relation* between them. A vast set (potentially infinite) of such triads is the starting point from which thinking and all scientific logic are built. We now come to the most crucial concepts in Matte-Blanco's ideas: the characteristics of asymmetrical and symmetrical relations, and his distinction between them. This is so important that it must be understood before going any further.

We begin with some examples of mental propositions about *asymmetrical relations*. These abound, every second, in conscious thought:

  (i) 'I am writing this page.'
 (ii) 'John is the father of Peter.'
(iii) 'B is smaller than, or precedes, 15'.
 (iv) 'The door is on the left side of the wall.'
  (v) '*A* is part of *B*.'
 (vi) 'You are a member of the British Psycho-Analytic Society.'

In all these there is a relation (given by a verb) between subject and object. What is more, you find that *the converse of each relation is not identical to it*. This is why it is called asymmetrical. Thus if we turn to the first example, 'I am writing this page', we find there are two 'somethings': 'I' and 'this page'; and one relation: 'writing'. Note that the 'something' called 'I' comes first or is to the left of the sentence, and the 'something else' called 'this page' comes in the second place. If we reverse the order of the 'somethings' then the new sentence makes no sense (or a quite different sense) unless we also alter the relation. So we might say: 'This page is being written by I (me)', but not 'This page is writing me.' The other sentences are also examples of asymmetrical relationships. All have converses different from the original relation. If we alter the order of the 'somethings' in these cases then the relationships must also be changed to make sense, for example: 'Peter is the son of John'; '15 is greater than or follows 8'; 'The wall has the door on its left side'; '*B* has *A* as a part'; 'The British Psycho-Analytic Society has you as a member.' By contrast, 'Peter is the father of John', '15 is smaller than or precedes 8', 'The wall is on the left side of the door', and 'The British Psycho-Analytic Society is a member of you', which are all the converses of the original relationships, mean something quite different or are puzzling.

There are, however, some relationships whose converse or inverse is always the *same* as the proposed relation. These are called *symmetrical* relationships. For example, '*A* is identical to *B*', 'John is different from Peter', 'Sarah is married to James.' When these relationships are inverted, the meaning stays the same. Some other relationships, such as those between siblings, are sometimes reversible and sometimes not. For example, the relation 'Paul is the brother of John' is reversible, but the relation 'Paul is the brother of Kate' is not. In general, symmetrical relationships of this kind are less frequent than asymmetrical relations. You may verify this for yourself.

Symmetrical logic and the principle of symmetry

In discussing Freud's ideas about thinking in the unconscious, we concluded with Matte-Blanco that ordinary thinking deals only with things which are in some ways distinguishable from one another and with the relations existing between such things. This uses bivalent logic, and we can now see that it uses asymmetrical relations. Through the examination of the characteristics of the unconscious Matte-Blanco showed that Freud made it clear that thinking of this kind is *retained* in unconscious processes, but is also accompanied by something which is not thinking of this sort. In fact, in *The Un-*

conscious as Infinite Sets (Matte-Blanco 1975a: 93–4) he put forward the idea that Freud's fundamental discovery was not the characteristics of the unconscious as such but a *symmetrical form of logic*. Freud did not state the principles of symmetrical logic directly of course, but it is Matte-Blanco's belief that his arguments were based on some implicit notion of its kind. In any case, Matte-Blanco sets out to demonstrate that, along with bivalent logic, symmetry provides a set of unifying principles which conceptualizes the forms of thinking and not-thinking which are fundamental to the characteristics of the unconscious.

Symmetrical logic is a loose general description used by Matte-Blanco to refer to a logical operation governed in part by what he calls the *principle of symmetry (PS)*. This principle states that *whenever somebody or something – let us call him or her or it 'A' – has a given relation to somebody or something else, then this latter (we may call him or her or it 'B') must also have or be treated as having the same relation to 'A'*. It has been mentioned that, in ordinary logical thinking, symmetrical relations are usually thought to apply to a limited number of defined situations, such as the relationship between two brothers. But here we are concerned with applying the principle of symmetry to *any* relationship that we might have in mind. In this case things are quite different. Take, for example, the statement 'Rose is the mother of Mary.' If the principle of symmetry (PS) is operating, then this is the same as 'Mary is the mother of Rose.' In these circumstances, like Alice in Wonderland, we find ourselves in very unfamiliar territory. Matte-Blanco thinks this is precisely the territory inhabited by the unconscious.

Matte-Blanco examines some important corollaries of the principle of symmetry (PS). From this he unfolds his main contention that the operation of a logic based on PS is indeed a defining characteristic of the unconscious as Freud has formulated it. To start with, PS is incompatible with the concepts of time, space, and movement. This is because PS is incompatible with what mathematicians refer to as the concept of *total order*.[5] Put another way, we can say that *the unconscious, in using symmetrical logic, often treats the converse of any relation as identical to it; it treats asymmetrical relations as symmetrical.*

The way the unconscious can deal with asymmetrical relations is the keystone of Matte-Blanco's work. It is, therefore, worth while to exercise ourselves and become thoroughly familiar with what is meant by a process of symmetrization. The first attempts we shall make may seem distinctly odd. There may be a temptation to dismiss the whole idea as ridiculous or to feel one is being driven mad. But if the argument is followed to the realm of *emotional* relations we hope it will become clear that Matte-Blanco has illuminated something very important.

Take a general example. Let us make a proposition using an asymmetrical relation, say, 'A is giving something good to B.' This involves an asymmetrical relation whose converse 'is being given' is not the same as 'is giving' (the original relation). But if, after the initial discrimination, we were to slip into symmetrizing, we would think: 'A is giving something good to B, and B is giving something good to A.' Ordinarily this is faulty logic, but emotional experiences like this are common. For instance, a patient can readily feel to himself, 'My analyst is giving me something good; I must be a good patient (giving him something good).' The same is often observed about a child who feels, 'My mother loves me, and I love her.' It is implicit in the phrase 'a loved child is a loving one'. This symmetrization is just as applicable with negative feelings. 'He hates me; I hate him.'

Let us now extend the argument by some further exercises – for example, to the idea that, if PS is applied to the concept of time, then it collapses. If an instant A precedes an instant B and PS holds, then B precedes A. As the conception of time is that of an order (a total order) called sequence of instants, in which each instant either precedes or follows any other given instant (an asymmetrical relation), then if PS holds we cannot construct the sequence of time. We are confronted with timelessness.

The principle of symmetry is also incompatible with the concept of space. If a point A in space precedes a point B and PS holds, then B also precedes A. As in the case of time, in such a case, space, which requires the concept of a sequence of points, disappears: spacelessness. Moreover, if space and time disappear when PS holds, then movement, because it is a displacement which occurs in time, must disappear too. Still more radically, under the principle of symmetry, awareness of *any process* at all must disappear.

There is another corollary to the operation of the principle of symmetry. When PS holds, a *part* of something is equal to *the whole* and is therefore indistinguishable from it. Expressed formally, if a is a part of A and PS holds, then A is a part of a. (In bivalent logic this conclusion is true only when the part is a so-called improper part, i.e. a part which is defined as identical to the whole.) Matte-Blanco thinks that this second corollary of PS is most important because the equation – that is, the symmetrization of the relationship – between the part and the whole of any object is frequently observed in clinical practice and ordinary life, as a few examples will show!

It is usual, in conscious logic, to recognize that the penis is a part of the body in a certain location. But in dreams and psychosis it is quite common to experience that penis, whole body, and self are undifferentiated. In muted form it is common, of course, in a neurosis; for example, when a patient feels when talking that he 'is ejaculating prematurely'. Part–whole equation is also noticeable in slang and swearing – for instance, 'Oh he's just a big prick.'

Next consider with Matte-Blanco the set of all human mothers, past, present, and future, and consider in a logical way a given mother, say Mrs Mary Higgins. She can be called an element or (more loosely, in order to avoid longer explanations) a part of this set. If PS holds in this set, then the set is an element or part of Mrs Mary Higgins. However, as we have just argued, with this symmetrization, the set and the elements or parts are identical to one another. As this identity must also hold for any other mother, and considering that two things identical to a third are, even in bivalent logic, identical to one another, it follows that, where PS holds, any mother is identical to any other mother and to the whole set of mothers. Thus, whenever we consider any of them we are considering the whole lot of them. Something like this seems to be happening when we diffusely have a feeling of 'motherliness' in a general way. Note, however, that the set of mothers is different from the set of daughters or of fathers or any other set.

The set of human mothers might be defined, in terms of bivalent logical thinking, as the set of all women who have given birth to a child. In so far as PS holds (and this need not necessarily happen) we may say that the set may become symmetrized so that all mothers are treated as identical to each other. As the elements or parts become indistinguishable from each other and from the whole set, we may also say that the set becomes *homogenized* by PS.

When such a homogenization is taking place in the mind, then, to the experiencer, every mother becomes the same as every other mother and the same as the whole class. As we have noted, under these circumstances perhaps all that is known is the vague feeling of motherliness. In such a case, Matte-Blanco believes we have a new type of *mixed* logic. The *set itself* is defined in terms of *bivalent logic*, as just mentioned; but the characteristics of the 'inside' of the set, i.e. all the elements contained in it, are, instead, *ruled by PS*. So here we have a curious combination of normal logic and PS, which acts to dissolve-unify-identify all concepts. As we have seen, Matte-Blanco called this mixture by the name of *symmetrical logic*. Later, as we shall see in this and subsequent chapters, Matte-Blanco investigated this mixing of asymmetrical logic and symmetrization in some detail. He calls the mixture *bi-logic*. We could say that when the conscious (asymmetrical) mind 'expects' a bivalently logical sequence, but symmetrization has been 'inserted', then we have a bi-logical structure.

It appears that a modicum of symmetry plays a part in *any* discrimination of a set or, in other words, in any normal classificatory act by the mind. To recognize, to see a similarity, and so on, is to classify; this is to register that two or more elements are equivalent (or the same) with regard to the defining characteristic of the class. Now equivalence, sameness, and similarity are all symmetrical relations. So the principle of symmetry functions in ordinary conscious logical activity. It is thus a (hidden) aspect of normal bivalent logic. It is when symmetrization *breaks the bounds*, as it were, of asymmetrical bivalent logic that we slip into bi-logic or, in Freudian terms, into the unconscious.

The concept of *symmetrization* is so important in Matte-Blanco's thinking that, even at the risk of repeating the last paragraph, we will stress its meaning again. When there is symmetrization within a particular category or equivalence class, the individual 'things' or elements collected together by some thought (propositional function), which regards them as sharing something in common, *become the same in every and all respects*. Ordinary asymmetrical thinking means that we regularly and normally form equivalence classes – rich, poor, tall, angry, dangerous – to categorize people or things. With symmetrization the differences within the class – more or less rich, and so on – are abolished. Anyone belonging to the same class becomes represented as the same. You will notice that we shall use the terms 'set' and 'class' as well as 'category' more or less interchangeably in what follows. Remember, we are always referring to a collection of 'things' formed by a thought (formally termed a propositional function) which 'sees' some similarity between them.

Matte-Blanco is clear that psychoanalysis has envisaged symmetrization similar to the kind described from its very beginning, only not explicitly. He takes one of the more recent examples. It is common to speak of a patient envying the breast. However, when we do this, we are not referring specifically to the envy, say, of the right or left breast of Mrs Mary Higgins or of any other woman, but to envy of all breasts of all women: envy of THE BREAST. Individuals have disappeared, and the only thing that remains is *breastness* – and not only physical breastness but psychological breastness as well. Matte-Blanco would describe the replacement of a specific, tangible breast by the concept of breastness (as comprising and being equal to all breasts) as a typical symmetrization. Matte-Blanco argues that, if there is greater clarity about this type of conceptualization by using his logical formulation, then much is gained in understanding and hence in the possibility of helping patients.

We have just said that the breast we consider in psychoanalysis is not a concrete breast but 'breastness'. In more general terms, symmetrization of any set entails the disappearance of the separate elements of the set and their replacement by the concept itself (in logic termed the propositional function). This concept becomes 'incarnated' in the elements of the set: motherhood, fatherhood, goodness, badness, beauty, 'doorness', 'chairness', intelligence, etc. Again this is an idea which is constantly implicit rather than explicit in psychoanalysis. But this is not the whole story. The establishment of concepts of 'breastness', goodness, badness, etc. does not, as we have already noted, necessarily violate the laws of scientific or bivalent logic. But another aspect is the identification of the individual with the whole set and hence with all the other elements of it, so that each mother, for instance, can be felt as not only herself but also any and all mothers and, indeed, motherhood. This derivative of symmetrical logic is constantly employed in psychoanalysis, but in a non-explicit and rather muddled way, which can lead to much confused thinking.

Freud's characteristics of the unconscious in the light of symmetry and asymmetry

Let us take each of Freud's characteristics of the unconscious in turn. We will start with and spend most time upon the first five given at the beginning of the chapter. These are the characteristics Freud considered to be the most fundamental in his paper 'The Unconscious' (1915b). We will be more summary with the other eight. (In this we have used both Matte-Blanco and a previous article by one of us: Rayner 1981).

(1) *The absence of mutual contradiction and of negation.* You will recall that Freud treats these as similar but probably not quite the same. Matte-Blanco discusses the issue in great detail (1975a: 43–53). By absence of contradiction Freud refers to wishes which are distinct, to the ordinary logical mind of consciousness, but which strangely do not contradict each other unconsciously. In its simplest form take the experience of two wishes; for them to be known as contradictory they must be consciously felt as in a relation where one *opposes* the other. Thus one wish will be different from the other, hence the converse of the relation between the two wishes is non-identical. This is essentially asymmetrical. But, when symmetrization

24

intervenes, only that which is the same between the wishes is known. Asymmetry disappears, so the knowledge of contradiction must disappear also.

Such experiences are well enough known in dreams – as when, for instance, a dreamer is glad or well satisfied that a relative is both long dead and yet alive; as when one enjoys a dream of being a child again and yet at the same time is being adult.

Absence of negation can likewise be seen as a function of symmetrization. For the act of negation essentially is the discrimination of a converse to a relation which is not the same as the original. This defines symmetry.

(2) *Displacement*. This characteristic is crucial since it lies at the basis of symbolization, transference, projection, introjection, sublimation, and probably condensation also.

Freud, of course, envisaged displacement in terms of the transfer of investment of mental energy from one object to another. Matte-Blanco is concerned about how the ordinary, discriminating mind, as it were, allows such transfers to happen, and frequently at that.

In displacement a person is seen by an outside observer to be shifting feelings and ideas from a primary object to a less primary one. But to the experiencer's unconscious both objects are identical. To him or her, they are registered as belonging to the same class and then, with symmetrization, they are conceived as identical. Defence (repression, denial, etc.) may come into play so that the idea or feeling is not recognized in consciousness as belonging to the primary object.

Here are a couple of examples with explanation by Matte-Blanco.

'If he feels his chief to be a dangerous father it is because he considers both to have the same characteristic, dangerousness. If we express this in terms of symbolic logic we may say that in his unconscious he treats both as elements of a class; it may also happen that he treats one as an element of another class, but in this case both classes are always subclasses of a more general class. For example, a mother who feeds belongs, let us say, to the class of women who feed materially; a professor who teaches belongs to the class who feeds mentally. When, on account of a process of displacement, an individual feels the professor as a mother who feeds he is, first of all, treating both classes as subclasses of a more general class, that of those who feed, either materially or mentally.'

(Matte-Blanco 1975a: 42)

These symmetrizations within the class are obvious here. These are just the first steps in displacement; Matte-Blanco goes on to define further functions involved in various defence mechanisms, but this will suffice us here. You will find more of this later in the volume.

(3) *Condensation.* It is possible that condensation and displacement have very similar mechanisms, for condensation does seem to involve displacements. As we saw earlier, here ideas derived from different times and different object relations are experienced as belonging to one object or idea.

This can readily be seen as a consequence of symmetrizations where, in specific ways, awareness of space and time disappears. Both of these are, as we have seen, dependent upon asymmetrical relations. Matte-Blanco makes plain, as we described when considering condensation early in this chapter, that symmetrization is *never* complete even in the unconscious. Symmetrizations are always local, as it were, mixed with ordinary asymmetrical relations and logic.

(4) *Timelessness.* This has already been considered. Time involves awareness of an ordered sequence. With symmetrization, order, which is by its essence asymmetrical, disappears, and so will awareness of time.

(5) *Replacement of external by internal reality.* The awareness of external reality involves the conception of space and boundary, of inside and outside. Both space and boundary involve asymmetrical relations; with symmetrization these can disappear, so that inside and outside become identical to the experiencer. However, to another person, an observer, the difference is still evident, so to him or her the experiencer seems to be replacing external by internal reality.

Now briefly, the eight further characteristics. They are dealt with more fully later by Matte-Blanco himself.

Co-presence of contradictories. This seems to be an extension of absence of contradiction, which has already been discussed.

Alternation between absence and presence of temporal succession. Here symmetrization alternates with the continuing presence of awareness of asymmetrical relations. It is a clear example of the working of bi-logic – of which, more later.

Logical connection reproduced as simultaneity and causality as succession. Here again, bi-logic can be seen working. In the first of these two characteristics, time seems to be symmetrized, while space remains intact. In the second, space is symmetrized, and time remains intact.

Equivalence-identity and conjunction of alternatives. Here too can be seen a mixture occurring between awareness of asymmetrical relations and symmetrization.

Similarity: the privileged relation. In this Freud saw how important recognition is in everyday life. It does not necessarily involve gross

26

symmetrization. But in so far as it involves the everyday registration of 'sameness' it might be said to be the essential 'normal' functioning of symmetry within well-defined asymmetrical limits.

Co-presence of thinking and not-thinking. As we have seen, thinking necessitates asymmetrical functioning. With symmetrizations, 'not-thinking' necessarily intrudes.

Profound disorganization of the structure of thinking. Here, Matte-Blanco considers that symmetrization is in the ascendant; as symmetrization increases, thinking and consciousness disappear.

3 The internal world

The bi-logical stratified structure

Our examination of Freud's characteristics of the unconscious has stressed that there is often a mixture of respect for bivalent thinking with its negation. We have seen that this makes it clear that bivalent and symmetrical logic can exist in various types of relationship with one another. This is therefore a process which submits, not to one logic – so far as does, for instance, all reasoning of arithmetic and science – but to two. As we noted earlier, this has been called *bi-logical reasoning* by Matte-Blanco.

All processes of thinking have a certain structure. They are sets endowed with various relations between their components. Bi-logical structures of thinking may be compared by considering how they differ in the way bivalent and symmetrical logics intertwine with one another. Moreover, Matte-Blanco suggests that our everyday ideas, thoughts, and feelings about people, things, and their relationships mean different things to us at what may be considered deeper and deeper zones or *strata* in our minds, conceptually differentiated according to the degree of symmetrization routinely present at that level. He suggests that at the deepest levels (in our unconscious) we all experience a unity, between ourselves and everybody and everything else. There is no asymmetrical thinking, and there are no distinctions. However, this is not incompatible with recognizing differences at less deep, more conscious, or more superficial levels. In these terms human experience can be conceived as structured by the existence of up to an infinite series of strata in which our capacity to recognize differences declines as the amount of symmetrization increases. At the limit, the deepest levels, is what Matte-Blanco calls the indivisible mode.

Putting the idea of stratification in formal terms, Matte-Blanco suggests that

'behind every individual or relationship – as perceived or given in a certain manner at a given moment – the self "sees" an infinite series (sequence) of individuals; all these satisfy the same propositional function (which may be a complex one, i.e. consisting of several sub-statements) under the light of which the individual or the relationship in question is perceived or seen or lived at this moment. If the attention of the observer remains focused on the first level, that of consciousness, then he will only be aware of the concrete individual; and if he lets himself be permeated by the underlying levels, this infinity will unfold itself before him, though in an unconscious manner. Embracing this infinite series (sequence) there is one unity: the class or the set. This, in its turn, is lived as one unity.'

(Matte-Blanco 1975a: 170)

If we conceive this stratification as a bi-logical structure, experience of it may be described quantitatively according to the amount of symmetrical or asymmetrical logic employed within each stratum. Although the number of potential strata is infinite, there being infinite scope for the subtlety of the gradations between them, Matte-Blanco delineates merely five strata in which there is a particular combination of symmetrical and asymmetrical logic to draw out some interesting implications. However, he also mentions gradations within them.

In what he terms the *first stratum*, experience is characterized by the conscious awareness of separate objects. At more conscious levels of this stratum there is conception or perception of concrete and well-defined things: a person, a material object, a precise thought referring to a concrete fact ('the temperature is rising'), or an abstract notion, such as the concept of freedom of the will. At this level thinking is mostly delimited and asymmetrical. A rather less conscious level of the same stratum would be that in which one becomes aware of or explores the relations between a concrete object under consideration and other objects. We would be aware of their similarities and differences – that is, the classes of equivalence to which the object belongs and those to which it does not belong. For example, one could be aware that Peter is a man (i.e. he is an element of the equivalence class of men), that he is not a woman (i.e. not an element of the equivalence class of women), that he is a psychoanalyst, that he belongs to such-and-such a school of psycho-analysis, and so on. At this level the object of the thinking can be linked or related to a potentially very great number of other objects or sets of objects. But here the linkages and relations are made consciously or at levels of preconsciousness that are easily susceptible to consciousness, for example by retrospection or consideration.

A *second stratum* can be defined by the appearance of a significant amount of symmetrization within otherwise asymmetrical thinking. It is the stratum in which more or less conscious *emotions* related to distinguishable and separate elements within a class are discernible: 'I like it', 'I hate him', 'I fear him', and so on. Matte-Blanco has for a long time argued that affects or emotions can be understood better with the help of the principle of symmetry (PS) (Matte-Blanco 1975a: 247). He has also succinctly demonstrated the similarity between the characteristics of the unconscious and emotions. Later in this chapter is included a brief description of the relation between emotion and the experience of infinity. Further reflection has led him to realize that emotions, like the unconscious, are in fact bi-logical structures. Here is one brief example. Take a young man in love. The natural tendency in such a state is to attribute to the beloved young woman all the attractions of wonderful woman: beauty, intelligence, goodness, tenderness, etc. In fact, being in love, he feels her as having *all* the characteristics of the class of beloved woman. This of course means that he has symmetrized and hence identified one element (his loved one) with the whole class of wonderful women. This is a part/whole equation.

At this second stratum, symmetrizations, such as that made by our man in love, are quite well delimited at the conscious level. For instance, while many people may feel that a person is *like* a tiger, one does not usually feel at this (fairly conscious) level that the person *is* a tiger. In the same way, a man in love, if his emotions are at this second level, is usually able to keep his head somewhat clear. Normal two-valued logical thinking will still obtain, and he will realize that his young woman also has limitations and defects. In other words, the emotion of love shows a mixture of both logics; it is a bi-logical structure.[6] At deeper levels, as we shall shortly see, much more symmetrization takes place; so that, in the example of a man in love, say, the loved one's qualities are ultimately felt to the maximum degree – at infinity, which Matte-Blanco calls the indivisible mode.

The next deeper, *third stratum* is one in which different classes are identified (thus containing a fair amount of asymmetrical thinking) but in which symmetrization is taking place to the extent that the parts of a class are always taken as the whole class, and vice versa. A constant feature is the symmetrization of the class. As we descend further into the strata of greater symmetry, things belonging to the same equivalence class become identical with regard not only to the property which defines the equivalence class in question but also to all properties. For example, everyone having 'blue eyes' is treated as the same in every respect as everyone else in that class. Similarly all doctors of philosophy, cruel people, people of the same race, tall people, and so on are indistinguishable amongst themselves or are the same. Eventually, each member of the class has become identical to all others in all respects; complete symmetrization has taken place within the class. Perhaps this level is rampant in gross prejudices.

A fundamental consequence of the sort of symmetrization that is observed in this third stratum is that, because the part of a class becomes the same as the whole class, each individual becomes the same as the class in question. Each individual becomes the potentiality of the class or set, up to its highest degree. Thus, if the set is that of 'angry mothers' then one individual mother or any part of her (for instance, her breast) will be felt as being immensely angry and hence dangerous. If it is the class of fathers that is felt to be angry and hence unendingly dangerous then the penis (as part of the father) will be felt as unendingly angry and dangerous as well as extremely penetrating. This will hold for a particular father and his penis. The same sort of generalized feeling would hold for goodness.

In this third stratum, simply because of the identification of individual and class, intensity tends towards infinite values. Because there is no difference experienced between the two, the first acquires all the potentialities of the second. As the classes (of angry mothers or fathers) can be infinite in size, so the individual can attain, at this level, an infinite degree of the class characteristic. Klein's observations of both adults and children (and particularly about the role of aggression and destructiveness) have masterfully explored this stratum. This has produced what Matte-Blanco describes as a rich harvest in terms of strange, almost incredible, yet true and stimulating findings about psychic life. Matte-Blanco will be discussing Klein's findings in terms of the concepts of bi-logic in Chapter 7.

Some degree of timelessness is also a consequence of the symmetrization of the class and thus a characteristic of this third stratum. This is because time is conceived as a set of instants with the same properties of preceding–following. After symmetrization of the class, instants become indistinguishable from one another.

The *fourth stratum* is defined by the fact that there is the formation of wider classes which are also symmetrized. However, some class differentiation, hence some asymmetry, remains. Because different classes or sets are unified, symmetrization becomes wide and more comprehensive. For example, the class of 'man' is a wider class than those comprising men, women, or children, and when symmetrized this means that to be a man is identical to being a man, a woman, or a child. Matte-Blanco thinks that this is a stratum where some schizophrenics tend to function. They treat as equal things which belong to subsets or substructures of a larger set or structure. The woman patient who said that a man was very rich because he was very tall is an example. Since both rich and tall can be considered subsets of the larger set of those who have something in a high degree it is through the formation and then the symmetrization of this higher class that she draws her conclusions: very tall = very rich.

In this fourth and rather deep stratum, a number of the features of the Freudian unconscious are also characteristic. There is an absence of contradiction: because a set, which contains all affirmations of an idea and also their corresponding negations of it, if symmetrized, results in the conclusion that any assertion is equal to its negation. There is no possibility of contradiction. For the same reason there is also an identity of psychical and external reality.

Finally, Matte-Blanco defines the deepest, the *fifth stratum* as that in which processes of symmetrization tend towards the mathematical limit of *indivisibility*. From this point 'downwards' the amount of symmetrization is so great that thinking, which requires asymmetrical relations, is greatly impaired. At the limit is what he calls the pure indivisible mode. Here Matte-Blanco envisages that everything is experienced as everything else. This is where the relations between things are all theoretically contained in any single thing which the intellect can grasp. An endless number of things tend to become, mysteriously, only one thing.

The stratified structure and normal development

The stratified structures which we have been discussing can be conceived as developmental achievements. The capacity in the human psyche for differentiated thinking (forming equivalence classes and distinguishing elements within them) may be considered as the product of the development of structured and relatively stable relationships between · the strata. Relationships between the five strata, Matte-Blanco thinks, may be formed in normal development so that they remain fairly distinct. Each stratum becomes relatively well differentiated from those above or below it. That is, the operations that occur in one stratum do not occur generally in those strata which are above or below it. For instance, in the first stratum, there is a well-delimited grasp of specific, almost isolated objects, relations, or situations. In the second, on the other hand, there is a great amount of interrelation between its elements. Meanwhile, the third stratum establishes, through symmetrization, identities between individuals, and this does not occur in the first two. As symmetrizations become more extensive, new characteristics make their appearance, which, as we have seen, were not present in the upper levels.

The structural relationship between the strata is also such that the 'normal' individual is able to perceive (feel) the continuity between the strata so that this is part of his or her taken-for-granted experience. Matte-Blanco gives an example. An experiencing individual knows, say, a specific visible mother, Mrs Rosa Torres. Behind and inside her the individual also recognizes a number of other mothers, such as his own mother and many other mother-images which have played a role in his life; and there also is the general idea, motherhood. These perspectives on Mrs Torres – that is, the individual's feelings about her – are possible while maintaining total respect for the rules of bivalent logic. In spite of the fact that she is seen from the perspective of both the second stratum (as other mothers) and the third stratum (as motherhood), there is no visible manifestation of bi-logic. In the midst of it the individual Mrs Torres remains consciously and socially perceived as an individual. Moreover, at deeper and deeper strata Mrs Rosa Torres, the individual, together with other mothers and motherhood, is also experienced as fatherhood, everyone, inanimate objects, and so on.[7]

Only in 'abnormal' states does the continuity of differentiation between the logical strata become fractured or confused. Bi-logic is then, of course, manifest at the level of conscious communication. For example, Matte-Blanco suggests that it is possible to describe in this way some of Schreber's problems, as described by Freud in his case history (1911, SE 12), as the result of a breakdown (short circuit) in the (unconscious) relationship between strata. While everyone may equate (by symmetrization) at deeper levels such representations as those of God and father, or son and Jesus Christ, Schreber made these equations quite consciously. In other words equations that existed at deeper levels persisted at more superficial or conscious levels, and there was thus for Schreber some kind of breakdown or short circuit in the relationship between the different zones. Schreber, therefore, could not, in consciousness, distinguish between his father and God or even between himself and his wife as potential mothers. Moreover, his feeling that human beings other than himself were shadows rather than real expressed how his representation of the world had broken down. Matte-Blanco thinks that Schreber did not feel related because his concepts of himself, other people, and all humanity were not separately experienced; it is only in this way that they could be appropriately linked together.

Some specific forms of bi-logical structure

The bi-logical stratified structure provides only one example of the way bi-logical concepts can elucidate unconscious processes. Matte-Blanco has delineated a number of other specific structures that can be met in clinical practice or even any day in conversation.

The first that he noticed can be observed as follows. In the course of a chain of ordinary bivalent logical reasoning, a symmetrical link (i.e. a step or link where a symmetrization occurs, termed PS) is introduced alternately with a bivalent link. For example, after he was bitten by a dog, a schizophrenic went to consult a dentist. It looks as if the reasoning which led to such a bizarre action might have gone as follows. First, that a dog has bitten A. has implied to him that he, A., has bitten the dog (PS). Second, since the dog has behaved badly he is a bad dog. However, this would imply that A. is also bad: a bivalent-logical reasoning which takes its starting point from a symmetrization. Third, it seems that because A. is bad (morally) his tooth is bad (morally); the part is treated as equal to the whole (PS). Note that in normal logic this would not follow. Fourth, a 'morally bad tooth' is an element of the class of all bad teeth; a physically bad tooth (caries) is another element of this class; bivalent logic is employed to construct the class. Fifth, if PS is now applied to the class of bad teeth, then 'morally bad tooth' is equal to 'physically bad tooth'. Sixth, since a dentist treats decayed teeth, that is the place to seek help (a deduction based on knowledge acquired by experience as seen in terms of bivalent logic). The feature of this patient's reasoning to attend to is the alternation between bivalent, asymmetrical reasoning and symmetrical thinking. For brevity, Matte-Blanco calls this type of thinking an *Alassi* (alternating asymmetrical/symmetrical) type of bi-logical structure.

A second type of reasoning process is that in which the same restricted piece of reality is seen *simultaneously* from the point of view of normal or asymmetrical reasoning and from a symmetrical point of view. For brevity's sake we may call it a *Simassi* type of bi-logical structure. Matte-Blanco gives another example of a schizophrenic, mentioned by Storch, who, upon seeing a door in the process of opening, felt frightened and exclaimed, 'The animals are eating me.' In the first place, there is a symmetrization in this comment because, as Storch (1924: 10) pointed out, in the German language *Tieren* (animals) sounds similar to *Thüren* (doors); the patient treats one sound as though it were the same as the other (PS). Also, the patient made his comment when the door was opening. Now the (horizontal) rotation of the door around its hinges with the consequent appearance of an opening or gap is quite likely to be thought of as similar to the vertical rotating movement of the jaw and the opening of the mouth. But the patient treats this similarity as an identity – this is another symmetrization which refers to the mouth and to the gap of the door. This equation is the starting point of a further symmetrization; from the identity of mouth and opening door he goes to the identity between door and animal: identity between the two on account of the (symmetrical) identity between a part of one and a part of the other. Note that, even if the identity between mouth and opening door were accepted, one could not conclude in bivalent logic that door and animals are identical. There are, therefore, three symmetrizations in this case of reasoning. In the second place, however, the patient, who was not a confused but a paranoid schizophrenic, knew quite well that the door was a door. In other words, he conceived it simultaneously as a door and as a dangerous animal: a Simassi bi-logical structure of 'reasoning'.

There is a third type of bi-logical reasoning which is frequently seen in dreams and also in waking life and which is connected to what Freud initially described as distinguishing marks of the primary process, i.e. displacement and condensation. When one displaces an aspect of a given person or of oneself on to another person (in the case of oneself it is a particular form of displacement called projection), one finds that, on the one hand, the displaced aspect appears as separate – i.e. as being in another individual – and, on the other, it still is the individual. The displaced aspect is at the same time outside and inside the person, only for certain, but not all, purposes it is considered as being only outside. Matte-Blanco now goes on to a new direction of reasoning which is developed fully later in his book. We can only allude to it here.

In the case of displacement, and that form of it called projection in particular, a characteristic is experienced at one time or another as all the following: as belonging to the self, as not belonging to the self but to another, and as belonging to both. Here a characteristic is 'seen' sometimes in one 'place' (self), sometimes in two (selves). In later chapters Matte-Blanco will discuss the similar conceptual problems raised by the widely used psychoanalytic concepts of projection and introjection, particularly in regard to Freud's under-standing of projection in the Schreber case and to Melanie Klein's concept of projective identification. When Matte-Blanco, describing the way Freud and other authors have struggled with the underlying logic, asks how phenomena of this kind can be best conceived, his answer is to suggest that psychic space should not be conceived as three-dimensional space but, borrowing once more from mathemat-ics, as a multidimensional space of *n* dimensions. This idea seems to us to be of great value for psychoanalytic thinking, but we intend to introduce it only very briefly here.

According to Matte-Blanco, mathematical ideas about the con-sequences of representing multidimensional space in a space of fewer dimensions help to overcome the logical difficulty of trying to remain precise and 'logical' while suggesting that 'selves' can feel in two or more places at once. The crucial point is that recognized by mathematicians when they argue that when a structure, of *n* dimensions, say, is represented by a structure in fewer dimensions, *n* − 1, say, then a *repetition* of points occurs. Take, for example, a simple triangle *ABC*, represented conventionally in two dimensions as in *Figure 1*. If we want to represent it as best we can in a lower number of dimensions, conventionally as a line, we get the result in *Figure 2* – a line *ABCA*. The point *A* must be repeated in order to represent a triangle on a single line. As Matte-Blanco will explore

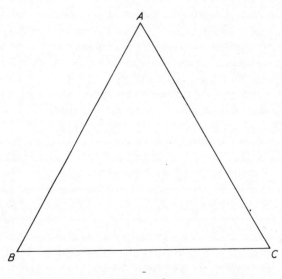

Figure 1

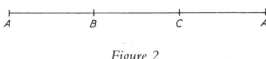

Figure 2

subsequently, the greater the number of dimensions upon which the reduction applies, the greater the number of repetitions of points. He shows in his discussion that the mind registers many different *qualities* in things and must thus absorb many dimensions. But it can *imagine* only in three dimensions. Thus the experience that selves are repeated, as in the phenomena of displacement and projection, is a function of the mind reducing its multidimensional experience to a three-dimensional imagination.

Returning to displacement, this takes place when, first, a given individual is split (into at least two individuals), and subsequently one of them is seen as separated from the original person. This suggests that the individual in question is conceived as isomorphic[8] to a *space of more than three dimensions* and is represented in terms of a space of fewer dimensions, with the result that volumes are repeated or multiplied. For this reason Matte-Blanco calls this particular type of bi-logical structure a tridimensionalized one, in short the *Tridim* structure.

The Tridim is a bi-logical structure for two reasons. First, one can see in it the presence of symmetrical logic in that two different persons are implicitly treated as only one; i.e. the original person and the person on to whom displacement takes place are really the same person in different 'incarnations', just as happens in a symmetrized class or set. Second, however, bivalent logic is present in that one sees the appearances of two quite different and separated persons; there is no identification. An example was discussed early in this chapter when Freud's analysis of his dream concerning a man with a fair beard was introduced. The image formed, Freud argued, a composite one because it stood for several people Freud knew, each representing several different ideas. Matte-Blanco suggests that the fact that the beard was blurred indicated a vague (asymmetrical) awareness of what had happened in the dream work. It is, in fact, only by means of the analysis of the associations that one can discover the (secret) identity of the two. This bi-logical structure is not of the Alassi type, because there is no alteration of bivalent and symmetrical logic, or of the Simassi type, because the same piece of observable or visible reality is not seen simultaneously in terms of the two logics. In the Tridim structure one can, at first sight, detect only the heterogenic asymmetrical mode. The indivisible mode is

36

dissimulated, precisely by means of a splitting-displacement, which makes one appear as two.

In condensation we also see that a given person, who appears 'normally' as three-dimensional, has the features of several different persons. It is as though these persons have all been catapulted and compressed into only one; in Freudian terms, it is a composite figure. This suggests that a being which is isomorphic to a space of more than three dimensions is made to appear as three-dimensional. The traces of a number of dimensions higher than three, however, are suggested in the different features of different three-dimensional persons. In the end we see that splitting-displacement and condensation both arrive at three-dimensionality, only by opposite paths.

These three bi-logical structures – Simassi, Alassi, and Tridim – are only the first few structures to be investigated by Matte-Blanco. It is probably in the region of investigating various defence mechanisms in terms of these structures that the most immediate clinical research might be done. Matte-Blanco has made a start in this volume by convincingly investigating projective identification. The problem for such future investigations may lie, we think, not in spotting symmetrizations, but in differentiating one form of structure from another. Looked at in one way they often seem of one sort, while looked at from another point of view the same structure can seem to be another sort.

A new perspective on the inner world: the basic matrix of projection and introjection

Having discussed asymmetry and symmetrization, strata created by degrees of symmetrization, and bi-logical structures, we can briefly take another look at the notion of *inner world*. Using these ideas of Matte-Blanco, it becomes plain that the usual concept of an 'inner world' is a tridimensional one. It involves definitive spaces and with it the idea of 'inside' and 'outside'. All these require highly articulated and fixed concepts of space and, therefore, the availability of asymmetrical relations. If this is so it can apply only in the relatively superficial strata of the mind where asymmetry remains consistently functional. At more general, deeper, or more symmetrized strata, the mind would not be operating with such ideas as 'inner' and 'outer', or, therefore, with 'self' and 'not-self'. Under Matte-Blanco's gaze our traditional view that the mind and the self function by having an inside and an outside looks distinctly simplistic.

Matte-Blanco makes it plain, of course, that at certain levels close to consciousness asymmetrical thinking is available and, therefore, that inside and outside distinctions present no particular difficulty. But, if we wish to understand mental functioning better, and particularly if we are to do justice to what we know about the characteristics of unconscious thought (i.e. to symmetrical logic), Matte-Blanco stresses that we must become able to think in more ways than of discrete objects in a three-dimensional space. Later in the book he will make particular observations arising from his conceptualization and will investigate splitting, projection, and introjection, particularly projective identification, in great detail, from the bi-logical point of view. Here we will do no more than indicate to the reader the thrust of his ideas.

We have just shown how one characteristic of the unconscious, displacement, rests upon a symmetrization. Matte-Blanco delves deeply into this to show in detail that projection is a particular form of displacement, as is introjection. Both thus rest upon a basis of symmetrization. A first step in projection, for instance, involves the self and an object being registered as belonging to the same class: having an attribute in common. They are then totally identified – symmetrized, in other words. When this has taken place, further functions operate to create the final form of the projection or introjection. There are thus several strata of bi-logic functioning at once. The level at which the symmetrization takes place, identifying the self with another object, he calls the level of the *basic matrix* of projection and introjection. The final path, as it were, of the projection as introjection, however, involves asymmetrical functions. For instance, projection does usually involve a movement from self to an outside object; this is a spatial change, which is asymmetrical of course. Actually Matte-Blanco envisages that projection partially retains spatial relations, but time is symmetrized. This stratum where asymmetry is used in the defence he terms the *level of happening* of the mechanism.

Using these ideas he examines the many different forms of projection that have been recorded and is able to throw light on some of the more puzzling phenomena: such as the way projective identification, its basis in the basic matrix of symmetrization, leads to a feeling of impoverishment.

As you will see later in the book, Matte-Blanco investigates many aspects of bi-logical structures. But this will suffice for us here, with one very notable exception. This is the question of infinity and the individual experience of it, to which Matte-Blanco attaches much significance.

Infinity as a bi-logical structure and its function in emotion and affects

You will remember that, when a symmetrization takes place within a class or set, then differences between its elements tend to disappear. All that is known, in effect, is the characteristic of the set. A consequence of this is that discrimination of any hierarchy (which is asymmetrical) in the set disappears. This in turn means that *a member of, or subset of, a set can be known only as identical to the whole class*. This, for instance, would occur in the (psychotic) thought that plants, animals, and humans are equally evil because they are alive and all living things are greedy, hence evil. A similar phenomenon was noted earlier in the experience of equating penis, whole body, and whole self.

Now Matte-Blanco does something very unusual. In contemplating this phenomenon of part being equal to the whole, he asks this question: 'In mathematics, when is a proper subset equivalent to (i.e. has as many elements as) the whole set?' The answer, which has been recognized mathematically for a good many years, is 'Only when the set is infinite.' By 'infinite' we mean a set in which, even conceptually, there is no limit to the continuing of it.

A little later in this book Matte-Blanco goes into this question in logical detail. Here is a simple illustration which will hardly satisfy a mathematician, but may make this striking oddity more comprehensible to others.

Take the set of all whole numbers 1, 2, 3, 4, etc. This is an infinite set. Now take a part of this set – say, the subset of all even numbers (2, 4, 6, 8, etc.). This subset is also infinite. Since both sets are the same, i.e. infinite, there must be a one-to-one correspondence between every number in each set. Hence, for every whole number there corresponds one and only one even number. For instance 1 corresponds to 2, 2 to 4, 3 to 6, and so on *ad infinitum*. There are as many even numbers as whole numbers. But the even numbers comprise a proper subset, for the set of whole numbers includes odd numbers as well. This whole–part equivalence characterizes only infinite sets.

By using similar but more sophisticated reasoning, Matte-Blanco concludes that mathematical infinite sets behave in a way which is similar to parts being identical to wholes when a symmetrization takes place. Matte-Blanco, as you will see later in the book, considers that, in the concept of the infinite, mathematicians have actually stumbled on a bi-logical structure. Up until now at least they have been content to leave this phenomenon as a paradox. Matte-Blanco argues that they have thus missed a great opportunity.

We, of course, cannot enter into this question here; let us just consider some general elementary ideas. There are many conceivable sorts of infinite sets. A line a millimetre long can conceptually be divided into an infinite number of smaller lines. When each of these lines is infinitely short and infinitely narrow it becomes that well-known idea, a point. A line is thus an infinite number of points. A circle can be bisected in an infinite number of ways. A leaf on a tree can take up an infinite number of positions; likewise a dance can be performed by an infinite variety of movements, while still conforming to the pattern of its music. Our minds can conceive of an infinite number of infinite sets.

In this way Matte-Blanco has introduced the idea of infinity and hence of *infinite experiences* into psychoanalysis. This was certainly not there before. Does it throw light upon psychoanalytic work?

Anybody, once alerted to it, will notice allusions to infinite experiences every day. *Omniscience* obviously has an infinite basis; 'there is no limit to my knowing'. *Omnipotence* likewise means 'there is no limit to what I can do'. *Impotence* also is based on 'think of anything and I won't be able to do it'. Here a negation is extended infinitely. In *idealization* the self tends towards the infinitely small, while an object is endowed towards infinite greatness in one way or another.

In all these there is an experience of *quantity*, albeit a very loose one, and it is upon this that the tendency towards infinity is based. Here, incidentally, we have more evidence for the existence of bi-logical structures in the mind.

With omnipotence, idealization, and so on we are clearly concerned with emotional experiences. Let us look at a few other emotions in this light. It seems that the stronger an emotion is, the more clearly does it contain infinite experiences. For instance, consider being in love. If a lover said, 'I am in love with you only for a finite time and in a specific location,' you would feel, 'Here is not a true lover but a cold fish.' Rather, at its height the true lover feels that the loved one's beauty is all beauty, and his love is all love. Such emotions may not be very logical but they are essential to most of us. Here infinities are ruling, time and space mean little, parts tend to be equal to wholes. We have long recognized that idealization dominates the state of being in love. Matte-Blanco has added a new dimension to both by demonstrating the part played by infinity.

You can examine for yourself the experiences of other extreme emotions, such as hatred, anger, fear, and grief. By introspecting we think you will quickly see how these emotions can irradiate out so that all things conceivable can get infused with the emotion. To coin a word, 'infinitization' is taking place.

If it proves to be the case that *any feeling*, even a muted one, contains these extremes as nuclei, but has them contained by relating them to other feelings and ideas, then we may conclude as follows: *all affects contain elements of infinity*. This in turn means that all affects contain symmetrization of thought. You will remember that Matte-Blanco came to the same conclusion by a different route when we considered his idea of logical strata of the mind. You will remember that it was at the second stratum that he thought that conscious emotions were experienced.

Notes

1 This particular chapter by the two editors of this volume arose out of difficulties in its presentation. We felt a simple introduction to the work of Matte-Blanco was needed to orientate the reader to the importance of Matte-Blanco's contribution to psychoanalytic thought. He whole-heartedly agreed with us in principle but felt it was wrong for him himself to surrender his way of presenting arguments. It was thus agreed that we should write the introductory chapter and use his ideas as we felt best. We have unashamedly borrowed wholesale from his writing (including various drafts), but blame for errors in this chapter must rest with us alone.

2 See Ellenberger (1970).

3 'The nucleus of the Ucs consists of instinctual representatives which seek to discharge their cathexis; that is to say, it consists of wishful impulses. These instinctual impulses are co-ordinate with one another, exist side by side without being influenced by one another, and are exempt from mutual contradiction' (SE 14: 186).

4 'In the great majority of cases, it must be confessed, the causal relation is not represented at all but is lost in the confusion of elements which inevitably occurs in the process of dreaming' (SE 4: 316).

5 The concept of *total order* requires asymmetrical relations and must break down if PS is employed. To explain, consider the set of natural numbers or integers in what is called its natural order, i.e. 1, 2, 3, 4, etc. One can easily see that, if we take any two numbers, with no exception, we find that one is greater and the other is smaller; it is then said that the relation between natural numbers is a connected relation, i.e. it applies to all the elements of the set of natural numbers; in other words, all natural numbers are connected by the relationship of being greater or smaller. By

convention a smaller number precedes, and a bigger one follows. Thus if, say, 3 is smaller than 14, then it cannot be bigger than 14: an asymmetrical relation. Similarly, no number can be greater or smaller than itself: what is known as an irreflexive relation. In this way, if, say, 14 is bigger than 10, and 10 is bigger than 3, it follows that 14 is bigger than 3: a transitive (asymmetrical) relation. A set with all these four relations or properties is said to be a totally ordered set. It is easily seen that if PS holds in such a set, the concept of total order collapses (3 would be greater than 14 as well as smaller than it, etc.).

6 In terms of what is to follow, one asks: what kind of structure? Matte-Blanco is inclined to think of it as being of the Simassi type.

7 Matte-Blanco considers this an example of how the indivisible is there but is invisible.

8 Isomorphic, i.e. corresponding in form and in the nature and product of their operations.

2

Bi-logical structures, the unconscious, and the mathematical infinite

Initial panoramic view

The protagonist of this book is the Freudian unconscious. Its nature and my reformulation of it will be found in the introductory chapter which Eric Rayner and David Tuckett have kindly written.

Further reflection about the subject has made me aware that the Freudian notion of the unconscious contains implicitly two essential aspects which, so far as I know, have not been explicitly mentioned before: the concept of bi-logical structure and that of the fundamental antinomy which is its most obvious consequence. This book devotes special attention to both. Once they are clearly understood, the reader may find that, together, they open up new ways towards a deeper understanding of human beings and of certain aspects of the world. This does not mean, however, that I intend to neglect other aspects of the unconscious.

This chapter and the next one describe these concepts. The rest of the book is devoted to the study of clinical examples of them, to widen their understanding, to see their various applications and possible developments, and, finally, to give some hints about their philosophical pertinence. (Both clinical and non-clinical examples are numbered consecutively throughout the book.)

If we translate Freud's intuitions about the unconscious into a more general, logical, and philosophical language, as I have tried to do, we become aware that such intuitions are only one expression of a fundamental epistemological problem which is also found in other fields, such as mathematics, philosophy, and probably also physics. The subjects of these disciplines are in themselves completely alien to

43

psychoanalysis, yet they seem to show, in some of their aspects, the same lack of respect for the rules of logic found by Freud in the unconscious (I mean logic as it is conceived and employed so far). Taken together with psychoanalysis, they open a door to a new epistemology which may bring those aberrant aspects of humans and the world into the realm, if not of human understanding, at least of the definable and circumscribable.

Since my reflections along the lines I have just hinted at reached a certain degree of development, I have been repeatedly and admiringly surprised to see that some of the things that had become clear to me, in terms of the new formulation, had already been said by Freud in a way which I had not grasped before and which is generally unnoticed. Some examples of this will be seen throughout the book. It seems pertinent to start with an example given by Freud himself:

Example 1
'July 12 [1938]. . . . "Having" and "being" in children. Children like expressing an object-relation by an identification: "I am the object." "Having" is the later of the two; after loss of the object it relapses into "being". Example: the breast. "The breast is a part of me, I am the breast." Only later: "I have it" – that is, "I am not it".'

(SE 23: 299)

This was written less than fourteen months before Freud's death. if we examine it, in terms of the two modes of being (see the introductory chapter), it is immediately seen that 'having' is the expression of the heterogenic mode, which is the mode through which thinking and perception are usually expressed in a clear way. On the other hand, the identity between breast and child ('I am the breast') is an expression of the indivisible mode. Note, furthermore, that if we also consider the expression 'the breast is part of me', which precedes it, we are confronted with two assertions which are incompatible in normal logic. It is as though we said: 'my right hand is part of me' together with 'I am my right hand'; it amounts to affirming the identity between a (proper) part and the whole, which is a violation of the rules of classical logic. This is a common occurrence in the unconscious, which abides by the principle of symmetry. So we conclude that these two assertions, if taken together, constitute an example of the Simassi structure (see section 2, below) and, as such, an example of the fundamental antinomy.

I think it is fair to tell the reader that a thorough understanding of Part One of this book requires a certain amount of work. As I see it, the main reason for the difficulty is due to the fact that it deals with the most difficult and yet the most important aspects of the Freudian unconscious. Such aspects are utterly different from everything our thinking and our perceptions are able to know and have accustomed us to know.

If a moment arrives when the reader feels discouraged, perhaps even irritated, when he or she contemplates something not immediately understood, I dare say that this is sometimes inevitable. The psychoanalytic movement has been working on Freud's contribution for nearly a century, and we are still struggling to understand all his intuitions.

The subject, however, deserves some effort to master it. At this point I dare to make a second suggestion to the reader. If you find that the next two chapters are too complicated and appear confused to you, do not try to understand them completely from the beginning. Go on with the reading and, when the need arises, return to them. You will then find that things are becoming more accessible, until a moment comes when you will feel yourself quite at ease handling the very notions which at a first impression seemed confused. I have had this experience many times in my study of mathematics.

Example 2

A schizophrenic patient told me, 'Your assistant is very rich.' I asked her how she knew it. She answered, 'He is very tall.' This process, of thinking shows: (a) The discovery of a general class to which those who are tall and those who are rich belong as sub-classes: principle of generalization (PG). It could be formulated as the class of people who have something (height, money, etc.) in a high degree. (b) Treating the sub-classes of this class as identical: principle of symmetry (PS). Therefore: very tall = very rich. Note that, without PG, PS could not be made to hold in this case.

The interweaving of PG and PS is seen in the characteristics of the unconscious, described by Freud.

In the light of later reflections, PG can now be seen as the expression of the indivisible mode which slips into the territory of classical logic with no contamination of symmetrical logic (part (a) of the reasoning just presented). Its constant presence in unconscious and schizophrenic manifestations suggests that there are aspects and times of human life in which the homogeneous mode is, so to speak, eager to come to the first, conscious plane. In such cases one 'uses' classical-logic bi-modality as well as bi-logic bi-modality, frequently both together. This is what we shall now consider (see also Chapter 3, sections 2 and 3).

1 Bi-logic and bi-logical structures

The utterances of the patient just mentioned show, on the one hand, a process of reasoning which strictly respects bivalent logic and, on the other, a reasoning based on symmetrical logic. It is, therefore, a process which submits, not to one logic – as so far do, for instance, all reasonings of arithmetic and science – but to two; it is *a bi-logical reasoning.*

All processes of thinking have a certain *structure*, i.e. they are sets endowed with various relations between their components. *Processes in the so-called deep unconscious are bi-logical structures.* The evidence in favour of this assertion is overwhelming. Emotion, so far as it is expressed in thinking-feeling, is usually a set of bi-logical structures (see also Matte-Blanco 1975a: part VI). The only possible exception could be the case of mild emotions, such as pleasure and well-being; but even in such cases it seems probable that this exception refers only to the presentational aspect of emotion, whereas the underlying aspects would always be bi-logic.

Bi-logical structures are most abundant. They are seen in the various ways of conceiving and living all aspects of human life, religion, art, politics, and even science, in the differences between psychoanalysts, and in every other aspect of life. Once one gets used to seeing them, *one cannot avoid the surprising conclusion that we live the world as though it were a unique indivisible unit, with no distinction between persons and/or things. On the other hand, we usually think of it in terms of bi-logic and, some few times, in terms of classical logic.*

2 Types of bi-logical structure

In spite of the fact that the concept of bi-logical structure is only a few years old, clinical experience has already begun to show that there exist a variety of different bi-logical structures, which I shall briefly mention.

Bi-logical structures differ in the way classical and symmetrical logic intertwine with one another. So far I am able to define fifteen quite different types.

● *Alassi (alternating asymmetrical/symmetrical)*
This structure is quite common. One observes that, in the course of a process of reasoning which respects classical logic, a *symmetrical link* is introduced, i.e. a step or link which abides by PS.

Example 3
After he was bitten by a dog, a schizophrenic went to consult a dentist. If we try to reconstruct the process of reasoning that led to such a bizarre action, we may say as follows. (a) A dog bites A. implies A. bites the dog: PS. (b) If the dog is bad (he behaves badly) on account of his action, this implies that A. is also bad: a classical-logical reasoning which takes its starting-point from a symmetriz-ation. (c) A. is bad (morally) implies his tooth is bad (morally); the part is treated as equal to the whole: PS. Note that in normal logic this would be a wrong conclusion following from a wrong reasoning. (d) A 'morally bad tooth' is an element of the class of all bad teeth; a physically bad tooth (caries) is another element of this class: classical logic. (e) If PS is applied to the class mentioned in (d), then 'morally bad tooth' is equal to 'physically bad tooth'. (f) A dentist treats decayed teeth: a knowledge acquired by experience as seen in terms of bivalent logic.

Hence, the decision to go to the dentist after having been bitten by a dog is a perfectly legitimate classical-logical conclusion of this particular bi-logical reasoning.

One can see that in the reasoning just described there is an alternation of asymmetrical (logico-bivalent) links of the chain with some symmetrical ones. For a brief reference I have suggested calling this structure an *Alassi type of bi-logical structure.*

● *Simassi (simultaneously asymmetrical/symmetrical)*
A second type is that in which the same restricted piece of reality is seen simultaneously from the point of view of normal or asymmetri-cal reasoning and from a symmetrical point of view. For brevity's sake we may call it a *Simassi type of bi-logical structure.*

Example 4
A schizophrenic, mentioned by Storch, upon seeing a door in the process of opening, felt frightened and exclaimed, 'The animals are eating me.' One can say, in the first place, that there is a symmetrization visible in this comment, and this for two reasons. (a) As Storch (1924: 10) points out, in the German language *Tieren* (animals) sounds similar to *Thüren* (doors); the patient treats one as though it were the same as the other: identity between two elements of the class or set of objects whose names have a similar sound: PS. (b) Note the the patient made his comment when the door was opening. Now the (horizontal) rotation of the door around its hinges with the consequent appearance of an opening or gap is similar to the vertical rotating movement of the jaw and the opening of the mouth. The patient treats this similarity as identity: a symmetrization which

refers to mouth and gap of the door. (c) This would be the starting point of a second symmetrization; from the identity of mouth and opening door he goes to the identity between door and animal: identity between the two on account of the (symmetrical) identity between a part of one and a part of the other. Note that, even if the identity between mouth and opening door were accepted, one could not conclude in classical logic that door and animals are identical. There are, therefore, three symmetrizations seen in this case.

In the second place, the patient, who was not a confused but a paranoid schizophrenic, knew quite well that the door was a door. In other words, he conceived it simultaneously as a door and as a dangerous animal: a Simassi bi-logical structure of 'reasoning'.

● *Tridim (tridimensionalized bi-logical structure)*
There is a third type of bi-logical structure which is frequently seen in dreams and also in the waking life and is connected to what Freud initially described as distinguishing marks of the primary process, i.e. displacement and condensation. When one displaces an aspect of a given person or of oneself on to another person (in the case of oneself it is a particular form of displacement called projection), one finds that, on the one hand, the displaced aspect appears as separate, i.e. as being in another individual, and, on the other, it still is the individual; the displaced aspect is at the same time outside and inside the person, except that for certain, but not all, purposes it is considered as being only outside. At other times a person may be seen as a father or mother, and in the deep unconscious, say, an authority is felt not simply as a substitute of the father, as is seen in classical logic; he *is* the father.

Displacement, therefore, takes place when, first, a given individual is split (in at least two individuals), and subsequently one of them is seen as separated from the original person. This suggests that the individual in question can be conceived as isomorphic to a space of more than three dimensions and is represented in terms of a space of fewer dimensions, with the result that volumes are repeated or multiplied (for further details of this particular aspect, see Matte-Blanco 1975a: 409–14, and Chapter 3 below). For this reason we may call this particular type of bi-logical structure by the name of *tridimensionalized or tridimensionalizing structure – in short, Tridim structure.*

Note that this is a bi-logical structure for two reasons. (a) One can see in it the presence of symmetrical logic in that two different persons are implicitly treated as only one; i.e. the original person and the person on to whom displacement takes place are really the same person in different 'incarnations', just as happens in a symmetrized class or set. (b) Classical logic is present in the fact that one sees the appearances of two quite different and separated persons: no identification. It is only by means of the analysis of the associations that one can discover the (secret) identity of the two. It is, therefore, a *dissimulated bi-logical structure*, which is neither of the Alassi type, because there is here no alternation of classical and symmetrical logic, nor of the Simassi type, because the same piece of observable or visible reality is not seen simultaneously in terms of the two logics. In the Tridim structure one can, at first sight, detect only the hetero-genic-dividing mode, while the indivisible mode is dissimulated, precisely by means of splitting-displacement, which makes one *appear* as two.

In condensation we see that a given person who appears as 'normally' three-dimensional has the features of several different persons. It is as though these persons have all been catapulted and compressed into only one; in Freudian terms, it is a composite figure. This suggests that a being which is isomorphic to a space of more than three dimensions is made to appear as three-dimensional. The traces of a number of dimensions higher than three, however, are suggested in the different features of different three-dimensional persons.

In the end we see that *splitting-displacement and condensation both arrive at three-dimensionality, only by opposite paths.*

● *The epistemological see-saw*
I have proposed this concept (see Matte-Blanco 1981: 498, section 13) to designate a curious alternation of manifestations of both modes, which has some similarity to both the Alassi and the Simassi types of bi-logical structures, without, however, being either of them. I shall discuss this concept taking an example of it seen in Bion (1975: 63).

Example 5
'CAPT. BION I stared at the speck of mud trembling on the straw. . . . Wot 'appened then? 'E fell on 'is arse. And 'is Arse wuz angry and said, Get off my Arse!. You've done nothing but throw shit at me all yore life and now you expects England to be my booty! Boo-ootiful soup; in a shell-hole in Flanders Fields. Legs and guts . . . must 'ave bin twenty men in there – Germ'um and frogslegs and all starts!'

As I see it, this piece – which recalls, with an amusing cockney humour, a grim experience – expresses subtleties which are not easy to understand. The humour of the first part seems connected with the strange and surprising relationship established between an individual and one part of his body. If we try to understand the cause of the comical effect we may say, to begin with, that the person who falls on his arse has an arse as a part, and experiences, we may surmise, an unpleasant sensation which has precisely that part as a starting-zone of it. Up to this point of the written text everything unfolds in complete respect of bivalent logic, and there are several asymmetrical relations visible in the text.

When "'is' Arse wuz angry and said, Get off my Arse!' we are confronted with a new, quite complex manifestation. In the first place, grammatically speaking, the 'arse' becomes the 'Arse', with all the dignity which the capital letter confers to a given person; the arse is promoted from the status of part of the body to that of an honourable person. 'He' then proceeds to speak, i.e. behave like a person. If we consider that it was not he – when 'he' was 'it' – who actually had the sensation, but its 'owner' and, furthermore, that the only thing we know about this latter is the fall in question, we become aware that the arse is reacting as if it were the owner, i.e. the whole individual: identity between part and whole, as seen in symmetrization.

Up to this point, therefore, the text shows the presence of classical logic and symmetrical logic. In other words, it shows a bi-logical structure. We now ask: of what type? We rule out immediately the Tridim structure, for there is nothing in the text that can be seen as tridimensionalization. We also find that the Alassi bi-logical structure does not correspond to this case; for, in this type, once a symmetrization is inserted as a link in a discourse (the schizophrenic bitten by a dog), it is immediately accepted and incorporated as something definitely established and it is used as such in the rest of the discourse (the patient and his teeth were bad, just as the dog was).

If it is not Alassi, it might be Simassi. Again, here, the text does not fit with the concept; for in the Simassi type a given reality is seen at the same time as symmetrized, hence as not having distinguishable parts (i.e. identity between parts and whole as we saw in the case of mothers), *and* as clearly formed of distinguishable parts or elements. This coexistence happens all along; at each point of it we see simultaneously distinction and non-distinction, i.e. classical logic and symmetrical logic. In this case, instead, we see a symmetrization which makes its appearance at a given moment; and, once the arse becomes the Arse, identical to the person, the symmetrization disappears and is no longer to be found. We are confronted with a new individual, initially with the characteristics of the man who gave birth to him; but immediately after, he becomes quite distinguishable from him, as is seen in what he says. In other words, once the Arse is born, so to say by gemmation – which in this case takes place after an instantaneous identification of the part with the whole – it becomes so distinguishable from the being who originated it as to quarrel with him and lament about the ill-treatment received by him when he was an 'it', i.e. an anus.

Note also (a) the nature of his order: 'Get off . . . '. It is evident that though this is an order to perform a highly asymmetrical action it could not be given by a person to his own anus nor by an anus or bottom to its possessor: only to another person. (b) His complaint: 'You've done nothing . . . ' likewise could not apply to the same individual but only to a different one. On the other hand, the action for which he is accused, when performed by anybody, is not an offence to his anus, which participates in a function which both is necessary and benefits the individual who performs it and, in consequence, also benefits his anus. All this shows that a clear distance is now established between the individual and his anus-become-person.

We conclude: this structure is different from all those we have already studied. That it deserved to be called epistemological see-saw is seen in the fact that whenever one of the modes is expressed, the other one comes forth and claims its rights, and so on. In the case we have studied we have seen that the discourse of the quotation starts asymmetrically, then a symmetrization sets in, and immediately afterwards asymmetry comes again, through the appearance of a new person, different from that whence 'it-He' came. It does not stop there, however, for the indivisible mode quickly butts in, still another time, as is suggested in the lines that follow, i.e. the identity of sound between 'booty' and 'boo-ootiful', to which attention is called; this suggests a renewed presence of non-bi-logical bi-modality. Furthermore 'soup' is the concept of something which, however much made of parts, is one thing: a bi-modal, non-bi-logical, presence of the indivisible mode. Immediately afterwards twenty different men, Germans and frog legs all mixed up, yet different: the heterogenic mode in action. But, even here, 'frogslegs' is one term with two meanings – the legs of frogs and the French people: non-bi-logical presence of both modes. Note also that the French were called Frogs by the English because of their proclivity to eat frogs' legs – an identification of a being with the object of one of its actions: he eats frogs' legs = he is a Frog: PS in action.

It seems, therefore, that the term in question gives account of the structure we have studied here.

As already suggested, it seems that the epistemological see-saw can be at times a bi-logical structure, and at other times the expression of non-bi-logical bi-modality. Perhaps it plays a role in normal thinking. But this is a question to be studied.

● *The molar bi-logical structure*
This is another type, which we shall consider in relation to the work of Melanie Klein in Chapter 7.

● *The constitutive stratified bi-logical structure*
A few words of introduction. When trying to disentangle the structure of the Schreber case (Freud 1911, SE12), I became aware that this could be done only in the light of a structure seen in all human beings. Subsequently I realized that, without being aware, I had described this structure in great detail in chapter 14 of *The Unconscious as Infinite Sets*. At the time I had not come to the concept of bi-logical structure and, therefore, I did not mention it.

My intention here is to complete the rather extensive discussion of the question undertaken in that chapter. So I shall only concentrate on the 'structure aspect' of the question.

To make the present discourse somewhat self-contained I shall begin with a quotation from chapter 14:

'behind every individual or relationship – as perceived or given in a certain manner at a given moment – the self "sees" an infinite series (sequence) of individuals; all these satisfy the same propositional function (which may be a complex one, i.e. consisting of several sub-statements) under the light of which the individual or the relationship in question is perceived or seen or lived at this moment. If the attention of the observer remains focused on the first level, that of consciousness, then he will only be aware of the concrete individual; and if he lets himself be permeated by the underlying levels, this infinity will unfold itself before him, though in an unconscious manner. Embracing this infinite series (sequence) there is one unity: the class or the set. This, in its turn, is lived as one unity.'   (Matte-Blanco 1975a: 170)

In this structure we may distinguish various strata, each with various levels conceived in terms of greater or lesser generality.

First stratum: conscious and well-delimited objects. A first conscious level of this stratum is that of the conception or perception of a concrete and well-delimited thing – a person, a material object, a well-defined thought referring to a concrete fact ('the temperature is rising'), or an abstract concept, such as the concept of freedom of the will.

This would be the level of delimited and quite asymmetrical thinking or perception.

A second, also conscious, level of the same stratum would be that in which one becomes aware of or explores the relations between the concrete object under consideration and others: their similarities and their differences,i.e. the classes of equivalence to which it belongs and those to which it does not belong: (a) Peter is a man, i.e. he is an element of the equivalence class of men; (b) he is not an element of the equivalence class of women; (c) he is a psychoanalyst; (d) he belongs to such-and-such current of analysis, etc.

It will be seen that at this level the immediate object in question becomes linked up or related to a potentially very great number of other objects or sets of objects. All of this happens at levels of consciousness or is susceptible of easy arrival in consciousness.

Second stratum: more or less conscious emotions. The distinctive trait of this stratum is that emotion makes its first easily visible appearance: 'I like it', 'I hate him', 'I fear him', and so on. Since emotions are bi-logical structures we may say that this level begins to show symmetrizations which are, nevertheless, quite well delimited at the conscious level. For instance, one may feel, 'this person is like a tiger'; but a normal person will not feel he is a tiger.

A third, deeper stratum: symmetrization of the class. As we descend further into the strata of greater symmetry, things belonging to the same equivalence class become identical not only with regard to the property which defines the equivalence class in question (for instance, the class of those who are identical with regard to the property 'having blue eyes', that of doctors of philosophy, of cruel people, those of the same race, tall people, and so on) but to all properties, so that each member of the class becomes identical to all others in all respects: symmetrization.

A fundamental consequence of such symmetrization is that each individual becomes the class and, hence, has all the potentialities of the class or set, up to its highest degree. If the set is that of angry mothers, then she or any part of her – for instance, the breast – will be felt as being immensely dangerous. If it is the class of fathers, the penis will be felt extremely penetrating and, as such, dangerous. The same holds for goodness.

This is the stratum where intensity tends to infinite values. Owing precisely to the identificaton of individual and class, the first acquires all the potentialities of the last and, hence, a potentially infinite degree of the characteristics of the class.

Klein has masterfully explored this stratum and has found a rich harvest of strange, almost incredible, yet true and stimulating facts.

Symmetrization of the class is also seen in an example quite different from those just mentioned: timelessness. The instants have all the same properties of preceding–following and, hence, become indistinguishable from one another.

Note that in this case the concept of intensity, in contrast to the other cases just mentioned, plays no role. Yet the stratum is the same: an interesting fact to reflect upon.

Fourth stratum: formation of wider classes which are symmetrized. Owing to the union of different classes or sets, these become wider, more comprehensive. Example: the class of men comprises that of women and children, so that, when symmetrized, to be a man is identical to being a woman or a child.

I believe this is a stratum where some schizophrenics tend to feel at ease, treating as equal things which belong to subsets or substructures of a larger set or structure. In example 2 a woman patient who said that a man was very rich, when asked why, answered, 'He is very tall.' Note: both were subsets of the larger set of those who have something in a high degree. Symmetrization results in: very tall = very rich. At this stratum of greater symmetry and correspondingly less asymmetry, the great aggressions of the preceding stratum are no longer found. *Intense aggression requires a good amount of asymmetry.* This is important to keep in mind the understanding of schizophrenia. Some tend to think that all the emotions of schizophrenics are extremely intense. This seems to be only partially true. Experience with such patients seems to be in favour of the view that patients with very extensive symmetrizations, which treat as equal classes which are not equal, frequently are quiet, 'serene' people.

Of course, at certain very deep levels everybody has the peace of the depth.

The following characteristics of the unconscious belong to this rather deep stratum:

- absence of contradiction – a set which contains all affirmations and their corresponding negation, if symmetrized, results in any assertion being equal to its negation: no possibility of contradiction;

- identity of psychical and external reality, for the same reason.

The deepest strata – their mathematical limit: indivisibility. From this point 'downwards' the amount of symmetrization is so great that thinking, which requires asymmetrical relations, is greatly impaired.

The conceptual end is the pure indivisible mode, where everything is everything else, and where the relations between things are all theoretically contained in any single thing which the intellect can grasp. The endless number of things tend to become, mysteriously, only one thing.

The relations between the strata. We now arrive at a very fundamental aspect of human nature. In normal development and structure there is a mysterious relationship between the strata, formed by two apparently incompatible properties:

(a) On the one hand, each stratum is well differentiated from those above or below, in the sense that in general what occurs in one stratum does not occur in those strata which are above or below. For instance, in the first stratum there is a well-delimited grasp of concrete, almost isolated objects, relations, or situations, while in the second stratum there is a great amount of interrelation between the elements of this stratum. The third stratum establishes, through symmetrization, identities between individuals; this does not occur in the first two. And so on, as an attentive reader may verify by himself. As symmetrizations become more extensive, new characteristics make their appearance, which, as we have seen, were not present in the upper levels.

(b) In spite of these neat distinctions between the strata, it can also be affirmed that *each stratum is present in a mysterious way in every one of the strata which are nearer to the surface.* But they are present in an invisible way which respects the characteristics of the stratum in question. To take one case as example, behind and inside a concrete visible mother, say Mrs Rosa Torres, there also are a number of other mothers, such as one's own mother and so many other mother-images which have played a role in one's life; and there also is motherhood. All this happens in the midst of total respect for the rules of bivalent logic, with no sign or visible manifestation of bi-logic; in the midst of it the individual remains always intact as individual, in spite of the fact that the second and third strata are in him.

This, however, is not the whole story, for behind and inside Mrs Rosa Torres, the individual, together with other mothers and motherhood, there is also fatherhood: fourth stratum. Behind and inside this, there are other *classes*, of inanimate objects, of abstractions and symmetrizations, i.e. all the deepest strata; until . . . until we find *that the indivisible is mysteriously present in the profound depth of anybody, however covered and asymmetrical the surface may appear; present yet not directly or immediately grasped. The indivisible is there but it is invisible.* And, if we force language to try to convey something so difficult to convey, we may add that the indivisible is also present behind any and all 'passages' from the most divisible to the pure indivisible. And so, despite the fact that between the divisible and the indivisible there is no intermediate, no passage, yet 'they' appear to us as passages in a similar but probably not identical way as in a film. Each recorded scene is static; the succession of them gives the impression of movement. And this coincides with the fact that in modern mathematics movement, as in the case of Zeno's arrow, is conceived as a succession of immobilities.

I believe that it was Laplace who said something like this: tell me what is happening in one point of the world, and I will tell you what happens in the whole world. He was referring, I suppose, to the material world. Starting from one small stratum of the world he would reconstruct the whole universe up to the most distant galaxy. Our problem, however, is not quite this; it is to find the whole world, even the most distant galaxy, in only one point of the world, and to find that all this is indivisible, alien to space and to movement. Remember that, in the theory of relativity, time is the fourth dimension of a four-dimensional *space*. Hence all instants are there in this dimension, just as all points are there in the other three dimensions: no flow of time. However, it would, perhaps, be necessary to reflect what $\sqrt{-1}$, a characteristic only of time, means in this theory.

I feel that it is through a meditative, thoughtful consideration of the observations made in psychoanalytic pratice that we have arrived at this puzzling conclusion, in front of which one has the feeling of having lost one's own bearings. Maybe, as we become more familiar with it, we shall gradually feel more at home in it. So far, there are two considerations that may help to show its reasonableness. The first is that of the mathematical infinite (see section 8, below) where (according to my own conclusion) we find that $1 = 2 = 3 = \ldots$ any number: a most strange conclusion, which reveals the indivisible in nature. This also means that each number, for instance 16, is itself *and* all other integers. In consequence, *as* 16 it is smaller than 17, 18, etc. . . . and bigger than 1, 2 . . . 15. *All this happens within itself, i.e. within 16; and also in any other number*: most strange, yet a legitimate conclusion from a legitimate, strictly classical-logical reasoning, i.e. a reasoning made in respect of the normal laws of logic. In other words, 'inside' 16 or any other number there is, in this case, an infinite number of asymmetrical relations. One asks: could it not be that this is the kind of thing that happens in the superficial layers of the stratified bi-logical structure?

The second consideration regards the representation or definition of multidimensional space in terms of space of fewer dimensions (see Matte-Blanco 1975a: ch. 32, esp. 411–13). In this case, what in a space of *n* dimensions *is* one thing (for instance, point *C* of a triangle *ABC*) in a space of fewer dimensions *appears* as several, up to an infinite number of things (see Chapter 3, section 8).

56

One asks: could it not be that these several, up to infinite, things in the visible surface may 'become', in the 'deepest depth' of the infinitely dimensional indivisible, only one thing – just *the* indivisible? In such a case the 'depth' may be multidimensional, up to an infinite number of dimensions.

And so we find, as in the case of the infinite, that our intellect is capable of discovering truths which the intellect itself is unable to understand. 'Memento homo . . .'

A comprehensive view of the stratified structure. It obviously is a structure because it refers to the relations between levels. It is a structure whose elements are structures, i.e. sets endowed with one or more relations. Its elements are the levels. It is a bi-logical structure because it could not be defined if classical and symmetrical logic were not available in it.

It is different from all other bi-logical structures so far known. It is different in more than one way. I shall mention only the following. (a) In contrast to all of them it is so very extensive – both 'horizontally' and 'vertically' – as to comprise the whole human psychic life. (b) It has the peculiarity that it 'starts' from pure classical logic and 'goes down' to symmetrizations, and these become more and more extensive until it 'ends up' in only one something which is both one and indivisible. (c) In the midst of it we may find all the other bi-logical structures so far known, some of them as *components* of it at a given level, such as some of the characteristics of the unconscious; others as (normal) relations between the strata (condensation, displacement: Tridim, Multidim, molar, inverted molar); others as alterations of the normal relations between the strata, such as the short-circuit or Schreber structure; and so on. This is a subject for further study. (d) It obviously *is* constitutive of human beings because it is an essential and inevitable aspect of human psychical life. This assertion does not imply either that it is or that it is not constitutive of some non-human aspects of the world. In fact in the deeper strata human consciousness merges into or is felt as merging into the world.

In later chapters I shall introduce further bi-logical structures to discuss various co-presences of symmetrical and asymmetrical modes, underlying what psychoanalysts describe as projective identification, bizarre objects, and so on.

After having studied the *internal structures* which distinguish various bi-logical structures from one another, we may now consider other aspects in which they differ. One is the *amount of symmetry* present in them. A frequent type of Alassi structure seen in 'normal' people has only one or two symmetrized 'steps' or 'links' in the process of reasoning, and the rest respects classical logic. This type is the daily bread of human life and accounts for the extreme variety of opinions about most subjects. In everyday parlance one might say that, if somebody has a prejudice due to emotion, this disturbs (partially) his or her view of reality. If this prejudice is taken as truth, a process of reasoning which takes its starting point from it may in all other respects conform to the rules of normal logic; in other words, it is an Alassi type of reasoning.

We each make our own symmetrizations. These are dependent, among other things, on the emotions which particular life experiences have provoked and which, through irradiation (due also to symmetrization) to a variety of other territories, end up by being an aspect of our individual mental structures.

At the other extreme we see, for instance in confusional states, that so many things are identified with one another as to make ordered thinking impossible. I have used the term *symmetrical frenzy* to describe this phenomenon.

Some bi-logical structures help one in life, provided these are not 'too bi-logical'. Examples of this would be seen in the (relative) idealization of one's partner in love, or of a given state of affairs or situation. Idealization furnishes the possibility of seeing beauty and goodness in human beings and in the world and to live, in some way, in contact with Supreme Beauty and Supreme Goodness.

Other bi-logical structures, instead, put obstacles in one's inner life as well as in one's relations with fellow humans. This is frequently seen in love relationships, where the mutual incompatibility of corresponding bi-logical structures may render life quite impossible to both partners. It is striking to note that what to an outside observer seem trivial differences of opinion may become the source of considerable unhappiness.

From this point of view, therefore, we may classify bi-logical structures as more or less vital or not vital. Symmetrical frenzy, for instance, is one which makes mental life impossible to a very great extent. There also are other, less striking structures which present great obstacles to normal life.

3 A brief remark about therapy

Sometimes it seems possible to change a non-vital (i.e. one which puts obstacles to living) bi-logical structure into another, vital one, which is isomorphic to it. This seems a promising avenue to explore for psychoanalytic therapy – one which may save much time, now spent in working through, and not always with success. I already have a certain experience of it, and so far the results are encouraging. For instance, one may change a masochistic activity into a domineering one and eventually into a tender one. I should like to say that for a long time I have been sceptical about the possibility of an increase of good therapeutic results only through an increase of certain aspects of our knowledge. For instance, I very much doubt that we now get better results than in the early days of psychoanalysis, in spite of our progress in understanding, say, introjective processes, the importance of orality, and so on. That *alone* is not sufficient, and this would be an interesting subject to study. I was also sceptical about the possibility that my own researches might help therapy. The recent insights I have mentioned, about isomorphic structures, have opened my eyes to the possibility of significant progress in psychoanalytic therapy which could lead to modifications, *by means of psychoanalysis*, of functional structures in the nervous system, which would put to good use the bad experiences – such as traumas and early frustrations – which remain, so to speak, embedded in the nervous system and impede the process of healing.

In other words, a knowledge of the isomorphisms of the psychological structures which remain adamant to change may lead, by psychological means, to putting to better use their physiological correlates. Such a task would not be possible without knowing the various bi-logical structures.

4 A retrospective general look at bi-logical structures

Personally I feel that the concept of bi-logical structure enables us to bring back to psychoanalysis the most creative of all of Freud's discoveries: the *nature* of the unconscious, submitted to strange laws which are not those of normal logical thinking and which, for this very reason (it is my guess), has been to a great extent cast aside in psychoanalytical thinking and practice. For instance, when we do hear in psychoanalysis any reference to atemporality or to the absence of the principle of contradiction?

For this reason the concept of bi-logical structure – which is nothing other than the reintroduction of the notions at the base of the conception of the unconscious – is bound to play a role in future psychoanalytic research. Furthermore, it furnishes the bridge from psychoanalysis towards mathematics and epistemology and offers the possibility of mutual fertilization of these fields.

But we are at the beginning. Most probably the notions put forward here will have to become more precise; new interrelations need to be discovered, and a more general view will, I hope, eventually emerge, which itself will lead to wider and deeper knowledge.

So much, however, remains to be done before we may reach that goal.

5 Redefinition of the Freudian unconscious: a set of bi-logical structures

The five characteristics in which Freud summarized the unconscious, as well as the other eight mentioned above, seem fairly different from one another. It is difficult to see what relation there is, for instance, between condensation and timelessness. The view I am putting forward here enables us to regard all the characteristics of the unconscious as various types of structure which differ between themselves but have one feature in common: they are all bi-logical structures. *The unconscious, therefore, is a set of different bi-logical structures which, as such, are isomorphic to one another.*

Seeing it in this light, one immediately becomes aware of the possibility of deepening our understanding of the unconscious. I shall now review all thirteen characteristics in the light of the two modes. To follow this review, the reader needs to go back to Chapter 1.

Absence of contradiction and negation. Note that if there is no negation there can be no principle of contradiction, for this is defined as the incompatibility between an assertion and its negation.

In itself as 'seen' in the deep unconscious this is not a bi-logical structure but the pure expression of PS: symmetrical logic. *As seen with the eyes of a 'classical logician'* who sees both the contradiction and its absence, it obviously is a Simassi structure as already defined. Note, however, that the unconscious, also is, at times, a classical logician.

Displacement and condensation. We have already described these as Tridim structures. Again here, from the 'point of view' of the 'deep unconscious' they are not bi-logical structures but an expression of symmetrical logic or the indivisible mode. In fact, in displacement the original thing and the thing towards which it is displaced (on account of having one or several features in common) are not two similar things but only one thing. In condensation the composite figure is also, in the deep, purely symmetrical unconscious, only one thing. Seen from the point of view of thinking, it may be conceived as being more than three-dimensional, whereas symmetrically it is only one adimensional thing. The three-dimensional figure with features of several figures appears to thinking as a multidimensional thing which has been three-dimensionalized.

Timelessness. In itself timelessness also is an expression of pure symmetry. If, instead, we look at it in the terms in which our thinking develops (Freud speaks of processes) and consider both together, we have, again, a Simassi structure.

Replacement of external by psychical reality. This is an example of displacement, already considered: a Tridim structure. Deep down, instead, psychical and external reality are the same.

Co-presence of contradictories. This characteristic is intimately linked to absence of contradiction in the sense that it is a playing with it: presence and absence. So it becomes pure symmetrical logic but also pure classical logic, which absence of contradiction is not; and, as this latter, it is a Simassi structure.

Alternation between absence and presence of temporal succession. If we consider one dream which shows this alternation, this would be a typical Alassi structure.

Logical connection reproduced as simultaneity in time and causality as succession. Again here, as in the co-presence of contradictories, we find a sort of playing with symmetry and asymmetry: keeping space and abolishing time, i.e. symmetrizing time and respecting the asymmetry of space. On the other hand, one could, perhaps, say that putting next to one another things which are logically connected amounts to treating logical connection as identical to spatial contiguity: a symmetrization. In conclusion, one sees here the presence of both symmetry and asymmetry, but this is probably done in a way we have not understood well, which deserves further study. Anyway this is obviously a handling of symmetry and asymmetry and as such is a bi-logical structure not very well defined. In the end: a symmetrization–confusion which, perhaps, could also be seen in terms of classical–asymmetrical logic: a subtle Simassi. We see in all this a process going towards an increasing symmetry.

There is a good deal more to think about it!

Equivalence-identity and conjunction of alternatives. This is a Simassi bi-logical structure in which one seems to observe an increasing prevalence of the symmetrical component.

Similarity: the privileged relation. This general observation of Freud is a very important discovery. In itself it is not a bi-logical structure but an understanding of the tendency of dreams towards identification of all things, passing through similarity. It implicitly contains an intuition of the indivisible mode.

Co-presence of thinking and not-thinking. Simassi structure, yes, but it must be added that Freud's description suggests a gradual 'falling' into the abyss of symmetry-confusion. This is very visible in the next characteristic.

Profound disorganization of the structure of thinking. It is most eloquently described. It is a Simassi structure with a much greater proportion of symmetry. It is also seen in mental confusion.

If symmetry increases, a moment arrives in which thinking and consciousness disappear.

6 Emotion: bi-logical structure

I have previously put forward the validity of PS in emotion (Matte-Blanco 1975a: 213–307, esp. 247) and have pointed out the similarity between the unconscious and emotion. Further reflection leads to the awareness that some psychological aspect of emotions are, like the unconscious, bi-logical structures. To explain briefly with one example. Take, for instance, a young man in love. The natural tendency in such cases is to attribute to the beloved young woman all the attractions of Woman: beauty, intelligence, goodness, tenderness, and so on. In fact, so far as he is in love, he feels her as having all the characteristics of the class of women – identification of class and element: a symmetrization. On the other hand her qualities are felt to be in a maximum degree: *infinitization.* All this is an expression of symmetrical logic in the person in love.

At the same time, if he is not swept by emotion and is able to keep his head clear, he will realize that his loved one has limitations and defects. This shows the presence of classical-logical thinking. In other words, the emotion of love shows a mixture of both logics, i.e. it is a bi-logical structure. What kind of structure? Perhaps it is of the Simassi type. However, it seems too early to arrive at clear conclusions; this is an entirely new territory of bi-logic and it deserves a careful exploration.

The relation between the unconscious and the psychological aspects of emotion is considered in Chapter 3, section 6.

7 A tool for psychoanalytic and other subjects of knowledge: the three logics

I have suggested (Matte-Blanco 1975a: 93–4) that Freud's fundamental discovery was not the unconscious but the symmetrical mode, which, as we now see, is particularly but not exclusively visible in unconscious manifestations. During the last ten years the study of the question of the interweaving of the two modes led, first, to the concept of bi-logical structure and, subsequently, to the awareness that various concepts in use in psychoanalysis are bi-logical structures. Among them I may mention projective identification, transitional objects, and bizarre objects.

We are gradually coming to see that the concepts of bi-modal and, in particular, bi-logical structures open up possibilities for understanding not only human beings but also the world (see section 8). Ever since human beings began to think and know about the world, we had only one instrument to acquire and develop our knowledge: so-called 'reason', respectful of certain laws or rules, which were laboriously discovered and formulated and which now can be roughly subsumed under the term 'classical logic'. This was the first logic at our disposal for understanding the world. It has helped to unravel innumerable enigmas, and, thanks to it, knowledge is in an endless process of expansion.

Yet Aristotelian or classical logic was not sufficient. In spite of the fact that all research showed that the world conformed to its rules, among which the principle of contradiction, it seems that human beings have always been aware that 'reason' is not sufficient to understand everything. This conviction is eloquently expressed in Pascal's *Pensées*: 'Le coeur a ses raisons que la raison ne connaît point.' Note that Pascal uses 'raisons' to refer to 'coeur': a suggestion or intuition of another logic.

Then, for the first time in the history of science, Freud made two fundamental discoveries: first, that the unconscious does not conform to the known logical rules, among them the principle of contradiction; second, he found and clearly described the various types of 'behaviour' of the unconscious, which he summarized in what he called the special characteristics of the system unconscious. Throughout the twentieth century psychoanalysis has worked within the frame given by Freud. But it has not explored it sufficiently, so as to discover its enormous potentialities.

On the other hand, roughly at the time when Freud was thinking about the unconscious, eminent mathematicians were reflecting

63

about the nature of their object of study, i.e. mathematics. The knowledge of the infinite and that of the concept of set were being submitted to a thorough scrutiny, and the same can be said of the foundations of mathematics. As a result the notion of formalization was developed. To mention only a few names, Cantor, Frege, Russell, Whitehead, and Hilbert were applying their brilliant minds to this task.

The all too understandable fact is that neither Freud nor the mathematicians knew of each other's work. Sooner or later, as psychoanalytic and the newly acquired mathematical insights became better known, a confrontation was bound to take place. It was my own lot to be one of those to undertake this task. By using some fairly elementary mathematical notions, which in the meantime had become common knowledge, I put forward (1959) a reformulation of the characteristics of the system unconscious in terms of the two principles already mentioned. This paved the way for a series of new insights which are now in a process of development.

From PS it was possible to formulate a new type of logic which was the joint result of classical logic, on the one hand, and of the dissolution of all logic and all distinctions which is observed where PS holds. This mixture, but not combination, is *symmetrical logic*. We now had not one but two logics.

It soon became evident that classical and symmetrical logic entered into various types of relationship with one another. The result was a process of reasoning conforming not to one logic, as had hitherto been considered in science, but to two: a bi-logical process. In the end, therefore, we have three logics at our disposal to study the mind and the world: classical logic, symmetrical logic and bi-logic. Note that their intertwining is a logical expression of an ontological fact: that there is in human beings and in the world (see section 8) a mode of being which expresses itself in the distinction between things, hence in their division; and another mode which treats any object of knowledge as if it were non-divided: the heterogenic and the indivisible modes.

The 'heterogenic road' does not and cannot, by its own nature, end at this point, nor anywhere else. The most recent studies begin to open up the possibility of unlimited, infinite combinations of the three logics, thus giving birth to *bi-logics* of the second, third . . . up to an infinite order. The infinite sequence of infinite cardinalities or alephs described by Cantor is an example of this assertion (see Matte-Blanco 1980).

Equipped with these new tools both psychoanalysis and knowledge of the world come to the possibility of having a wide general view, which enhances the possibilities of understanding and of subsequent action.

8 Mathematical infinite: a Simassi bi-logical structure

At first sight it would seem that this section might be omitted for our purposes. At second sight, however, such omission would impoverish our understanding of the subject of this book, for the following reasons. (a) Because the infinite is omnipresent in psychoanalysis, as we shall see in section 9 of this chapter. (b) Because the infinite is omnipresent in the understanding of nature, owing to the fact that this understanding is reached to a very great extent by means of infinitesimal calculus, which is based on this notion. In fact, without infinitesimal calculus the understanding of nature would be enormously reduced. From this we conclude that nature and mathematics have something in common; they have some sort of morphism, at times an isomorphism between them. (c) Because, if the mathematical infinite is a bi-logical structure, we then conclude that the indivisible mode is present in mathematics and, for the reason just mentioned, also in nature, and this is something at the same time important and new in science. (d) Because the conclusion just mentioned leads us to understand, with surprise, that there is some sort of morphism between the psychical structure of humanity and the structure of nature. (e) Last but not least, because the conclusion that the mathematical infinite is a bi-logical structure has been reached after the discovery of the concept of bi-logical structure, which has itself sprung from the study of the unconscious: a contribution of psychoanalysis to mathematics. I consider it highly improbable that mathematicians not conversant with psychoanalysis could have reached this conclusion. It is the logical strangeness of the unconscious that, in the end, led to it.

Let us now tackle the question. Consider the set of natural numbers or integers in their natural order, i.e. $\{1, 2, 3 \ldots\} = N$. It is an infinite set that, if seen in a certain way, is formed of two proper subsets (i.e. subsets which do not contain all the elements of the set). These are the (infinite) set of even numbers $\{2, 4, 6 \ldots\}$ and the (infinite) set of odd numbers $\{1, 3, 5 \ldots\}$. Note that both common sense and the mathematical definition of proper subset tell us that the number of integers is greater than the number of even numbers: in fact, one would say, twice as great. Yet if we take the elements of these sets one by one we find that for the natural number called 1 there corresponds the even number called 2, and vice versa. For the

65

natural number 2 there corresponds the even number 4, and vice versa, and so on till infinity. In other words, there is a bi–univocal correspondence between both sets, and this is normally interpreted as meaning that the set of natural numbers is equinumerous with its subset of even numbers. It is also equinumerous with its subset of odd numbers, as a reasoning identical to the one just made shows.

Consider again the set of natural numbers, N, again in their natural order. It is obvious that this set is equinumerous with itself. Now we may study the correspondence with the same set, i.e. with itself but this time in the following order: $\{1, 3, 5 \ldots 2, 4, 6 \ldots \}$. It would seem that N in this new ordering should be equinumerous with itself in its natural order, because both *are* the same set, only ordered differently. In other words, the way of ordering a set should not change the number of its elements. Yet we find that for each element of N in its natural order, there are two elements of N ordered according to the second procedure. In fact, for 1 in the first set there are only 1 and 2 in the second, and for 1 and 2 in the second there is only 1 in the first: a 1:2 correspondence; and for 2 in the first set there are only 3 and 4 in the second, and vice versa; and for 3 in the first there are only 5 and 6, and vice versa; and this 1:2 correspondence goes on towards the infinite. We must, therefore, draw two conclusions: (a) if for every integer in the infinite set of all integers there are, in the same set, two integers and vice versa, then for every two integers in the infinite set – never in a finite set of integers – of all integers there is in the same set only one integer; (b) considering that the total number of integers is the same in both cases, we have no alternative to accepting in classical logic that, in this case, i.e. in the infinite, $1 = 2$. That this conclusion is inevitable was pointed out (in another way) 350 years ago by Galileo, and is, so far, ignored in mathematics. (c) Card. (card. = cardinality, i.e. number of elements) $1 \cdot N = $ card. $2 \cdot N$, N being the set of natural numbers or integers. This is a paradox, which is actually quite easily accepted in the mathematics of the infinite, without any apparent perplexity about the colossal problems it brings with it.

Take now card. $1 \cdot N = $ card. $2 \cdot N$. In any equation of this type in the mathematics of finite quantities one can simplify by the factor that both sides have in common. It is said that in the case of the infinite this is not acceptable, and I have not found any real reason for this prohibition except that it leads to antinomies. For example, if in our present case one simplifies by N one arrives at $1 = 2$, which *seems* to lead to a total destruction of mathematics. In fact, if $1 = 2$, then $1 + 1 = 2 + 1$, i.e. $2 = 3$; for, if to two numbers which are equal is added a third number, the same in both cases, then the resulting numbers are also equal.

Now, if $2 = 3$, then $2 + 1 = 3 + 1$, i.e. $3 = 4$. We may continue this procedure and in the end we arrive at the conclusion that any number is equal to any other and to the whole set of them: indivision of the set of numbers!

I will add, very briefly, that, since such catastrophes never happen in finite sets, mathematics really remains just as it is. The facts of the infinite not only do not destroy mathematics but open the door to a *bi-logical mathematics*. And all of this ultimately springs from the findings of Freud about the unconscious.

One step further. One could arrive in a simple manner at this (apparent) catastrophe by means of PS. Take the set $\{1, 2\}$, which is a subset of N. We may call it SsN. Symmetrize it. Then 1 is an element of SsN, and SsN is an element of 1, which leads to the conclusion that $1 = $ SsN. In fact the reasoning which leads to this conclusion is more complex, but I shall omit it here. The same holds for 2. If $1 = $ Ss$N = 2$, then $1 = 2$, and in consequence $1 = 2 = 3 = 4 \ldots$ as just seen.

We could have arrived at the same conclusion with any other subset of N formed by two contiguous numbers, say $\{55, 56\}$, as the reader may easily verify. More surprising, it can be proved (though I shall not do it here) that the same result would be obtained if *any* two integers or natural numbers are chosen, however distant from one another. In other words, symmetrization of a subset formed of any two integers leads to the dissolution of the distinction between numbers. We have already seen that the same happens if we symmetrize the set of mothers or any other set. But, as we saw, the propositional function which defines the set, which is the classical-logical aspect of it, remains. If we apply this to the present case we conclude that the concept of number remains in a symmetrized N, but each number is now equal to any other and to all of them, i.e. to the set.

We now return to the mathematical concept of the infinite. Mathematics has prohibited the simplification of $1{\cdot}N = 2{\cdot}N$ but has accepted that even numbers are as many as natural numbers. With all due respect I dare say that it has repressed the fact that accepting the equinumerosity of both these sets brings as a necessary consequence all we have just seen. Put more precisely, it has accepted a *partial symmetrization*, i.e. $1{\cdot}N = 2{\cdot}N$, and has put a dam (the prohibition to simplify) to stop the avalanche that follows from it: a very illusory dam indeed. On the other hand, as just seen, we do not need to simplify to arrive at the same result.

Instead of prohibiting simplification, I suggest doing something else: allow it and then look at the question in terms of classical and symmetrical logic *at the same time*. From the point of view of the second logic, there is in this case no way of distinguishing the numbers; from the point of view of the first, everything remains as always, and each number is different from any other. Accept both assertions. Then you have a Simassi type of bi-logical structure.

I think that this is exactly what the mathematical concept of the infinite is.

We have already seen an example of Simassi in the case of the schizophrenic frightened of opening doors. We also see the same in art, especially in poetry. If we reflect about this fact, we fancifully could say that *the infinite is the schizophrenic and the unconscious of mathematics but also is its poetry*.

There are many other aspects of this question to consider, but that is not necessary here (see Matte-Blanco 1980, 1984). I should like to say only that the use that mathematics makes of the infinite, mainly through differential and integral calculus, is extremely subtle; it avoids all its antinomies. I shall not explain here the reason for this assertion, and will add only that, even in such a case, the antinomies remain and they cannot be solved in terms of the normal mathematical logic, which holds in the case of finite sets.

In a similar way, science before Freud had avoided considering anything which does not respect the laws of logic. Now, the reformulation of Freud's unconscious in terms of the simple notions I am putting forward offers psychoanalysis and other sciences the possibility of venturing into the exploration of vast, hitherto inaccessible regions.

9 The unconscious as infinite sets. The mathematical infinite – a substructure of the logic of the unconscious (but not of the unconscious itself!)

There are two groups of facts that make one reflect about a possible relation between the concept of the unconscious and that of the infinite. The first refers to something which the unconscious and the emotions have in common. In moments of great intensity one fears to be overwhelmed by an emotion which breaks all dams and becomes all-invading. Emotion is then felt or construed as having infinite intensity. This holds for any kind of strong emotion, positive or negative.

The second group of facts is connected with the identity between part and whole, seen in dreams, in schizophrenics, and in other manifestations of the unconscious. As already mentioned, the principle of symmetry accounts for this property in logical terms. Identity between part and whole means identity of all the properties that both the part and the whole have. One of these properties is the number of elements. According to it, if a part has, say, five elements, and the whole ten, and if PS holds, then, as the observation of the cases just mentioned tells us, part and whole are treated as having the same number of elements, i.e. as being equinumerous. This property is precisely at the base of *Dedekind's famous definition of an infinite set: a set is infinite if and only if it can be put in bi-univocal correspondence (i.e. if it is equinumerous) with a proper part of it.* We conclude that the unconscious treats its object as if it conformed to the mathematical definition of infinite.

In mathematical reasoning about the infinite, equinumerosity is the only property in which the proper part and the whole are treated as identical. In fact a simple reasoning (which I shall not present here) shows that, if we accept equinumerosity, this leads to the identity of all the properties. In the mathematical conception of the infinite, however, this is ignored. So, if seen as mathematics treats the infinite up to now, we may conclude that mathematics deals with a very limited aspect of the identity between part and whole, i.e. only one property, number of elements, whereas the unconscious deals with a much more extended and radical identity: identity of all properties. We may, therefore, *legitimately conclude that the present mathematical concept of the infinite is only a substructure of the logic of the unconscious, seen as a set of bi-logical structures*; and also is a substructure of any symmetrized set formed of whatever number of whatever objects.

Deep down, both the infinite and the unconscious are human attempts, independent of one another, at understanding something which is indivisible and, as such, unthinkable.

The reader may find some additional notions in Matte-Blanco 1975a: ch. 13.

3

The fundamental antinomy of human beings and world

1 The concept, and three examples of it

Foreword. This antinomy, also mentioned in the subtitle of the book, is the basic fact which inspires and permeates this study and constitutes its guiding line. It is, in my opinion, a summary expression of Freud's discoveries about the nature of the unconscious. In this chapter I shall try to explain what is meant by it and what its concept involves or implies, so that, when further on we come across various examples, it may easily be seen that they are manifestations of it.

Definition. By 'antinomy' I intend the usual meaning of the word, i.e. the incompatibility between two assertions which can claim equal rights to be true. 'Incompatible' means, according to the Oxford Dictionary, 'mutually intolerant; incapable of existing together in the same subject'. Now, we saw in Chapter 2 that the Freudian unconscious is a set of bi-logical structures. This means that one aspect of them corresponds to the rail of classical logic and the other is the expression of the principle of symmetry, which constitutes the second rail along which psychoanalysis develops, and describes the violations of this logic precisely in the same aspect of the same argument. Therefore, it can be affirmed that there is in the very structure of humans a fundamental antinomy resulting from the co-presence of the two modes of being which are incompatible with one another and, in spite of this, exist and appear together in the same subject. This is incomprehensible to our normal thinking. They appear together yet remain incompatible and never fuse to form a wider unitary concept which comprises both. They are, in this sense, like the nitrogen and oxygen in the air: together, yet separate, and never combining into dioxide of nitrogen.

This antinomy is fundamental because it seems to be present not only in human beings but, so far as I can understand, also elsewhere. In fact, we saw in Chapter 2, section 8, that the mathematical concept of the infinite is a Simassi bi-logical structure and, as such, is antinomic. On the other hand, the considerations put forward there about the relations between this concept and our knowledge of physical nature explain why we can affirm that the antinomy is also present in the world. I would like to add, but not explain here, that according to the very respectable opinion of the mathematical logician Max Jammer (1987), the paradoxes of Zeno, in spite of so many efforts throughout many centuries, have never been solved. On the other hand, it seems to me that these paradoxes, which show the impossibility of reconciling the approach to movement in terms of the infinite with that in terms of finite quantities, are also the expression of the same antinomy; they are bi-logical structures.

I suspect that some of the strange findings in atomic physics are one more example of the same antinomy.

I think that the preceding considerations are sufficient to conclude that there is a fundamental antinomy in human beings as well as in the world.

All the examples of the basic antinomy, in particular all the bi-logical structures presented here, have been found in the study of patients: they are clinical researches and reflections. This is so obvious that there seems to be no reason to mention it in the subtitle. Yet there is and, in my opinion, an important one: behind and further than these appearances I have kept in mind their philosophical implications. A comparison may help to explain what I mean. I fancy that this book is like the mythological two-faced Janus. Look at it from one side. You see the patients, their emotions, their thoughts, their actions, their bi-logical structures. Look at it from the other side and you find that all these examples are also illustrations of fundamental philosophical questions which psychoanalysis is bringing to the fore. Therefore, to speak of clinical reflections about the fundamental antinomy of human beings and world seems fully justified.

The concept of being, as applied to humans, is intimately and inextricably linked to the concepts of thinking and feeling. These considerations explain the reason, meaning, and sense of the title of this book as well as the general framework within which this study will unfold.

Perhaps the meaning of this book will become more clear if I add a

71

further comment. I view it as the second of a trilogy. The first (Matte-Blanco 1975a) was an attempt to reformulate the Freudian unconscious in terms of some simple logico-mathematical concepts. This one is a further development which puts forward some new notions; in particular that of bi-logical structure, and its use in clinical psychoanalysis, plays a preponderant role. At the same time the philosophical and epistemological implications of Freud's discoveries about the unconscious are present and detectable in the clinical studies presented here. In order to bring these implications to their full light I hope to write *si Dios quiere* ('if God wishes it') the third book of this trilogy, devoted to the prolegomena of a bi-logical epistemology.

A final remark which is important to complete the description of our basic antinomy. Every time we are in front of a bi-logical structure we are in front of the fact that the same reality is simultaneously treated, on the one hand, as if it were divisible or heterogeneous, formed of parts, and, on the other, as if it were one and indivisible. This is probably the most important insight which follows from Freud's discovery of the laws which rule the unconscious, especially the non-respect of the principle of contradiction. This book can be seen as an unfolding of this frequent encounter with that feature of the basic antinomy.

I shall now give three examples of the antinomy.

Example 6

As we have seen in Chapter 1, Freud affirms that the processes in the unconscious are atemporal. One may immediately object that a process is by definition something which unfolds in time. Therefore, how can it be atemporal? The following answer is certainly right, even though its meaning is incomprehensible to thinking, precisely because we are in front of an antinomy which thinking is, so far, unable to resolve. You look, in terms of classical logic, at a certain unconscious manifestation and you see it as evolving in time. Study the same thing under the light of the indivisible mode – which expresses the distinctive feature of the Freudian unconscious – and you discover that it is now seen as atemporal. Therefore we are confronted with something which, in the same aspect of the same argument (temporality), is both temporal and atemporal: precisely an antinomy.

Example 7

Freud also says that the unconscious does not respect the principle of contradiction. Suppose you consider the following sum: $2 + 2 = 4$. It is obvious that it is right. Then you conclude that $2 + 2$ does not equal 4. This would be right if, instead of ten numbers, the numerical system had only three, for instance 1, 2, 0. In such a case the counting would go as follows: 1, 2, 10, 11, 12, 20 . . . and 2 + 2 would be 11. Note that this number corresponds to 4 in the decimal system. So we would have the same result called by a different name, and the principle of contradiction would be respected. This is not what Freud affirms. In the present example his finding means that the unconscious ignores the distinction between the assertion '2 + 2 equals 4' and the assertion '2 + 2 does not equal 4', which is the negation of the first. From the fact, discovered by Freud, that the unconscious does not know the concept of negation, it follows that an assertion and its negation are not distinguishable and, therefore, are treated as if they were exactly the same thing; the principle of contradiction is ignored.

Freud did not speak of a fundamental antinomy but discovered and described the facts which lead towards its formulation. Personally I am certain that, if I had not had at my disposal the intuitions of his genius, I would never in my life have arrived at the antinomy. It is his radically new discoveries that implicitly contain and open the door to a completely new view, not only of human beings but of the world. He was obscurely aware of it, and he shows it in various parts of his writings. To give only one of several examples, in the *New Introductory Lectures* (SE 22: 74) he remarks that the atemporality of the unconscious furnishes 'an approach to the most profound discoveries'. Such awareness leads one to understand and confidently affirm that he is the pioneer, the beginner of a new epistemology. Perhaps with his formulation, as he gave it, it would have been difficult to reach this point. It is in the light of the conception of the two modes of being in human beings and world that this possibility becomes more accessible. Personally I can say that I was reflecting upon the Freudian unconscious when this conception dawned upon me all of a sudden one day in Torremolinos. I now am fully aware that the two modes were implicit in the Freudian conception of the unconscious, and the antinomy was implicit in the conception of the two modes. At that time, however, I had no idea that the latter was implicit in the existence of the two modes, and it took me several additional years to arrive at its explicit formulation.

Example 8
A patient of mine, a student of philosophy, was following a course on psychology as part of the curriculum. At the time I am going to discuss he was passing through a very intense period of the psychoanalytical therapy. He was reliving in his relationship to me

some very disturbing experiences he had in his childhood in connection with his parents, who had deprived him of various things which were most important to him at that period of his life. In terms of a very happy expression of Melanie Klein (1957: 5), in the transference situation he was having 'memories in feelings'. I shall mention one example. I had promised to give him a fourth weekly session as soon as I could. When the time came to abide by my promise, it so happened that the only session I could give him was very early in the morning, a time which was not agreeable to him. With rage and in the midst of great distress he accused me of things which had a resemblance (were isomorphic) to various frustrations imposed upon him by his parents. Following my custom in such cases, i.e. to make quite clear the reality aspects, so that afterwards we could better focus on the so-called transference situation, I explained, as much as I deemed it convenient, the reasons why I had no other possibility than the particular hour I had offered him. This did not satisfy him, and he began to draw various erroneous inferences about my preferential behaviour, on this subject, towards other patients. I explicitly pointed out where his inferences were erroneous and added that I was not prepared to give any further explanations because this would entail giving details of the organization of my work and of that of my patients, and this was, for obvious reasons, out of the question.

He continued for several weeks, angry, accusatory, and depressed to a point which I intuitively felt no longer helped but, on the contrary, disturbed his therapy. He had become stuck reliving a period of his life for a longer time than seemed convenient. At a certain moment I decided to try to see whether I could find him a new hour while at the same time respecting the needs of the other patients and my own. I told him of both aspects of my decision and added that I was not sure that I would succeed.

The result was impressive. His anger and depression began to fade away like the clouds dissolve at times under the effect of the sun. He was able to smile and even laugh and told me that his change had been caused by his becoming aware of my attitude towards him.

This example is interesting in various ways, in particular to understand the relation between a bi-logical structure and therapy. At the present moment, however, I shall try to complete the story only in those aspects which are pertinent to the example of the fundamental antinomy which it offers. At a certain moment of the course in psychology he was following, the teacher began to develop a subject about which I had written a paper. My patient was aware of the existence of this paper but had not read it. Laughingly he told me that he would mention it to his teacher, obviously with the intention of showing him that he was not as well informed as he felt. It so happens that this limitation was not of the type attributed to me but was, instead, in keeping with some complaints about his parents which he had previously made, in a rather vague manner. On the other hand, precisely those days he had been angry and critical of me in other aspects which, he felt, were similar to those of his parents. So we may say that he had suddenly stopped criticizing me, perhaps prematurely if the question is seen from the point of view of his feelings on that aspect, and had shifted his complaints on to his teacher. This amounted to continuing having me as a target, only this was done in such a way as not to make me appear as myself, but in the person of the teacher. In psychoanalytical parlance we may say that he had displaced his criticism of me on to his teacher. He was aware of the humorous aspect of this situation.

I feel that what I have already mentioned is sufficient for the purpose of giving a clinical example of the antinomy. To explain, it is in the first place evident that my analysand knew quite clearly that his parents, myself, and his teacher are entirely different and well-delimited persons. On the other hand, he accused me of the frustrations which his parents had imposed upon him in his childhood. This identification was visible in some aspects of his complaints about the hour of the session. Another patient would have, for instance, decided that, unpleasant though it might be to get up early, he would accept it because the benefit was worth the effort. Alternatively, he could have preferred not to make the effort, and the question would have stopped at that. This person, instead, poured over me the anger which he had towards his parents since his childhood to this day and which referred to their refusing to give him things that he intensely desired and felt they could easily give him: precisely the same accusation he made against me. In this aspect I was like his parents and in other aspects I was different from them. In his feelings, however, *I was his parents.* And the professor of psychology was myself, guilty of offences about which he was completely innocent. In the end we find that the patient behaves on the one hand as being fully aware that his parents, myself, and the professor of psychology are quite different persons; and, on the other, he behaves as though we were only one person. This is precisely an example of the constitutive antinomy.

Note that the patient knows we are different but feels that we are the same and treats us accordingly. This fact shows that in some obscure way his feeling is a form of knowledge. This is an important question which I shall not discuss in detail here, contenting myself with only a few comments. On three different occasions (SE 8: 206; SE 15: 174–75; SE 19: 45) Freud tells the story of a blacksmith who had committed a crime which deserved the death penalty. He was the only blacksmith in the village, and his function was necessary. On the other hand, there were three tailors in the village. The problem was solved by hanging one of them. The grim humour of the story is based on the existence of a profound abyss between thinking and feeling. In terms of thinking, the tailor is not the blacksmith and, therefore, cannot be punished for a crime committed by this latter. Feeling, instead, can treat both as though they were the same person and, therefore, punish one for the crime which thinking attributes to the other. We know, on the other hand, that thinking is the purest expression of the heterogenic mode; feeling, instead, is highly saturated with the indivisible mode: the abyss of the incompatibility between the ways in which both modes of being live the world. However incomprehensible, full of problems, and imperfectly expressed this insight is, it nevertheless points towards something very real in human nature. And we cannot escape the evidence that these two incompatible modes of being coexist in humans.

Feeling is not normal logical thinking but also contains or expresses some type of bi-logical thinking. When Pascal said that the heart has its reasons which Reason does not understand, it seems to me that, in addition to what we have already noted in Chapter 2, section 7, he also was, unawares, referring to the fundamental antinomy of human beings and world!

Throughout this book we shall be constantly using several terms: 'unconscious', 'thinking', 'feeling', 'classical logic', 'symmetrical logic', 'bi-logical', 'indivisible or symmetrical mode of being', 'heterogenic or asymmetrical mode of being'. Some of the relations between these terms are already known, more or less. Others, instead, are not explicitly stated and deserve a clearer definition. Finally, there are some which we know to exist but are so obscure as to leave us with a sense of dissatisfaction and a desire to know more.

The remainder of this chapter will be an attempt at throwing as much light as possible on these important questions. Considering the difficulty of the subject, it seems reasonable to expect that, even if some problems will be solved or, at least, better understood, much will be left in the dark. My hope is, however, that if we succeed in clearly delimiting the nature and the extension of their darkness, we shall be in a better position for further progress in our knowledge – in particular, our knowledge of the antinomy.

2 Modes and logics

It seems premature to try to define with precision the concept of mode, intended in the sense we are employing it in our study. We must, at this stage, content ourselves with getting as clear ideas as we can on this difficult subject. We may begin by noting that this concept is more vast than that of logic, which refers to the principles, laws, or rules which are implicit in thinking-reasoning. In other words, logic deals with the frame within which thinking develops. A mode of being, instead, refers to all aspects of being, one of which, but only one, is thinking.

Classical logic is for the heterogenic mode similar to the constitution of a country, whose rules and norms must be respected. It is obvious that a country is something considerably more vast and multifaceted than that aspect of it called its Magna Carta or constitution. Correspondingly, the heterogenic mode appears and is expressed in full respect of classical logic but only in those aspects of conscious life which regard thinking and perception. In fact, emotions, conscious or unconscious, do not always respect classical logic. This assertion seems useful for the understanding of our problem. Just as the constitution of a country is not the country but an expression of it, the same thing can be affirmed of the relation between this mode and its logic.

In Chapter 1, the corollaries of the principle of symmetry are described, and the reader may have become aware that all of them also refer to aspects of classical logic which are not respected in symmetrical logic.

Mutatis mutandis, a corresponding relation holds between the indivisible mode and symmetrical logic, which is the expression of the principle of symmetry. This assertion, however, requires a careful explanation, otherwise we may fall into an abyss of misunderstandings. It must be said from the beginning that the principle of symmetry and so-called symmetrical logic do not reveal the essential traits of a logic in the manner in which the principle of contradiction and the other rules alluded to in the preceding paragraph make us aware of the nature and frontiers of the territory of classical logic. The principle of symmetry is, instead, a statement, made in terms of classical logic, which permits us to identify in a simple way, through its corollaries, *all* the destructions or cancellations of classical logic which we find in what we have called the symmetrical or indivisible mode. In contrast to what is seen in classical logic, the principle of symmetry does not refer to a *must* but to a *how* the indivisible mode is revealed to us; it is precisely from the radical violations of logic that we infer the existence of a mode of being.

If all relations are treated as having the symmetrical property, this means that the concept of asymmetrical relation does not exist when the principle of symmetry holds. In order to understand and discover the existence of this mode, we must therefore consider any aspect of the world which is defined in terms of classical logic, and see what happens when the principle of symmetry holds.

I must confess that I feel intrigued and puzzled when I consider that the strange and most varied features which the indivisible mode shows to our thinking are all, including the non-respect of the principle of contradiction, the expression of one single fact: the unavailability of asymmetrical relations at various points of a process of reasoning in terms of classical logic. I feel that a continued reflection about this almost incredible (for me) fact could open up new and fertile perspectives.

Among other things, the principle of symmetry, the pure and radical expression of the indivisible mode, cancels all the possibilities of abstraction and generalization, because, when this principle holds and two or many things have a single property in common, this fact is sufficient to consider them as identical – that is, as though they had all the other properties in common. This includes precisely those properties which in normal thinking permit us, first, to establish the various differences between them; subsequently to single out, that is *abstract*, from the set of all such properties precisely those which they have in common; and finally, starting from a few examples, to define a class or set which contains all the things which have one or several properties in common: a process of *generalization*.

Curiously indeed, we know on the one hand that abstraction and generalization are manifestations of the heterogenic mode; and, on the other, they constitute precisely the presence of the indivisible mode in classical logic. Note, furthermore, that they are the expression of co-operation between the two modes, and this is possible only when the principle of symmetry is absent: bi-modality which is not bi-logical.

If we consider more closely this bi-modality which is not bi-logical we become aware that in abstraction we can detect, on the one hand, the process of finding some form of identity and, hence, non-distinction between various things: the presence of indivision. This identity is immediately circumscribed by the awareness that such things have a great many properties which distinguish them from one another: the presence of the heterogenic mode. In other

78

words, before identity can appear as total, it is made to become, so to speak, identity with regard to one or a few properties.

The same thing may be said in the case of generalization. So we may conclude that in both these cases each mode claims its rights and does not give them away. This gives birth to a coexistence of both, whereby the invading nature of each is reined by that of the other, and the result is that both are simultaneously expressed in the same piece of reality. We may call it a non-bi-logical bi-modal structure or, for the sake of simplicity, simply a *bi-modal structure*. It *looks* like a form of co-operation between both modes. In fact each of them, so to speak, ignores the other; it only tries to express itself. This is an example of what was discussed in section 1 of this chapter; each mode is incompatible with the other, ignores it, and remains solitary. Incompatible, separate, and solitary, yet always together. Only ourselves, as fully bi-modal beings, are able to see the advantage of this mutual setting of barriers.

We have just seen that abstraction and generalization are expressions of the restraint imposed by the heterogeneous mode on the indivisible mode. I will now discuss an example of the opposite, i.e. the indivisible mode invading the field of the heterogeneous mode. Take the example of the symmetrization of a set formed by the numbers 1 and 2, discussed in Chapter 2, section 9. We saw there that this very circumscribed presence of the symmetrical mode leads, in classical logic, to a mathematical catastrophe: each number 'contains', so to speak, each and every other number, so that when we have one number we have all the numbers. In other words, it is sufficient in this case to have one very localized symmetrization to transform the whole set of natural numbers into an indivisible unit.

Note that the symmetrization just mentioned, which brings as a consequence a very great and extended transformation which covers the whole set of integers, remains, however, in the realm of integers. Put more generally, the consequences of symmetrization remain within the territory where the principle of symmetry is applied. Take a wider, more comprehensive set or class and let this be the set or class of all the inhabitants of the British Isles. Symmetrization results in a situation which is wholly absurd in terms of classical logic; what to this logic is a single individual is for symmetrical logic each and all the individuals of the British Isles. As such, if seen in terms of classical logic, he has both sexes, all possible ages, lives at the same time in all the places where the various people live, may at the same time be completely ignorant and know all the science of all the most cultured people of the islands, and so on.

I shall not enter into a detailed discussion of all the differences between a 'normal' set or class and a symmetrized one. I shall mention only two points. First, in a symmetrized set or class many concepts which are essential in classical logic do not exist. Among these we may mention time and space, negation and, hence, contradiction. The extent of this ravage depends on the extent of the symmetrizations introduced in the set in question. This is a large and, so far, mostly unexplored question.

The second point I wish to mention is that, the larger the classes where symmetrization reigns, the wider and more radical are the identities between totally different things. In the end we arrive at the strange consequence that the whole world is one and only one indivisible thing within which are all the things which our thinking discovers. A strange consequence indeed but a fully justified one because it is the result of a rigorous process of reasoning which has its starting point in the concepts implicit in the characteristics of the unconscious discovered by Freud and which can be daily confirmed in psychoanalytical practice.

Looking back over the various aspects of this section I personally have a feeling that, the more we know and understand, the more complex and incomprehensible the reality we are studying appears. It is like getting further and further into a mysterious jungle, seeing new things and feeling lost and alone. However unpleasant and distressing this situation is, we must continue along the same path, in the midst of things we find and do not understand. Perhaps it is all a question of intelligence. If instead of having an intelligence quotient which varies around the number 100 of our present measures of it, we had a quotient varying about 10,000 – something that no one of us humans could ever reach – then we would see all our problems in a much more simple, lucid, and comprehensive way. And the problems we are now discussing would be so obvious as to be practically non-existent.

So, let us go forward into this jungle.

If we take the results of the reflections in the two preceding paragraphs, we may get the following additional small insight about the fact that the modes are mutually anaclitic on one another: each of them can unfold the fullness of its nature only if it leans on the other. In fact, we have just seen that abstraction and generalization, which are the most subtle and fundamental expression of the heterogenic mode, are the result of its 'taming' the indivisible mode to make it serve its highest purposes by putting in its own activity a small grain of indivision. Correspondingly, the indivisible mode would not be known to us if we were unable to observe the ravages of the principle of symmetry upon the heterogenic mode. The more destruction we observe the more of the indivisible we find. If the whole world becomes one and indivisible, to our limited intellect this amounts to the complete disappearance of the heterogenic mode; like a ferocious beast, the symmetrical or indivisible mode has 'eaten up' all that was there to eat!

The preceding reflection provokes a disquieting feeling that the nature of the fact it expresses is alien both to thinking and to feeling and that it hangs in a state of suspended animation in no man's land. Maybe I am wrong, maybe I do grasp something of something which is mostly unknown.

3 Logics, the modes, and the unconscious as 'realm of the illogical'

I now wish to refer to another group of facts which helps to show certain things in their proper perspective. Freud has written that the unconscious is 'the Realm of the Illogical' (SE 23: 168–69) – a very striking and illuminating insight. For a correct understanding of this phrase, however, one must keep in mind another Freudian finding (see Chapter 1) where he affirms that critical thought activity plays a role in the formation of dreams. Now, critical thought activity is a manifestation of classical logic and, hence, of the heterogenic mode. It appears not only in dreams but also in other manifestations of the unconscious. We also saw that the Freudian unconscious, as described in its characteristics, is a set of bi-logical structures. Finally, if we inspect carefully the characteristics of the unconscious, we find that the participation of classical logic in such structures varies from one to the other. In other words, the principle of generalization is not the only presence of classical logic in the unconscious, and the reader may find in the preceding chapters the various aspects of this logic seen in the bi-logical structures found in the unconscious. From all that precedes we conclude that both modes are constantly present in the unconscious as components of bi-logical structures.

We know that whenever we come across a bi-logical structure we come across the fundamental antinomy. So we conclude that the unconscious is the privileged seat of this antinomy. On the other hand, we already know that the Magna Carta of the heterogenic mode is classical logic and that the distinctive characteristic of the indivisible mode is the principle of symmetry, that powerful acid which, wherever it is present, destroys classical logic in its various aspects. From all this we can, therefore, conclude that *the heterogenic mode is the realm of the logical. The symmetrical mode is the realm of the illogical. The Freudian unconscious is the realm of bi-logical structures and, as such, the realm of the antinomies.*

It must be added, however, that this conclusion is the result of a reflection in terms of classical logic which, so far, is the only logic we employ in our usual thinking and reasoning. If, instead, the question could be seen in the light of a unitary super-logic, which is not yet available (see sections 8 and 9 of this chapter), the conclusion just mentioned might no longer be true.

4 The sense-organs and the two modes

In section 2 of this chapter we considered mainly the relations between logic and the two modes. I now shall complete this study by means of an approach from another angle.

Our sense-organs put us in contact with various aspects of the surrounding world. It is interesting to become aware that the normal or usual functioning of these organs furnishes us with two types of knowledge which have different relations to logic: sensation and perception. We may start with the perceptive information. This is structured in respect of the laws of classical logic. It does not employ this logic in a process of reasoning but in the discovery of the nature of the world external to us. Its findings, however, may be used in various ways and for various purposes, including that of thinking.

We proceed now to consider some examples of the activity of perception. If it informs us that 'this wall is white', it will never tell us at the same time that it is not white: respect for the principle of contradiction. If it tells us that Peter is taller than John, it will not add that he is smaller than John: use of asymmetrical relations. If somebody is sitting on a chair, perception will never tell us that somebody else is sitting in the same chair at the same time and in exactly the same position: respect for the principle of incompatibility. If we perceive the objects of a room, each one will have its own identity and will not be considered to be the same as another. For example, normal perception will never con-fuse and treat as identical a chair, a book, and a pencil. Perception is always discovering new and different objects in the surrounding world; it is fully heterogenic.

Recapitulating, we may say that *thinking-reasoning and perception are quite different manifestations. Both of them and each in its own territory are structured in respect of classical logic.* We may add that perception and thinking are extremely heterogenic, in the sense that they are always discovering new objects, material ones the first, abstract ones (relations) the second.

If we compare our perceptions when we are awake with those during dreams, we become immediately aware that these latter are not structured in terms of classical logic and conform, instead, to the characteristics of the unconscious. In other words, their structure is bi-logic.

If we now consider the 'raw material' of perception, i.e. sensation, we soon become aware that the role of classical logic is much smaller than in perception and probably in most cases it is totally absent: thinking and sensation are two different kinds of psychical happening. Sensation is utterly alien to logic but in the process of perception it is submitted to a process whereby, in a sort collaboration with classical logic, it ends up by becoming, so to speak, an ingredient of perception. In itself, however, it would seem that sensation may be experienced just as itself, with no connection with logic, for instance in the case of a pain. At other times, however, it may become the starting-point of an elaboration in terms of symmetrical logic. So, in the end, we may conclude that sensation may appear alone, lead to perception, or furnish the opportunity for the development of a process of vaguely shaped reverie which shows the same characteristics of the logic of the unconscious.

5 The relation between feeling-emotion and the unconscious

We saw in Chapter 2, section 6, that the psychological aspects of emotions are, like the unconscious, bi-logical structures. So we ask: are emotions a form of manifestation of the unconscious? Alternatively, are they the same thing, or is the unconscious a new aspect of emotion, not known before Freud?

We may start the discussion of this difficult question by considering the three illuminating pages devoted to it by Freud in his paper on the unconscious (SE 14: 177–79). He writes:

'I am in fact of the opinion that the antithesis of conscious and unconscious is not applicable to instincts. An instinct can never become an object of consciousness – only the idea that represents the instinct can. Even in the unconscious, moreover, an instinct cannot be represented otherwise than by an idea. If the instinct did not attach itself to an idea or manifest itself as an affective state, we could know nothing about it. . . .

. . . It is surely of the essence of an emotion that we should be aware of it, i.e. that it should become known to consciousness. Thus the possibility of the attribute of unconsciousness would be completely excluded as far as emotions, feelings and affects are concerned. . . .

. . . In the first place, it may happen that an affective or emotional impulse is perceived but misconstrued.'

It seems clear that the misconstruction in question can ultimately be seen as the expression of the distortions present in the bi-logical structures. These are seen both in emotion and in unconscious thinking. In consequence, if emotion and the unconscious coincide in this aspect, we must seek elsewhere for a possible difference between them. One asks: where? We may try in pure sensation and perception. In fact, it seems that an emotion may appear as a result of a process happening in one or more of three situations: thinking, logical or bi-logical, as just seen; pure sensation, which leads to bi-logical developments; finally, perception, which, having provoked an emotion, also leads to the same result.

In the end nothing is found which leads to a clear and neat psychological distinction between emotion and the unconscious. One could then think of a last aspect where such a distinction might exist: the physical correlatives of each of them. We know a good deal of the physical aspects of emotional manifestations. I do not know anything corresponding to such aspects with regard to the unconscious. There surely are some physical correlatives to every unconscious manifestation. I doubt that one could ever arrive at a circumscribed group, in the way, for instance, one could say that the physical correlatives of the emotion of fear are tachycardia, paleness, and so on. Even the hypothesis itself seems a strange formulation of the question.

The conclusion of this discussion is that the differences between emotion and the unconscious, if any, are yet to be defined. One remains with the feeling that there are a number of preliminary questions to be solved before one can arrive at a proper perspective of the respective fields of emotion and the unconscious. In the following sections we shall consider some of them.

6 The logic of the unconscious or bi-logic and its relation with emotion, the Freudian unconscious, and the mathematical infinite

I begin by declaring that my intention here is modest: to put forward the beginning of a contribution to the study of the fundamental question of the nature of the unconscious.

There is one thing we know for certain about the relations between the concept 'the unconscious' and the concept 'emotion': both coincide in being bi-logical structures. Such structures can also be found in other manifestations which have nothing to do with the unconscious. An example of this is the mathematical concept of the infinite, which is at the base of our understanding of the world. And it is obvious that the concept 'the infinite' is not the same as the concept 'the unconscious'. Both, however, are different expressions of bi-logic.

On the other hand, the systematic use of the logical and ontological conceptual frames we are considering leads to an increasing awareness of the omnipresence of the principle of symmetry or, if expressed in terms of its 'brotherly' counterpart, the omnipresence of the indivisible mode, which we have found in all the characteristics of the unconscious, and now we find in every aspect of human life, always together with the heterogenic mode, mixed with it in the various types of bi-logical structure. I say 'increasing awareness' because, to my surprise, I never finish finding some new and recondite human manifestation where this principle – more generally put: total indivision – is surreptitiously present in the most varied ways. In fact, it is easy to see that all human beings think most of the time in terms of bi-logical structures which intermix in various ways with classical logic. Mathematical thinking, if we exclude the concept of the infinite, is the only constant exception to this rule; it is a pure expression of classical logic.

We conclude, therefore, that the logic of the unconscious or bi-logic permeates all human psychical manifestations, and it is difficult to say whether it is the unconscious or this logic, i.e. a more general concept, which is at their base. Furthermore, this logic is present in the mathematical infinite, which obviously has some fundamental relation with the structure of the world. All this means that the indivisible mode is a constitutive component not only of humans but also of the world.

7 Is the principle of symmetry the expression of a falsehood; is the unconscious a form of pathology?

Is the principle of symmetry the expression of a falsehood? If not, is the unconscious a form of pathology? If not, where do we go from them? In 1956 (see Matte-Blanco 1959) I put forward the idea that the characteristics of the unconscious found by Freud were the expression of the principle of symmetry and of a representant of classical logic, which I called the principle of generalization. Subsequent studies have led me to become consciously aware that various other aspects of classical logic are also present in the unconscious; this was visible in my book on the subject (1975a), but I was not personally aware of it. The concept of bi-logical structure has taught us to discover various ways in which classical and symmetrical logic intermix.

Throughout these three decades the principle of symmetry has survived unmodified. Nothing has appeared which led to the conviction or at least suggested that this principle was an inaccurate expression of the Freudian unconscious. On the contrary, I believe that much has been found which illuminates various aspects of questions about the unconscious. So the conviction that the principle of symmetry is, so far as it goes, an accurate expression of the unconscious mode of being is reinforced rather than shaken.

At the same time many years' research with the help of this principle has confronted us with an increasing number of strange findings which do not fit in with normal processes of reasoning, or which even show a complete neglect of their most elementary rules. I think it is fair to affirm that the more we advance in this research, the more fascinating and disconcerting our findings become. In the end one feels uneasy; the appearances of these findings are more strange than those of the happenings in *Alice in Wonderland*. So one asks whether we are not embarked on an illusory adventure, and we should at this point re-examine the whole question. Therefore, let us face this task.

I have already mentioned that everything points, so far, to the principle of symmetry being a faithful expression of the Freudian unconscious. It seems, therefore, reasonable that, until we find some reason which suggests abandoning it, we must keep it and search elsewhere for a solution. The first thing that comes to our mind is the similarity between the reasonings of schizophrenics and some unconscious reasonings, and this poses the question whether the unconscious is not, after all, the expression of some form of pathology.

It seems easy to give an answer. Considering that manifestations of the Freudian unconscious are present in all human beings, with no exception, if the unconscious is a form of pathology, we should conclude that the normal thing for humans is to be ill! A strange conclusion indeed and one which is no less strange than the things we find under the light of the unconscious.

A second alternative is that our research has led us to discover the fundamental antinomy – the unconscious is, after all, the most important testimony of it – and that this is not understandable in terms of our present knowledge. As a consequence, when we find something meaningful, we discover that its meaning is not comprehensible in terms of our present frames of thinking. This does not mean, however, that it will never be.

This subject leads us to the following section of this chapter.

8 Why is the Freudian unconscious unconscious?

The answer to the question of why the Freudian unconscious is unconscious is relatively easy if it refers to the repressed unconscious: owing to one or more of various reasons, the possibility of entering into consciousness may be barred to a given unconscious content. Once this prohibition is cancelled, the content in question may become conscious. Naturally, this leaves unanswered a number of questions about the process of entering consciousness. But this is not the problem I intend to discuss here.

The unrepressed unconscious, on the other hand, cannot enter consciousness owing to its own nature. All the characteristics of the unconscious, in contrast to thinking, tend to unite and fuse things which for conscious thinking are different and fully distinguishable from one another. Readers may find in the introduction the details of this behaviour in the case of each of the characteristics in question; and in Chapter 2 they may see what the violations of classical logic seen in each of them are.

I now wish to put forward a possible explanation, in terms of spatial dimensions, of the impossibility of access into consciousness in the case of the unrepressed unconscious. To explain this we may consider a painting which represents a jug. It may be so well drawn that it gives the impression that it is three-dimensional. We know it is two-dimensional, and if we try to pour milk into it we shall fail. The reason is simple; milk is a three-dimensional substance and cannot enter inside a two-dimensional 'jug'. The same thing can be said in the case of a picture of a tray which contains some oranges. If we wish to add some 'real' apples to put next to the painted oranges, we shall also fail.

In order to get a better understanding of this question we may now consider the drawing of a triangle in *Figure 3* (page 88). Take the point *C*. It is one and only one point. Let now accept a convention which permits us to represent the triangle, a two-dimensional figure,

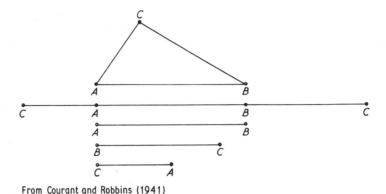

From Courant and Robbins (1941)

Figure 3

in a line, i.e. a one-dimensional space. This convention requires us to rotate to the left the side *AC* of the triangle and to rotate to the right the side *BC*, and to do it until *AC* arrives at the line which is a continuation to the left of *AB*, while *BC* also arrives at the same line, this time at the right of *B*. In the end we have represented the triangle *ABC* in the line *CABC*. Note that in this representation of the triangle the point *C*, which was one and only one in the two-dimensional space, becomes two *different* points in a one-dimensional space. The initial point is defined by a number which represents its distance, in the abscissa, from the origin; and by another which expresses the distance from the origin in the ordinate. Each of the other two is defined by only one number, i.e. in the abscissa. The fact that the three corresponding numbers in the abscissae are different between themselves means in geometrical terms that the three points are different from one another.

In other words, if we represent a triangle, a space of two dimensions, in terms of a line, a space of one dimension, then the point *C*, 0-dimensional, appears twice. Note that the number of repetitions is equal to the difference between the number of dimensions of the triangle (two dimensions) and that of the point (zero dimensions).

Consider now the case of the cube, as seen in *Figure 4*. If we represent it in terms of a plane, the cube will look like a flat cross. Children use this property to build a cube from a piece of paper. In this case each of the vertices of the cube appears three times in the plane, and this number is the difference between the number of dimensions of the cube and that of the point. Here again it will be seen in the drawing that each of these new points is defined by coordinates which are different, not only from those of the original point, which has a greater number of coordinates to define it, but also from those of the other 'sons' in a lower-dimensional space, each of which is defined by the same number of coordinates as the others, only the numbers defining each of the points are different from those of the others.

We may continue this reasoning towards the infinite. We will then see that, the greater the number of dimensions and the distance, in terms of number of dimensions, between the starting point and its 'descendants', the greater will be the number of the 'descendants' of this point in each space of fewer dimensions. Furthermore, we will find that the same thing happens in the case of the 'inheritors' of figures of any number of dimensions, be they points, lines, volumes, or other 'portions' (in geometrical terms: sub-spaces) of n-dimensional spaces. For instance, a given n-dimensional figure may yield a

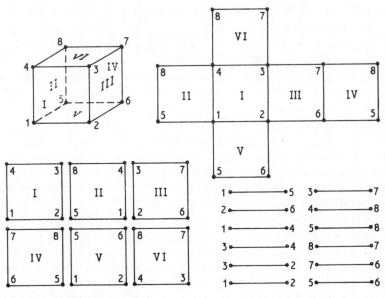

From Courant and Robbins (1941)

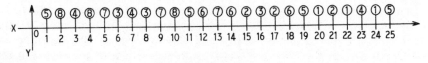

Figure 4

89

greater or lesser number of (say) cubes if its distance, in number of dimensions, from the final space is, respectively, greater or less.

If we generalize we may say that the greater the difference between the number of dimensions of the initial geometrical figure and of the final one we are considering at a given moment, the greater the number of the figures which are 'born' from the original figure will be. Note also that none of them has the same coordinates that their starting figure, we may call it their ancestor, had; and the same holds with regard to their 'sisters'. In other words, what in an *n*-dimensional space was only one geometrical figure will become a number of different figures in a lower-dimensional space.

After all these necessary preambles, we may return to the question asked in the title of this section. If we reflect about the fact that the unconscious tends to unify many different things into only one, and in fact treats them as if they were only one, we become aware that this 'behaviour' seems to go in exactly the opposite direction of the representation of a higher-dimensional space in terms of a lower-dimensional one. If we invert the procedure, we could say that many figures which were different in the lower-dimensional space become one new figure in a higher-dimensional space, a figure which is different from all of them. So we ask: could it not be that the unconscious deals with a number of dimensions greater than that with which our conscious thinking can deal? And could it not be that, if we were able to think in terms of more dimensions, then all the strange behaviour of the unconscious could easily enter into our consciousness and have a logic of its own?

In order to understand the problem better it is necessary to consider some aspects of the nature of our intelligence and of our self-awareness. Regarding the first I wish to refer to an important insight of Henri Bergson. He writes (my translation): 'All the operations of our intelligence tend towards Geometry, as the term where they would find their perfect achievement' (Bergson 1906 [1970]: 229). It may be added that our intelligence seems to be at ease in our perceptive world. Of course, it can conceive spaces of more than three dimensions, but its access to them is through a process of reasoning which establishes a contact with such spaces, a contact which is quite different from that established with the three-dimensional perceptive world which evolves in time: a direct, intuitive contact, with no intermediation of a process of reasoning.

Something similar may be said with regard to our self-awareness, i.e. the awareness of our own psychical happenings. We can have a direct experience of our sensations and perceptions. Note that when we perceive we take for granted the ordinative action of classical logic, which organizes our sensations and, through this process, makes us aware of the existence of certain relations in the external world. Furthermore, our internal perception may make us aware that we are thinking. In this case, however, when we become aware that we are thinking we interrupt momentarily the process of thinking that occupies us, in order to concentrate our attention and realize that *we* are thinking: we cannot think about something and at the same time think that we are thinking about that something. In spatial terms we could, perhaps, say that we do not have at our disposal a sufficient number of dimensions to experience both simultaneously.

Finally, when we wish to introspect about a given emotion that we are experiencing at a given moment, we must interrupt momentarily the conscious *experience* of our emotion in order to become aware that we are experiencing it: our thinking cannot be aware of more than one thing at a time. We must add something more: our awareness of our perceptions and of a process of thinking gives us precise information about them. The proof of it is that we can describe with precision what we are perceiving or thinking. In the case of most emotions, instead, we can never have a very precise definition of what we are feeling. With the possible exception of very strong emotions, such as joy, sadness, or rage, the best we can do to describe the intimacy of our feelings is to employ various and more or less vague explanations or comparisons. *Our descriptions of our feelings are always hazy.* And this seems to be true also in the case of strong emotions. Such a situation is probably due to the fact that emotions are bi-logical structures, and, as such, we can know about them but we cannot have, so to speak, a macular vision of them, as we have in the case of perception or thinking. They seem to have a greater number of dimensions than that with which our self-awareness is capable of dealing.

I believe all that precedes also holds for the unconscious. If we were to summarize these reflections we could say:

The symmetrical aspect of the bi-logical structures of our unconscious operates or thinks in a space of a higher number of dimensions than that of our perceptions and conscious thinking. This is the reason why we cannot be aware of it or, put in another way, this is the reason why it is unconscious for us; our lower-dimensional thinking cannot grasp it, just as a painted tray cannot be a recipient for real apples. If we had a consciousness capable of containing processes of thinking of a higher number of dimensions than that required to think in terms of classical logic, then we would be aware not only of our classical-logical thinking but also of our symmetrical thinking. In such a case we would be directly aware or conscious of what we now call our un-

conscious. This leads to the understanding that our symmetrical unconscious is itself a potential consciousness of a higher number of dimensions than that of our actual consciousness.

9 From bi-logic to a unitary super-logic?

It is both interesting and important to note that both modes are always intertwined but never fuse or combine to form one super-mode or super-logic which would comprise both modes or, respectively, both logics, as integral aspects of a more general mode or logic. To express this idea with the help of a comparison with chemistry, we may say that the modes, or the logics, appear mixed, like nitrogen and oxygen in the air, but never combine to form, in our example, a new substance such as dioxide of nitrogen.

From what we saw in the preceding section we may suspect that it is possible to conceive a higher-dimensional logic which would have symmetrical and classical logic as sub-structures in sub-spaces of it. In such a case, instead of defining symmetrical logic in terms of the violations of classical logic, we could define it in terms of this wider conception or super-logic. This new logic would not be obvious in an intuitive way to our intelligence, as classical logic is. To explain with two examples, you do not need any study to conclude that, if a sheet of paper is white, it cannot at the same time be not white; or that, if something is a pencil 15 centimetres long, it cannot be a house of a height of 20 metres. The unitary super-logic would not be spontaneously and immediately 'perceived' as classical logic is, but this does not mean that it would not be understandable through a process of reasoning.

I just wanted to pose this problem. Its possible solution waits in the future, some or many years of hard work ahead of the present.

10 Miscellaneous thoughts about the two modes of being

● Which is a wider concept: indivisible or symmetrical?

The principle of symmetry is useful to study the logical aspects of the symmetrical or indivisible mode. The concept of indivision serves, instead, to deepen the understanding and to further the development of the fundamental ontological aspects of the insights of Freud contained in his descriptions of the various characteristics of the unconscious. The indivisible mode may appear in the absence of the principle of symmetry. So we conclude that the concept of indivisible mode covers an area which is larger than that of the principle of symmetry. If we succeed in arriving at the concept of a super-logic we shall probably see new aspects of this assertion, not understandable at present.

If the reader wishes to get some additional information about the relations between the two formulations, he or she may see Matte-Blanco 1975a: ch. 28, esp. 353–58.

• When in chapter 28, pp. 349–52, of *The Unconscious as Infinite Sets* I was putting forward the notion of the two modes of being in man, I wrote: 'the homogeneous, indivisible totality'. Further reflection led me to drop the word 'homogeneous', and I now tend to speak just of an indivisible totality or of the indivisible mode. The reasons for this change need not be considered in detail here, and I shall say only that I have begun to understand that homogeneity is not an essential characteristic of indivisibility. Take, for instance, the concept of the mathematical infinite as a Simassi bi-logical structure. If any number, for instance 7, is all the numbers, then it must contain an infinite number of relations in it. As 7, it is bigger than the six numbers which precede it and which are in it; and it also is smaller than each one of the numbers which follow it and which also are in it. The result is an infinite number of relations. So it seems that we should say that 'symmetrical 7' is all the numbers, is indivisible, and at the same time has in itself an infinite number of relations.

I am not sure, however, whether what I have just affirmed is the result of a judgement of a bi-logical happening made in terms of classical logic or is, instead, a bi-logical assertion or, finally, an assertion which would be accepted in the super-logic we have imagined.

I am aware that all these reflections may seem to many, perhaps to most, people as foolish hair-splitting which leads nowhere. Needless to say, I do not share this view. On the contrary, I believe, to give another example, that the refusal of the truth of the antinomy of Galileo – that square numbers are considerably less than the total number of integers and they also are just as many – has closed the possibility of opening up vast new ways towards the understanding of the world. One of these new understandings might be that it is illusory to think that this antinomy can ever be resolved in terms of classical mathematical logic, and, instead, it would not be antinomy in this super-logic we are hypothesizing. I also think that these reflections, however disquieting and absurd they seem, may lead to these new ways of understanding.

- Something which is indivisible and not necessarily homogeneous: to affirm this seems self-contradictory and, therefore, incomprehensible, strange, and unacceptable. Yet it may be true. I feel, however, that this matter needs further reflection – a great deal more. And I also believe that its study may be very rewarding and may open up vast new fields of knowledge. I mean knowledge of the presence of something important but not necessarily its understanding. Anyway, this subject seems to me a fertile reserve for future meditation.

- I wish to repeat, with some new shades of meaning: thinking which abides by classical logic is never bi-logical and is, at least sometimes, bi-modal, as in abstraction and generalization; mathematical thinking is its purest example. The everyday thinking of *all* so-called average human beings is a mixture which respects the laws of classical logic in a greater or lesser amount, according to the individual, and which is *always* interspersed with greater or lesser amounts of *symmetrical links* in the chain of reasoning. This undeniable fact explains the enormous differences of opinions existing about most of the things with which human thinking deals.

- It is interesting to note that the choice of the symmetrical links interspersed in a piece of reasoning is a function of the constitution and of the personal history of each individual.

- Each and all forms of human psychical manifestation can be considered as various forms of bi-modality, bi-logical or not. In other words, *the conception of both modes covers all the range of psychical manifestations*.

- We may consider a view of the heterogenic mode which in some of its aspects was, perhaps, implicitly suggested but not explicitly asserted in the preceding book. In the first place, this mode may be said to be the same in the logical and in the ontological formulation; in both cases it is expressed through classical logic and always unfolds within the frame provided by its rules, which, we may say, constitute its framework. To put it bluntly: expression of the heterogenic mode = classical logic. I deliberately say 'expression' because it is this mode of being and not the logic it uses that is hetero*genic*. Logic is in itself passive in the sense that it can take no initiative; it is an instrument; whereas a mode of *being* can. And here we are considering a mode of being: something extremely more comprehensive than logic.

Furthermore, though the logic which the occidental culture has historically chosen is the so-called classical logic, this does not mean that it is necessarily the only one which can be employed in the understanding of nature. I personally am unable to find a reason intrinsic in the nature of humans and of the world whereby the only way to think should be that which is within the frame of classical logic. In order to avoid misunderstandings I may remind readers that in the two preceding sections we have seen the reason why this logic has been, historically, the first: because we live in a world which is, to our perception, three-dimensional plus time. Of course, it seems obvious that no possibility of *human* thinking exists without the principle of contradiction and of various other rules of classical logic. This, however, does not mean that humans could not develop another, more comprehensive logic – one, for instance (one instance among others), which would include classical and symmetrical logic as aspects of it.

● The most important distinguishing logical traits of the heterogenic mode belong, all of them, to classical logic. Furthermore, it may easily be seen that, whereas the principle of symmetry leads to ignoring the existence of asymmetrical relations, these are essential in thinking. Owing to this we frequently speak of the heterogenic mode as *the asymmetrical mode*. The reader will become aware that this denomination amounts to naming a thing in terms of one and only one of its characteristics. If we keep this in mind, we may say that the choice is useful because it confronts the mode with its counterpart, the symmetrical mode, which fully deserves its name because all its characteristics can be defined in terms of the principle of symmetry. This, however, does not exclude the possibility that, instead of defining it in terms of violations of classical logic, we could define it in terms of its positive features.

● I think it will be rewarding to stop for a moment to consider the heterogenic characteristic of the heterogenic mode; it is always discovering new facts or new things, and establishing the relations between them. The story of atomic theory is a good illustration. Twenty-five centuries ago Leucipus and Democritus gave birth to the notion of atom: something so small as to be incapable of further division. The notion remained the same, faithful to its etymological meaning, until the nineteenth century, when it was thought that the atom was formed of two parts, the proton and the neutron. Continued and intense research has led in about a century to a conception of the atom as formed of a great number of particles.

● An interesting hypothesis: it seems highly probable to me that the heterogenic mode has no limit to its finding new different aspects in every piece of nature towards which human beings direct their attention in a 'heterogenic frame of mind'. This supposition deserves further study. The indivisible mode, instead, is always *there*, and from its point of view we humans see every set of things as one and only one thing. If we are aware of this aspect of our nature, we shall be able to see the constant presence of one mode balancing the other.

● To continue with this very mysterious state of affairs which, in spite of all, is always 'there': the indivisible mode seems to be the background or the basis of everything, and this fact becomes extremely visible in an attentive study of emotional manifestations. The heterogenic mode is also always, or perhaps only almost always, there, finding diversity in the indivisible. From this point of view it seems that our efforts to understand reality in terms of classical logic – i.e. in terms of the heterogenic mode – will always lead to an endless road; the heterogenic mode points towards the infinite. I may add that, in my opinion, *the concept of the infinite is the expression of the desperate efforts of the heterogenic mode and its logic to try to understand the indivisible.* Not being able to 'get inside' its nature, it conceives it as being infinitely divisible. In other words, it tries, unsuccessfully, to bring the indivisible into its own realm, the divisible and heterogeneous!

11 Thinking, imagining, feeling, being, and discovery or invention

The preceding sections, taken together, confront us with a general question which is in intimate connection with the contents of this book: what is the relation between the two modes in our approach to the world and in particular to other human beings? This is a subject which deserves to be thoroughly studied. At this moment, however, I shall make only a brief comment about some aspect of it, in order to have it present as a background to our study. I shall try to explain what I mean by making some comments about two examples.

Example 9
The first refers to some research conducted by the French mathematician J. Hadamard (1945) into the psychology of invention in the mathematical field. The answer given by Einstein to his questions is most illuminating and, I dare say, is a beautiful example of what I would call *the basic antinomy harmoniously at work.* He writes (pp. 142–43):

'In the following, I am trying to answer in brief your questions as well as I am able. I am not satisfied myself with those answers and I am willing to answer more questions if you believe this could be of any advantage for the very interesting and difficult work you have undertaken.

(A) The words or the language, as they are written or spoken, do not seem to play any role in my mechanism of thought. The psychical entities which seem to serve as elements in thought are certain signs and more or less clear images which can be "voluntarily" reproduced and combined.

There is, of course, a certain connection between those elements and relevant logical concepts. It is also clear that the desire to arrive finally at logically connected concepts is the emotional basis of this rather vague play with the above mentioned elements. But taken from a psychological viewpoint, this combinatory play seems to be the essential feature in productive thought – before there is any connection with logical constructions in words or other kinds of signs which can be communicated to others.

(B) The above mentioned elements are, in my case, of visual and some of muscular type. Conventional words or other signs have to be sought for laboriously only in a secondary stage, when the mentioned associative play is sufficiently established and can be reproduced at will.

(C) According to what has been said, the play with the mentioned elements is aimed to be analogous to certain logical connections one is searching for.

(D) Visual and motor. In a stage when words intervene at all, they are, in my case, purely auditive, but they interfere only in a secondary stage as already mentioned.'

To make a brief comment: in his reply to the enquiry of Hadamard – which, in his case, refers to his fundamental conception of physics, i.e. a new and revolutionary view of the world – Einstein speaks of 'psychical entities which . . . are . . . signs and more or less clear images' and adds that 'the desire to arrive finally at logically connected concepts is the emotional basis of this rather vague play'. Note that his calling it a 'rather vague play' coincides with our reflections at the end of section 8 about the haziness of emotion. In these and also in all his other comments he is informing us that his research starts with an emotional playing with images. Once his play is well established, he passes on to a laborious search for words which are analogous to the logical connections implicit in the play.

Following along this path he arrives at his mathematical formulation. In other words, he informs us in a beautifully clear manner that it is starting from an emotional state expressed in images and sensations that his searching leads him to a purely intellectual and highly abstract conception. In other words, he is telling us that '*emotion is the mother of thinking*' (Matte-Blanco, 1975a: 303).

Example 10
The second example is taken from Freud. He writes (SE 18: 239):

> 'Experience soon showed us that the attitude which the analytic physician could most advantageously adopt was to surrender himself to his own unconscious mental activity, in a state of *evenly suspended attention*, to avoid so far as possible reflection and the construction of conscious expectations, not to try to fix anything that he heard particularly in his memory, and by these means to catch the drift of the patient's unconscious with his own unconscious. It was then found that . . . the patient's associations emerged like allusions, as it were, to one particular theme and that it was only necessary for the physician to go a step further in order to guess the material which was concealed from the patient himself and to be able to communicate it to him.'

Freud is speaking here of research into the patient's unconscious. As research for a clearly defined result, to discover what is in the patient's unconscious, this work is not different from the work in which Einstein was engaged. In both cases the finding was something well delimited and susceptible of being formulated in terms which conform to the laws of scientific thinking.

Einstein speaks of emotion as the guide which leads to thinking. Freud speaks of the unconscious and of the communication between the patient's and the analyst's unconscious as the guide which leads to a specific definition of an aspect of the patient's unconscious. One asks: are these two ways of arriving at thinking really different? To answer this question one would have to have a clear idea of the relations existing between emotion and the unconscious. As already seen in section 5, the least that can be said about emotion and the unconscious is that they are very similar if not identical. Emotion is expressed in terms of the same violations of logic which we observe in the unconscious. Neither of them is a pure expression of the indivisible mode, but both of them are highly saturated with it. So, from the point of view we are discussing, we may also say that the unconscious, which respects so little the laws of logical thinking, is nevertheless the father of logical thinking. And again we find here the co-presence of the two incompatible modes of being: the fundamental antinomy which, in this case, we see at work and as the source and the expression of the highest creative activity. This is the aspect I wanted to show.

Somebody asked Edison how he had managed to make so many important inventions. He replied that the formula was 2 per cent inspiration and 98 per cent perspiration. It will be seen that this answer is similar to that given by Einstein when he speaks of laborious searching for words. I believe that anybody who tries to understand some aspect of nature has the same experience. So far as I am concerned I have it. In fact, every time I sit down to revise what I am writing, I find that I must make some cancelling, corrections, additions, altering the order in which to put forward a train of thought, change the words until I find the best expression of what I am trying to understand and express, and so on. This process is repeated several times until, after much effort, I arrive at something which, I feel, is a clear, acceptable, and harmonious translation of the various things I wanted to say. It is only then that I may rest satisfied. But only more or less. To give an example: the chapter you are now reading is the twenty-fourth version. And if I went on working on it the result would be different. For the time being, however, I am more or less satisfied.

Projection, introjection, and internal world

Explanation. The concepts of Part Two, as known today, are inconceivable without the fundamental discoveries of Freud about the nature of the unconscious and without his contributions to the essential problem of inside and outside. The more specific concept of internal world starts with Ferenczi (1909), continues with Abraham (1924), and has a new, explosive, and fundamental development in Melanie Klein. As is easily understandable, the concepts developed here are mainly in the atmosphere of Freud and Klein. Starting from them, our hope is to go further in the explanation of this puzzling and fascinating world.

4

Freud's concept of projection in the light of the three logics

1 The initial ideas: the Fliess papers

Freud seems to have been the first author who used the term 'projection' with a psychiatric or psychological meaning. Apparently the first reference to it was made on 24 January 1895, in Draft H of the *Extracts from the Fliess Papers* (SE 1: 209). Freud wrote: 'The purpose of paranoia is thus to fend off an idea that is incompatible with the ego, by projecting its substance into the external world.' He then went on to give a series of examples from which it seems opportune to quote (p. 210):

'The litigious paranoiac cannot put up with the idea that he has done wrong or that he should part with his property. He therefore thinks that the judgment was not legally valid. . . .

'The "*grande nation*" cannot face the idea that it can be defeated in war. *Ergo* it was not defeated; the victory does not count. . . .

'The alcoholic will never admit to himself that he has become impotent through drink. . . . So his wife is to blame – delusions of jealousy and so on.'

In Draft K of the *Fliess Papers* (SE 1: 226–28) and later in 'Further remarks on the neuro-psychoses of defence' (1896, SE 3: 184–85) Freud returns to the problem and adds something which seems important and to which I shall refer later on: the projected self-reproach returns as a thought or as hallucinations, and the ego attempts to explain these by means of delusions which Freud calls *assimilatory delusions* and which are the beginning of an *alteration of the ego*. The ego tries to remodel itself by means of *protective delusions* (megalomania). The fundamental thing to gather from these latter remarks is that the ego is modified as a result of its attempts to deny and project something pertaining to it. This is an important insight.

I suggest that from these quotations and from the rest of what Freud writes in these two drafts we can see that when he discusses projection he refers to at least six different things quite distinct from one another:

(1) An internal state according to which the individual finds himself having an idea which is incompatible with the ego: *an intra-psychical conflict*.
(2) A way of dealing with this conflict within the mind: 'fending off'. Today we would rather say 'splitting'.
(3) A reason for this fending off: the incompatibility of the idea with the ego; in modern parlance we should say that the reason or scope would be to keep the integrity of the ego-functions and we should describe this scope in terms of the characteristics of tolerating no contradiction, in terms of the synthetic function, and perhaps in terms of other aspects of ego-functions as well.
(4) A mechanism with which further to deal with the unpleasant, split idea: 'projecting its substance into the external world'. It would, therefore, seem that (2) is not identical to (4) but that this latter is rather a subsequence or possibly a consequence of (2).
(5) Yet another mechanism with which to deal with such ideas: their denial. This is clearly visible in Freud's example of the *'grande nation'*. It will be seen that this example is different from that of the alcoholic who has become impotent, in which we clearly see an example of projection.
(6) A process in the ego as a consequence of all these happenings. This, again, is by no means simple. Freud speaks (a) of assimilatory delusions and of protective delusions; (b) of the fact that they constitute an alteration of the ego.

It is of interest to note that many years later the question of the alteration of the ego was taken up by Melanie Klein, who wrote of the weakening resulting from massive projective identifications (1946 [1952]: 301). This latter concept has been important in the understanding of certain clinical realities. It will be seen that this Kleinian description makes an implicit though quite clear use of the concept of contiguity and non-interpenetrability and, more essentially, of asymmetrical relation; if the individual projects something on to the outside, he is correspondingly the weaker or poorer for it. Such an assumption implies that 'what is outside cannot at the same time be inside'. This applies very well to the physical world, but we must study carefully the meaning it may have – if any – when applied to mental processes and happenings.[1] We might add that it is not quite clear from the paragraph quoted that this was exactly the sort of thing Freud had in mind here; anyway it is obvious that according to him the ego was altered as a consequence of projection and that it (the ego) tried to compensate for the upheaval resulting from projection by means of the assimilatory delusions and of megalomania, which would be a way for the ego to protect itself from 'a sense of the ego's littleness' (SE 1: 227), observed in melancholia. As can be seen, the idea of weakening or impoverishment seems to be a component of this conception, as is suggested by the word 'littleness', though we cannot be sure whether such an idea corresponds exactly to the Kleinian remark, i.e. weakening as a direct result of projection. On the other hand, some twenty-five years later Freud explicitly discussed the question of impoverishment or enrichment and came to different conclusions from those which Klein, in her turn, drew some further twenty-five years later (see Chapter 6, section 5).[2]

The conclusions we may draw from a consideration of these early writings of Freud on projection are that he describes the subject as being quite complex, and that together with the concept of projection he discusses a series of other concepts that in a precise formulation must be considered different from it: intrapsychical conflicts, splitting (not yet called by this name), reasons for splitting, denial, and alterations of the ego.

Furthermore, so far as I can see, all the mental properties, feelings, and behaviours found and described by Freud in these studies 'move' comfortably and are naturally contained in a form of thinking which develops in respect of the laws of 'normal', i.e. Aristotelian or classical, logic. Whether a more thorough examination of the implications of this study would reveal some bi-logical structure is an open question which has yet to be tackled in detail. Note, however, that Freud refers to the patient's thoughts which are permeated with emotions. These latter, in their turn, are bi-logical structures. This, however, does not detract from the fact just mentioned, i.e. that *the Fliess papers move essentially in the territory of asymmetry*.

It is also interesting to consider that all the studies in question refer to research conducted at least three to four years prior to the publication of *The Interpretation of Dreams*, where Freud put forward his revolutionary discoveries at great length, and it is these latter that lead to bi-logic. One wonders what happened in between.

Finally, as Strachey points out (SE 3: 184, n.), the first published use of the word 'projection' seems to be that seen in 'Further remarks on the neuro-psychoses of defence' (1896, SE 3: 159). Thirteen years later it makes a passing appearance in 'The Rat-Man' (1909, SE 10: 231–32) and the following year in '"Wild" psychoanalysis' (1910b, SE 11: 221–22).

All these cases so far mentioned treat projection as a pure asymmetrical affair.

2 The case of Schreber

Foreword. Freud's study of the case of Schreber (1911, SE 12: 1–82) has many aspects, among which we may mention his phenomenological description; his view as to the 'intense work of delusion-formation' (p. 38) and its relation to homosexuality; 'the exciting causes of his illness' (p. 35); and a number of interesting passing remarks about various subjects such as megalomania, narcissism, and points of fixation. Here, however, I want to concentrate exclusively on the aspects which are pertinent to the scope of this chapter: the relation of Freud's concepts on the subject to the three logics of the internal world. In other words I now shall focus upon the structure of the case of Schreber.

We have just seen that Freud's early concept of projection seems an essentially asymmetrical affair. The understanding of the structure of this case, instead, requires the concepts of the three logics. I have chosen to study it by means of a succession of comments.[3] The piecemeal insights obtained in this way can then be integrated into an all-round view of the structures. I must warn, however, that I shall limit myself to bare essentials and not even to all of them but only to a few.

From the case history I shall take some excerpts which are pertinent for our purpose.

The conception of God presented by Schreber is a very curious mixture of a superior being who is extremely powerful and dangerous and at the same time a fool and stupid. Schreber is the only one who has the right to scoff at him; to other men 'He remains the almighty creator of Heaven and earth, the first cause of all things . . . to whom . . . worship and deepest reverence are due' (SE 12: 28). This strange mixture is visible in various parts of his history (SE 12):

'When the work of creation was finished, God withdrew to an immense distance and, in general, resigned the world to its own laws. . . . In creating anything, God is parting with a portion of

Himself or is giving a portion of His nerves a different shape. The apparent loss which He thus sustains is made good when, after hundreds and thousands of years, the nerves of dead men . . . once more accrue to Him.'

(pp. 22–3)

'It was not until very much later that the idea forced itself upon my mind that God Himself had played the part of accomplice, if not of instigator, in the plot whereby my soul was to be murdered. . . . From this apparently unequal struggle between one weak man and God Himself, I have emerged as the victor.'

(p. 19)

'The consequence is that, now that the miracles have to a great extent lost the power which they formerly possessed of producing terrifying effects, God strikes me above all, in almost everything that happens to me, as being ridiculous or childish. As regards my own behaviour, this often results in my being obliged in self-defence to play the part of a scoffer at God, and even, on occasion, to scoff at Him aloud.'

(p. 27)

Flechsig was seen by Schreber as his doctor, persecutor, seducer, and soul-murderer – as different from God and also as 'God Flechsig' (SE 12: 39).

The sun is in intimate relation to God (SE 12: 22); at other times Schreber identifies the sun with God (p. 54).

Note also: (a) Every time he refers to God, Schreber writes 'He', 'Him', and 'Heaven' with capital letters. (b) On the other hand, Freud writes: 'Through the whole of Schreber's book there runs the bitter complaint that God, being only accustomed to communication with the dead, *does not understand living men*' (SE 12: 25).

(c) Dr Weber, his physician, writes:

'Whatever the subject was that came up for discussion (apart, of course, from his delusional ideas), whether it concerned events in the field of administration and law, of politics, art, literature or social life – in short, whatever the topic, Dr Schreber gave evidence of a lively interest, a well-informed mind, a good memory and a sound judgement. . . . So, too, in his lighter talk with the ladies of the party, he was both courteous and affable, and when he touched upon matters in a more humorous vein he invariably displayed tact and decorum. . . . Indeed, on one occasion during this period when a business question arose which involved the interest of his whole family, he entered into it in a manner which showed both his technical knowledge and his common good sense.'

(SE 12: 15–16)

(d) Several decades after Freud's study of the case of Schreber, Niederland (1959) and Schatzman (1971), quoted by Bowlby (1973: 174–77), have produced evidence which supports the hypothesis that many of Schreber's corporal delusions are to be related to strange and cruel treatments to which his father, a physician, submitted him in the interest of his physical and moral education.

I now shall try to put some order in the material I have quoted, and shall also refer, without quoting them, to other aspects of the case mentioned throughout the study, in order to see whether all this can be viewed in a unitary light. I repeat that I am not concerned in this discussion with the question of genesis but only with that of structure; in this context I shall use some other psychoanalytical notions, mentioned by Freud, only so far as they contribute to understanding the structure.

A first meaningful fact is that Schreber's father, Flechsig, and the sun were, for him, very important father images. In terms of classical logic they were representatives of the class of fathers, and this is seen in some of the Schreber's comments. The validity of PS, however, can be seen in the fact that the features or properties commonly present in the class of fathers, i.e. in the propositional function which defines it, *were present in them to a maximum degree*. For instance, they had the power in an infinite degree, and as such both Flechsig and the sun became respectively and explicitly God Flechsig and the Sun God, and the same can be said of Schreber's father. Though he was not present explicitly in his delusions, if we use the knowledge that we now have about him, it is evident that these delusions were modelled on the features that the child Schreber had felt his father had. All this shows an evident symmetrization of the class.

This fact is not, in itself, abnormal and it is found in everybody. At a deep level all authorities are felt in an obscure way as being omnipotent, i.e. having the maximum quality of the whole class and not only of an element of it (see Matte-Blanco 1975a: ch. 14, 161–67). In normal individuals, however, the deep levels, where the individual tends to merge into the class, are quite different and separate from the superficial levels, where each individual is himself – with all his qualities and limitations – and no other. In other words, *there is in such cases no immediately visible contamination of the superficial levels with the deep levels*. In the case of Schreber, instead, to take one example,

Professor Flechsig bcomes God Flechsig, which is a peculiar condensation into a unity of the superficial level, where he is only a professor, and the deep level, where he is (supposed to be) God. In this sense God–Flechsig is identical to Schreber's father, to the sun, and to all other elements of this symmetrized class, which becomes formed of only one element, and this identical to the class. This seems at first sight a Simassi structure because there is in it the presence of PS as well as asymmetry. But it is not, because in Simassi we find two parallel but different and incompatible ways of seeing the same reality. What is peculiar to this case is that there are, in this manifestation, no two ways but only one way of seeing Flechsig, i.e. as God–Flechsig and not as God *or* Professor Flechsig, according to the logic used. The converse is also true: one way of seeing God in this case, i.e. as God–Flechsig and not as God alone. In normal logic one would say that God is the inaccessible limit (as in mathematics) to which Schreber's father, Flechsig, the sun, and all other elements of the class tend but do not reach. Here, instead at a certain level, individual and the limit to which it tends are the same thing: God–Flechsig or Flechsig–God.

This, however, is not the whole story. God the '*almighty* creator of Heaven and earth, the first cause of all things' is at the same time a rather grotesque figure full of defects, 'ridiculous or childish'; and Schreber the 'weak man' 'emerged as the victor'. It is very difficult not to see in this description the view that the child Schreber formed of his father, who imposed upon him such extravagant and ridiculous procedures in the name of his physical and moral welfare.

So we see, at the same time, two incompatible views, that of an omnipotent being and that of a highly limited and ridiculous being, fused into one being which has the features of both; incompatibility has given way to compatibility! I do not believe this is visible in anything which is not extremely pathological.

The short-circuited stratified structure. We are now, I feel, in a position to define the distinctive characteristic of this aspect of the case of Schreber: *a short-circuiting of two strata of the stratified structure* (see Chapter 2, section 2) *which occurs in such a way that they are not connected in an alternation as in the Alassi structure; neither are they two different but parallel registrations – respectively, symmetrical or asymmetrical – as in the Simassi structure; but they are* fused *in a way that such features which are symmetrical, and as such cannot be asymmetrical, have in this case at the same time and on the same aspect both symmetrical and asymmetrical, hence incompatible, aspects: no simultaneity as in Simassi, but fusion into a new unity.*

This is a new product not seen in the normal structure of humans, a bi-logical structure different from all others so far known, and also most obviously different from projection when this is seen as an asymmetrical affair. I propose to call it the short-circuited stratified structure.

Once we have reached this view of the case, we can go a step further and try to understand other aspects of it. We may begin with a quotation taken from Freud.

'At the climax of his illness, under the influence of visions which were "partly of a terrifying character, but partly, too, of an indescribable grandeur" (73), Schreber became convinced of the imminence of a great catastrophe, of the end of the world. . . . He himself was "the only real man left alive", and the few human shapes he still saw – the doctor, the attendants, the other patients – he explained as being "miracled up, cursorily improvised men".
. . .

'. . . If we base ourselves on our theory of libidinal cathexes, and if we follow the hint given by Schreber's view of other people as being "cursorily improvised men", we shall find it not difficult to explain these catastrophes.* The patient has withdrawn from the people in his environment and from the external world generally the libidinal cathexis which he has hitherto directed on to them. . . . The end of the world is the projection of this internal catastrophe; his subjective world has come to an end since his withdrawal of his love from it. . . .

'. . . What forces itself so noisily upon our attention is the process of recovery, which undoes the work of repression and brings back the libido again on to the people it had abandoned. In paranoia this process is carried out by the method of projection. It was incorrect to say that the perception which was suppressed internally is projected outwards; the truth is rather, as we now see, that what was abolished internally returns from without.'

(SE 12: 68–71)

'* Cf. Abraham (1908) and Jung (1907). Abraham's short paper contains all the essential views put forward in the present study of the case of Schreber.' (Freud's footnote)

From the passages quoted above I shall single out for discussion the following ideas:

(a) The patient has withdrawn his libidinal cathexes, his love, from people in his environment and from the external world generally.
(b) 'The end of the world is the projection of this internal catastrophe.'

(c) 'His *subjective* world has come to an end since his withdrawal of his love from it' (my italics).
(d) The process of recovery 'brings back the libido again on to the people it had abandoned. . . . this process is carried out by the method of projection.'
(e) 'It was incorrect to say that the perception which was suppressed internally is projected outwards; the truth is rather, as we now see, that what was abolished internally returns from without.'

An attempt at understanding Freud's views. I find it far from easy to understand completely what Freud means in the statements I have quoted. If, furthermore, we consider that they all occur in the same study and with very few comments between, the problem becomes more acute. We may start from the more obvious in order to try and reach the core of his thought. There is no need to point out that (b) is in blatant contradiction of (e), because Freud himself says so in (e). But also (d) seems at first sight to be in contradiction of (e), because in the first Freud maintains that there is a projection of the libido, back to the people it has abandoned; whereas in (e) he expressly says that what was abolished internally returns from without. Perhaps such a statement is not a contradiction, because in the first case it is the libido, which has abandoned the people, that returns to them, whereas in the second it is the perception, which was abolished internally, that returns from without. If we try to be very rigorous in our efforts to understand this, we might say that here there are two different processes at work: on the one hand, the withdrawal of the libido which was originally directed towards people in the outside world; this would be a movement from the outside to the inside. On the other hand, there would be an internal suppression of a perception. This perception returns from the outside, but Freud insists that it is incorrect to say that it was projected outwards.

We find here a curious linking of two facts in an apparently contradictory way. (e) He describes (and seems to insist upon doing so) the process in terms of 'outside' and 'inside'; in other words, he employs the concept of contiguity to refer to these psychical processes. (b) But the curious thing is that while doing so he comes forward with a notion which is in blatant contradiction of the concept of contiguity, which he himself is using: something which has been suppressed internally, and about which it is incorrect to say that it has been projected, returns, mysteriously, from the outside.

If we continue to study Freud's words we come across some other interesting facts. The assertion that the end of the world is the projection of an internal catastrophe clearly suggests that Freud is referring to the end of the external world (i.e. the external world as seen by Schreber); this is indicated by Freud's use of the adjective 'external' shortly before in that same paragraph, and is confirmed by the comment that the end of the world is the projection of Schreber's internal catastrophe, i.e. something that happens outside. But also Schreber's subjective (i.e. internal) world had come to an end since his withdrawal of his love from it. We must, therefore, conclude that, according to Freud, the internal world had come to an end, for the reason he describes, and this had resulted in or coincided with an end (for Schreber) of the external world, a process which Freud first describes as projection. Subsequently, however, he affirms that it is incorrect to suppose that the perception which was suppressed internally is projected outward. On the other hand, in (e) he affirms that what was suppressed internally returns from the outside. We could reconcile this assertion with what we are now considering if we assume that the end of the world happened internally and not externally and that what was suppressed internally returns from the outside, where it has always remained intact. But this would not be a *return* and, anyway, seems to be in clear contradiction of Freud's description of the case.

Discussion. I shall now comment on various aspects of the case. The reader will realize, I hope, that, though they appear separate from one another, all converge into a unitary view in terms of the concepts I am putting forward.

(a) I do not see how we can escape the conclusion that, in terms of relations of three-dimensional outside and inside, which he, like everybody, was implicitly using, Freud contradicts himself. One could, alternatively, think that his comments are confused. If, instead, we think that in his comments he was trying to describe faithfully the deeper realities that he saw behind the appearances in the case of Schreber, we come to another, unexpected, and fascinating hypothesis: without being much aware, or perhaps even being totally unaware, he gave a faithful description of the clinical reality at the cost of contradicting himself through his use of spatial concepts which were obviously insufficient to 'contain' the reality which he was trying to describe. This provokes in me an admiration for his genius, and for the faithfulness with which he described the deep reality of the mind, even when he did not have the adequate tools to describe it with precision. The more we get to know about the mind, the more the genius of Freud unfolds itself to us.

I have tried without success to impose some order on, and to understand, Freud's remarks in the light of the terms in which he formulated them. I believe the task is hopeless. If, instead, we look at

112

the problem from another angle, we realize that he was trying to picture an elusive reality. To clarify what Freud may have been struggling towards, the first thing we must do is separate his description of the facts (which we may call his *phenomenological approach*) from his interpretation of them in terms of the libido theory (which we may call an *interpretative approach*), with the help of which, we may say, he intends 'to explain these catastrophes'. In his presentation both are intermixed, and this is one source of confusion. For our purposes we may leave aside his considerations in terms of libido, which, I believe, at the present moment throw no further light on the study of the structure, and would lead us away from our present subject.

If, instead, we consider his phenomenological description, we find some contradictions which I believe can be solved by resorting to a wider frame of reference. Briefly we may say that Freud maintains, first, that as a result of some internal catastrophe the external world, as was shown in the way Schreber saw it, had also come to an end. Note that when he speaks of the external world he can mean only Schreber's vision of the external world. Second, in the process of recovery both the internal and the external worlds were restored to their former state. Thus, from a purely phenomenological point of view, Freud is describing the existence of a perfect parallelism between the internal and the external changes as seen by Schreber. But he gets into difficulties and contradictions when he tries to describe this in terms of something that goes towards the outside (starting from the inside) or of something that 'returns from without'. In other words, the facts which he is studying do not lend themselves to being described in terms of 'either three-dimensional outside or three-dimensional inside'. This was perfectly possible, indeed necessary, in the cases Freud had studied fifteen years before; for instance; the alcoholic who refuses to blame himself for his impotence, and blames his wife, is a perfect case of 'either or'. Put in terms of inside or outside, it is a case of 'what is outside is not inside'. In more general terms, it is the assumption of contiguity. In still more general terms, it is a question of having asymmetrical relations available.

In Schreber's case, instead, something which is inside is *at the same time* outside, and vice versa. This can be understood in more than one way. A first way is to consider that the relations of outside and inside do not apply in this case and that what we are trying to do is describe in terms of such relations of contiguity – that is, asymmetrical relations – something which does not conform to it at all. A second way, for us, might be to see Freud's description from the perspective of a multiple-dimensional space expressed or represented in terms of space of a lesser number of dimensions. In this case, spaces of a number of dimensions smaller than that which is being considered may appear to be repeated. If a plane (two dimensions), for instance a triangle, is expressed in terms of lines (one dimension), then the points (zero dimension) appear repeated (see *Figure 3*, page 88). If a cube (three dimensions) is expressed in terms of planes, as when we undo a paper cube, then the edges or lines appear repeated (*Figure 4*, page 89). And so on. In this way a representation in terms of volumes (three dimensions) of a space of more than three dimensions may lead to the repetition of volumes. If we assume that psychical reality has more dimensions than three, then it is not surprising that in a geometrical representation it may appear duplicated in terms of the volumes which may represent it.[4]

Let us suppose, therefore, that the facts which Freud discusses do not happen in or, as it might be stated more formally, are not iso-morphic to a three-dimensional space. Instead, they might be isomorphic to a four-, a five-, or an n-dimensional one. In this case, what to us, who 'look with three-dimensional eyes', appears as two different regions of a three-dimensional space, i.e. external and internal, may, in a higher-dimensional space, be only one zone; these two three-dimensional volumes become one four-dimensional 'volume'.[5] In short, in this aspect of the case of Schreber, we are confronted with a three-dimensionalized or Tridim bi-logical struc-ture (see Chapter 2, section 2).

(b) Once we have reached this insight, several aspects of what Freud is explaining about the Schreber case seem to become much clearer. For example, we become aware that the contradiction between, on the one hand, 'the end of the world is the projection of this [Schreber's] internal catastrophe' and, on the other, 'it was incorrect to say that the perception which was suppressed internally is projected outwards; the truth is rather, as we now see, that what was abolished internally returns from without' no longer exists. It is a contradiction only if the facts are seen exclusively in terms of three-dimensional space. It is not a contradiction if the first statement is seen in that light only, and the second as a 'reading' in terms of a three-dimensional ('returns from without') something which was four- or more-dimensional. Something that, in a higher dimension, appears as only one and the same thing *unfolds*, in three dimensions, into external and internal, and the incompatibility-contradiction is solved.

(c) Another aspect which, I think, can now be understood is that of the 'cursorily improvised men', which seems to have been important for Schreber and which, if I have understood correctly, Freud explains in terms of withdrawal of the libido. I believe that without questioning this interesting explanation, which would be a dynamic one, we could add a structural point of view to understand it. In fact, in the normal stratified bi-logical structure (Chapter 2), we find that, 'underneath' the 'presentational aspect' or surface of each individual, there normally is, as already seen, a sequence of deeper and deeper strata with greater and greater amplitude and symmetrization. Normally, without being aware of it, we feel in an obscure way that the beloved woman is not only our wife but also our mother and, in a deeper stratum, all lovable women and, at a still deeper level, she is a goddess; deeper still, she is ourselves; and so on till we approach the full expression of the indivisible mode, at which point everything tends towards being the same as everything else.

(d) None of this is thought or felt consciously. Nevertheless it is there as a characteristic of our unconscious being and if, for whatever reason, we do not feel it, then the person or thing in question is voided of his, her, or its background or of the pyramid on which he, she, or it rests. As a consequence, there is no longer a he or she or it but only a shadow in which much is missing. This is, I believe, at least one structural meaning of one of Schreber's delusions: not real human beings but shadows, images of the real persons, 'cursorily improvised men'.

(e) The fact that Schreber was 'the only real man left alive' suggests that in a certain way the stratified structure is more preserved in what regards himself and is more disturbed in what regards his relations with the external world. Perhaps a study of this could lead to new insights about this structure.

(f) The imminence of a great catastrophe, the terrifying grandeur, may correspond to an acute, more conscious perception of the third zone of the stratified structure.

(g) The 'miracled birds' or 'talking birds' (SE 12: 35–6) confuse and treat as the same thing 'Santiago' or 'Karthago', and 'Chinesentum' or 'Jesum Christum'. We here see an identity which starts from similarity of sound: a symmetrization which, however, is used at a higher level of the discourse – a short circuit, as already described.

(h) Schreber's idea that he must become a woman, something which he both rejects and desires and which he integrates into a divine project to save the world (he also identifies with Jesus Christ (SE 12: 28)) is another clear example of a short circuit between a deeper and a superficial level and the formation of a synthesis of both levels into a new unity and not simultaneity as in Simassi: another example of the short circuit.

115

Still another short circuit in this aspect of this delusion: his wife cannot give him the children he so much desires, *ergo* he becomes a woman and not only gives birth to new generations but, in so doing, redeems the world. Note that Freud's idea of a 'genetic relation' (SE 12: 34) between Schreber's transformation into a woman and his favoured relation to God is an important insight. I repeat, here I am studying only the structural aspects.

This aspect of Schreber could be studied in much greater detail.

(i) The very curious mixture of ideas of what God does to him – searing his anus, believing he becomes an idiot – conveys an idea of God who is, to use Schreber's own words, 'ridiculous or childish'. I would add that Schreber himself, as seen in this light, appears pathetic. One cannot but think that all this is an elaboration of his reactions to the very bizarre actual behaviour of his own father. From the structural point of view this constitutes another example of forming an idea of the 'almighty creator of Heaven and earth' (SE 12: 28) by mixing/short-circuiting in a grotesque manner levels of experience and feelings which normally are never mixed in a conscious, earnest, and 'absolute' way as he does; at most the deeper levels may make their appearance as either jokes or obsessive ideas.

(j) Schreber obviously is an intelligent man, some aspects of whose mental life have gone astray. As a consequence, 'we can gauge in retrospect the wealth of sublimations which were brought down in ruin by the catastrophe of the general detachment of his libido' (SE 12: 73). To this genetic explanation we may add the structural description: all this happened through a shunting introduced in the stratified structure. And, I believe, various other things may be understood better if seen in the light of the concepts put forward here.

(k) Freud mentions the word 'projection' on three occasions in this study. The first (SE 12: 66):

' . . . projection. An internal perception is suppressed, and, instead, its content, after undergoing a certain kind of distortion, enters consciousness in the form of an external perception. . . . For when we refer the causes of certain sensations to the external world, instead of looking for them (as we do in the case of others) inside ourselves, this normal proceeding, too, deserves to be called projection.'

This precise description makes use of the concepts of internal and external but does not use the concept of 'from the internal to the external'; no displacement is at stake, as it usually is in the concept of projection. In other words, Freud has chosen to be very faithful to the phenomena observed (a *phenomenological description*) and has abstained from making an *interpretation* (from . . . to) which is not, in this case, a fact of observation. This results in this description fitting in very well with a conception of the simultaneity of two registrations of the facts; internal and external may coincide in a four- or *n*-dimensional space and not coincide in a three-dimensional representation of this space. Confronted with this description, together with that of the preceding quotation, one is tempted to ask whether, after all, Freud knew of spaces of more than three dimensions. If he did not know consciously he seems to be implicitly using both concepts!

The other two uses of the word 'projection' are already contained in a previous quotation ('At the climax . . .': see page 110). Note that in the second he uses the word 'returns', which suggests movement and corresponds to the asymmetrical conception of projection.

Conclusion about the case of Schreber. We have found two structures in this case: the short-circuit structure and the Tridim structure. It is natural to ask what the relation, if any, is between them in this case, if seen as a whole. A first thing that comes to mind is that the Tridim structure establishes relations between spaces of different dimensions which, as such, can be seen as corresponding to different levels or zones of depth: more unifying and, as such, 'deeper', in the case of more than three dimensions; more 'superficial' in the case of three dimensions. This is in keeping with what one finds in the normal stratified structure. Therefore, that aspect of the case corresponds to or is, in Schreber, a normal structural aspect; there seems to be no pathology in it as such. What strikes us is: (a) that at times it is replaced by a short circuit, and we then see the pathology; (b) that at times, when it is missing, Schreber seems to 'notice' its absence, for instance when he speaks of 'cursorily improvised men'.

So we may say that *the short-circuit structure seems to be the main characteristic of the case of Schreber, and the Tridim structure, which can be seen in normal behaviour, provides an opportunity for a pathological interpretation, as just mentioned.*

I cannot resist introducing a theoretical consideration which, it seems to me, may open new and very wide perspectives in the understanding of nature. I have given the reasons which lead to describing the Tridim structure as a bi-logical structure (see Chapter 2, section 2). On that occasion we considered different aspects of the *same* person which appeared 'incarnated' in different persons. In the case of Schreber, instead, we find that a multidimensional conception of the world unfolds into, or is tridimensionalized in terms of, external and internal; in three dimensions they are quite different; in a space of more dimensions they are one and the same thing. This strikes me as a new piece of knowledge which I wish to put on record here to reflect about when one becomes more familiar with it. I will, however, add that this may lead to a great new insight in our present conception. Bi-logic, which is so clearly and abundantly found in psychoanalysis and represents – in Freud's words, as used in relation to the unconscious (: a set of bi-logical structures: see Chapter 2) – 'the Realm of the Illogical' (see Chapter 3, pages 81–82), would, if this line turns out to be correct, be only a zone of a unitary logical conception, possibly a logic which, perhaps, would not be just classical logic (which seems to be essential unidimensional or, anyway, not more than three-dimensional plus time) but a multidimensional logic. And both bi-logic and unidimensional classical or bivalent logic would be substructures of it, both of them embraced in a higher synthesis. Note that when I speak of multidimensional logic I do not mean multivalued logic, because this latter has more than two truth values, whereas multidimensional logic could still have two truth values.

Thrilling indeed! More soberly said: hard work ahead to clarify this question.

A final remark. It becomes clear from the preceding reflections that the case of Schreber requires concepts which are entirely different from those we saw in Freud's earlier writings. The time was not yet ripe for developing the concepts required, and Freud could not consider the possibility of a more sophisticated use of the duality internal–external in terms of a multidimensional space, simply because such a possibility was, at the time, available to only a limited group of mathematicians. For similar reasons he did not broach the problem of spacelessness or the concept of bi-logical structure.

3 Freud's subsequent writings on projection

In subsequent writings Freud uses 'projection' in the first and best known of the meanings of the term which were developed by him. For example: 'The defence against it takes the form of displacing it on to the object of the hostility, on to the dead themselves. This defensive procedure, which is a common one both in normal and in pathological mental life, is known as a "*projection*"' (Freud 1913b [1912–13], SE 13: 61). Note that he affirms that projection is a form of displacement and that projection is common in both normal and pathological mental life.

A little later he speaks of 'the repression of the unconscious hostility by the method of projection and the construction of the ceremonial which gives expression to the fear of being punished by the demons' (SE 13: 63). This phrase seems ambiguous because it may be interpreted as meaning that projection is a method for repression, whereas it seems more accurate to say that projection is linked on to repression in order to dispose of the repressed material, i.e. to get rid of it. In other words, projection would be, in such a case, a mechanism which would facilitate the maintenance of repression. It is to be kept in mind, however, that when Freud wrote this paper the distinction between repression and other methods of defence had not yet reached, in his mind, its explicit and final formulation (see Strachey in SE 20: 174).

In the same book, in a footnote, Freud writes: 'The projected creations of primitive men resemble the personifications constructed by creative writers; for the latter *externalize* in the form of separate individuals the opposing instinctual impulses struggling within them' (SE 13: 65, my italics). So far as I am aware, this is the first of only two occasions on which he uses the concepts 'externalize' and 'externalization' in connection with projection and, as I understand, as synonymous with it – the second occurs in 'A metapsychological supplement to the theory of dreams' (1917b, SE 14: 223) – in which he describes projection as 'an externalization of an internal process'. This is of some interest because there seems nowadays to be a tendency to employ the term 'externalization' with a meaning which is similar, though perhaps not identical, to that of 'projective identification'.

Notes

1 See the contrast, for instance, with the expression quoted by D'Annunzio: 'Soltanto ho quel che ho donato' ('I have only what I have given'). We shall discuss that matter later.
2 It is curious to note the coincidence of the length of these intervals: (approximately) twenty-five years in both cases.
3 Freud's presentation of the case is woven by the interlacing of Schreber's own writings with Dr Weber's reports and Freud's own description and comments based upon the first two. In order not to render the discourse unnecessarily cumbersome, I shall not specify which of them I am quoting.
4 For further details see Matte-Blanco 1975a: ch. 32, and also Chapters 14 and 16 of this book.
5 I have inserted the inverted commas because, it seems to me, to speak or not of a four-dimensional *volume* is a matter of convention.

5

Identification and projection

This chapter aims at being a brief introductory reflection on a subject which will be repeatedly considered later.

1 Melanie Klein's and Elliott Jaques's comments on Freud

It is interesting to note that in his later years Freud once again turned his attention to problems which, like those in the case of Schreber, could not be entirely understood in terms of the antithesis between three-dimensional inside and three-dimensional outside, which was the only one available to him. And again he added to our understanding. These new insights are contained in *Group Psychology and the Analysis of the Ego* (1921). Melanie Klein, who put forward the concept of projective identification (1946 [1952]: 300–01; 1952: 207), comments (1955: 313, n. 3) that on re-reading the book just mentioned it appeared to her that Freud 'was aware of the process of identification by projection, although he did not differentiate it by means of a special term from the process of identification by introjection'.

Klein also refers to Elliott Jaques (1955: 480–82), who, on his part, deals with the same question in more detail. He mentions, quite rightly, the distinction made by Freud 'between identification of the ego with an object and replacement of the ego ideal by an object' (Freud 1921, SE 18: 134), and adds that in his opinion the first is identification by introjection and the second contains implicitly the conception of identification by projection, i.e. projective identification. As an illustration Jaques cites an example given by Freud, i.e. when the Assyrians take flight on learning that their leader, Holofernes, has had his head cut off.

2 Confrontation with a quotation from Freud

So far so good. I would like, however, to put forward the following points.

(a) Klein and Jaques are right when they say (essentially) that Freud differentiates projective from introjective identification without employing the first term.

(b) The concept of projective identification as developed by Klein gives account of only one part of the clinical reality which is studied in terms of this concept, i.e. that part which is describable in terms of outside and inside. The observation of patients, however, frequently confronts us with aspects which do not fit in with this antithesis. If we try to describe clinical reality only in terms of projective or introjective identification we leave aside most meaningful aspects of it, simply because we do not succeed in seeing them.[1]

(c) A careful reading of the paragraphs in *Group Psychology* which deal with the question leads to the conclusion that Freud discovered certain aspects of clinical reality which cannot be expressed in terms of the alternative three-dimensional/outside–inside, which was the only one known to him; and that he managed to convey these aspects in spite of the fact that his frame of reference was so inadequate. Moreover, not only was he faithful to clinical reality but he succeeded in putting forward new ways of understanding it. The evidence in favour of my assertion is contained especially in the following paragraph (1921, SE 18: 113–14):

'It is now easy to define the difference between identification and such extreme developments of being in love as may be described as "fascination" or "bondage". In the former case the ego has enriched itself with the properties of the object, it has "introjected" the object into itself, as Ferenczi expresses it. In the second case it is impoverished, it has surrendered itself to the object, it has substituted the object for its own most important constituent. Closer consideration soon makes it plain, however, that this kind of account creates an illusion of contradistinctions that have no real existence. Economically there is no question of impoverishment or enrichment; it is even possible to describe an extreme case of being in love as a state in which the ego has introjected the object into itself. Another distinction is perhaps better calculated to meet the

121

essence of the matter. In the case of identification the object has been lost or given up; it is then set up again inside the ego, and the ego makes a partial alteration in itself after the model of the lost object. In the other case the object is retained, and there is a hypercathexis of it by the ego and at the ego's expense. But here again a difficulty presents itself. Is it quite certain that identification presupposes that object–cathexis has been given up? Can there be no identification while the object is retained? And before we embark upon a discussion of this delicate question, the perception may already be beginning to dawn on us that yet another alternative embraces the real essence of the matter, namely, *whether the object is put in the place of the ego or of the ego ideal.*'

Comments. A careful study of this dense paragraph shows, I think, the following.

(a) Freud is evidently comparing what is frequently called identification by introjection, with one example of what Klein would possibly call projective identification. The example chosen by him is that of being in love; it is clear that it could be replaced by that of the relation of the soldiers to their leader or by the case of hypnosis: the actual problem is the comparison between both types of processes.

(b) When Freud follows his research in terms of putting inside or sending outside he is faced with the question of enrichment or impoverishment of the ego. When some years later Klein described projective identification she also found the problem of impoverishment. Closer consideration of the question, however, led him to the conclusion that such description is not satisfactory and that there is no question of enrichment or impoverishment.

(e) But the most important conclusion Freud reaches is (though not put in these words) that *the state of being in love cannot satisfactorily be described in terms of either projective or introjective identification.* In fact he affirms that an extreme case of being in love is a state in which the ego has introjected the object into itself. On the other hand, he questions the idea that in identification the object cathexis has been given up. Note that if it has not been given up then we have the *same* object in two places: outside and inside. The concept of a space of more than three dimensions may come to our rescue in our efforts to solve this problem.

We may at this point choose to replace the concepts of identification by projection or by introjection by the more general concept of movement from the inside towards the outside of the person and vice versa. In that case we find that Freud seems inclined to think that both types of movement are found in being in love and in identification. If we were to express this in Kleinian terms we should say that projective and introjective identification take place in being in love, and in identification as well. The trouble is, however, that such a formulation forces *all* reality into a (double) distinction – on the one hand, between outside and inside and, on the other, between identification by 'sending outside' (projective identification) and identification by 'bringing inside' (introjective identification) – which corresponds only to one part of the total reality. It is, therefore, understandable that Freud did not coin either of the two terms.

I would add that Freud obviously finds it difficult to describe in terms of movement in either or both directions the elusive reality he is studying. However, he is, at least, less hampered if he does not use the terms 'introjective' or 'projective' identification, which cover a limited territory. I may anticipate at this point that *neither can one ever succeed in describing accurately in terms of movement outwards or inwards a reality which does not refer to movement.* And the interesting thing one observes is that at the end of the paragraph Freud obviously avoids the notion of bringing inside or sending outside (introjection or projection) and replaces it by that of putting the object *in the place of* the ego or ego-ideal. This new notion clearly may be coinsidered as more general than that of (three-dimensional) space but it can also be put in (bi-univocal?) correspondence with it. So, though some further understanding of clinical reality has been gained from this formulation, the problem still remains. It seems to me that a more abstract formulation of the concepts of space, inside, and outside, as well as of the spaceless–timeless aspects of the mind – which Freud himself discovered and actually made fully explicit in the case of timelessness – may lead us away from 'material' three-dimensional space and bring with it deeper insights, some of which, I hope, will be seen in this book.

Note

1 For details see Parts Three, Four, and Five.

6

The notion of internal world: problems and hopes

1 Internal–external: why?

The concepts of internal and external usually refer to spatial happenings. In what sense do we use them when we speak of psychical processes? This question, however abstract and unnecessary it may appear, is of vital importance for a proper formulation of the problem. At first sight one can think that the concept of space, and therefore those of external and internal, has nothing to do with psychical processes. In fact, such an impression is wrong. We must reflect why.

It is easy to verify that this notion is used, in a simple way, in everyday language. Examples:

- 'We carry our beloved ones *within* our hearts.'
- 'After suffering this injustice I felt disconcerted and depressed. Then I gradually became aware that a tremendous rage *had begun to accumulate in me.*'
- 'I am *filled* with love and admiration for you.'
- 'I am not so *gullible*[1] as to accept your story as true.'
- 'I find that the subject you are explaining is very difficult for me *to digest.*'
- 'He speaks of things he has read a lot about but obviously he has not understood; it is *undigested reading.*'
- 'When you are near Mary you live and *breathe in an atmosphere of love.*' Note that this suggests the notion of 'inhaling' and 'exhaling' love. Otherwise one would have said 'you feel her loving nature', etc.

124

- 'I had to get rid of this feeling and express it *outside* myself in actions.'
- 'Why don't you *get it out of your system* and do something about it?' This may refer to any type of feeling.

- 'Und wenn Ich sah mein armer Vater beraubt und blind von der Barmherzigheit mildtät'ger Menschen lebend, Da weint ich nicht.
  Nicht in ohnmächtgen Tränen
  Goss ich di Kraft von meinem Schmerzen aus:
  In meiner Brust, wie eine teure Schatze,
  Verschloss es hin und dachte nur aus Taten.'

  ('And when I saw my poor father robbed and blind,
  Living from the charity of generous people,
  I did not cry.
  Not in impotent tears
  Poured I the strength of my pain:
  I locked it in my breast as a precious treasure
  And only thought of action.')

  (W. Schiller, *Wilhelm Tell*)

- A patient under analysis said that she had developed a very positive feeling towards her analyst. She felt protected by him and fantasied that she was very, very small and was lying on a very, very small couch inside the chest or the heart of her analyst. As can easily be seen, this fantasy expressed a psychical relationship by means of an image referring to the inside of the body.

All the above are obvious examples of expressing psychical experiences by 'comparing' them to something which is put inside, kept inside, or expelled. In other words, they are examples of the use of the concepts of 'internal' and 'external', i.e. of spatial notions, with reference to purely psychical processes.

The above is an initial simple approach to the problem of internal and external. We now pass on to express the same thing in a more precise way.

All thinking activity and all its expressions in language make use of the concept of logical relation, and in particular that of asymmetrical relation, and this concept is intimately linked with those of space and time. Take, for instance, the expression of a fairly simple thought: 'I drank an orange juice.' 'I' comes *first* (time) or *to the left* (space) of 'orange juice', which comes after or to the right of 'I'. The relation 'to drink' is asymmetrical because if we use the same relation as inverse, 'the orange juice drank me', it has no sense. So one can say that 'no logic can be actually built without the concept of space—

time' (Matte-Blanco, 1975a: 325). On the other hand, thinking cannot take place without making use of an underlying logical structure.

The previous assertion becomes in a certain way reinforced by the fact that the concept of space entails that of dimension, and this, in its turn, that of sequence. On the other hand, any sequence is generated by a transitive asymmetrical relation (see Russell 1903 [1948]: 463). In this way we arrive at the conclusion that there is an intimate relation between thinking and space–time; this latter underlies every thinking activity and, in consequence, every psychical *activity*.

The relations just mentioned, between space and thinking, are, however, something that remains, so to speak, in the background, one might say the philosophical background, of the question. There is, instead, a third reason why the concept of space, and therefore of internal–external duality, is very important in the study of psychical phenomena. The fact that human beings have a body determines in a basic way all their psychical life, *which appears as built from bodily and material experience as a starting point*. Furthermore, the fact that the material world appears, at least at first sight, as three-dimensional (length, breadth, and height) – plus the dimension time, which is not, however, identical to spatial dimensions – brings as a consequence the fact that the conception of psychical life, which springs from experience, and also the scientific conception, begins by being that of a three-dimensional world. Ultimately, if we bear in mind that imagination is capable of working only with three dimensions – neither more nor less – this fact anchors human beings still more to the three-dimensional world. We thus become aware that *all unconscious phantasies,[2] the majority of our thoughts, and a great part of our scientific conception of the world are deeply rooted in the conception of a three-dimensional world.*

But thinking can escape from this world – though only up to a point – and use imagination in this adventure, and so it becomes possible to discover spaces of zero, one, and two dimensions and of more dimensions than three, up to an infinite number. It is then discovered that *unconscious phantasy, which can furnish only three-dimensional images, in fact employs certain procedures which succeed in transmitting the conception of a space of more dimensions than three.[3]*

The earliest phantasies refer to corporal experiences or to the experience of the external sensory world. Rascovsky (for example, 1960: 67–8) has pointed out that before birth internal perceptions are already taking place and that these precede perception of the external world (see also Rascovsky 1960: 80–90).[4] Paula Heimann (1952: 155–60, my italics) writes:

'An inner world comes into being. The infant feels that there are objects, parts of people and people, inside his body, that they are alive and active, affect him and are affected by him. *This inner world of life and events is a creation of the infant's unconscious phantasy, his private replica of the world and objects around him.* (My italics.)

'. . . the infant has only his body with which to express his mental processes.

'. . . The phantasies about the inner world are inseparable from the infant's relation with the outer world and real people.

'. . . gradually the "internal objects" assume an abstract character. Phantasies about living entities within the self develop into ideas and mental work with concepts, a process which begins in quite young children.'

It is from this experience of the body and of the external world that our psychoanalytical study starts. But it should not stop just there, i.e. with only the consideration of material space.

2 What is internal and what is external?

It seems important at this point to clear up a potential misunderstanding about the meaning of the word 'internal'. Alix Strachey, quoted by Brierley (1951: 66–70), points out that the word 'internal' may be used to mean (1) 'mental', (2) 'imaginary', and (3) 'as actually imagined inside (the body)'. If the considerations just put forward are kept in mind, it is easy to understand that the concept of 'mental' has a close connection with that of space. It refers above all to the fact that every psychical activity, feeling included, is linked to thinking and that there cannot be thinking without implicitly employing the concept of an asymmetrical relation, which is so closely linked to the concept of space. Perhaps feeling in its not-thinking aspects is also related to space. The fact that imagination 'works' in three dimensions, however, is not by itself sufficient to explain how the concept of space may be employed in the study of the mind; and the same may be said of 'imagined inside the body', which refers to a fantasy and does not necessarily apply to the structure of the internal world seen as spatial structure.

I wish to point out as a consequence of what precedes that *the expressions 'internal world' and 'external world' will be employed in this study to denote spatial structures, and that the concepts of external and internal will be understood here in exactly the same sense in which they are understood in geometry and topology,* as we shall define them in Chapter

15. I am of the opinion that any tendency to escape from this meaning leads to a useless and misleading imprecision. I must warn, however, that we shall not limit ourselves to considering the structure of so-called material space, which is three-dimensional, as psychoanalytical research has done so far. On the contrary, the scope of all this study is to try to go further.

3 Some pertinent definitions

This section intends to offer some simple definitions for those readers who are not psychoanalysts and, therefore, are not working daily with these questions.

This is an initial step. More of it will come throughout the book.

- *Projection*:
  'The adscribing to the outer world mental processes that are not recognised to be of personal origin.'

  (Jones 1938: 621)

  'In the properly psycho-analytic sense: operation whereby qualities, feelings, wishes or even "objects", which the subject refuses to recognise or rejects in himself, are expelled from the self and located in another person or thing.'

  (Laplanche and Pontalis 1973: 349)

- *Introjection*:
  'Absorption of other personalities into the self, so that external events are reacted to as though they were internal, personal ones.'

  (Jones 1938: 621)

  'Process revealed by analytic investigation: in phantasy, the subject transposes objects and their inherent qualities from the "outside" to the "inside" of himself.'

  (Laplanche and Pontalis 1973: 229)

- *Projective identification*:
  'Projective identification is the result of the projection of parts of the self into an object. It may result in the object being perceived as having acquired the characteristics of the projected part of the self but it can also result in the self becoming identified with the object of its projection.'

  (Segal 1964: 126)

- *Object* (see Chapter 14).

4 The challenge of introjection and projection

I hope the preceding sections have clearly established that, in various ways, we link our mental experiences to physical happenings. This is in keeping with Freud's characteristic of the unconscious of replacing external by psychical reality. So far so good. But we are unable just to leave the question fixed at this point. It is precisely our use of the concepts of projective and introjective processes, which has been a stimulus to the development of our knowledge about human mental life, that has made us better aware of the difficulties regarding the present formulation of certain basic notions. We must, therefore, face this question squarely.

To start with a recent question which is of both theoretical and practical importance: the distinction, if there is one, between projection and projective identification has not, in my opinion, been clearly established, with the result that the latter term is now frequently employed in circumstances in which previously one would have used the former. In fact the term 'projection' seems to have gradually disappeared from certain sectors of the psychoanalytical literature, in spite of the fact that Melanie Klein herself, who put forward the concept of projective identification, continued to employ it.[5] One cannot help wondering whether both *concepts* are different, whether they greatly overlap, or whether they are even the same; and also whether the recent *term* is a better or more explicit way of describing the same facts. There is still another possibility: lack of precise definitions, which gives each author the freedom to follow his or her own inclination in the use of the terms.

On the other hand, since 'Mourning and melancholia' (1917a, SE 14) psychoanalysts have become more aware of the fundamental role played by the mechanism of introjection both in human mental growth and in adult psychical life. To give an example, the whole Kleinian conception of object relations is inconceivable without the concepts of introjection and projection. At the same time this development should lead to an awareness of extremely serious problems, even though, unfortunately, these have been to a great extent ignored or bypassed. To give an example, the small baby introjects the breast – so it is usually repeated – as a way of overcoming the frustration resulting from not having it always at his disposal. This means either a fantasy or a hallucination about the introduction of a material object, the breast, into the body, in order to satisfy a material need, that of milk. So far so good. But things do not stop at that. Introjection soon becomes something which, though never alien to references to bodily processes, is applied in the depth of the unconscious to things completely alien to the material world. The trouble is, however, that all observations about introjection show that it is treated in the unconscious as though it were indistinguishable from a material phenomenon of incorporation. This poses a series of conceptual questions of a very fundamental order. To take one of the many examples, if somebody introjects a parental *image* towards which he feels aggression, it may then be difficult for him to *keep it inside*, and he may proceed, as one of the possible solutions, to *expel* it or project it. Instead of images one may speak of *objects*, either partial or whole. In both cases one may ask: maintain what inside what? Expel it where? What is a mental object or image? How can they be *kept inside*? For it should not pass unnoticed that the phrases employed to describe these psychical processes are identical to those which would be used to describe a corporal process; but they are intended to describe a psychical one: the unconscious identity between psychical and physical, which does not exonerate us from trying to understand what that means in logical conscious thinking. We also say that the introjected object may be destroyed or split into innumerable pieces, pulverized by explosions, reconstituted in its parts; and we also speak of a process of *reparation*, a word which in its more primitive meaning designates a material action. We must recognize that the various vicissitudes of the introjected object, its destructions and recompositions, are an adequate description of one aspect of the facts but, on the other hand, seem more apt to describe material destruction or the work of a skilful mender of precious vases than the intense life of the mind. Such descriptions are both true – so far as they point towards things which clinical experience confirms daily – and false – so far as it is only crudely that they describe these realities.

Marjorie Brierley (1951: 69) writes:

'Now it is quite possible to imagine a person being dismembered, since persons and things can be dealt with in fantasy in any way human imagination can devise, but it is not possible to conceive of a mental object being literally shattered – one cannot take a hammer to a mental object. But this impasse is largely artificial, a consequence of mixed thinking. If the metapsychological mental object is thought of as a system of mental processes, it can be conceived as being more or less well integrated and as more or less liable to disintegration. Such a system can also be conceived as either integrated with, or excluded from, the major ego-organisation.'

The necessary distinction presented in this quotation and required

130

in scientific thinking confronts us with the definite task of giving a precise meaning to terms such as 'metapsychological mental objects' and 'system of mental processes'. When one tries to tackle the question one finds that it is not easy to get rid of the problems connected with the use of the physical image of object, even if we try to purge it (in our theory) of all its physical connotations.

What really is a mental object or system? Those who are not familiar with the analytical experience may easily dispose of this question by resorting to the simple expedient of ignoring it, together with the reality it tries to picture. Yet clinical experience confirms every day the deep truths contained in the initial descriptions of Freud, and the subsequent developments of Melanie Klein. It confronts us at the same time with the conceptual problems raised by such findings. And it must be recognized that psychoanalytical literature as a whole is strikingly silent about – and even uninterested in – these problems. The fundamental question remains: *what do we mean when we describe a psychical phenomenon in terms which are suitable for describing physical happenings? What do we mean when we speak of the 'inside', and the 'outside' of the mind, of 'taking to pieces' or 'destroying' objects, and when we use other similar expressions?*

The question becomes still more acute when we consider that the fear of an introjected object may be expressed by diarrhoea or vomit, which for the mind have the significance of expelling it. How can a *psychical* object be expelled by diarrhoea or vomit? And the curious thing is that, whatever the conceptual difficulties of such formulations, the facts which have led to them are undeniable, unavoidable, and familiar in psychoanalytic clinical experience; we must, therefore, try to understand them.

Still further complications arise when we consider certain details of clinical observation. The prototype of introjection is oral incorporation. If we compare the physical phenomenon of the incorporation of food with introjection – its carbon copy, so to speak – we soon find that, though the terms employed are the same, there are fundamental differences between the two processes. Eating develops through a series of actions which require (small) displacements in space and which take a certain time: to take the food into the mouth, chew it, swallow it, and then the slow, that is to say, temporal, process of digestion. In other words, oral incorporation, in the physical meaning of the expression, is framed in space and time, or rather *is* a spatio-temporal process. Introjection, however, 'behaves' in an entirely different way. In the first place, we do not find in it any activity which develops either in space or time, as all activities do. All the spatio-temporal aspects of the physical model, eating, have disappeared. An interesting metamorphosis has taken place whereby eating is performed without chewing, salivating, or swallowing; and everything takes place in what *appears* to us as an instant. *Introjection makes us think of despatialized and detemporalized eating*, which, of course, is no longer eating. And this applies even to those aspects of it which appear to be copied from some detail of the physical process. There can be, for instance, a biting introjection, but this does not necessarily contain the details of the physical act of biting, such as the sensation of physical resistance when digging the teeth in, the sensation of having the bits inside the mouth, and so on. Correspondingly, the same may be said of an introjection copied from the prototype of sucking or of scooping.

Time and timelessness. When we say that introjection takes place in an instant, further reflection will show that this is only a manner of speaking. An instant is a little 'piece' of time, however small; when we speak of it we are already speaking of time. In introjection, in contrast, if we sharpen our observation, we find that at a certain moment of time we do not find it, it is not 'there' and at the next moment it is already 'there'. It is an illusion to think that it took place or developed 'passing' from one moment to another; it simply made its appearance without the mediation of time, and if we tend to frame it in time this is due to the fact that we do not know what to do with or how to look at a psychical 'phenomenon' which appears as though it were coming from nowhere (neither space nor time) like characters of fantasy films, or the genie in Aladdin's lamp.[6]

I do not know whether I have succeeded in making clear this characteristic of introjection which is shared by all deep psychical processes. It is so difficult for us humans to get rid, in our thinking, of time and space that we are led to misrepresent our observation of certain psychical phenomena by framing them only in space–time, even when they are not only spatio-temporal. In other words, some psychical manifestations obviously appear only as spatio-temporal, while others do not appear so; but we tend to think that all of them are spatio-temporal. If we remember Freud: 'the processes of the system Ucs are *timeless*' (SE 14: 187), we then become aware that introjection may be viewed as a process, i.e. something which develops in time, and *also* as being timeless. This is very strange but it is so.

Summarizing this part of our reflections, we may conclude that introjection behaves in a very peculiar manner with regard to space and time; the same can be said of the objects of its activity, the objects that are introjected. It is a mechanism in which the physical aspects – apparently so insistently present in its essence, that of introducing something inside, as it is done in the body – have become dematerialized, despatialized, and detemporalized. In other words, *in introjection we detect the characteristics of the unconscious.*

Similar but not identical considerations can be made of its counterpart, projection. In short, we may conclude that *introjection and projection are striking and important examples of the fundamental antinomy of human beings and world.*

How to understand this fascinating behaviour? The problems which I have outlined represent a challenge to our intellect. It can safely be said that if we can find our way towards their solution we shall have succeeded in increasing our understanding of some fundamental aspects of human beings and of the world. My aim in this book is, among other things, an attempt at making some conceptual proposals, delimitations, and precisions which, I believe, may increase our mutual understanding of the various views that have been expressed on the subject. I also aim to try to organize some of the very many observations so far made on these matters, by applying the concepts I am proposing and by trying to delimit clearly the various levels of 'depth', without which, it seems, no clear comprehension can ever be reached.

5 Internal world and the unity of the self

It is important for a general perspective of our argument to stop for a moment to consider this aspect of the question. Freud uses the word 'introjection' very infrequently, as Strachey points out (SE 14: 241, n.). He uses the term 'introjected object' still less[7] and, so far as I know, never 'internal world' in the sense in which Melanie Klein intends it. The concept of 'introjected object' appeared, among all his writings, only in *Group Psychology and the Analysis of the Ego* (1921, SE 18: 108–09, 113–14, 130, 133–34, 143). The concept in question is used only six times and in all cases in a way which is not completely explicit, because Freud speaks in fact of *identification through introjection of the object.* This seems to mean that introjection of the object and the introjected object are, in Freud's view, aspects of or connected to the process of identification. It is obvious that *identification is a process which preserves the unity of the individual.* It would seem that Freud thought that this preservation is fundamental in the conception of the human mind. Perhaps one could find here the clue to explain the scarce use which he makes of the concepts of introjection and of introjected objects as things in themselves.

It is pertinent at this point to quote Freud. We start with his use of the concept of introjected object (Freud 1921, SE 18):

'First, identification is the original form of emotional tie with an object; secondly, in a regressive way it becomes a substitute for a libidinal object-tie, as it were by means of introjection of the object into the ego.'

(pp. 107–08)

'Identification with an object that is renounced or lost, as a substitute for that object – introjection of it into the ego.'

(p. 109)

' . . . the ego has enriched itself with the properties of the object, it has "introjected" the object into itself, as Ferenczi [1909] expresses it.'

(p. 113)

Contemporarily one can see his attention to, one could even say his concern about, the multiplicity in the ego and the problems that it raises (Freud 1921, SE 18):

'They show us the ego divided, fallen apart into two pieces, one of which rages against the second.'

(p. 109)

'Each of the mental differentiations that we have become acquainted with represents a fresh aggravation of the difficulties of mental functioning, increases its instability, and may become the starting-point for its breakdown, that is, for the onset of a disease.'

(p. 130)

It seems, therefore, fair to say that the Freudian conception clearly shows awareness of the nature of the problem; it is, however, difficult to foresee from it the subsequent Kleinian developments.

The natural evolution of Melanie Klein's views, in contrast, has led to a conception in which the multiplicity inside the individual plays a preponderant role. When followed to its ultimate consequences, this conception raises important problems about the survival of the unity of the mind in the midst of this internal world filled with so many objects: just the problem mentioned by Freud. The vicissitudes of the introjected objects – later on called simply the 'objects' – have been studied in a detailed way. The concepts of 'fragmentation' of the objects, of 'explosion', 'invasion', 'angry objects', 'bizarre objects', 'reconstitution', 'embedding', and various others have become quite familiar, together with those of 'container', 'internal breast', 'introjective dependence on the breast', 'relation with the internal objects', interaction between internal and external world, and 'external object encapsulated in the self'.

Contemporarily to the development of these ideas there has been a gradual theoretical evolution in which the threefold conception, i.e. Freud's description of the mind in terms of ego, id, and super-ego (cf. *The Ego and the Id*, 1923, SE 19), became imperceptibly replaced by an alternative conception, that of 'object relations'. The relation between these two ways of conceiving psychical structures has not been sufficiently clarified. Probably at the present moment there is a mixture of elements of both conceptions implicit in the work of many analysts. Many of them do not seem to worry about an explicit definition of one or the other.

It is necessary at this point to avoid a misunderstanding. Though I am of the opinion that the Freudian effort to save the unity of the individual is of great importance for an integral comprehension of the mind, I do not mean to say that Klein and her disciples have chosen to follow a wrong path which ends in chaos. I am, instead, of the opinion that the Kleinian approach has been extremely fertile and has led to a deeper understanding of meaningful facts, which otherwise would not have been understood and perhaps would not have been discovered. At the same time this approach has brought to the fore a question which Klein herself mentions (see Appendix, quotation (24)) and which by now has become quite clear and needs to be further studied.

On the other hand, the way in which facts have been, at times, reflected in the present use of Kleinian discoveries implies, from a certain point of view, a gross distortion of psychical reality, because it jeopardizes the basic *unity* (oneness) of the self, which is in fact always preserved, even in serious cases of splitting or in schizophrenia. Sometimes one has the impression that these descriptions give an image of the mind as a bag full of objects, good, dangerous, or not worthy of trust and the mind is not a bag.

This situation should not lead us to abandon the path undertaken. The problems raised *can* be put in a more satisfactory perspective with the help of a further refinement and subtilization of present-day conceptions, and with a more rigorous formulation than that so far in use. *It would be essential, above all, to try to delimit very well the boundary between what we know and what we do not know, and between psychical reality and our way of expressing it in concepts.* It is only through such an effort that we shall have the opportunity of finding our way towards a solution of the problems mentioned.

6 Conclusion

Our clinical work confronts us every day with facts which cannot be understood and ordained in terms of the usual naïve conception of internal and external which, without substantial modifications, has up to now been applied in psychoanalytical researches about the internal world. We must make a qualitative jump forward, and a new formulation may open the way to the understanding of old problems.

There is much evidence which confirms the assertion just made, although the difficulties raised are far from easy to solve. If we wish to develop a conception capable of expressing clinical reality in a satisfactory way, which may lead to new understanding, it will be necessary to consider seriously the notions of geometry and topology. But this is not enough. We must become aware that present mathematical concepts are not sufficient. They are, no doubt, useful to introduce precision in the heterogenic aspect of the constitutive antinomy. The other, the indivisible, must be faced, and we shall have to create new concepts in order to enable our intellect to use its own heterogenic nature in the impossible task – impossible for our intellect – of getting, in some way, to live the indivisible.

This task must necessarily be tackled through a co-operation of thinking and feeling, because this latter is our only way to be indivisible. *Thinking, feeling, and being are our only hope.*

My hopeful impression is that a deeper understanding of the spatial dimensionality of psychical phenomena may lead to fundamental new insights about humanity. Among other things, I believe the so-called body–mind question, so little understood and so badly mishandled in recent times – when it is said simply that it is a false problem, in spite of the fact that, to give a simple example, a mathematical reasoning is obviously different in 'nature' from, say, a muscular contraction – may disclose a new and simple solution. The body, a three-dimensional structure, might, for instance, be a substructure of something which has more dimensions than three.

We shall return repeatedly in the book to the question of dimensionality as an approach to the fundamental question of our antinomic nature.

Notes

1 Oxford Dictionary: '*gull*: 1. To swallow. *Gullible*: capable of being gulled, easily duped.'

2 When the word 'phantasy' appears in the text I refer to the unconscious process. 'Fantasy', instead, refers to a conscious one. I am willing to abide by this convention, only at times I either forget it or I am not able to decide which term to use.

3 See Chapters 15 and 16; and Matte-Blanco 1975a: chs. 32 and 33.

4 I believe that recent studies of the foetus by means of echography confirm this early intuition of Rascovsky.

5 In *Envy and Gratitude* (1957) Klein uses 'projection' fourteen times and 'projective identification' five times. In *Narrative of a Child Analysis* (1961) the proportion is thirteen to eleven. On the other hand, in Meltzer's *The Psychoanalytic Process* (1967) the proportion is nought to twenty. The early writings of Bion seem to show a tendency similar to Meltzer's. In Bion's later work, instead we observe a much more comprehensive approach, in which the infinite and spacelessness play a role which, however, remains implicit to a great extent.

It will be seen that a more comprehensive view clearly leads to a new perspective on the theoretical and practical importance of projection and projective identification: because, as usually formulated, they refer exclusively to the realm of *happening* while they should be seen as only one aspect of a wider reality. Naturally, the same holds for introjection.

6 I think the following is food for thought for students of introjection and projection. On the one hand, the reflections of Saint Thomas Aquinas (1880: Vol. I, question LIII, art. II) regarding the possibility that an angel may first be in a place and later on in another without having to pass through the intermediate places: it seems to me that psychology would benefit if, leaving aside the context in which Aquinas's remarks are made, it applied the underlying ideas to its own subject matter.

On the other hand, some distinguished mathematicians starting with Weierstrass (cf. Russell 1903: ch. XLII; Kline 1953: ch. 25) have come to agree with the assertion of Zeno that the arrow is at rest at every instant of its motion; movement would be 'composed' of a sequence of immobilities!

7 In *The Psycho-Analysis of Children* (1932), Klein uses the term 'introjected object' twenty-five times, and introjection nine times. In *Contributions to Psycho-Analysis* (1948) 'introjection' appears sixty-one times in the index, while 'object' is mentioned (if I am not wrong) three hundred and seven times in the index. In *Envy and Gratitude* (1957) 'object' appears also far more frequently than 'introjection'.

7

A perspective on Melanie Klein's contribution

Foreword. This chapter is, on the whole, more of a panoramic perspective than a complete review.[1] My feeling is that in order to arrive at this latter one would have to comb carefully all Klein's writings, a task which I have not attempted and which would take a long time; I have only drawn from my own reservoir of the knowledge I have acquired and from the impression gathered throughout the long decades of acquaintance with her writings.

I am aware that the way I deal, in this chapter, with Melanie Klein's contribution may at first sight appear as not having anything to do with her discoveries as explicitly formulated by her. Yet, as in the case of my reformulation of Freud's unconscious, what I am doing is making explicit some concepts which are implicit in her writings, even though at first sight she would most probably have been surprised at what I am affirming of her research. I fancy, as I also do in the case of Freud, that on second thoughts she would have come to see that the assertions just made are true. So far as I am concerned – again, as in the case of my study of Freud – it is in the fact of living in the atmosphere created by him, on the one hand, and by her, on the other, that I arrived at my present formulation, through the interaction of their ideas with my interest in other, different subjects.

My hope is that what I am putting forward here is one way of continuing along the path which Klein had the courage to discover and pursue, so as to venture further into it and explore the views it discloses.

I see this chapter as a coherent as well as a serene homage to Melanie Klein.

138

1 A preliminary impression

When one reads Melanie Klein, one finds it is far from easy to grasp the implications of the various aspects of the concepts she puts forward, and the exact hierarchy and variety of recesses and hidden corners within them. The reader is frequently dazzled by the wealth, both of the phantasies she describes and of her observations; so much so that at times one finds it difficult to make a distinction between essentials and details. Perhaps the comparison with an exuberant, dense, attractive, mysterious, exciting, and frightening tropical jungle conveys something of the experience of getting to know Klein. Her descriptions confront us with the mystery and fascination of the inside of the mother; in fact they are, in some ways, isomorphic to the unconscious conceptions of it, which itself is – for the intellect – isomorphic to the tropical jungle, as just mentioned. On the other hand, for a deeper aspect of the unconscious, seen as a set of bi-logical structures, Melanie Klein, her descriptions, and the tropical jungle are, all three, *the same thing.* We have seen (Chapter 3, section 11) that bi-logical structures play an important role in scientific discoveries and conceptions, and this is above all true of psychoanalytical research. The permanent contact with unconscious fantasies inevitably pushes the psychoanalytic researcher to give an important role to bi-logic in the workings of the human mind, even if one chooses to formulate it, not in terms of bi-logic, but in terms of the unconscious, projective identification, and so on. And, remember, bi-logical structures are the expression of the fundamental antinomy.

At times, it must be recognized, bi-logic surreptitiously slips into psychoanalytical *scientific* formulations which, as all science, should be made in respect of 'the laws of thought' (Boole) even when bi-logic is discovered in an unconscious manifestation; *bi-logic is in the facts under study, and should not be in our present-day conceptual formulations.*

What I have just affirmed is particularly true in the case of Melanie Klein's studies. When reading her, there are some moments during which a feeling arises that everything, or almost everything, seems to be everywhere, or almost everywhere. This is apt to lead to disorientation and, at bottom, to an intense desire of the mother, and to anxiety.

I beg the reader to be indulgent if and when he or she finds that bi-logical expressions such as emotions have slipped into my own perspective of Klein's contribution and have led to misinterpretation.

I hope that, however imperfect my view may be, it may nevertheless serve as stimulus to a further understanding of her work.

On the other hand, when reading Klein, it is possible to discover another reason why one gets a feeling of fascination. She introduces us into an intense real personal experience of both fusion and separation or separation and fusion. These are, I believe, some of the unconscious reasons for the great impact she is having on psychological thinking, and also a reason why at times she is violently rejected. Actually her impact seems to be inseparable from the fact that the zone of life which she describes awakens deep anxieties in most people.

I still recall very vividly my student days in London, and the feeling of fascination which I experienced with *The Psycho-Analysis of Children*. When her first paper on 'Manic-depressive states' appeared in 1935 and I read it for the first time, I was clearly aware of feeling anxious. I soon found, to my relief, that other students or analysts had a similar reaction.

2 The infinite in Klein's writings and in her conception

As I now see it, one of the deepest causes of the anxiety felt at times when reading Melanie Klein is that her writings deal with and move at a certain special level of psychical happening, i.e. the level at which the indivisible mode is *translated* in terms of heterogenic experiences which are bi-logical structures, hence antinomic, and, as such, do not respect the laws of classical logic, or are felt as being of an intensity which tends towards infinite values. This corresponds to the third and fourth strata of the constitutive stratified structure discussed in Chapter 2. Both cases are at bottom the same, for the mathematical infinite is a bi-logical structure. Briefly said, *Klein's research deals with, and actually her own thinking, as seen in her writings, is constantly exploring, a highly bi-logical 'territory' of the mind.*

The infinite provokes a feeling of fascination and fear; if this happens even when we consider its most 'purified' expression, the mathematical infinite, it happens all the more when we face emotions, of aggression or love, of an intensity which is felt as tending towards the infinite. In such cases the experience of emotion leads one to feel the possibility of a catastrophe, of disintegration. To explain, if the paradoxes of the infinite, which already provoke anxiety, are related to the identity between the part and the whole with regard to only one property (equinumerosity), one can easily understand how much stronger such anxiety must be when there is identity between part and whole on all properties: symmetrization and bi-logical structure. It seems that the laws of thinking have gone to pieces and that one has lost one's bearings.

Consider the following quotation from Klein:

'The ideas of an infant of from six to twelve months trying to destroy its mother by every method at the disposal of its sadistic tendencies – with its teeth, nails and excreta and with the whole of its body, transformed in imagination into all kinds of dangerous weapons – presents a horrifying, not to say an unbelievable, picture to our minds. And it is difficult, as I know from my own experience, to bring oneself to recognize that such an abhorrent idea answers to the truth. But the abundance, force and multiplicity of the imaginary cruelties which accompany these cravings are displayed before our eyes in early analysis so clearly and forcibly that they leave no room for doubt. . . . This element of *intensification* of impulse seems to me to be the key to the whole matter . . . we can readily understand that the destructive cravings which are fused with the libidinal ones and cannot be gratified . . . should lead to a further intensitifcation of sadism and to an activation of all its methods.'

(Klein 1932: 187–88)

Now, this paragraph, which clearly refers to the third and fourth zones of the stratified structure, confronts us with an intensity of impulse and phantasy which provokes amazement and horror not only in Melanie Klein but in many people confronted with similar circumstances. One *feels* that the intensity is frightening, and, without formulating it explicitly, one also feels, though in an obscure manner, that it has no limit. In other words, it *tends towards the infinite*, just as 1, 2, 3, etc. do, only in the case we are considering the emotion is much more intense than, say, the 'dizziness' that people experience when they consider something that goes on and on and on, without ever ending. The difference is, I think, understandable if one remembers that the mathematical infinite is a substructure of the logic of the unconscious or of a wide symmetrized set (Chapter 2, section 9).

In the case of Melanie Klein's work it is not only our intellectual considerations that are at stake but our individuality and our relations with our fellow beings, father and mother images, and so on. It is my contention that *The Psycho-Analysis of Children* (1932) moves in this atmosphere. There are several lines along which the concept of the infinite is implicit:

(a) *Intensity of feeling.* There are so many examples of it, the book is so much permeated with this idea, that it seems useless to make quotations.

(b) *Variety of intense impulses and their corresponding fears*: oral cannibalistic, sucking, scooping, emptying, biting, anal sadistic, and so on. Quoting on this subject would amount to quoting a great part of the book.

(c) Correspondingly, *multiplicity of objects and consequently of dangers*. Take three comments on p. 206 as examples:

(i) 'a multitude of persecutors inside its body';
(ii) 'the child's fears of subterraneous attacks upon itself on the part of its introjected and external objects become more manifold';
(iii) 'Its anxiety spreads out and is distributed over many objects and sources of danger in the outer world, so that it now expects to be attacked by a great number of persecutors.'

It is of interest to consider the multiplicity of objects described by Klein in the light of an interpretation I have put forward of the meaning of the mathematical infinite (Matte-Blanco 1984). When thinking is confronted with the indivisible, it finds itself incapable of understanding it, because thinking can deal only with that which is divisible, formed of triads of something, something else, and the relation between them (Matte-Blanco 1975a: 330–49). It then excogitates a curious and ingenious way of grasping it: it conceives the indivisible as formed of a number of elements whose counting cannot come to an end. In this way it creates the concept of the infinite, which is in itself an attempt to transform something which is outside the very notion of concept, because it is indivisible, into the concept of infinitely divisible.

It seems to me that Melanie Klein, as shown in these quotations, presents a beautiful picture of the child who finds himself surrounded by something mysterious, awe-inspiring, intense, incomprehensible, and tries to grasp the mysterious indivisible by means of making it infinitely varied in the ways Klein describes.

(d) *Variety of the nature of the attacks*: biting, scooping, cutting to pieces, pulverizing, blowing up into innumerable pieces, cataclysmic explosions, and so on. One can see here both extreme intensity and extreme division of the attacks against the object. Once more the infinite appears in an implicit, suggested way.

At this point I should like to make a personal reference. *The Psycho-Analysis of Children* played a very important role in my analytical training in London. I remember the many evenings when I read it, with fascination and anxiety, and tried to understand and absorb it. Many years afterwards, in the late 1960s, I came into contact for the first time with the details of the mathematical concept of the infinite. I was very struck by its mystery and I can now see that my initiation in Melanie Klein's writings, in the middle 1930s, represented in the middle 1960s the basis upon which I was able to establish a connection between the mathematical infinite and psychoanalysis. On the other hand, I suppose I have always had in mind – how much of it consciously and how much unconsciously I do not know – the mystery of Freud's conception of the 'true psychical reality' of the unconscious and its so strange characteristics or laws. It is starting from Freud and Klein that I was able to write *The Unconscious as Infinite Sets*. Without their teachings and their inspiration I do not think I would have been able to write it in a hundred years. My gratitude goes to them. I now can see and live a synthesis of both with no detriment to either one. Sometimes I feel that an opposition between Freud and Klein is quite unnecessary even though it is visible in the opinions of some analysts.

3 Bi-logical structures in Klein's writings

I have not made a study of *The Psycho-Analysis of Children* in the light of the concept of bi-logical structure. The reason seems to be that, at the period of my development during which this book played its greatest role in my development, the intensity of feelings and fantasies described in it was the aspect more obvious to me and which apparently struck me most. Looking back, I now suspect that most probably, and being utterly unaware of it, the presence of bi-logical structures contributed as much, if not more, to my strong interest in this book and to the anxiety it sometimes provoked in me: the fundamental antinomy. Remember at this point that, as I see it (Chapter 2, section 8), the mathematical infinite is a bi-logical structure and, as such, an expression of this antinomy.

Melanie Klein's later writings have been more on the front line of recent Kleinian psychoanalytical research, and it is starting from them that I now shall make my comment. However, I believe that a thorough study of *The Psycho-Analysis of Children*, in the light of my proposal, may lead to the discovery of a number of new bi-logical structures described in it but not named as such. I also think that the same would happen with a study of Klein's later writings. It seems to me that what I am discussing in this chapter may be compared to a rapid gleaning[2] of a rich field. Better some than none.

A Simassi bi-logical structure. When Klein writes (see Appendix, quotation (3)), 'Together with these harmful excrements, expelled in hatred, split off parts of the ego are also projected . . . *into* the mother' (1946 [1952]: 300), one may – too easily – reject this assertion as absurd, for 'parts of the ego', just as the square root of −5, cannot be expelled or projected *together* with excrements. Yet clinical observation shows that this description may correspond in certain cases to the actual truth of the patient's mind. When this happens we are confronted with a Simassi bi-logical structure (see Chapter 2), which Klein is implicitly describing. The symmetrical aspect of it has to do with identification of psychical (parts of the ego) and physical (excrements), a characteristic of the unconscious described by Freud. The *simultaneous* asymmetrical aspect, instead, lies in the assertion of their differences, hence the conflict, in terms of classical-logical reasoning: the fundamental antinomy. Some people may resolve the problem by simply rejecting Klein's assertions (I have even seen somebody become literally angry for what he felt were her 'absurdities'). Others, with psychoanalytical knowledge, will accept them. In the first case, rejection is a defence against the anxiety provoked by the fundamental antinomy implicit in equating psychical and physical reality. In the second, one remains more at the mercy of anxiety, due ultimately to non-viable bi-logical blending of the two modes (see Chapter 2, section 2) that leaves the intellect – which, to employ with only a slight difference of meaning an expression of Freud, 'is in the last resort our one beacon-light in the darkness' of this world (SE 19: 18) – badly shattered.

Note, however, that Melanie Klein speaks of *expelling* the excrements and *projecting* the part of the self. This is, I think, a clear sign that, as a scientific thinker, she wanted to stress that a part of the ego cannot be defecated; therefore, her own discourse is not bi-logic: only what the patient feels is, and this is shown in the preposition '*together*', which seems to express a hint at identification or at least that the self can be expelled, as faeces can. The result is that the sentence quoted seems, in a very subtle way, to be put *between* bi-logical and non–bi-logical bi-modality (see Chapters 2 and 3). This poses most interesting questions, but I shall refrain from entering into them here.

Note that when the intellect or thinking appears defeated or invaded by something alien to it, i.e. the indivisible, this leads to *confusion*; and this is a fundamental cause of anxiety when one has no alterations of consciousness (as are present in confusional syndromes).

In the last resort, the anxiety of the infinite is the same thing as the anxiety of the unconscious, as seen in the case we are studying; in both cases we are confronted with a 'clash', instead of harmonious co-operation between both modes of being: again the fundamental antinomy. In such a case we cannot think clearly, i.e. we have lost our classical-logical understanding, which is *the* potent tool which human beings possess to face and conquer nature. In the case of the mathematical infinite we witness only a partial 'abolition of reason', whereas in the case of unconscious manifestations we see a much more radical one and, therefore, we react with greater anxiety.

I suggest that this more radical anxiety is frequently aroused when we read Melanie Klein, for she explores precisely *those* bi-logical 'regions'. Eventually anxiety gives way to a feeling of fascination, frequently observed when studying Klein.

Incidentally, the quotation just referred to is an example of my assertion, made above, that Klein's scientific research moves in a highly bi-modal territory. Of course, it would be easy to 'establish order' by saying that the child *feels* that 'portions of the ego . . . ', and that is what she actually implies. Things, however, are rather more complex, as we shall see later in this chapter.

Another example. In the same quotation, Klein says that these

> 'excrements and bad parts of the self are meant not only to injure but also to control and to take possession of the object. Insofar as the mother comes to contain the bad parts of the self she is not felt to be a separate individual but is felt to be *the* bad self.'
>
> (1946 [1952]: 300)

My comment: in so far as the bad parts of the self injure, control, and take possession of the object, they are considered as being different from it (splitting and projection). At the same time, in as much as these parts are inside the mother (i.e. the object) she is not considered as being separate from the bad self but, as Klein says, is felt to be *the* bad self. In other words, there are two simultaneous but different and incompatible ways of looking at them; on the one hand the bad self and the mother are quite different; on the other they are only one thing. Two ways or modes of being coexist here – one for which reality is divisible and one for which (psychical) reality is indivisible; two persons are the same person. This is a Simassi bi-logical structure.

Melanie Klein does not speak of two modes, but her description points implicitly to the formulation just suggested. If we are more explicit about this we can solve various difficulties and furnish a better understanding of clinical reality.

She also writes: 'Much of the hatred against parts of the self is now directed towards the mother' (1946 [1952]: 300). This seems a clear description of Freud's initial conception of the mechanism of projection, i.e. as exclusively asymmetrical. In this case one gets rid of the hatred towards the self by displacing it on to the mother. Note, therefore, that at this point Klein is referring to a thoroughly asymmetrical *process* (any process is asymmetrical!). It leads, however, as just seen, to the disappearance of the limits between self and mother, i.e. to a symmetrization. If we do not look at both sides of the question our understanding remains incomplete.

I believe it is important to become aware that Melanie Klein is constantly making use of asymmetry as well as symmetry without, however, pointing it out in an explicit manner. The time was not yet ripe to do that. With the concepts now available to us, we can be more precise and detailed in our study, can understand an internal structure and its relation to other objects of knowledge, and can thus have access to general laws which increase our understanding. Eventually this may lead to a greater possibility of our modifying Nature. The influence that humanity has acquired over Nature has always come along the road of understanding. I have ever so many times heard from psychoanalysts the following remark that 'We are saying the same thing in different ways', when the truth was that they were referring to the same subject at different levels of understanding. Another remark is: 'What is the use of it if, after all, we already know it?' It is said that when Benjamin Franklin made his first discoveries about electricity, from the study of lightning, he was asked what the use of his discovery was. He replied something like, 'What is the use of a child? Wait until he grows up and you will have the answer.'

4 Projective identification: a bi-logical structure

The fascination of PI. Kleinian analysts seem to have been almost literally bewitched by PI.[3] Old Freudian projection has practically disappeared from their writings and has been replaced by the ubiquitous new term. Its use seems to cover a much wider territory than could be assigned to the initial Freudian concept of projection. The same, however, cannot be said of the concept of projection implicit in the Schreber case. Furthermore, the importance attributed to PI in psychical life seems to be much greater than what could be inferred from Melanie Klein's own remarks on the subject. Judging from what one reads, it now would seem that PI is the clue to a radically new and profound understanding of the mind, and whoever does not realize this is left 'way behind' on the road towards this understanding.

Yet nothing in the *explicit* formulations or definitions of PI, of

146

either Klein or her followers, seems to warrant such an ambitious implication. Whatever justification of it so far made has been worded in such an obscure way that not even the distinguished authors who are enthusiasts of PI succeed in adequately justifying it. This does not necessarily mean that this implication is not justified. Reflecting upon this question I have come to realize that PI is felt as so fundamental because it points to, and implicitly gives a place to, the indivisible. But it does so in an obscure way.

PI: a bi-logical structure. I shall broach the question by means of an analysis of a quotation we have already used in this chapter (Klein 1946 [1952]: 300) which precisely furnishes the opportunity to consider a fairly simple case. We are told in it of a series of movements from the self towards the mother (object), who becomes 'an extension of the self', 'a representative of the ego'. Such processes are, Klein says, the basis for PI or identification by projection. One can see that she is referring to three things, which must be considered as different from one another:

First, 'the object becomes to some extent a representative of the ego'. The situation Klein describes is like that of an ambassador, who may represent the president of a country, who in his turn may represent the country. In other words, the qualification 'to some extent' helps to stress the fact that object and ego are not identical, which is clearly true. The function which country, president, and ambassador exercise is the same throughout, but the three entities just mentioned are different from one another. As for the word 'becomes', it clearly indicates that Klein is speaking of a process.

Next she says: 'makes it into an extension of the self'. Here there is a step forward; the mother remains different from but becomes subsidiary to the self. The self has, in this case, priority over the object; it 'uses' it. In a case like this one can hardly speak of identification of the two parties. There is rather a *process* whereby the object (mother) is first taken possession of by the self and then made an extension of it. A process is something which evolves, and in this case it starts with two separate entities, self and object, and ends in the latter becoming an extension of the first, like a colony. It seems that in both the initial and the final state one must distinguish between self and object as one does between 'mother country' and colony.

Now consider the phrase 'identification by projection'. The invader-controller is now the same thing as the invaded; they are identical. Note that not much is said about identification in the following quotation:

147

'The phantasied onslaughts on the mother follow two main lines: one is the predominantly oral impulse to suck dry, bite up, scoop out and rob the mother's body of its good contents. . . . The other line of attack derives from the anal and urethral impulses and implies expelling dangerous substances (excrements) out of the self and into the mother. Together with these harmful excrements, expelled in hatred, split-off parts of the ego are also projected onto the mother or, as I would rather call it, *into* the mother. These excrements and bad parts of the self are meant not only to injure but also to control and to take possession of the object. In so far as the mother comes to contain the bad parts of the self, she is not felt to be a separate individual but is felt to be *the* bad self.

Much of the hatred against parts of the self is now directed towards the mother. This leads to a particular form of identification which establishes the prototype of an aggressive object–relation. I suggest for these processes the term "projective identification".'

(Klein 1946 [1952]: 300)

At the end of the first paragraph it is clearly said that the mother is not felt to be a separate individual but *the* bad self (Klein's italics).

In other words, the first two are processes (Klein herself calls them by that name) which maintain the distinction between self (or ego) and object (mother), and which are 'the basis for identification by projection'. This latter therefore, is something different from these processes. It is not easy to see whether, according to Klein, PI is or is not the result of these processes, or is itself a process or a state.

Note, furthermore, that when she writes that excrements, a physical substance, injure the self, a psychological entity, this would be inconceivable if one did not accept the identity between psychical and external reality, i.e. one of the characteristics of the unconscious described by Freud, which becomes more visible with the help of my logical formulation of the unconscious.

The general conclusion one draws is that *Melanie Klein's concept of PI is an attempt at picturing contemporarily two different things which can, however, be grasped clearly only if they are definitely treated as being different from one another.*

On the one hand, a series of movements *from* the inside *to* the outside and vice versa (for instance, phantasied attacks of the object), and also *in* the inside: these require the distinction between outside and inside, between the various directions of the movements, between self (or ego) and object, between whole self and its various parts, and so on. Such movements require a great variety of asymmetrical relations. They are isomorphic to classical-logical

148

thinking, (a) in the sense that they can be described accurately by thinking, and (b) in the sense that their structure itself entails relations similar to those seen in the structure of thinking.

On the other hand, there is also something quite different in PI: a state or mode of non-distinction or indivision of self and object, and of part and whole. Such indivision is *in itself* completely alien to thinking; there can be no correspondence whatsoever between something indivisible and thinking, because this latter is not possible if no distinction or division is made between something and something else. Nothing, however, prevents us from thinking *about* this unthinkable thing.

Therefore, the concept of PI contains the concept of indivision and also that of distinction; the object and the self are the same *and* are different. In other words, PI is a bi-logical structure: again the fundamental antinomy.

The question now arises: what kind of bi-logical structure is it? Upon reflection one concludes that it is not any of the structures already mentioned in Chapter 2. In order to answer the question I must refer at this point to a simple mathematical notion, that of vector, i.e. of a *quantity* which has (1) direction, for instance vertical, horizontal, or depth (we may use as an example the horizontal), (2) sense (in this case *either* from left to right *or* from right to left), and (3) magnitude. A vector is usually represented as shown in *Figure 5* (p. 150).

In this diagram we see three vectors represented. The first goes from the point 3,6 to the point 5,7, and its sense is upward and to the right. The second goes from the point −2,4 to the point −5,2, and its sense is downwards and towards the left. I have chosen the third to represent the relation between mother and child as described by Melanie Klein in the case of projective identification. We may choose to say that the child is located at the point 2,3. At first he projects on to the mother, represented by the point 7,3. The sense of the projection is from left to right. The original persons are represented as inside a rectangle. Once the projection takes place, the mother becomes the bad self of the child. This is represented by the word 'child', under mother . Then there is the movement from the mother -child to the child (sense from right to left) in the form of aggressions (it also may be love). The result is that, just as the mother has become the child, the child has also become the mother: identification. We see in the two other examples in the graphic that the starting point and the point of arrival remain separate, and the sense is only one in each case. In contrast, in the case of the mother and child we find that both the mother and the child are in both points. In so far as this happens, the child *is* the mother, and vice

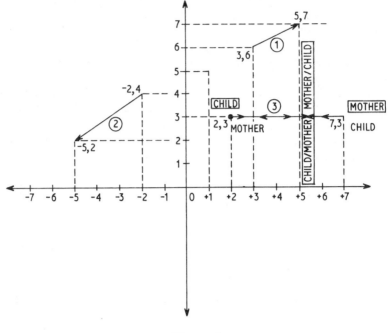

Figure 5

versa. In the representation, the sense of the movement is from one to the other and vice versa in so far as they are different. But when they are the same, since the distance between them has disappeared, there is no displacement, and everything happens within the mother-child-child-mother. All movement of love or aggression has ceased, yet it is active inside the 'new' person resulting from identification; *there is movement and there is not movement*: a Simassi bi-logical structure.

We have represented the relation between child and mother, as seen in PI, by means of a vector. When we are speaking of only projection the representation works well as a comparison. When there is identification, instead, mother and child become the same. It is as though the respective points have become one and the same, because the movement from mother to child and vice versa is from one point to the same point: disappearance, in this case, of the notion of distance. What is more, the movement from one point to the same point is no movement, hence disappearance of movement. In other words, a symmetrization has occurred. If there is no movement there is no sense of the vector.

150

We therefore find that the vector representation works when we consider projection; there is a point of departure and a different point of arrival, a sense, and a magnitude (distance). When identification sets in, then all the defining characteristics of a vector disappear, and this is the result of making identical two persons who are not identical to classical logic: a symmetrization.

Conclusion. I would summarize the preceding analysis of PI by saying that *projective identification as described by Melanie Klein is a bilogical structure isomorphic to a symmetrized vector, which results in a Simassi bi-logical structure. In short, PI is a symmetrized vector Simassi structure, the fundamental antinomy once again.*

I feel there is much more to understand about this question but at this moment will not venture any longer on this difficult and exciting task. I shall only mention that it seems to me that symmetrization of a vector, as just described, leads to a corollary with which we have become familiar in certain aspects of the case of the infinite: any distance becomes identical to any other distance, and this cancels the concept of distance.

Someone may ask: what is the use of complicating matters when we know already what projective identification is and we know how to use it to help our patients?

The answer would be something similar to this: Leucippus and Democritus conceived the atom more than two thousand years ago. After such a long time it was only during the nineteenth century that some curious people began to 'complicate' matters and postulate components of the atom. The complication has continued to the present day, when many particles of the atom have been found. We now know much more about it than Leucippus and Democritus could ever have dreamt about, and it looks as though the search for further understanding and discoveries about the atom will never stop. All research is endless in the sense that the knowledge acquired leads to new questions, and when these are solved new problems emerge. Think of the development of physics from Copernicus to Newton to Einstein to the atomic theory of the beginning of the twentieth century to the present day. This fact of increasing and never-ending knowledge poses fundamental epistemological problems.

It may be objected that all this concerns only the beauty of thinking. One then asks: could it be said that both the two imaginative pioneer Greeks and all their followers have indulged in useless fantasies? The answer is: obviously not. The fact is that without such fantasies, which initially had no connection with action, the fission of the atom could not have taken place. In consequence, we would not have at our disposal any of the developments that have followed from fission, which have brought humankind into a new era of its history.

To return to Melanie Klein. She discovered PI, and our thinking about it starts from that point. Now, as always in science, it will develop. Surely no one will think that what Klein knew about it and its meaning will remain for ever immobile. Nor are we able to affirm that the possible therapeutic use of her insights will always remain condemned to a static repetition. In my view, *one* way to assess and develop new possibilities of understanding our patients is to study clinical reality in terms of the wider conceptualization I have put forward.

Freud and PI. Two quotations from Freud, also quoted by Melanie Klein (1955: 313, n. 3), describe a similar bi-logical structure to that I have suggested for PI. In *Group Psychology and the Analysis of the Ego* (SE 18: 112–13) Freud writes:

> '(We see that the object is being treated in the same way as our own ego, so that when we are in love a considerable amount of narcissistic libido overflows on to the object. It is even obvious, in many forms of love-choice, that the object serves as a substitute for some unattained ego ideal of our own.) We love it on account of the perfections which we have striven to reach for our own ego (and which we should now like to procure in this roundabout way as a means of satisfying our narcissism).'

(The parts between the brackets enclose words from Freud which were not quoted by Klein and were not between brackets in Freud's text.)

In the same work, a little further on (p. 113), he says:

> 'the ego becomes more and more unassuming and modest, and the object more and more sublime and precious until at last it gets possession of the entire self-love of the ego, whose self-sacrifice thus follows as a natural consequence. The object has, so to speak, consumed the ego.'

As seen in these quotations, the object is treated as the ego: a timid way of non-distinguishing between object and ego. This points to, or implies, the indivisible mode. On the other hand, libido flows, the object is loved as a substitute for some unattained ego-ideal, and so on. Here various distinctions are being made, which presuppose ample use of asymmetrical relations and, hence, of the heterogenic mode. We also see in this quotation that the ego becomes more and more unassuming and modest and that it is in the end 'consumed' by the object. This is a typical happening (asymmetrical) and it presupposes the distinction between ego and object, which is inconceivable in the indivisible mode. But it ends in disappearance, i.e. in non-division. Note that this Freudian idea of impoverishment is also used by Melanie Klein, as is that of enrichment. Both refer to one aspect of reality, that of happening, an important one in certain cases. This can and must be completed with another important aspect of reality: the peaceful 'immobility' of being-with-no-happening. Here there is no process or movement. With no asymmetrical relations there is neither impoverishment nor enrichment.

Additional comments on projective identification. Melanie Klein's comments about greed deal eloquently with the asymmetrical aspects, i.e. those in which we see a clear separation between self and mother. It is important to keep in mind that there are other aspects, i.e. those relating to non-differentiation or indivision of self and mother:

> 'At the unconscious level, greed aims primarily at completely scooping out, sucking dry, and devouring the breast: that is to say, its aim is destructive introjection; whereas envy not only seeks to rob in this way, but also to put badness, primarily bad excrements and bad parts of the self, into the mother, and first of all into her breast, in order to spoil and destroy her. In the deepest sense this means destroying her creativeness. This process, which derives from urethral- and anal-sadistic impulses, I have elsewhere defined as a destructive aspect of projective identification starting from the beginning of life. One essential difference between greed and envy, although no rigid dividing line can be drawn since they are so closely associated, would accordingly be that greed is mainly bound up with introjection and envy with projection.'
>
> (Klein 1957: 7)

We see again a description of a happy relationship, in asymmetrical terms, in which symmetry, i.e. non-distinction, is hinted at, in her reference to internalization:

> 'A happy relation to the first object and a successful internalisation of it means that love can be given and received. . . . Introjective and projective identification, when not excessive, play an important part in this feeling of closeness, for they underlie the capacity to understand and contribute to the experience of being understood.'
>
> (Klein 1963: 112)

The conflicts and anxieties connected with PI are, in my opinion, connected with the fear of losing one's own (asymmetrical) identity and of being 'sucked up' into indivision, which is felt as annihilation.

This is an expression, in terms of asymmetrical concepts, of a symmetrical experience. This is beautifully seen in pp. 143–44 of *Narrative of a Child Analysis* (1961) (where we see the anxieties of the incompatibilities of both sides of the fundamental antinomy: a subject which deserves a thorough study) and also in the following:

> 'For the individual to feel that he has a good deal in common with another person is concurrent with projecting himself into that person (and the same applies to introjecting him). These processes vary in intensity and duration and on these variations depend the strength and importance of such identifications and their vicissitudes.'
>
> (Klein 1955: 341)

In this latter case the identification-fusion-indivision between the individual and the other is felt as positive, constructive, and not anxiety-arousing.

Projection, the Schreber case, and PI. The first concept of projection formulated by Freud around the turn of the century referred to an essentially asymmetrical affair. On the other hand, the Schreber case (Freud 1911) presents, without mentioning it, a bi-logical structure which is different from PI and all other bi-logical structures (cf. Chapter 4, section 2).

As a conclusion from the study of PI in the light of bi-logic it seems important to become aware that there are many new possibilities of studying the co-presence of both modes and their intertwining in bi-logical structures. This, in its turn, leads to a more sober way of looking at PI; it points to one among many bi-logical structures – an important one, however, because the conflict between both modes (fundamental antinomy) becomes very clear to somebody who reflects about the facts.

5 The intertwining of both modes and their relation to Klein's discoveries: bi-modality, order, and grammar

Foreword. At the beginning of this chapter I mentioned the difficulty of reaching a clear grasp of the hierarchy of the various concepts put forward by Melanie Klein. One gets the impression of finding oneself in the midst of many ideas, and at the same time of a certain lack of obvious and well-defined logical connections, such as those found in other types of scientific writings. I believe this may be due in part to the fact that Klein's method of presentation has a certain correspondence to the structure of the subject which she studies. But it also may be due to the anxiety that her findings – which refer to anxiety-arousing zones – may provoke, with the consequent blurring of serene understanding. In fact, Klein leads her readers to the 'cauldron full of seething excitations' (Freud 1933, SE 22: 73), i.e. the third and fourth zones of the stratified structure (see Chapter 2), where so many anxious as well as exciting things are lived.

I must warn the reader that the subject of this section is a new territory which I myself am only beginning to explore. I feel sure that what I am going to say here will have to be completed. It may also be that some aspects of it should be modified. It is a fertile territory. I offer it in the spirit of a stimulus towards further research.

Bi-modality, order, and grammar. I will begin with a comparison which may be helpful. Mathematical writing or language tends to be precise and concise and it has a correspondence with its subject matter, which is formed of well-delimited concepts, such as a concept expressed in a theorem. For instance: the sum of the three angles of a triangle equals 180 degrees. Something similar can be said of writings on physics. The concepts employed in sociology and psychology, in contrast, are frequently less clearly defined than those used in mathematics.

Psychoanalysis is frequently not precise, among other reasons because the use of symbols and their symmetrization enlarges enormously its territory and makes its concepts more difficult to delimit. Sometimes psychoanalysts employ notions which are apparently more precise but which may impoverish psychoanalytical insight if used unwisely, because they leave out many things which actually belong to it. The castration complex, libido, and good breast are examples; to view human beings rather exclusively in terms of such notions gives a poor and limited idea of their inexhaustible capacities, unless each of these concepts is enlarged to cover many other notions which are isomorphic to them. To do this one has to include the entire equivalence class to which each of the notions just mentioned belongs. This might include: the class of all structures equivalent but not identical to the castration complex, or the class of all structures equivalent to the structure 'breast and its functions, real or phantasied', and so on.

Poets and schizophrenics are frequently concise but usually not precise, and this is connected with the fact that they tend to put in so many things – as a limit: the universe – even when they speak of small, well-circumscribed subjects.

The attempt to specify the differences between these various types of language leads to further insights, and I now shall try to tackle this question.

Molecular and molar language. Order presupposes asymmetrical relations. In the mathematical concept of total order the relation 'less than', or its converse 'greater than', enables us to distinguish an infinite number of numbers. In psychoanalysis we employ verbal language, and one can easily see that, the greater the number of asymmetrical relations available, the greater are the possibilities of distinguishing various phenomena between them. Another point to be kept in mind is that, in order to use such (asymmetrical) relations for the purpose of understanding, language itself needs to have a structure, grammatical or otherwise, that also is highly asymmetrical. Mathematical and in general scientific language is relatively well structured. Schizophrenic language, in contrast, as well as (in some cases) the language of modern poetry, appears less structured in terms of classical logic. It is perhaps more accurate to say that it is differently structured, as a result of more or less frequent symmetrizations, which treat certain things which scientific thinking differentiates from one another as one and the same. Since such symmetrizations refer to the single links of a chain or process of thinking, we may call them *molecular symmetrizations*. Their existence points to bi-logical structures, to which they belong, i.e. it points to the fundamental antinomy.

By using a set of molecular symmetrizations employed as links in a bi-logical structure, it is possible to construct a message (language) which as a whole, in what I will call its *molar* aspects, is perfectly asymmetrical and hence within the realm of ordinary comprehension. This is *bi-logic in the service of classical-logical understanding*. This is frequently observed in schizophrenia and modern poetry where, with a series of obscurities, they may transmit a clear, classical-logical message. It also is the case of many dreams, as Freud (SE 4: 275–76) has beautifully shown. In dreams we usually find that a given object or thought is expressed by another one which is structured in a way that is isomorphic to it, i.e. by another element of the same equivalence class, which may, however, appear quite different at first sight.

Alternatively, in other cases a highly classical-logical or asymmetrically structured discourse at the molecular level may also convey at the molar level a very general, highly asymmetrical structure. This is usually the case with mathematical thinking.

Finally a writing or utterance may be highly asymmetrical at the molecular level, while at the molar level it is both highly asymmetrical and simultaneously highly indivisible, i.e. bi-modal, but not bi-logical. In other words, while being highly asymmetrical at the molecular level, it may in certain aspects of the molar level be quite asymmetrical or heterogeneous but also strongly redolent of the indivisible, even though not bi-logical. This manifestation may in some cases be a high human achievement, the expression of a noble blending of both modes. Possibly some mystics reach it.

Note that one cannot exclude a priori the possibility that greater or lesser visibility of bi-modality may not run parallel to a greater or lesser presence of it.

The molar bi-logical structure. A mental manifestation may *appear* highly asymmetrical at the molecular level and show at the molar level a non-bi-logical bi-modality, *together with some participation of bi-logical bi-modality.* This may be the case of some schizophrenics. *I believe it is more frequently also the case in the reasonings of the majority of human beings at most times.* The enormous amount of differences between people with regard to social, philosophical, and religious questions may be found to lie in that in each one of us, in the midst of an *apparently* classical-logical reasoning, an unnoticed indivision slips in at the molar level, and the result is a bi–logical reasoning. Note that this may be a bi–logical structure different from the others I have described. It may appear mixed with other types, for instance when symmetrization occurs also at the molecular level with respect to one or more single links of the reasoning (Alassi type).

As the symmetrizations chosen differ from one individual to another, in this way we come to the situation so vividly described in the following sentence: God handed over the world to the disputations of men.

One asks: how is it possible for a symmetrization to slip in at the molar level with no symmetrization at the molecular level? It is not easy to explain, and perhaps an example may help. Some religious people convey the impression of being pathologically severe towards themselves and others on general moral issues. Yet, when each concrete issue is examined in itself, they may appear tolerant and broad-minded, putting the accent on God's love. 'Molarly', however, this is not visible. They appear like Nazi Germany (as the story goes) when it was prohibited, in the early 1930s, from rearming; the Germans built a factory to make spare parts for toys, another to make spare parts for kitchens, and so on: all innocent. When all these spare parts were put together, the result was an armoured car: molecularly innocent, molarly aggressive.

The possibility of building a bi-logical structure at the molar level by utilizing *only* classical-logical links is a very interesting one and commends itself for further research. At first sight it would appear that to do so would be the very negation of the concept of bi-logical structure. However, when one has many relational links to work with, it does not seem impossible to connect them in such a way as to suggest not only a non–bi-logical bi-modality but also a bi-logical one. In other words, it does not seem impossible to use relations between relations in such a way as to convey a sense of indivision. For example, it seems possible to speak of a genital desire (a highly asymmetrical thing) towards a woman by means of references to oral desires (also highly asymmetrical) in such a way that, underneath, the sensation may be conveyed that having sexual intercourse with this woman is the same as eating and hence becoming fused with her, i.e. a state of indivision. In this way we would have here a *molar bi-logical structure formed of purely asymmetrical links related in a way which suggests indivision.*

It is convenient to keep in mind that the case we are studying contains, at times, not only molar but also molecular bi-logical structures, and these would also be highly dissimulated. We frequently see this in religious, political, and social reasonings.

It is particularly relevant for our present purpose to become aware that it is possible to use a highly classical–logical or asymmetrically structured language at the molecular level and yet to succeed in transmitting at the molar level a curious sense of partial or total absence of structure. The great Mexican actor Cantinflas uses this type of discourse to make people laugh. The same type of thing is also visible in some people whose (serious) discourse is difficult or impossible to follow because no guiding thread is easily discovered in it, even if the various parts of it may be understandable. It would also seem that some philosophers are not entirely free from writing in this manner.

It is interesting to reflect that this way of thinking resembles, but does not seem to be identical to, what is known in psychopathology as circumstantial thinking. Some patients furnish at times evidence of it. The lack of hierarchy and organization suggests the presence of the indivisible mode. This would, however, be an unsatisfactory result and not a high achievement, as we considered in the case of mystics. It strikes us in fact as disharmonious or discordant, and it would be the expression of a failure of an attempt to reach the category exemplified in mystics.

Finally, schizophrenics probably show symmetrizations and bi-logical structures at both the molecular and the molar level. This corresponds to more blatant pathology. The symptoms of schizophrenia described in psychiatry are usually bi-logical structures. This subject, however, requires a special study.

The work of Melanie Klein as seen in the light of both modes. Klein has defined a good number of fairly well delimited notions, such as her concepts of PI, envy, defences against envy, paranoid–schizoid and depressive position, and so on. She uses these and many other psychoanalytical concepts in her descriptions. Her examples of interpretation are frequently extremely precise. With these detailed (molecular) highly asymmetrical bricks she constructs a general (molar) conception which, as a scientific conception, is asymmetrically structured. But what is interesting is that at the same time she manages to convey a feeling or impression that the patient is in the midst of both separation and fusion–indivision with the object (mother, etc.). At times this is expressed in terms of molar bi-logical structures in the patient, as, for instance in her description of PI, which I have shown is a symmetrized vector bi-logical structure. At other times, however, she seems to be describing essentially non-bi-logical bi-modality.

This subject is worthy of a thorough study, which, I feel, may lead to a better understanding of the subtle intricacies of unconscious manifestations.

An extraordinary feature of Melanie Klein's writing, given her fundamental preoccupation with the symmetrical mode, is that it is, I believe, mostly asymmetrical at both the molecular and the molar level. I do not exclude, however, the possibility of some bi-logical molecular or molar structures in her thinking, as is the case of all human beings and even of scientific writings, as already noted. It is also striking to note that, although she has made meaningful contributions to the understanding of schizophrenia, she has not, so far as I am aware, considered the classical symptoms of schizophrenia as described by Kraepelin and the German classics. These appear as molecular bi-logical structures of the various types mentioned in Chapter 2; but they also are molar bi-logical structures. They play, and rightly so, a central role in clinical psychiatry, and are completely ignored by Klein, not only in the sense that they are never mentioned explicitly but also in that the concepts entailed in such symptoms are ignored. This is all the more striking when one realizes that such symptoms are so much related to the special characteristics of the system unconscious. These latter are not, so far as I remember, explicitly considered in Klein's scientific conception, not even as psychoanalytic insights. Yet she uses these characteristics all the time.

This comment has no intention of being polemic, but only to point out an obvious and curious fact, and to add that, in spite of this great absence, Klein's study of the schizo-paranoid phase and position, however incomplete, is meaningful. And this holds for all her writing. I think this is a real feat.

6 Order and grammar

As a more general proposition I suggest that, in order to transmit at the molar level a bi-modal experience (one involving both modes), especially if this contains bi-logical aspects, it may become necessary to use a language whose grammar differs somewhat from that employed, for instance, in a piece of algebraic or geometrical reasoning. I do not intend to suggest that this grammar necessarily violates the rules of grammar as seen in textbooks, though I do not exclude this possibility. I mean rather that the construction of sentences and especially the way the various sets of sentences are presented (i.e. the molar, long-term aspects of the discourse) are different in both cases. I do not know if there are any studies of this type. I believe a study of Melanie Klein's writing style from this point of view could furnish meaningful information about the level of co-presence she is studying; and, perhaps, also could put new questions to linguistics. Klein is, I feel, definitely not a tidy writer who conveys precise ideas in an organized way as a mathematician or other academics would do. Rather, she manages to create *an atmosphere* and envelop the reader with it. In the case of what she writes about schizophrenia, I believe this is due to some correspondence between her language and that of schizophrenics, however different they actually are. There is some morphism, though I am not able to say whether it is an isomorphism or a morphism of a 'weaker' type.

All this requires further research. The fact remains, however, that what Melanie Klein writes, though clear, has not so far been easy to systematize or present in a satisfactorily ordered way. What is more, I have noted that reading her also awakens strong feelings of enthusiasm, devotion, anxiety, rejection, and so on. This underlines my point that, despite its asymmetrical structure, her work constantly invokes bi-logic.

It is interesting to note that Segal's (1964 [1973]) presentation of Klein's ideas also shows some lack of logical order. The point I am making is illustrated by the difficulty of knowing about her work. If one wishes to know just a little about Klein, one can acquire certain basic notions of hers about the Oedipus complex, the various positions, PI, and so on. If one wishes to know a great deal, one has to go through a process of almost literally learning every phrase in which she (or Segal) presents the details of the problem, and this makes one think that *something is missing regarding the connections between the parts of the discourse*; for one can understand and repeat a clearly ordered discourse without having to learn it by rote. If one wishes to know still more, one has no alternative but to try to get to the foundations or bases of Klein's researches, and this leads inevitably to a more general formulation and to new insights as well as to new facts. This is what I am trying to do. Something is undoubtedly gained from this type of work. Perhaps there also is something lost.

I want to stress that, so far as I am concerned, the above comments are an indication of Melanie Klein's wealth. She has succeeded in transmitting certain intuitions about the depths of the mind not only through intellectual description but through feeling. This is an admirable achievement. It must be recognized that it has drawbacks. The fact that it raises strong emotions creates difficulties for classical-logical thinking. Perhaps it is possible to follow her lead and transform her method without destroying it. Perhaps Bion has done something of this.

All thinking is bi-modal. It is becoming increasingly clear to me that fundamental progress in our understanding of human beings and the world will take place when the possibilities that bi-logical structures offer for this understanding come to be explored. What is, so far, quite clear to anybody who examines the question in the terms proposed is that *all human beings frequently think bi-logically and are all the time bi-modal. Scientific writings are not free from bi-modality. At times, some aspects of scientific writing are bi-logical.* This is, I am sure, a fact but also a challenge. Why not accept it, explore it, and try to see where it leads?

7 Freud and PI

As already seen in Chapter 5, Melanie Klein and Elliott Jaques point out that Freud had a clear notion of the concept of identification by projection, although he did not call it by that name. This assertion deserves one further comment: the Freudian concept seems to refer exclusively to identification of the whole individual, whereas the Kleinian one also comprises identification of parts of the self, as quotations (1) and (3) of the Appendix clearly show. Behind what may be considered an insignificant detail there is the fundamental question, which deserves careful reflection, of the meaning of the notion of part object. Suffice it to say here that a part which exercises control is actually a part which behaves as a person, i.e. as a whole; I shall discuss this question in Chapter 12.

8 Klein and the concept of the unconscious

It is interesting to note that Melanie Klein does not seem to show an interest in referring *explicitly* to Freud's greatest and most revolutionary discoveries, i.e. the characteristics of the unconscious. She uses them profusely throughout her work but on the whole, I believe, she does not mention them.

I suspect that this difference is due to the difference of sex. Freud's thinking is highly masculine; he tried to arrive at a general theoretical formulation of his clinical findings. Melanie Klein's thinking is highly feminine; she tries to grasp, up to the finest details, what is happening to the patient, i.e. her child, and is not interested in abstract formulations.

I think psychoanalysis, just as human life, may be enriched by the differences in the contributions of both sexes. Men cannot do certain things that women do. Women cannot do certain things that men do. *Honi soit qui mal y pense.*

9 'Memories in feelings': an unexpected contribution to the solution of an old problem

The problem. Traumatic experiences in early life – either single and dramatic, or repeated and not so urgently dramatic – are frequently found in analysis. They obviously play an important role which to a considerable extent hampers in some cases the development and the success of analytic therapy.

In the heroic early period there was the hope of 'recuperating' these – as it was thought, repressed – reactions and memories by means of the analysis. In most cases this hope was not satisfied. For myself, in about fifty years of analytic experience I recollect only one case of recovery of forgotten important happenings; and I am not even sure that this was fully genuine.

Some people have tried to recover such events by means of hypnosis or hypno-analysis. This was quite successful and it led to a cure of the traumatic war neurosis *provided that it was performed a short time after the trauma.* Later on the results were not satisfactory. Here and there one finds a case where the history reveals a certain knowledge about a traumatic experience. I have never seen in such cases a success in recovering clear memories of such experiences by either expert psychoanalysts or hypnotists. One is always left with the feeling that, if this could be done, there would be a dramatic

162

improvement in that aspect of the case where such experiences play a role. And it is not a negligible aspect in psychoanalytic practice.

Almost in passing, Melanie Klein proposes a solution to this problem when she writes in a footnote on p. 5 of *Envy and Gratitude* (1957):

'All this is felt by the infant in much more primitive ways than language can express. When these pre-verbal emotions and phantasies are revived in the transference situation, they appear as "memories in feelings", as I would call them, and are reconstructed and put into words with the help of the analyst. In the same way, words have to be used when we are reconstructing and describing other phenomena belonging to the early stages of development. In fact we cannot translate the language of the unconscious into consciousness without lending it words from our conscious realm.'

I have a number of cases where something like this seems to have happened in a very intense way for years. They all were persons who were severely traumatized in early infancy. I find it very hard work because the wrath of hell seems to fall on the psychoanalyst for years and years. I remember that when I was a student of psychoanalysis Susan Isaacs treated a person at the Psycho-analytical Institute. We all heard the very loud shouting and roaring of the patient throughout the sessions and were surprised and full of admiration when, at the end of the session, Mrs Isaacs came out serene and with a sweet smile.

I have come to see that the expression of these 'memories in feelings' is fundamental in the treatment of some cases. Without them these patients could not be cured. Some of the patients I am referring to had some memories of their (repeated) traumatic situations, others not. No increase in memories *of the happenings* was obtained. The feelings, instead, were abundantly and repeatedly discharged over a long time. I feel that this repeated expression of most varied feelings connected with the episodes and persons concerned, now made towards a basically respectful and tolerant analyst who tries to understand the meaning of the emotional expression and its connections with the details of early experiences and actual relationships, is the real healing factor. There is here, in my opinion, an important reason for a (moderate) optimism in the long run.

So far as I am concerned, I have had, at times, quite intense counter-transference feelings in front of repeated and, I felt, unjust attacks made with a violence which, somehow, reached me in some depth of my being. I did express these feelings, at times vividly, but soberly, and with no comment about the personal meaning they had for me. Subsequent detailed discussion of both the patient's and the analyst's reactions, and of their meaning in the interpersonal relations between patient and analyst, is, I feel, a corrective and maturing emotional experience: for both patient and analyst.

I think that the following is an important point: consider the emotions towards a person or situation. These can be expressed towards another situation or person which or who, however different in many aspects, is in some way isomorphic to the original ones. For the unconscious, through symmetrization this isomorphism becomes identity. This holds, I feel, not only as regards the situation or person towards whom the transfer develops. It also happens in the case of the patient's replacing the original *expression* of an emotion by another expression isomorphic to it and, therefore, owing to symmetrization, identical for the unconscious, but not so for conscious thinking. The new expression may, in this way, satisfy the unconscious 'zone' where it is identical to the original one; and may also satisfy the conscious organization of the personality because it is much more satisfactory in everyday conscious life. This may lead to an important therapeutic result.

So one comes to realize that the indivisible mode plays a saving therapeutic role in certain difficult cases. This insight springs from the footnote quoted above.

I wish to call attention to a most interesting fact. Nowhere is the expression 'memories in feeling' found in the alphabetical indexes of Melanie Klein's writings; not even in *Envy and Gratitude*, where this notion was introduced. But there is one, only one, exception: *Narrative of a Child Analysis*, where it is mentioned six times. I have a hypothesis: it was towards the end of Klein's life that she had an 'illumination' which led to the explicit formulation of this important therapeutic insight. The fact that it appears in the case of Richard is not without meaning. As for myself, since I began to take seriously this concept, I began to understand certain behaviours of some of my patients towards me.

Further understanding and use of this question may lead to important improvements in psychoanalytical therapy.

10 Concluding remarks

I hope this study may serve, especially for young people of both sexes, as a stimulus to deepen the important discoveries Melanie Klein has made. I also hope that my formulation may be a help towards the realization of this aim.

11 Postscript: a personal impression of Melanie Klein

I think it is pertinent to the subject of this chapter to relate the following so that the reader can judge. I had the good fortune to attend Melanie Klein's seminars in London in the middle 1930s. My memory is that at least some of these seminars were in her house, with a large, complex, and nice living-room. She always impressed me as charmingly feminine, with a nice, relaxed, and viscerotonic face, a beautiful complexion, and a smiling sense of humour.

Honesty prompts me to add that, though from the beginning of my study of her writings I conceived a great admiration for her, this, however, was far from being free of ambivalence. Now, in my old age, I can see how intense in all senses was the storm that Melanie Klein awakened in me. It took me several decades to arrive at a more serene attitude towards her.

I suspect that what happened to me also happens to other people. There was something in her personality – and it was reflected in her writings – which brought one to descend with her to the abysses of being; it was like going down the Niagara Falls. One survived, at times with some initial bruises and, eventually, with reflection and admiration.

Some years after I left London, I gave one of my students a letter of introduction to her. She answered with a kind and stimulating reply. I was very pleased and I re-read it every now and then.

Notes

1 My ideas on Melanie Klein's contribution (and particularly her idea of projective identification) have been clarified by the work of my wife, Luciana Bon de Matte. Her paper, originally given at the Institute of Psycho-Analysis in Rome on 27 February 1970, and published in *Psyche* (1970), is the source of many of the quotations I use in this chapter. Any reader who is not thoroughly conversant with Klein's own use of her concept of projective identification will find Luciana Bon de Matte's paper very useful, and for this reason I have included it as the Appendix to this book.

2 *Glean*: '3. To gather or pick up in small quantities' (Oxford Dictionary).

3 See Matte-Blanco 1976a; this, however, was written at the beginning of the development of the concept of bi-logical structure.

PART THREE

Projective and introjective processes: a bi-logical point of view

Explanation. The aim of Part Three is to show that projective and introjective processes can be seen in a new, fruitful way if the dichotomy 'in–out' is enriched with the help of the concepts of bi-logic.

8

Some guiding concepts for understanding clinical reality

1 Normality, pathology, and levels of aggression

In spite of the fact that Freud and other authors have expressly affirmed that projection is also observed in normal conditions, there is a tendency to link this mechanism with pathology or with something undesirable for a normal individual. It is difficult, for instance, not to think that this is implied in Meltzer's (1967) proposal to call projective identification by the name of intrusive identification. There is also a tendency among some people to use the notion of paranoid reaction or paranoid attitude in a promiscuous way. This may spring, at least in part, from an unnecessary use of the conception of the paranoid-schizoid position. This is a tendency which restricts openness of thought.

Projection and projective identification are not just emergency mechanisms which function only when anxiety and conflicts are at very high levels, but are regularly present and play a central role in mature and well-balanced adults. They may be very important both in the maintenance and expression of the normal personality as well as in its development. An instance of this would be parents who satisfy, in an ego-syntonic, non-ambivalent manner, some of their own desires through the achievements of their children.

Next let us consider aggression and the question of levels. There is a tendency to associate only pathology with extreme aggression, without taking into consideration the distinction between the structural strata of the mind (first, second, third, fourth, deeper) which I introduced in Chapter 2, section 2. It seems clear to me that aggressive wishes which are extremely strong at the first or presentational level (Matte-Blanco 1975a: 167–68) are incompatible with normality. However, it seems possible that aggression may tend towards an infinite degree of intensity at deep levels and yet be perfectly in keeping with peaceful normality.

The conception of mental life in terms of a varying proportion between symmetrical and asymmetrical relations leads us to a new view of conflict. I suggest the following convention: the more the symmetry, the deeper will the level be. Aggression, real or fantasied, always requires (more or less violent) actions which are real or fantasied movements. These are events which, as such, must be intrinsically connected with the notions of space and time. As we have noted before, these notions require asymmetrical relations. The superficial levels (what I have called the first, second, and third strata) are the levels of consciousness, the preconscious, and the first symmetrizations. Asymmetrical relations are available in profusion in these strata. Thus the possibility of visible aggression would be at its maximum there. It must be kept in mind, however, that aggression is feared in proportion to the intensity which it is felt to have, and this is connected with its being 'seen with symmetrical eyes'. In other words, the actions (asymmetrical) by means of which aggression is expressed are felt, symmetrically, as tending to infinity. This seems to happen mainly in what I have called the third stratum. Now, at the superficial level the synthetic ego-functioning, which is associated with the self (Matte-Blanco 1975a: 122–24), usually succeeds in smoothing out and coordinating opposing wishes; this fact results in these conflicts becoming less visible. But if there is an 'invasion of symmetry' (from a lower level) into higher (more conscious) levels, then the aggression will be felt as dangerous.

If we study the 'descent' from more superficial to lower levels, with increasing proportions of symmetry, we find a succession of changing circumstances. When asymmetrical relations are still amply available, when differentiation between various desires and between various concepts is still great, but at the same time things are increasingly seen symmetrically, then conflict is at its highest (the third and fourth strata). There is a certain depth at which aggressive tendencies are felt to tend towards infinite magnitude. As we proceed towards still lower levels, the notion of aggression begins to lose its meaning. Indeed, at the level of spacelessness–timelessness (absence of asymmetrical relations) aggression and conflict are both alien and inconceivable; so, also, is thinking. We can thus conclude that *the same individual may appear, at any one time, well balanced and peaceful, filled with aggression, or alien to aggressiveness, according to the strata being considered.*

170

It is interesting to note that at the intermediate strata we encounter some symmetrizations which tend to infinity in two ways. First, the number of elements of the class defined by a given propositional function tends to infinity. This is because of the process through which there is the creation of very wide and ever increasing equivalence classes which gather together, for instance, the class of fathers, that of teachers, of professors, or of dangerous police, and so on. Second, there is also a tendency towards infinite magnitude of the intensity aspect of the propositional function itself. As a consequence, aggression, since to the mind it is recognized by a propositional function, may be felt as having, so to speak, a force greater than a nuclear explosion. It seems infinite. From another angle, however, it is circumscribed and is, therefore, an infinite within finite limits. I think that clinical experience confirms both these views; aggression does tend to be felt as very intense, and equivalence classes tend to become very wide.

2 Libido and object–relations theories

Freud described projection, and more especially introjection (Freud 1917b [1915], SE 14), in terms of the investment or detachment of libidinal cathexes. Melanie Klein chose to work with the concept of object. This is usually conceived in a quite concrete manner, starting from the image of the first object, the material breast. We know that libido theory refers to the Freudian conception of energy and that object-relations theory is related to the Freudian topographical or spatial image of the mind. It does not seem that both alternatives, though different, are necessarily mutually exclusive. Despite appearances to the contrary, they are not incompatible. They are also the only ones in use so far, though this need not be necessarily so.

The promising impetus provided by the concepts of libido and object seem to have run out of steam, for there has been little subsequent theoretical development of the initial notions. In fact the only things we see repeated about the first refer rather vaguely to energy cathexes, to their withdrawal, and so on; and nobody seems to know much about what psychical energy, cathexis, investment, or withdrawal are. Obviously these two latter terms refer to notions which imply a very general concept of movement – but where and into or away from what? If I say that I invest my money or that I withdraw it, or if I speak of expenditure of heat or mechanical or electrical energy in a given work, you know quite well what I mean; not so in the case of the libido.

Practically the same is, at present, true of the concept of object, which also seemed to hold so much promise. Sooner or later the use of this notion must lead to clarifying some fundamental questions: what is an object, what does it mean to put inside, introject, expel, or project? One thing, however, is certain in the midst of these difficulties: projection and introjection are concepts which presuppose space, an outside and an inside of the individual. This concept should, therefore, be defined with greater precision. On the other hand, as I mentioned in Chapter 6, paradoxically enough we seem to have no use for the notion of time in our descriptions of introjection and projection. It seems to make no sense to describe a given introjection or projection in terms of seconds, minutes, or weeks. However, it does make sense to say that the paranoid-schizoid phase, i.e. the initiation of the paranoid-schizoid position before the emergence of defensive feelings, takes so many weeks or months and that certain projection–introjection mechanisms are typical of this phase.

We must conclude that these theoretical descriptions, however much they reflect important observations, are very imperfect ways of portraying the underlying phenomena.

It will be easy to see that my presentation of the subject is based on the concept of object and its various relations, and not on that of psychical energy. The reason for this is that the idea of an object seems much nearer to the clinical realities under study, if developed along the lines I am suggesting. What is more, I really do not know how to reach a precise and fertile way to handle and develop the concept of psychical energy, which is quite obscure to me.

3 The general functions of defensive processes

I want in this section to try to clarify certain notions required for an understanding of introjection and projection as defensive processes. Initially Freud considered repression as a defence against impulses which were feared or disapproved of. Later on he suggested that repression was not the only way of dealing with such impulses and introduced the more general concept of defence, of which repression constituted only one example.

Further experience led to a wider view. According to Anna Freud, this was expressed by Hartmann at a meeting of the Vienna Society:

'in the Vienna Society in the discussion following the presentation of my first two chapters of *The Ego and the Mechanisms of Defence* in

1936, Hartmann showed himself appreciative on the whole, but he emphasised the point that to show the ego at war with the id was not the whole story; that there were additional problems of ego growth and ego functioning which needed consideration. My views were more restricted at the time, and this was news to me which I was not yet ready to assimilate.'

(A. Freud 1969)

As can be seen from this quotation, many years ago Hartmann realized and pointed out that the concept of defence did not cover or exhaust all the functions that so-called defence mechanisms fulfil in psychical life. It is pertinent to mention here a concept of his which has an important bearing on the subject. He writes: 'Through what one could call a *change of function*, what started in a situation of conflict may secondarily become part of the non-conflictual sphere' (Hartmann 1964: 123).

In a paper read in 1939 before the British Psycho-Analytical Society (Matte-Blanco 1940), I studied the functions of the mechanisms of defence and introduced the concept of *utilization*:

'in the physical world work is obtained by a fall of energy from a higher to a lower potential only if an obstacle is in the way: in the case of a waterfall by interposing a hydraulic wheel, and by means of a steam engine, if I am dealing with heat moving towards cold. In a similar way, in the mind we have, at one extreme, the id-impulses and, at the other, their satisfaction. The ego, directed by the super-ego, puts some obstacles in their way. The impulses passing through those obstacles provoke the so-called defence mechanisms. Thanks to this arrangement the ego can utilise the energy of the id-impulses in activities of all kinds (wishes, desires, feelings, actions) which would not have been developed had the impulses been allowed to find direct gratification.

'Thus, from the energic point of view, it can be said that defence mechanisms represent *the utilisation mechanisms for the id-energy* – the heat engine of the mind. . . .

' . . . There is a group of id-impulses that, ideally speaking, can never find completely adequate satisfaction, on account of the individual's lack of the proper organs necessary to provide it. I am referring to the bisexual impulses. Consequently, these are always forced to find a diverted means of discharge. The diverted means of discharge, both in the bisexual and in the pregenital impulses described above, are provided by the defence mechanisms; thanks to these, the possibilities of satisfaction are diversified and increased. It is usually said that the ego exerts the defensive

173

function as a protection against the onslaught of instinctual drives. But it is equally true to affirm that instinctual drives are discharged by the defensive arrangements, sometimes by one, more often by a combination of several of them. A dam represents a protection against flood, but is also useful for purposes of irrigation. Similarly, the defence mechanisms fulfil a function of utilisation of id-energy, both for internal and external activities. . . . By devising systems of defence mechanisms, human beings have been able to enlarge their range of interest, thus permitting the activities of civilisation to develop.'

(Matte-Blanco 1940: 5, 6–7)

The role of symbols. Commenting on my view then, I would say now that, since the notion of psychical energy has still not been developed and understood, it is still not easy to advance along the lines proposed in that paper. But the underlying ideas can help in our understanding if, instead of framing them in the concept of energy, we integrate them in another context. We might start by saying that instinctual desires can be satisfied by means of some symbolic activities. In fact it is a matter of daily observation that large (logical) classes are formed in the unconscious, for instance the class of oral satisfactions, of genital satisfactions, and so on. Each of these large classes has various sub-classes; in each of these there is a sub-class of primitive specific bodily activities and various sub-classes of corresponding symbolical activities. In other words, the mind defines each large class by a propositional function which explicitly or implicitly, consciously or unconsciously, contains various aspects. Thus under the large class of oral activities the mind will define actual primitive activities such as sucking, chewing, and biting and also various symbolic oral activities such as reading and listening to a teacher. When the principle of symmetry holds in a large class, then any sub-class becomes identical to any other and to the whole class; in contrast to what is thought in ordinary classical logic, I suggest that *the psychoanalytical concept of symbol is that of a symmetrized equivalence class in which an object and all its representatives are treated not only as equivalent but as identical.*

In fact, the mind recognizes symbols in two ways. First, it does so through classical-logical formulations; here the mind registers that bodily activities with their objects have something in common with their symbols but are different from them. Second, it does so through symmetrization; here all objects and activities in a class are experienced by the mind as identical or the same thing.

A particular aspect of this view deserves consideration. If we look

174

at physical space from the point of view I have set out we can see that any physical structure in space and a mental structure that are in any way isomorphic with each other (classical logic) are experienced as the same thing at deeper mental levels (symmetrical logic). Hence the fundamental antinomy in the form of a Simassi structure. Take two problems from earlier chapters. In introjection and projection, the breast and any symbol of it become identical. In this way instinctual desires can find their satisfaction by means of symbolic activities. (Obviously certain limits to this are determined by biology; one cannot, for very long, satisfy hunger by reading!)

I will summarize by saying that symbolic satisfaction of instinctual desires is in fact utilized to develop various kinds of psychical activity (psychical organization) as well as in psychical growth and development. This is sublimation. By this approach we avoid the thorny question of psychic energy, for the time being at least.

Challenge and response. I once put forward the possibility of applying some ideas of Toynbee (1948) on history to human individual development. According to him the various civilizations known throughout history have emerged as a response to a challenge. Take Egyptian civilization as an example. At the end of the Ice Age the ice of northern Africa began to melt, and the cyclonic belt shifted northwards. This caused a gradual drying up of the region, which eventually culminated in its transformation into the deserts of Sahara and Libya. The human hunters who lived there found themselves confronted by a serious challenge: their sources of food began to disappear, and they had no alternative but to emigrate, in search of better living conditions. Some of them went east and found the marshy plains of the Nile; and they were forced to drain and cultivate them in order to survive. The response to the challenge of these circumstances was the Egyptian civilization.

The parallel with individual development is striking. The challenge of frustration leads to anxiety. This, as Klein has shown, leads to the development of symbols, and these, in their turn, play an important role in the development of the ego-functions.

Mechanisms, processes, and levels of defence. The broader view of the mechanisms of defence initiated by Hartmann (1964) has been subsequently expressed, probably with various shades of added meaning, by several authors, among whom are Lampl-de-Groot (1954), P. J. Van der Leeuw (1969), and R. Schafer (1968). Guntrip (1968: ch. XV, esp. 398–99, 410) has objected to the term 'mechanism' and has pointed out that Klein's contribution has meant, among other things, that psychical processes must be considered in their own right and not in terms of physics or biology.

175

Personally I doubt whether Klein would have liked the idea of separating her conception from its biological basis. On the other hand, Guntrip is, I think, right when he points out that the word 'mechanism' may be used as meaning something too closely connected with physics. However, if instead we adopt the term 'process', which he in fact employs (Guntrip 1968; 402, 403), we are only a bit better off, because 'process' is also a spatio-temporal metaphor. What seems important is always to keep in mind that both terms are, like 'object', used in psychoanalysis in a broader sense than in physics, i.e. to mean a sub-class or substructure which in its propositional function also comprises the physical meaning of the word. There probably is an isomorphism between both sub-classes, if seen as structured sets, but this does not necessarily mean that they are identical. So we can use 'mechanism' or 'process' as representatives of an abstract structure.

This formulation has the advantage of bringing to the forefront the need to define this isomorphism more explicitly. We must tackle the unavoidable and fundamental issue: what is the meaning of the use of space–time when referring to mental processes?

Regulation and growth. Further reflection leads, I think, to the conclusion that so-called defence, the wider concept of utilization, and the other concepts mentioned can be subsumed under two general functions: psychical regulation and psychical growth. The first refers essentially to what I have described in the quotation from my paper (Matte-Blanco 1940): the utilization of wishes or emotions in the service of well-being and of mental activity. Psychical growth refers to the possibility, through these processes, of increasing the range of emotional life, of understanding, and of establishing contact with other human beings and the world in general. This takes place through what may be compared to a *metabolic process*; so that the growth function of defence mechanisms can be seen from this point of view. Both the regulating and the growth functions can take on various simultaneous or successive expressions in the same mechanism.

4 The particular functions of projection and introjection

I want first to pay attention to the levels of experience at which the distinction between outside and inside is clearly made – that is, where asymmetrical relations are firmly established (I refer to the first and second strata: see Chapter 2, section 2). At such levels introjection and projection fulfil definite defensive functions as well as that of utilization of primitive instinctual wishes for the psycho-biological well-being and growth of the individual. The functions of defence are so obvious that we need not dwell upon them long. I shall only mention that introjection may be used defensively to control conscious experience of a dreaded object or to protect a loved one. Projection coupled with splitting is frequently used for the same purpose. As for the function of utilization and diversification of activities by means of the symbols of the primary objects and situations connected with instinctual desires, we have already seen that Melanie Klein has shown that anxiety, which provokes defensive reactions, is instrumental in the development and diversification of symbols; this fact obviously applies in our present case.

Projection may also be used to promote welfare and growth. At a given moment it may be convenient to project a part of oneself in order to recover it later and in this way better to regulate intrapsychical events. The growth function of projection is discussed by Anna Freud (1969) in her view of externalization. A particularly important example of a growth function may be seen when a child projects something on to his mother, who keeps it in 'store', for it to be recovered when the right moment comes to use it in the process of growth. As is well known, another aspect is the splitting of the object into good and bad and the corresponding projection of the latter. According to Klein this splitting and projection are one of the fundamental processes of early growth and lead to the stable establishment of the good object within the self.

I think it is pertinent to remember here that splitting, like introjection and projection, is possible only through the availability of asymmetrical relations, which are instrumental in the establishment of differences; whereas a preponderance of symmetrical relations leads, at these levels, to confusion.

Introjection and projection as metabolic processes. The handling of introjected and projected aspects of objects results in a distinction of the different characteristics of the objects. This can lead to an integration of these components in new configurations. Here a transformation takes place so that they may combine with one's own or others' inner *Erlebnisse* (a word which, for lack of a better term, is usually and imperfectly translated by 'experiences') so that they are utilized in defensive, self-regulating, or mental growth processes. Sometimes they are not integrated in this way but 'expelled' as undesired or harmful. These activities, viewed as a whole, can be described, as Abraham has proposed (1924 [1942]: 464), as processes of psychic metabolism. I believe this constitutes a central aspect of introjection and projection, which for this reason can be truly called the *metabolic mechanisms*.

177

I suggest that an important line of progress in the conception of introjective and projective processes could be made by a detailed study of the metabolic vicissitudes of introjected objects, as suggested by Abraham and, unfortunately, not developed. By using a comparison with the metabolism of nutrient substances we may see how an object is eventually destined to be katabolized into its constituent aspects. These are then incorporated into highly personal mental structures.

Perhaps one finds here and there in Klein some reference to this process, without, however, giving it the name used by Abraham. Many years ago I myself began to study this question (Matte-Blanco 1940) but have not followed it up. Goethe has given a beautiful and profound example of this process of katabolism as well as anabolism of the 'objects':

Selbstbildnis

Vom Vater hab ich die Statur,
Des Lebens ernstes Führen,
Vom Mütterrchen die Frohnatur
Und Lust zu fabulieren.

. . . .

Sind nun die Elemente nicht
Aus dem Komplex zu trennen,
Was ist denn an dem ganzen Wicht
Original zu nennen?

Self-Portrait

From Father have I the stature,
The serious conduct in life,
From darling Mother the good-humoured nature
And the pleasure of fairy tales.

. . . .

You must not separate
The elements from the whole,
Otherwise what can be called
Original in the poor, unhappy subject?

5 The integration of projection and other defence mechanisms

There are certain mechanisms which, here and there, constitute a prerequisite for the appearance of projection. Among these would be repression, disavowal (denial), and splitting. When an individual is going to project an aspect or feature of himself, he may frequently start by repressing, denying, or disavowing this aspect with regard to himself. He may also split it in order (for instance) to protect it or himself from internal dangers. Subsequently he projects it, in order to get rid of it, to handle it better elsewhere, or to send it 'in custody' to a safer place. Sometimes this seems to be a purely asymmetrical work, while at others, as in projective identification, it would be a bi-logical structure of the 'symmetrized vector' type. If we keep these simple facts in mind we shall, I feel, be in a better position to understand clinical reality.

6 Ethology, assimilation, introjection, and projection

I would now like to comment on some aspects of a view expressed by Bowlby (1973: esp. ch. 11). He points out that psychoanalysts frequently tend to invoke projection to explain fears which do not seem warranted in the situation in which they appear. In his own approach, instead, 'projection is given a much smaller role as an explanatory principle. A solution is found in the relationship that the natural clues bear to danger and safety' (Bowlby 1973: 170). He proposes to keep the term 'projection' 'to denote the process whereby a person (male or female) attributes to another (male or female) some features of his own self, especially some aspect of himself that he dislikes or is afraid of' (p. 172). It will be seen that this definition is essentially the same as that given by Jones (1938: 621), to which I referred in Chapter 6, section 3.

Bowlby points out that projection is often confused with assimilation but that they are in fact very different processes. Assimilation was introduced by Piaget 'to denote our propensity to perceive any object in terms of some model we already have, even though the model may fit the object imperfectly: the new object of perception is said to be assimilated to the existing model' (Bowlby 1973: 172). Bowlby remarks that if the meaning of the term 'projection' is restricted to that just mentioned, then it can be said that psychoanalysts, especially those who follow the 'Kleinian system of thought' (p. 173), frequently invoke this process as an explanation of situations which can be seen from various other points of view. In clinical work this has the harmful effect of 'directing attention away from a person's real experiences, past or present' (p. 173). He adds that a person's fear that somebody may harm him is 'explicable in at least four ways' (p. 173):

(1) The person has become aware rightly of hostile intentions in the other.

(2) In his childhood he has actually learnt that hostility may be hidden behind outwardly friendly claims. Through assimilation he may see in later life hostility where it is not present.

(3) As he may be aware of his own lack of friendship or hostility towards the other, he naturally expects them to be the same towards him.

(4) He is not aware of his own hostility and considers that while he has a friendly attitude the other is hostile.

Bowlby considers that, if the term 'projection' is used in the sense of attributing to others unwelcome features of the self, only the last of these four ways can be properly called projection. As can be seen, from this point of view projection is a form of *misattribution*, but by no means the only one.

Bowlby then refers to recent studies of the Schreber case, especially the one by Niederland (1959), which I have already mentioned in Chapter 4, section 2, where it is suggested that 'Schreber's delusory beliefs regarding the way God was treating him were derived from memories of how his father treated him when he was a child' (Bowlby 1973: 176–77). Bowlby concludes the chapter with the following comment:

> 'Meanwhile, enough has been said to show that, when the actual experiences they had had during childhood are known and can be taken into account, the pathological fears of adult patients can often be seen in a radically new light. Paranoid symptoms that had been regarded as autogenous and imaginary are seen to be intelligible, albeit distorted, responses to historical events.'
>
> (p. 177)

I find Bowlby clearly convincing when he shows that the concept of projection alone is insufficient for the understanding of fears that are not objectively justified. All four of the ways that he mentions contribute to our understanding and probably others as well. I would, therefore, like to conclude the chapter by relating Bowlby's views to the bi-logical structures.

Ethology and symmetrization. As I see it, today's biology offers us so far a series of observations which are formulated only in terms of classical logic. But there is another aspect of the question which should not be neglected. Our *biological* nature is expressed at the mental level in terms of a potentially infinite number of complexities and subtleties which in a highly developed form are found only in human beings. *Some of these complexities respect classical logic, but most of them are bi-logical. The great wealth of bi-logical structures seems an evolutionary privilege of humans.*

To explain: biology offers us, so far, a series of observations which are formulated in terms of only classical logic. It may be doubted, however, that *all* biological facts can be completely formulated in terms of this logic. There is, in fact, some evidence of bi-logic also in biology. To be, life requires death, and in a way both are co-extensive. Freud's concept of the death instinct is a fascinating but not altogether satisfactory attempt at formulating this problem;[1] and if one applies it in clinical work without much care, just as it is sometimes applied, it is even more unsatisfactory and it distorts the reality of human beings. This, however, is not what I wish to discuss here, but rather the fact that bi-logical structures are, quantitatively speaking, the most important aspect of our daily mental life. Psychoanalytical practice furnishes ample evidence confirming this assertion, if one knows how to look for it. What I have just affirmed is another, I believe more precise, way of saying that the unconscious is omnipresent in every human manifestation. *And it is in terms of these structures that, at times, we must observe biological facts in human beings.* We cannot escape from this requirement. To give an example, we can understand introjective and projective processes only in a very superficial way if we do not look at them in these terms.

Finally, I should like to point out that Piaget's concept of assimilation seems to correspond to the mathematical conception of equivalence class in which the various elements of the class have something in common and something that separates them. But there is here a fundamental fact to consider, without which understanding of human psychology remains very rudimentary. *The unconscious grasp of the existence of common aspects, together with the application of the principle of symmetry, leads to the identity between the various elements of the class: symmetrization, hence non-distinction between the elements of the (symmetrized) class.* The result of this process, if the question is looked at in terms of classical logic, is con-fusion.

To take another instance, if the recent discoveries about the relationship between Schreber and his father (Freud 1911, SE 12) are looked at in terms of bi-logic, then we can better understand the confusion between Schreber's father, Flechsig, and God; all three are representatives of an equivalence class which was symmetrized. They have, therefore, become identical. This is, of course, quite different from projection.

To explain a little more. There are cases which may be described as examples of Piaget's process of assimilation, and in which one could see the following: first, forming an equivalence class with various objects which are similar but not identical between themselves; the 'model may fit the object imperfectly'. This is an example of abstraction, of singling out one propositional function which fits both the model and other objects. All this happens within normal logic: the discovery of an equivalence, but not identity, between these different objects. Second, through the application of the principle of symmetry any element of the equivalence class becomes identical to the whole class and, hence, to any other element of it. Third, owing, perhaps, to the phenomenon of imprinting, the whole class which has been subjected to the action of the principle of symmetry – and, hence, all its elements – is 'coloured' with the characteristics of the object which was its first representative.

It seems clear that all three aspects are seen in the case of Schreber, and it is the third that explains why Schreber felt that God was treating him in the same way as his father treated him. It seems equally clear that the fact, so well established by the recent studies of Schreber quoted by Bowlby (1973), of the connection between the way Schreber felt about God and his early life events (the way his father treated him) would in itself, if taken alone, furnish no satisfactory explanation of why Schreber felt that God treated him as his father did. And it also seems clear that the last paragraph quoted from Bowlby refers to an important insight on the question, which must, however, be integrated with the other aspects of the question, just mentioned. Otherwise we risk arriving at only a partial understanding that is liable to provoke criticisms which may, in their turn and unjustly, lead to ignoring the insight offered by the point of view Bowlby is developing.

These problems will be touched on, here and there, throughout the book.

7 An important epistemological principle

An important epistemological principle stems from psychoanalytical knowledge and is constantly seen in introjective and projective processes: *at certain depths the unconscious tends to treat anything as if it were human.* A striking example is seen in so-called animism, but we may also observe the same thing, though less obviously and at an unconscious level, in every case of understanding and establishing contact with some aspect of the world. The breast described by Klein in *Envy and Gratitude* (1957), for instance, has all the characteristics of a human being.

Two other examples of this principle are the reactions to projective tests and the phallic phase. They will be discussed in the next chapter.

This principle is the expression of a characteristic of the unconscious found by Freud: replacement of external by psychical reality. If we formulate it in terms of the principle of symmetry, then we may say: identity of psychical and external reality. This is a manifestation of the fundamental antinomy; these realities are the same and they are not.

Finally, remember the fundamental role of emotion in scientific discovery, as discussed in Chapter 3, section 11, where we saw that Einstein made his discoveries about the physical world by means of an emotional play with images!

Notes

1 Cf. Matte-Blanco, Le quattro antionomie dell' instinto di morte (1972 [1973]).

9

Levels of depth: a working scheme for use in clinical practice

Foreword. I have been pointing out how the studies of Ferenczi (1909), Freud, Abraham (1924), Klein, and others have led to the formulation of the notion of projective and introjective processes. As a consequence of this pioneer work there has been, in a comparatively short time, a considerable accumulation of clinical observations. But these can no longer be accurately expressed in terms of the concepts so far in use. The result is that various facts are frequently suppressed, distorted, or simply ignored, because they do not fit into the existing frame.

The purpose of this chapter is to put forward a scheme for observation, research, and work with patients which, I believe, both avoids the disadvantage just mentioned and provides opportunities for further growth of the subject. It will, I hope, become apparent that this scheme starts from and preserves the relevant knowledge so far acquired.

The reader will see that some ideas put forward here apply mostly or exclusively to projective processes. Later some aspects which apply mostly or exclusively to introjection will be added. Here, however, both types of process can be considered from a more general point of view, because, though one of them goes outwards and the other inwards, the basic factors at work may be the same in both cases.

1 Three regions or levels of projection–introjection

In Chapter 8 the notion of levels was defined in terms of the proportion of symmetrical and asymmetrical relations present in a given mental manifestation. This concept, which is closely allied to, but not the same as, my concept of strata, will now be used in our conceptual scheme.

The proportions of symmetry and asymmetry can assume an infinite number of values; thus the number of levels at which this proportion is distinguished in any one person can likewise be very large. However, for practical purposes these may be referred to under only three loose regions.

First, there is a more superficial region, which could be called the *region of happening*. In a wide sense every happening implies movement, i.e. some displacement, physical or psychical, which takes time: a change. As we know, happening or change (movement) is conceived in terms of space and time, and these too, in their turn, in terms of asymmetrical relations.

On the other hand, as pointed out in Chapter 6, the concepts of introjection and projection seem to be alien to the notion of time but not to that of space, if this latter is understood in terms of a more comprehensive structure than that of a three-dimensional one. *Psychical space would then be isomorphic to a space of more than three dimensions.* Bearing this in mind, the question arises: how should we refer to something which is isomorphic to space, is alien to time, yet makes its appearance, with certain features, at certain given moments, while at other moments shows other features? In fact, we have to recognize that introjection and projection, however timeless, do not appear static. They are rather like a sequence of photographs in a film: each individual photograph portrays something at rest, and the sequence of them portrays movement. Just as Zeno pointed out, and Weierstrass and Bertrand Russell agreed,[1] the movement of an arrow is conceived as being formed by a sequence of immobilities, so also introjective and projective processes may be conceived as formed by a sequence of timeless 'pictures'. Note that we may speak of process or happening with the same right as when we speak of movement as happening. I conclude that *introjection and projection are isomorphic to spatial yet timeless 'happenings' or changes which result in 'timeful' (i.e. developmental) changes in the person in whom they take place.* Such a conclusion follows, I think, simply from the observation of clinical reality. It is an expression of the fundamental antinomy; they are processes (in time), yet are timeless. As such, this conclusion poses difficult and fascinating problems. It must, furthermore, be pointed out that the use of asymmetrical relations is essential not only in connection with space but also in the distinction between individuals, between things, and between aspects of the self.[2]

185

In summary, the more superficial region, that of happening, is characterized by a most ample use of asymmetrical relations. Owing to this fact it is the region where we find the greatest respect for classical logic and, therefore, for the distinctions between inside and outside. I do not mean, however, that bi-logical structures never slip in at the levels of this region.

At the opposite extreme there would be a region where asymmetrical relations are non-existent or almost non-existent, and where symmetrical relations prevail. This is visible in a sort of dissolution (or, more precisely, non-appearance) of space–time and of the distinction between the subject and the outside world, between people and between things. I propose, for present purposes, to call this the region of the *basic matrix* of introjection and projection. This, being the region 'nearest' to the strata of the mind in which total symmetry predominates, would show more confused and wide bi-logical structures because of a greater participation of symmetry.

Finally, between these two regions there is a third which gathers from all intermediate levels, where we can observe different proportions of co-presence of asymmetrical and symmetrical relations. It is possible to conceive a sequence of strata from one extreme of greater asymmetry to another of increasing dissolution or unavailability of asymmetrical relations. We may call this the *intermediate region*. This would be the region where the bi-logical structures which are more familiar to us thrive.

Observation shows that clinical manifestations are frequently a complex mixture of these three regions and of several levels in each, especially in the intermediate one. One can discover something of the nature of this mixture if one is prepared to look for it. I will now consider each of these regions in turn.

2 The region of happening

Happening is essential in projection. Observation shows that it is frequently impossible to describe a given clinical manifestation in terms of only one of the concepts current in the literature, such as Freudian projection, Kleinian projective identification, or so-called introjective identification. If, instead, we see a clinical manifestation as a complex process in which several components[3] are at work, things become more clear. An analysis of some of the pertinent literature on the subject, especially of Freud and Klein, made in the light of experience with patients and of the concepts put forward in this book, has led me to identify three components in happenings of a projective–introjective nature. The reader may easily see what I have taken from others, especially from the authors just mentioned, and also what I have changed or added.

First there is *the disavowal-denial-expulsion component* of projection. This occurs when a piece of psychical reality, which, for whatever reason, disturbs the person, is first denied or split off and subsequently projected (expelled) on to another person, who becomes, for the subject in question, the 'owner' of this unpleasant reality. Any connection between the individual and the piece of reality in question is denied or disavowed, if seen from the viewpoint implicit in this component.

Strachey translated Freud's *Verneinung* by 'disavowal', but since the translation of this German word by 'denial' is by now also several decades old, I have coupled the two translations together to avoid misunderstanding. I believe, however, that in the present connotation 'disavowal' gives the meaning more faithfully.

I will mention two examples of fairly pure manifestations of this component.[4]

Example 11

A patient who worried about his body odour: he disavowed it in himself and projected it on to his girlfriend, who then became, for him, the bad-smelling one.

Example 12[5]

A small boy was with his grandfather looking with great interest at the lions in the zoo. One of them made a loud roar. The boy then pulled his grandfather's sleeve strongly and said, 'Let's go away from here, Grandfather, because you are very much afraid.'

With regard to *its structure*, the process involved in this component takes place in two quite distinct steps. First, there is disavowal-denial, which expresses itself by some form of splitting at the service of disavowal-denial.[6] Second, there is the expulsion on to somebody else of the split-off part. Alternatively this may be described as the attribution of the disavowed-denied part to somebody else. These two alternatives are not the same, and if we were very rigorous we could call projection or expulsion only the first of the two, for there would be no movement in the second. I believe, however, that to treat both as the same is, so far, permissible, because it does not lead to gross practical distortion. This component is exclusively asymmetrical in its logical structure; it strictly conforms to classical logic.

In regard to *its function and instinctual roots*, disavowal-denial-expulsion fulfils a double function. It serves, first, to get rid of what is unpleasant or not accepted as part of the self at the moment; and, second, to attribute it to somebody else. The first function, i.e. getting rid, may, in theory, take place without the second, but in this case it would not be a component of projection as the term is intended in clinical work.

The most obvious instinctual prototype of this component is related to a faecal expulsion. However, to restrict its origin only to this function is unwarranted and would narrow the meaning of the component itself. The emission of vomit, urine, or air and the elimination of skin products are other models, and not necessarily the only other ones.

If we consider another aspect of the question we become aware that this component is frequently but not always connected with aggression. A non-aggressive instance would be when a certain need, which has been felt to be both necessary and good, may at a given moment become unwanted. This is the case for any small child who is outgrowing the need to be helped by his mother and is beginning to prefer to do things by himself. He then may disavow his still present wish to be helped and attribute it to his younger brother, say, not because the wish in question is felt to be aggressive but because it makes him feel helpless and also because it blocks development.

You will note that disavowal-expulsion on the whole corresponds to Freud's early descriptions of projections already mentioned in Chapter 4. It is also present as a component, though never explicitly described as such, in Klein's concept of projective identification. It is the 'classical-logical vector' aspect of it (see Chapter 7).

A second component of projection is *the delegating-gift component.* In its pure form, which is rather an abstraction, this might be described as follows. When an individual does not want to have in himself, for whatever reason, a certain piece of psychic reality, but at the same time does not want to sever all relations with it, he may then proceed to split it from his self and project it on to another person. This person then becomes the bearer, host, or custodian of this reality. But he is always a proxy, delegate, or representative in charge of it, not its rightful 'owner'. The connections or links still remaining between the individual who has projected and the piece of reality in question may at times be very obvious and at other times quite disguised, but it is possible to trace them back and establish them clearly. Through the existence of these links we realize that the subject has not relinquished his 'ownership' of that reality.

With regard to the function of delegation-gift, I shall here follow, with some modifications, an illuminating study by Grinberg (1963) and take from him three of the five causes or motives which he thinks lead to projective identification. On my part, I will add three others. I prefer to use the term 'function' because it refers more directly to the action of the mechanism and not to the (unconscious) intentions or desires of the person who employs it. In the case of the present component we may consider the following functions.

(a) *Preservation of the object* (Grinberg): to protect the object or the piece of reality in question from the dangers that it may encounter within the individual, on account of strong destructive tendencies. This is comparable to the wartime practice of taking works of art from places where they are in danger of being destroyed and putting them temporarily in a safe place.

(b) *Destruction* (Grinberg): this function acts in the opposite sense to preservation; a destructive tendency is delegated in order to have it satisfied by means of the actions of another person; in this way the individual disavows all responsibility and guilt. An example of this can be seen in what Grinberg calls the *inductive finality* of projective identification, which is seen in psychopaths who manage to make others do what they themselves want to do. Such behaviour was also studied by Grinberg (1962) in relation to analytic therapy; here the patients' projective identifications with the analyst may induce the latter to act as the patient wants him to. It was Grinberg who first pointed to this process and gave it the name of *projective counter-identification*.

(c) *Self-protection*: to avoid exposure to danger or inconvenience in the pursuit of the satisfaction of one's desires. The delegating component serves this purpose very well. Note that (b) is always linked to (c), but (c) not always to (b). As already hinted in the description of this component, we frequently but not always find examples of disavowing combined with delegating. Thus disavowal may be used in avoiding responsibility for an action, while the action itself is accompanied by some subtle delegation. There is a Spanish saying which clearly expresses this idea in a picturesque way: to take the chestnuts out of the fire with the cat's paw.

(d) *Reparation* (Grinberg): by projecting good parts of oneself on to an object, it is possible to heal or repair the object.

(e) *Supplementation (supportive function)*: when a child does not feel capable of doing something by himself he may, in his fantasy, make his mother do it. This may refer to various kinds of actions, among which could be included those referring to reparation. This function amounts to the self being replaced by a proxy or representative who can do something the individual is not able, or willing, to do. This may be a delegation which is in no way connected with disavowal but rather with a realistic unconscious judgement that somebody else can do something for us better than we can ourselves. Examples of this kind may be seen (in both directions) in the parent–child relationship, in the relations between man and wife, and in many other cases. This type of procedure may greatly enrich psychical life and greatly benefit human relations.

(f) *Gift*: delegation may also be used when a child wants to make a gift to his mother. It seems that early in life a child's gift is usually, so to speak, subject to a return ticket. If the child likes what he gives, he often wants it back after a little time. He then gradually learns to give up the thing which he wishes to give the loved person. The delegating component always seems to play an important role in the first steps of the process of learning to give. Perhaps even when an adult gives something precious for love, he often consoles himself by 'descending' to the deepest region (the basic matrix of introjection–projection) in the sense I have described earlier and in which there is no distinction between self and not-self; in this way be recovers what he has given. At an early stage of their development all my seven children expressed their love for their parents by offering good things they did not want at the moment, for instance food they no longer wanted to eat. They were clear, open, and affectionate about it. Perhaps this represents a step forward in development, from delegating to the first stage of straightforward giving. A later, more mature stage would be that of giving, with no return ticket, something one likes and wishes to keep. Delegating and giving seem in this case so intimately connected with each other as to justify calling the component in question the *delegating-gift component*.

As can be seen, the processes connected with this component are by no means simple. But all of them have the element of delegation in common. This justifies subsuming them under the same name. One aspect of the progress of understanding is to discover the common features of apparently disparate phenomena.

I suggest that Klein's concept of projective identification may, in one of its aspects, be viewed in terms of this component with regard to the gift aspect – that is, to the projection of good parts of the self. However, it is not completely clear whether this is so, because the various stages of the process of learning to give are, so far as I know, not explicitly differentiated by Klein. The result is that it is difficult to know clearly what actually corresponds to delegating a gift and what is a gift with no return ticket. To explain further: the possibility that the delegated part may return to the self is important in the conception of the delegating component, whereas it does not seem to be included in Klein's explicit description of gifts (Klein 1946 [1952]: 301) in connection with projective identification. I do not know whether she does it elsewhere.

On the other hand, it does seem that the notion of delegation, in the sense that a part of the self is in somebody else, is clearly essential in Klein's concept. I believe this example shows that there is something to be gained in precision from the notion of component, and its clear definition.

As for the projection of the aggressive parts of the self, Klein's words (1946 [1952]: 300–01) seem to correspond rather to the disavowal-expulsion component. But the fact that Klein did not make the explicit distinction between these components results in her descriptions being difficult to read in the terms I am putting forward. What is more, all the elements of the processes at work cannot easily be disentangled from one another.

Among the various functions of this component which I have mentioned, destruction (b) is visible in the Kleinian concept of projective identification, as well as gift (f), possibly also reparation (d); whereas preservation (a), self-protection (c), and supplementation (e), as I have defined them, do not seem to correspond to Klein's conception of projective identification.

It seems pertinent to point out here that the bi-logical structure of projective identification, that of a symmetrized vector (see Chapter 7), is not the same thing as either the classical-logical structure of these components or their functions. If we use all the three aspects just mentioned we get a better all-round understanding. The same holds, it seems, in the case of other bi-logical structures.[7]

A review of Freud's writings under this light reveals in *Group Psychology and the Analysis of the Ego* (1921) that there clearly is a delegating component in the notion of ego-ideal represented by the leader. The process considered by Freud, however, seems more complex and probably cannot be fully understood through the notion of delegation alone.

The robbing-plundering or conquest component of projection refers to the activity or phantasy whereby an individual, so to say, invades another, for instance the mother, in order to take possession of her or of her contents. Accordingly, he may have the phantasy of acquiring those of her characteristics which he desires. Note that here in his phantasy the individual extends the limits of his self or increases his riches through invasion. In the case of the delegating component, if the process is viewed in spatio-temporal terms, we saw how he takes a part from himself and delivers it to others.

Now when we come to the notion of delivering we naturally are reminded of the issues concerning the impoverishment of the ego which I have had cause to mention in earlier chapters. Here you may recall that Klein and others have insisted that the individual may feel impoverished as a consequence of massive projective identification. I suggest that the concept of impoverishment through projection is important only at the levels of the region of introjection–projection where asymmetrical relations are preponderant. At these levels, if I give something, I lose it. In contrast, at the levels where symmetrical relations are preponderant, such an 'accountant's inventory' is no longer valid, for I may give something and at the same time keep it; and also because what is mine also belongs to the others, and vice versa. At these levels D'Annunzio's mention of an old saying, which I have quoted before, applies: 'soltanto ho quel che ho donato' ('I have only what I have given'). Moreover, even in terms of asymmetrical relations the question of impoverishment decidedly would not apply to this third component, because, in this case, to go outside, to project oneself, aims at, or results in, an increase of one's riches.

I believe that considerations such as these suggest that some projective identifications may be felt as impoverishment and others as enrichment. I would like to suggest that instead of speaking of projective identification to cover a great many complicated problems we consider, first, the three components I have described; second, the level (symmetrical–asymmetrical) of the psychical reality under study; and, third, the bi-logical structure of the manifestations. If we do this we shall be able to grasp a great many subtleties which would otherwise escape us.

I will now consider *the functions of robbing-plundering*. The most important is that of acquiring, which is the essence of the component. None the less, in order to acquire it is frequently necessary to gain control of the desired object, not only to prevent retaliating counter-attacks but also to obtain the full results of plundering. In fact, at times it is necessary not only to possess or invade the object but also to make it act according to the desires of the plunderer. The comparison with the invasion of a country is illustrative; in order to plunder and rob a neighbour it is necessary to conquer it, if only temporarily. In order to avoid the risk of losing what has been conquered, or what has been plundered if the booty is kept in the country, it is necessary to establish some form of control.

I should like to point out that Grinberg's (1963) distinction between an adaptive control, which functions at a mature level, and an omnipotent control, which functions at more regressive (lower) levels, is pertinent here. Obviously, the phantasies of plundering attacks are frequently accompanied by a great deal of aggression and anxiety, and this corresponds to levels with a relative preponderance of symmetrical relations. Here the experience of great magnitudes, hence omnipotence, is in full swing. It is at these levels that we find omnipotent and not adaptive control.

Yet it would seem that the assertion just made is not always true. However strange this may seem, there are cases in which plundering may be accomplished in phantasy with a view to acquiring which may not be accompanied by a great awarenes of guilt for the effects on the person plundered from. This would depend on the relations existing in such a case between, on the one hand, love and especially self-love and, on the other, the desire to take possession by plundering.

Robbing-plundering corresponds very closely to the description of the process by Marjorie Evans commented on by Melanie Klein (1946 [1952]: 300, footnote 2). This component of projection plays an important role in the Kleinian concept of projective identification, as may easily be seen in her descriptions. In contrast, it does not seem to be present in Freud's conception of projective processes. Reflection upon this fact leads to an interesting awareness. This component is quite different from the other two in that, in this case, there is nothing of the individual, which is sent outside. In the case of the first component (disavowal-denial-expulsion), a part is expelled. In the second component (delegating-gift), a desire or tendency is delegated. In our third component there is a question of extending the individual's possessions and limits. The three cases may be considered as substructures of a wider structure, but the similarities between the first two are greater than the similarities between these and the third.

Observation perhaps furnishes more examples of the participation of *several components together* in a given clinical manifestation rather than a pure manifestation of each. In my experience, however, it is the first and second that are more frequently met with, either pure or mixed. This may be a question either of chance or of my greater personal difficulty in finding the third component.

3 The region of the basic matrix of introjection and projection

The region of the basic matrix is that in which symmetrization exerts a major influence on representation and is the region of the deeper unconscious. To grasp what I now want to pursue it will be necessary to keep three ideas in mind. First, time is absent in the system or deeper unconscious. As Freud put it explicitly (1915b, SE 14: 187), in the unconscious there is 'no reference to time at all'. In fact, we are probably incapable of imagining timelessness, because the perception aspects of our being (imagination seems to reflect them) are like frames which are spatial in nature but where time is, in some way, 'enclosed'. But we can think it, though we must recognize that it is very difficult to handle such a concept. To say that something is atemporal means that it has no past, no present, and no future. Second, although Freud never spoke directly of the lack of space in the unconscious (see 1921, SE 18: 28, and 1933, SE 22: 74), the reader will remember that a corollary of the principle of symmetry and the consequent unavailability of asymmetrical relations means an absence of space. Third, as a consequence of what I have already said, it follows that at the deepest layers of the unrepressed unconscious we know no happenings. So, *in the deepest unconscious, things – including those which, if looked at from the outside, appear as introjection and projection – do not happen, but simply are.*

As soon as we try to study the levels of the basic matrix we encounter serious obstacles, for we can consider it only with our conscious thinking. With regard to this, Bergson (1906 [1970]: 625) has pointed out that 'Our intelligence, as it emerges from the hands of nature, has the unorganized solid bodies as its principal object.'[8] He then adds:

> 'All the operations of our intelligence tend towards geometry, as if to the point where they reach their perfect achievement. . . . It is evident that it is a latent geometry, immanent in our representation of space, which is the great springboard of our intelligence and which makes it work.'
>
> (1970: 674)[9]

I shall not pursue Bergson any further. Suffice it to say that, in our context, we find that what in the deepest unconscious is aspatial and atemporal is grasped by the ego-functions of the self – and by the scientific methodology which psychoanalysts, forgetting Freud, employ nowadays – as happening. The result is that when we begin to explore this stratum and think that something belongs to what we call the inside, but find that it may equally correctly be said to belong to what we call the outside, we tend to solve this difficulty by saying that this something has been projected outwards. Correspondingly, if we see a property of what we call outside felt as though belonging to what we call inside, we then say that it has been introjected. Both assertions are, however, spatio-temporal ways of describing something which is alien to space–time. In fact, if we describe as happening something that is not happening, then it is equally legitimate or illegitimate, and in any case equivalent, to say that it is a question of introjection or, alternatively, of projection; both are equally alien to this 'region' of the unconscious.

It becomes visible from the preceding comments that the 'region' of the basic matrix is a pure manifestation of being with no happening, where outside and inside do not exist: the indivisible mode. We tend, however, to view it in terms of happening. The result is a most vivid expression of the fundamental antinomy. If we tried to look at this indivisible 'depth' just as it appears, and not as we read it in terms of space and time, we would learn more about it. And this would be a source of new and deep understanding.

To continue, at the level of the basic matrix, because of the characteristics of the unconscious, no distinctions whatsoever are made between putting inside (introjection) and sending outside (projection). It is for this reason that I call it the basic matrix of introjection and projection, i.e. 'a place or point of origin and growth' (Oxford Dictionary). Only when our observations proceed upwards from this matrix shall we, at more superficial levels, be able to differentiate introjection from projection.

The deepest strata of the mind described in Chapter 2, section 2, are ones where no conflict is experienced. The latter can exist only when opposing forces are struggling: something which requires, even if on a purely symbolic level, both space and time. If infant development is related to the basic matrix, we can see that current views on the ferocity of aggression in the earliest period should be modified. Clinical observation reveals that the early periods may be conflictual only at the superficial levels; deep down, they are peaceful. This is, I believe, a more accurate view of the beginning of life.

4 The region of intermediate levels of introjection and projection

Between the extremes of the basic matrix and the region of happening which I have described there are other intermediate levels. At these levels asymmetrical relations and therefore the concept of space–time prevail. At the same time these are the levels in which space–time is dissolving, where, as we go down in depth, symmetrical relations are gaining the upper hand. The variety is considerable. We can detect various types of incomplete or partial use of space-relations which sometimes gives a sensation of strangeness. Some of the examples given (see Chapter 10), particularly those illustrating the region of the basic matrix, really illustrate these intermediate levels.

The limits of symmetry. Another essential point in the view presented here is that, with only symmetrical relations, thinking cannot take place. *Total symmetry means the confusion of everything with everything else.* Since I have discussed this idea in earlier chapters I shall only remark here that the observation of unconscious processes clearly suggests that the use of symmetry is frequently confined to 'the inside' of a given set or class and that classes or sets are frequently distinguished between themselves in the bi-logical structures which constitute the unconscious. This implies the use of asymmetrical relations. It must be added, however, that the deeper the level, the larger the classes. This leads to the identity of many things which in conscious thinking are clearly distinguished from one another.

I suggest that the concepts I have introduced lead us to understand the distinction between various types of projection and introjection in relation to the region in which such processes take place. Here I should like to mention three examples of manifestations which seem to be related to the deepest level of the basic matrix.

Projective tests. The first refers to so-called projective tests, such as the Rorschach, which are based on the fact that the deepest unconscious identifies self and not-self. To explain: it is obvious that when an individual looks at the Rorschach blots he sees there something of himself, for instance his own conflicts, whatever these may be. What he sees of himself belongs to the strata of asymmetry, of space–time. He would not, however, see himself or his conflicts in the plates if in some obscure way he did not see the plates, a part of the external world, as though they were himself. So, the very possibility of the existence of so-called projective techniques depends on the fact that one aspect of the mind 'sees' the external world as if it were itself. This is usually expressed by saying that the individual projects himself on to the plates. It would, however, be equally accurate or equally inaccurate to say that he introjects the plates and treats them as part of himself. If, instead, we consider that the distinction between outside and inside is non-existent at a deep region, we can understand better the fact that one reads one's own life in the plates. This case also shows, interestingly, that we seem not to be surprised at the fact that people should see their own selves in something which appears so alien to them. Such a fact is not explained at all in terms of outside and inside.

196

There is another important fact to note. The idea of projective techniques is that the individual picks up an aspect of the Rorschach blot, say, because it is isomorphic to something in him. Others may not see this aspect because there is not that isomorphism between them and the plate. In the deepest layers this isomorphism becomes an identity.

The phallic phase. My second example is that of the phallic phase, which, at least in the male, clearly shows some characteristics of the deepest unconscious. As Freud described it, an early aspect of this phase is that a child finds it impossible to accept that somebody else is not built like himself. This is quite a deep level of symmetrical functioning. When a young boy sees a woman and believes that she has been castrated, he is implicitly formulating a series of bi-logical reasonings, which are absurd from the point of view of biology and of simple classical logic. The bi-logical idea is that, if a human being has no penis, this necessarily means that the penis has been removed. In other words, he sees the other as though the other were himself: 'the other is built as I am', which deeper down is identical to 'the other is myself; hence, if the other has no penis, I am castrated'. At deeper strata: 'there is no other'. Deeper still: 'I am'. At these last two levels there is no castration anxiety, because being is not felt in terms of parts of oneself (head, penis, body, and so on); there is no distinction between part and whole.

From this we can see that the anxieties of castration, which are obviously set in motion by aggressive fantasies, presuppose, first of all, the impossibility of differentiating between self and not-self. This impossibility has its origin in an innermost part of human nature and is, nevertheless, blatantly contradicted by actual observation made in terms of classical logic. Contradictory as it may seem, this impossibility goes together with the existence of a sufficient number of asymmetrical relations as to be able to distinguish the 'parts' of the body-self (for further details see Matte-Blanco 1975a: esp. ch. 28, section 2). I would suggest that variations in the importance of the phallic phase may be dependent (among other factors, such as the amount of aggression) upon the varying degrees in which the deepest symmetrized layer of the unconscious (the indivisible reality) becomes more obvious and interacts with superficial asymmetrical layers.

It seems that we should add *the symmetrical or indivisible character type* to the various character types described in psychoanalysis. The indivisible character would be distinguished by the greatness of the role which symmetrical thinking plays, in a more or less disguised way, in the most varied superficial psychical manifestations. These are probably mostly bi-modal, but I would not exclude the slipping in of some unnoticeable vital bi-logical structure.

Animism. The third example is that of so-called animism, which can be observed both in children and in primitives. In order to avoid misunderstandings I wish to point out that by animism I mean that manifestation characterized by the attribution of human properties to inanimate objects and natural phenomena. For example, a child may feel that a table or a chair suffers from pain if hit, or may, like the primitive, attribute human emotions to natural phenomena; the sky may be angry, sad, and so on. It is obvious that, however much the attribution of certain concrete emotions or actions to nature may be the expression of a conflict about these emotions in the person who makes this attribution, this way of viewing things would not be possible if the identification of self and not-self did not previously provide the basic ground upon which the rest is built or developed.

Being in love. The example of being in love has been the subject of several discussions about projection to which I have alluded in earlier chapters. I now want to turn attention to the deepest levels and to consider being in love from the viewpoint of the theoretical framework I have set out. The first point is that in that aspect of being where symmetrical relations are almost the only ones available, love is a way of being in which the individual who loves is loved as being one with the beloved. The verb 'to love', which denotes some form of action (asymmetry), is, hence, the expression of a more superficial level, for at the deepest levels the distinction between individuals is non-existent. In that part of our being – our ego-functions, our consciousness – which uses asymmetrical relations profusely, these forms of being are grasped as happenings, for instance (in the case we are considering) as incorporation or introjection. Conversely, when somebody does not love, this amounts at the deepest levels to the non-recognition of the existence of the other, either within the self or outside: a non-presence.

At a certain depth, love does not distinguish between self and the other, but the 'I-you-everything' is there. Nor does not-love distinguish between self and the other, but in this case the other is not present; it would be like 'I-everything' with no 'you' as 'constitutive' of the indivisible reality in which no distinction exists between anything and anything else. This may sound absurd. In fact it is not absurd. It is the expression of unavoidable bi-logical thinking, due to the fact that as soon as we 'think' the homogeneous indivisible reality, we divide it. This may be grasped at the superficial levels as an expulsion, a projection.

What I have suggested is the inevitable consequence of the fact that our ego-functions are constituted in such a way that they can know only happenings or events.[10] When they come across other manifestations of being, they treat these as though they were happenings. They clothe, so to speak, indivisible being with happening; that is, they cover and replace the whole by one part of it, i.e. the part which is available to the ego functions. Viewed from this angle, *consciousness – which is built upon the physiological model of vision/hearing/touch/smell and as such is suitable for 'seeing' spatio-temporal phenomena – is really a deceit which replaces indivisible being by happening*! So far it has been a useful deceit because it has permitted humanity to see, although only in as unsubstantial a form as Plato's 'shadows', aspects of its inner nature which otherwise would have escaped it. Usually we are able to live the inner reality of our unconscious in its indivisible aspects. But, owing to the fact that our ego-functions 'dress' it with happening, our consciousness, by seeing the indivisible reality as happening, has enabled us to get into some other form of contact with it: that of 'seeing' it with the intellect.[12] It is precisely this kind of experience that permitted Freud to broach the problem of the 'innermost nature' of the unconscious, which he called 'the true psychical reality'. Perhaps now is the moment to take a step forward and begin to consider these things with the help of conceptions more suited to their true nature. To do this, however, we must formulate the principles of a new epistemology.

Notes

1 For Weierstrass see Russell (1903) 1937. Note also that in the four-dimensional conception of the world, as in the theory of relativity, time is a spatial dimension (it has, however, some peculiar aspects); it does not flow, it is just there.

2 This raises interesting problems regarding the relationship between the concept of space and the awareness of distinction between individuals, between things, and between part and whole.

3 The notion of 'component' was developed in this case by drawing inspiration from Sheldon's studies (1946) on constitution.

4 I wish to thank my wife Dr Luciana Bon de Matte, Professor A. Armando, Professor M. Princivalle, Dr M. Rechichi, and Dr G. Sassanelli for their generosity in furnishing (a number of years ago) some examples to add to my own in this and in the next chapter. Though the description made here is faithful to the information given me, the perspective in which the cases are presented is entirely my own responsibility.

5 Mentioned by E. Mira y Lopez (1946: Vol. I, 26).

6 Note that it is perfectly possible to split off for a purpose different from the one we are considering, for instance to protect an aspect or part of the self which is actually recognized as belonging to it.

7 Meltzer's concept of toilet-breast (1967: 20–32) seems to entail aspects of this as well as of the disavowal–expulsion component. It must be added, however, that this Meltzerian concept is more complex and it is not exhaustively explained or understood just in terms of these components.

8 'Notre intelligence, telle qu'elle sort des mains de la nature, a pour objet principal le solide inorganisé.'

9 'Toutes les opérations de notre intelligence tendent à la géométrie, comme au terme où elles trouvent leur parfait achèvement. . . . il est évident que c'est une géométrie latente, immanente à notre représentation de l'espace, qui est le grand ressort de notre intelligence et qui la fait marcher.'

10 This assertion is intended only as a reference to the initial psycho-biological exercise of the ego-function of the self, which tends towards knowledge and mastery of the physical reality, i.e. spatio-temporal reality. It does not intend to maintain that knowledge of events or happenings is the self's only potentiality. In fact, thinking can conceive aspatiality and atemporality, and this is a potentiality that evolution seems to be developing in humanity. Just as human beings are beginning to go further than the Earth, so we are capable of going further than space–time. And we may grow more capable.

11 Here we touch upon a problem which was considered by Lotze in his *Mikrokosmus* (1856 [1909]: 243–44), probably starting from the opposite extreme: humanity's total contact with the world vastly surpasses the contact given it by Logos (for more details, see Matte-Blanco 1975a: 164, n. 1).

10

The fundamental antinomy as seen in clinical examples

Foreword. I want to use this chapter to present some examples which illustrate the use of the working scheme for conceptualizing projection and introjection and the levels of depth of symmetry–asymmetry, that I put forward in Chapter 9. The examples will also provide the opportunity for developing some additional points which may lead to a better understanding of the issues.

Fairly pure manifestations of each of the three components of projection–introjection were mentioned in Chapter 9. In this chapter I will study the details of the way the three components can be related to one another; the intertwining (never combining!) of asymmetry and symmetry, and, therefore, the availability of space–time and other asymmetrical relations, in any particular example; and the structures, bi-logical or not, which result from the foregoing combinations.[1]

1 Pure disavowal–denial–expulsion

It seems that the only component which may appear alone is disavowal–denial–expulsion. In addition to the examples given in the last chapter the following is another.

Example 13
During a period when some unpleasant aspects of his character were being analysed, a patient felt that all the analyst's interpretations missed the point, and repeatedly commented, 'You don't understand.' It was evident from the context that it was he who did not

want to understand, denied this feeling, and projected it on to the analyst.

This seems to be a purely asymmetrical activity and, at first sight, it does not appear to be a bi-logical structure, even if the 'reasons' for it may be.[2]

2 Disavowal-denial and delegation

Example 14

At a certain period of an analysis attention became focused on a particular problem. This was that the patient had married on the condition that the couple were not to have any children; his wife had accepted this. To explain this decision he made use of some obvious rationalizations. I shall not go into the details of the various meanings of his rejection of parenthood. During the treatment his repressed longing to be a father began to be evident. Naturally the roots of his anxieties on this point were studied. One day he expressed the following criticism of the analyst: 'All right, you may have found out these things about me, but there was no need for you to tell me about them.' The meaning of this phrase, as gathered from his associations and various other circumstances, was that he had come close to realizing the experience of desiring to have a child but had immediately rejected it. He then had projected this desire on to the analyst, to whom, so to speak, he entrusted it. In this aspect, analyst and patient were identical. At the same time he denied such identity. He therefore protested against the analyst's efforts to make him conscious of his wish.

This is a combination of disavowal-denial and delegating; the first is asymmetrical activity, and so also is delegating, but this results in an identification. This is obtained by the symmetrization of the vector 'patient→analyst', to become also 'analyst→patient': a return of what was projected. Note that *this final symmetrization is achieved using elements of purely asymmetrical activities*: denial, projection, and delegation. In the end the patient satisfies his own desire for paternity secretly by means of being the same as the analyst. This is a highly unsatisfactory non-vital bi-logical structure. We need not enter into the details of the underlying meanings or causes of the attitude which created this structure.

Example 15

A patient dreamt that his son was kidnapped. He ran after the kidnappers, fought with them, and called the police. After this he said to his wife, 'You want to get rid of your son.' The patient loved his son very much but also had recently felt some conscious jealousy towards him. The dream shows the conflict between these two tendencies. His son is kidnapped; somebody in his dreaming, which thus won't be him, gets rid of his son. At the same time he tries to prevent this happening. The negative feeling is also disavowed and projected on to his wife, who becomes the bearer of his unconscious wish to get rid of the child. On the other hand, the fact that he refers to their son as his wife's son suggests that together with the disavowing component there is a disguised delegating component. For otherwise he might have said, 'You want to get rid of him', which is a phrase with no reference to parenthood, in which he was clearly a participant.

At first sight there is no obvious participation of symmetrization in this example. In fact all the mental activities here, as well as the corresponding dream actions, are quite asymmetrical. The patient experiences two desires which, to him, are incompatible, and deals with the problem by means of splitting and projection of the rejected aggressive desires. This is a highly asymmetrical process and one at the service of the unity of the self: a vital function. However, the fact that he projects his aggressiveness on to his wife and the way he does it suggest that this aggressive desire returns to him by means of his identification with her. We may see this particular part of the dream, i.e. delegating and identification, as a bi-logical structure of the symmetrized vector type which leads to his becoming, in this aspect, his wife.

Example 16
A girl had an intense love relationship which satisfied her in various ways. But it also provoked negative and critical attitudes towards her partner, which were connected with some frustrating aspects of his behaviour. It was repeatedly pointed out that she was trying to ignore these negative reactions, for fear they would spoil everything. Her comments showed that she was reluctant to admit it. She went through a short period in which she would say that she was sure the analyst would disapprove of a given aspect of her friend's behaviour and would hasten to add that, of course, she could not be in agreement with the analyst. It was evident that she had disavowed her own criticisms and had dealt with them by the mechanism of negation as described by Freud, because they could not be dismissed so easily. She also split them from her, projected them on to the analyst, and continued to fight them in him. This behaviour showed that she did not want to drop them altogether.

In other words, disavowal and delegation were acting in conjunction. Incidentially, it was through this combination that this subject achieved what Freud described as the function of negation in psychical life: a piece of psychical reality can be utilized in thinking 'on condition that it is negated' (Freud 1925a, SE 19: 235). Like the previous example, this seems a case of a symmetrized vector type of bi-logical structure.

3 Symmetrized vector and Tridim structures. The future of research

The three examples I have just discussed appear as bi-logical structures of the symmetrized vector type. However, they also can be seen, from a certain angle, as the result of an effort to three-dimensionalize higher-dimensional psychical happenings. This would be done in order to keep the self or the ego free from conflicts. Therefore, the question arises whether they rather are Tridim structures or both. So far as I can understand, the Tridim structures I have seen differ in some aspects from the structures of these last three cases. One could think of a greater precision and wider concept in the definition of Tridim structure which would allow the inclusion of other types under the same concept. However, this would not necessarily mean that they are not of the symmetrized vector type. And so the question becomes very complicated.

So far as I can see, to understand this problem at a more meaningful level we would have to know a great deal more about the relations between various different n-dimensional spaces in the human mind, and about the relations that such relations have with the concept of the unity of the self: a very difficult yet most meaningful problem.

A second aspect to consider is that, behind the first, more immediate appearance, there may be other different things. A. Siracusano (personal communication) has recently shown that, behind the typical Alassi structure of the schizophrenic who was bitten by a dog and consulted a dentist, one can discover other non-Alassi aspects. Such considerations lead to the conclusion, already suggested by many other observations but rendered more poignant by these, that, to one's great surprise, we are deeply immersed in the constitutive antinomy of being.

There is much food for thought here. I think we shall never be able to reach complete understanding but will, however, understand more and more, with no end to this progress.

4 Disavowal mixed with delegation to the ego-ideal

Example 17

A patient surrounded himself with a group of women who were definitely unattractive to him or actually, according to what he said, lacking in femininity. Though he had also courted attractive and feminine girls, it always turned out that either these girls were severely disturbed or he chose them because he was in some way unconsciously aware that they would not pay much attention to him. I had pointed out that his putting together a sort of harem made of dilapidated specimens of femininity was the expression of a fear of having attractive women for himself because he felt that these belonged only to his father, with whom he did not dare to compete. One day he asked me to give an appointment to one of these girls, with a view to the possibility of an analysis. I refused, for obvious reasons. He encouraged the girl to telephone me all the same. I interpreted this behaviour as offering me one of his women. He then told me that his grandfather had once made sexual advances to the wife of his (the patient's) uncle. He was very critical both of his grandfather, whom he called an imbecile, and of the man's two sons, the patient's father and his uncle. He remarked how weak and cowardly the uncle had been because he had not reacted adequately to the grandfather's behaviour.

At this point I interpreted that he had behaved towards me in much the same way as his uncle, a father-image, had behaved towards his grandfather. He had submitted to his father in fear and let him make advances to his wife. In fact he had gone further by offering me, symbolically, one of his girls, and had then proceeded to criticize the cowardice of his uncle.

The behaviour just reported appears very complex, but the following aspects could be singled out. There is disavowal of the patient's own feelings (not actions) of cowardice and submissiveness. Second, there is a projection of these feelings on to his uncle as a father-image, consequently seen as cowardly and submissive. This aroused his criticism of him. Third, there is displacement towards his grandfather – a more distant and, therefore, less feared image – of the rage felt towards me as a dangerous father. In fact, the patient gave further evidence for this interpretation when he commented that when one of his girls went to his home she would sit next to his father, while the patient took a more distant chair. In other words, he behaved in a way which resulted in being pushed aside by his father.

After this interpretation the following associations occurred to him: 'This must be connected with the relation with my mother. At times when I was in my bedroom speaking with my mother, my father came to search for us, to see what we were doing, obviously feeling displaced.' I interpreted that he intended to appease his father's reaction to his phantasy of stealing his mother from him, by offering his girl to him.

Consideration of the patient's confident description of the attitude which he felt the uncle should have adopted towards his father, and of how he himself had definitely not adopted it either towards his own father or to me, allows me to make a fourth point. One realizes that he consoled himself for his cowardly feelings by identifying with an ideal image of himself which he had created. In other words, he spared himself the feeling of failure and self-deprecation by identifying himself in phantasy with an ego-ideal built by himself, but very distant from his actual behaviour and not represented in any real person.

The first two processes I have identified, if taken together, can clearly be described as a disavowal-expulsion component and correspond exactly to the first concept of projection implied in Freud's writings. It is a variety of displacement of the projective type. The third process, however, is obviously not a projection but a displacement of an emotion towards another object. Here we see, as we always do in displacement (Matte-Blanco 1959 and 1975a), that one member or element of a class is identified with the whole class (in this case, identification of the father with the class of fathers). The replacement of this element by another then takes place (in this case, the replacement of the father by the grandfather). This second element is, according to symmetrical logic, like any element, identical to the whole class.

The fourth process I have noticed constitutes identifying with an ideal image and is clearly a delegating type of projection. Here something which the individual wishes to do and feels he cannot do, or which it is more convenient for him not to do, is projected to an outside object which is then allotted the function of doing it. The interesting feature of this case is that *the object which fulfils the wish in question is not a specific person, fantastic or real, but an ideal behaviour which is not personified in anyone. It is an ego-ideal which has no human shape but only the shape of a behaviour.* One can see that such a process shows the stamp or seal of the unconscious, which deals with general concepts (classes, sets) rather than with specific concrete persons. Freud wrote (1915b, SE 14: 204) that the schizophrenic's mode of thought 'treats concrete things as though they were abstract'. Viewed from this angle, our example constitutes a rather 'clean' solution. It is, paradoxically enough, an elaborate asymmetrical manifestation of a deep unconscious level which, being so symmetrical, would not be expected to be so subtly elaborated with asymmetrical relations.

I am not able to say whether this example would fall into the category of what Grinberg (1963) calls 'projective identification of aspects of the ego-ideal'. If I have understood correctly, Grinberg seems to have in mind cases where a certain aspect of the ego-ideal is projected on to another person; in our example, instead, it is the individual who identifies himself projectively with an ideal behaviour not represented in any concrete person. Both phenomena, however, obviously belong to the same general category discovered by Grinberg. Reflection shows, I think, that the so-called ego-ideal is, at least in part, often formed through this mechanism of delegation-projection.

This example teaches us, I believe, that a highly asymmetrical and well-delimited course of thinking and behaviour is based upon bilogical structures such as displacement, and on an aspect of symmetrical logic such as treating the individual as identical to the class and, hence, to other individuals who are also elements of this class. In other words, what in each bit of the process of thinking appears as classical logical ends up in what I have called a bi-logical structure of the molar type (see Chapter 7). In our case (example 17), the patient identifies himself with his father and grandfather; and he identifies his father with his grandfather, in spite of the fact that, to his conscious thinking, he considers them so different from one another and, in some ways, quite opposed.

5 The relation between repression–denial and levels of awareness (consciousness)

Example 18
A candidate says in analysis, 'You are thinking that this period (of the analysis) is arid.' Analyst: 'Do you think it is?' Candidate: 'Yes.' Analyst: 'This looks like projective identification.' Candidate: 'But I am aware of it; it is not unconscious.'

This dialogue between a 'learned' analysand and his analyst brings to light a significant problem. Defensive processes are considered to be unconscious, while here a person is aware of one of such processes. In this particular case it was a feeling which was not disturbing to the ego. The candidate's attributing to the analyst something which happened to him was not the result of his desire to disavow-deny this process in himself. It was more a question of giving sharpness and clarity to the feeling he had at the moment and of investigating the reactions of the analyst. In short, *it was more a strategy of the utilization of a feeling than defence against it.* This seems to happen in cases of ego-syntonic proxy or delegation. The aspect of disavowal or denial, so fundamental in other cases, is clearly absent in this case. It must be pointed out, however, that, when the interchange in question took place, the individual was not fully aware of everything that was going on in him. The conception, planning, and realization of the process described went on at a level below consciousness. In this case, it seemed to be at a preconscious level; for it was unrepressed and not denied. This, I believe, is seen in the analysis of primitive impulses of a non-aggressive nature, in which the patient easily recognizes their existence as soon as it is pointed out to him; once the process has taken place, the patient becomes aware of it, in this case with the help of the analyst.

If we follow the candidate's way and see projection from the point of view of consciousness, we find that the 'amount' of conscious awareness depends on the proportion between the various components, and also on the magnitude of each one of them. Delegating seems more compatible with awareness than plundering or disavowal. The latter seems, on the whole, the most incompatible of all.

I am unable to find a bi-logical structure in this example; everything appears asymmetrical.

6 Disavowal-delegation of plundering

Example 19
A patient dreamt that his wife, instigated by him, had sexual intercourse with one of his friends, who had a very big penis. The associations to the dream, as well as the information already gathered in his analysis, led to the following formulation. This patient had various homosexual fantasies, the purpose of some of which was to increase his own potency by acquiring that of virile men, including the friend in question. He attributed to his wife, in spite of her denial, the desire to have a man with a penis bigger than his. He also frequently spoke about the possibility of exchanging wives with his friends. In the dream he seems first to have delegated his wife to acquire the potency of his friend's big penis; then he satisfied his own desire through hers. If she had relations with his friend and then with him his own potency would be increased.

At first sight there was only a small amount of disavowal in the process just described, for the patient was fairly aware of his tendencies and did not reject them altogether. Further reflection, however, showed that things were not that simple. If we turn our attention to the process of delegating his own 'potency-catching' function to his wife, we become aware that it had two different aspects: first, delegation to his wife of his desire to increase his potency; secondly, entrusting her with the function of receiving the penis inside herself – a thing which, anatomically, he was not well equipped to do. His phantasy could subsequently find and take possession of the penis inside her. However, this is not the whole story. I have said that his desire to have the potency of other men was not severely disavowed because he was fairly conscious of it. But the satisfaction of this by means of another desire, that of having the penis inside him, as a woman can have it, was something much more rejected. This strongly disavowed feminine wish was projected-delegated on to his wife. So in the end we could see the delegation of two quite different desires related to the acquisition of the potency of men: one scarcely disavowed, yet delegated, and the other strongly disavowed and also delegated, in part on account of the disavowal and in part on account of the better posibilities of having it satisfied through a woman, i.e. his wife.

There was also a third component: plundering-robbing. This is connected with but not the same as acquiring potency, however intimately the intertwining of both may be. Acquiring potency can be compared to going to a petrol station to get some energy. The plundering aspect, instead, would, correspondingly, amount to the patient's taking possession of the station itself and having it all for himself. In spite of his protests of great cordiality towards his friends, he obviously had a strong fantasy of robbing them of their potency, which he delegated to his wife.

It was evident that in these various aspects he disavowed or denied his tendencies and projected-delegated them but in no way did he abandon them. I may add that his plundering-robbing tendencies were very visible in the transference situation as well. As for the structure of the process seen in the dream, we find in it (a) disavowal-splitting (an asymmetrical process); (b) delegating projection (a vector type of asymmetrical process); (c) identification (partial) with his wife, i.e. symmetrization. In short, this case is best understood in terms of a symmetrized vector type of bi-logical structure.

7 Almost pure plundering-robbing with a small amount of denial-delegating

Example 20

A candidate in analysis reported the following dream. He was driving his car near his home; several people were with him in it. They arrived at a little village a short distance from his own village. It was twilight, and the street was crowded with people. He stopped in front of the house of some distant relatives which was on the top of a hill. The housewife, a very fat lady, got into the car, and the patient closed the door. When he was about to start, he noticed that the brake had stopped working.

He then found himself going to his own village in a ferry boat. He had two suitcases full of things. He left them for a moment and when he returned he found that they had been opened with a knife and emptied. The cases did not contain objects of value, only his linen and some books by Freud. He saw a man with a big bag trying to get out of the boat in a hurry and he went to the purser and asked him to have the man stopped. The purser took no notice of him. He then decided to explore the boat to see whether he could find the stolen objects; he went to the dining-room and searched the drawers where the food was kept, but could only find some soap (*detersivi*). So he gave up the search.

His associations were as follows. The distant relatives were very rich people who owned several factories where they made cheese, beer, and wool fabric. When he was a child he felt envious of them and wanted to be liked by them. It became clear through this and other comments that the first part of the dream represented a sort of robbery of the fat lady. She was the mother of this rich family, who was literally taken away in the car. It was a plundering excursion which yielded the lady herself and two full bags.

The fact of his search in the dining-room for the contents of the bags clearly suggests that these bags, which, he said, contained linen and soap, were also symbols of breasts full of edible things, like the cheese and beer made in the factories of these wealthy relatives. The bags also contained another symbolic food: Freud's books.

What we see here is a clear distinction between wealth, food, and books and at the same time an identity between them. This is a Simassi bi-logical structure based on the identity of psychical food (intellectual contents of the book) and physical food. All are riches.

The fat lady entering the car suggests a massive introjection of the mother with all her contents. In this way he took possession of her and all her goodness. In the dream the mother agreed to it, as is shown by the fact that she herself got inside the car. At the same time there was a suggestion of robbery, seen in the fact that it was he who closed the door of the car and also in the fact that the car now had no brakes, and was bound to run downhill quickly; both details suggest the idea of escaping.

The suitcases made him think of his testicles, which he under-valued, as is shown in his insistence that the cases were cheap. The suitcases were testicles and also suitcases, i.e. identity and distinction: *a second Simassi structure*. Note that at first sight this structure is not directly formed, as the first is, through the use of the equality of psychical and physical reality. In fact, what the testicles may symbolize (potency, power, and so on) is another question which is, so to speak, in the background of the dream and also is *a third Simassi structure*: potency = testicle; and potency is not a psychical reality but a physical manifestation. The very disguised and subtle Simassi structure here is the identification of the testicles with their function, a thing which cannot be taken for granted in classical logic. The unconscious everywhere!

In fact, Freud's books reminded the candidate of two things: first that he had invited me to visit him in his village and second that my own house had actually been robbed. He knew this because the thieves had broken through the window of my consulting room, and he had seen the damage caused. He had been impressed by the episode and had asked what had been taken away. Actually, I answered by telling him that apparently the thieves were frightened by noises from inside the house and had run away quickly. The only thing found missing from my study was a book by Anna Freud. The man who came to see about the repairs said jokingly that it was a consolation to think that at least the thieves would benefit from reading the book. I was amused by the remark and repeated it to the candidate. He was concerned about future robberies and had recommended me to install an electric alarm system.

It is evident from all these associations that the dreamer had had the phantasy of entering inside my study and, through symmetriz-ation, inside me, lived as a mother. In his phantasy he wanted to rob me of my analytical knowledge, symbolized in Anna Freud's book as well as in Freud's books in the dream. These latter also represented the symmetrized class containing the father's penis as well as all phallic symbols which, on account of symmetrization, were all the same thing. All were inside the mother: symmetrization-identification, of physical and psychical inside, while maintaining the difference. In other words, this phantasy is *a fourth Simassi structure*. This appears quite directly, on the first plane of the associations.

On the other hand, as we have seen, the first part of the dream suggests he had taken various foods from his relatives' factory and run away with the booty. The booty is also personified by the mother, the fat lady, who herself was also a content of the larger mother-factory. This is another example of symmetry which makes a fat mother equal to several important factories. There is both identification and distinction between content and container and of a human being with a set of factories; it seems that the fat lady is a part of the set of factories and also symbolizes and deeper down *is* the whole set of them. This is 'facilitated' by the fact that she is fat, and thus contains many things inside her. This is *a fifth, more complex Simassi structure*.

The fact that the brakes of the car went wrong just at that moment, when he was on a hill, is a nice example of disavowal-denial of the plundering combined with delegating. It was the 'responsibility' of the car, and not his, that the car had no brakes and, as a result, could run downhill. This seems to be a delegation to the car of the patient's own intentions: a purely asymmetrical bit of the dream.

This candidate had had some phantasies of magically becoming an analyst in a day and had felt frustrated because at a certain stage of his training he had felt he was being held back by problems which had arisen about the formal training rules and regulations. This had revived in him feelings he had in his high-school days, when he eagerly wanted to be promoted and became very angry if any obstacle were put in his way. In this context he had relived old phantasies of obtaining what he wanted by plundering and robbing. When he started to treat patients by analysis, he had some phantasies of being devoured by them. It was obvious here that he had projected his own devouring tendencies on to his patients and at the same time had identified himself with his analyst. The result was that he feared that he, as an analyst, might be robbed and devoured by the patient, in the same way as he, as patient, had wished to rob and devour me. He was also afraid that I might disapprove of his way of conducting analysis. All this corresponded to an aspect of himself which was very much repressed; one may, perhaps, say split off. But, judging from the information given by him, it seemed to me that his performance as a young analyst was quite satisfactory, as was his behaviour in his work, love life, and relations with people. It was

212

only after a prolonged period of analysis that we were able to reach these deep phantasies of robbing and devouring. This led to a substantial increase of inner freedom and clarity about psychological processes.

The case I have been discussing gives a fairly 'pure' example of the plundering component. It is mixed with a certain amount of denial, seen in the fact that the suitcases do not appear to be directly filled with the 'oral booty' taken by him in phantasy but with his own linen. The fact that he searched for them in the dining-room, instead, clearly suggests food. This was replaced by a symbolic substitute in the form of Freud's books, which as a candidate he was allowed to read. Furthermore, denial–delegating can be seen in the fact that he appeared as the victim and not as the perpetrator of the robbery.

The inverted molar bi-logical structure. With regard to the structure of the dream, we find no visible violations of classical logic in its manifest content, nor in the immediate aspect of his associations. At the presentation level bi-logic is not visible, not even to an analyst; for everything, actions or thoughts, is expressed in respect of classical logic. It is only the analysis of the interrelations between the various parts of the dream and a study of the deeper meaning of the associations that permit the discovery of the component bi-logical structure: *five Simassi structures.* In the end we can see that the total structure of the dream appears respectful of classical logic, while some of its parts are, instead, bi-logical. This situation is exactly the opposite of what we find in the molar bi-logical structure in which the details are expressed in terms of classical logic but the whole is bi-logical. We may call it a set of Simassi bi-logical structures which do not appear at the presentational level but are present in the details and at the molar examination of the materials. In short, it is an inverted molar bi-logical structure.

The question of psychotic phantasies. Another interesting feature of example 20 is that the dreamer was quite a normal person. Contrary to what is frequently believed, plundering phantasies are not necessarily highly pathological nor connected with great aggression. They may be the expression of intense oral desires which in themselves need not be very disturbing nor very aggressive. It seems that *normality or pathology as well as aggression or peacefulness are dependent not on the type of phantasy but on the way the various levels of symmetry–asymmetry are organized. They are a function of structure and not of content*, as it is sometimes wrongly suggested when analysts speak, for instance, of 'psychotic phantasies'. A phantasy is in itself neither psychotic nor neurotic, and these adjectives are a function of the role the phantasy plays in the whole psychic organization, and not of the phantasy itself. Any normal person may have, at deeper levels, the 'wildest' of bi-logical structures. This subject needs a great deal of further study.

8 Plundering reversed into violent getting out

Example 21

The same candidate had the following dream.

'I was in a little villa near a small lake. It was twilight, and the place was very quiet. Three girls, who were at the edge of the lake, called me in a state of agitation and fear because they had seen an enormous monster emerge from the water. I understood that it was a question of the projection of their unconscious and reassured them. I myself was quite unworried.'

Among the associations, he commented that the three girls were the three women patients he was analysing at the time. The monster emerging from the lake reminded him of the Loch Ness monster, which in his phantasy looked like a prehistoric animal, a sort of dinosaur with a very long neck.

I frankly cannot remember but among other things I interpreted that the three girls represented the feminine aspects of his own personality which he had sent to placate the monster. After this interpretation he developed a conscious fantasy of being inside the abdomen of his mother, the small lake, from which he said, 'I emerge, tearing it with evil violence. It was as if it were a sheet of paper torn and punctured by a finger. I felt evil anger and experienced great anxiety.'

After some days he reported:

'When I was going to sleep I tried to reproduce the state of mind of the fantasy which I described to you and I soon succeeded in reproducing it. I was again seized by a strong anxiety and fear of destroying and being destroyed; I succeeded in controlling the situation and on two or three occasions I managed to bring this destructive fantasy into focus in my consciousness and then dismiss it. I think that this anxiety may be similar to experiences one has when the ego is about to be overwhelmed. Finally I became sleepy, satisfied with the experience I had just had, and slept calmly.'

A few days later he reported the following dream.

214

'I went down a steep path towards a small beach bounded by vertical walls of rock falling towards the sea. The rock was worn away by the dampness and spray of the sea, and small niches had been hollowed out in the walls; they contained the mummified bodies of various people which had become smaller than lifesize.'

On associating, he immediately thought of the walls of his mother's uterus having the mummified bodies of his siblings.

As a general comment on these dreams it is worth bearing in mind in the first place that the subject was a candidate attending lectures and seminars and was, therefore, in the midst of trying to 'master knowledge about the deep unconscious'. This may account for a certain artificiality and learnedness in his associations. Another fact, however, was more important than this. As already remarked, he behaved quite normally in his everyday life and was admired and liked for his ability to get on with people, for his efficiency in his work, and for various other aspects of his personality. During the analysis we had worked on his character structure, whose most striking feature was a certain rigidity and lack of spontaneity. Gradually we had come to see that as a child he was very sensitive, emotional, and prone to suffer from external psychological stimuli. To protect himself from over-exposure he had developed an outward toughness, a sort of hard crust. In his analysis he had, so to speak, resumed his development, precisely from the point where he had become rigid. He was very anxious to accelerate the process and this explains his desire to push his emotions to their utmost limit, as was shown in the 'experiment' mentioned above, of trying to bring out his feelings into the open. As a consequence of all these reactions there was a certain artificiality in his associations, behind which, however, one could detect his intense real feelings. In other words, it was possible to see that behind his learnedness there was a real correspondence between the associations and his inner processes.

An attempt at gaining insight. In the first dream and in its associations we see the unconscious phantasy, not of entering but of violently getting out of his mother's inside. In his phantasy he identifies with the father inside the mother, and wants to make a hole in his mother's abdomen to get out. In other words, we see, *not a violent penetration but a violent getting out.* This corresponds to unconscious phantasies of being trapped, as a counter-attack against his plundering activities. The plundering component of projection is seen, therefore, indirectly through the phantasy of fighting his way out, which suggests that the mother responds against his own invading attack by trapping him inside her. We here see the projection, on to the mother, of his invading violence; as a consequence, this plundering violence reappears in the mother but in a reversed form: trapping.

The example illustrates a curious and rather complex process. First, the violence is disavowed-denied and projected on to the person against whom it is directed. As is well known, this is a common occurrence. Second, the projected violence changes direction; the mother does not attack him by plundering, as would be the case in projective identification, but traps him inside. Note that he had projected himself as a plunderer on to his mother, and, since in his phantasy he was inside her, she had, in consequence, become not the representative of the patient but the patient himself. We may surmise this as happening at a deep level and not at the presentational level. This is shown by the fact that at the manifest level, as it appears in the dream, plundering had changed into trapping, which clearly indicates that the mother still retained her own identity and defended herself from the attack. We may call this a condensation: the image of the mother was both the patient and herself, but only this latter aspect appeared at the presentational level. An interesting thing here is the fact that one of the elements of this condensation is the opposite of the other: getting out becomes being trapped. This is a new structure in which one of the elements or components employed to form it is actually not present in it from the beginning but is a new element resulting from changing or reversing an initial element into its opposite. In this sense the patient becomes identical to the mother in the fact of defending himself, only she does it by trapping and he by trying to get out.

In the last dream about the small beach we see some aspects of the nature of his attacks: the corroding urine, the destruction and complete paralysis of his siblings, their reduction in size. It is interesting that he was the eldest child.

I cannot find any traces of the delegating component in this material. One can detect a certain disappearance or dissimulation of the dreamer's identity, which becomes that of his mother. Penetrating her and being trapped by her seem to be equivalent, and this suggests an abolition or at least a confusion of spatial relations, of dreamer and mother. On the surface, however, these dreams move within the zones in which things conform to the laws of ordinary space. Even the apparent confusion between entering and being trapped can be described in terms of retaliation rather than of fusion. In the depth, instead, we see important con-fusions: the dreamer with his mother, plundering with being trapped.

In short, dealing as it does with aggressive fantasies, the last dream appears to be essentially structured in terms of asymmetrical relations and is, therefore, to be located in the region of happening. This provides an illustration of the concept that aggression, which entails actions in the physical world, belongs to this region. As I have pointed out several times, without asymmetrical relations there cannot be aggression. However, as we go deeper into the unconscious we enter an increasingly immobile stratum where we find the two confusions just mentioned. Deeper still, in the realm of pure symmetry, with no movement, there cannot be aggression. This deeper aspect of the dream belongs, therefore, to an intermediate or superficial region.

I find it very difficult to understand the dream's structure and I must leave the reader to consider it for him- or herself. I do think, however, that a number of points need to be kept in mind:

(a) the presentational asymmetry;
(b) the reversing of plundering into trapping;
(c) the suggestion of deeper levels where we find the identification of plunderer and victim, who becomes defendant and, with her, so does the plunderer. How dizzy are the deep levels! As if to make the situation more provocative, they appear dressed in such asymmetrical terms as plundering and trapping.

If any of my readers think that what I am discussing here is a thoroughly disposable figment of my imagination, I invite them to re-read Freud's chapter 6 of *The Interpretation of Dreams*, and in particular SE 4: 312, second paragraph. What he says there is no less wild than what I am discussing. And it is true. I feel at times like Benvenuto Cellini when he went to the Colosseum to witness a seance in which the demons were called. At a certain moment he and his companions were surrounded by demons who wanted to attack them. Trembling, trembling, trembling, trembling, they defended themselves inside a circle of fire which kept the demons at bay!

I feel that we will gradually get more used to the dizziness of the deep unconscious so eloquently described by Freud and vividly recalled by Klein. But we will have to face still more difficult problems in the coordination of such dizziness with rigorous thinking. I have little doubt that we will succeed eventually and find some clear roads to advance along with relative safety. The reward will be another spark of Truth and the consequent, reverent admiration and joy.

9 A reflection on the death instinct[3]

I believe the comments I have just made may be pertinent to a reassessment of the concept of the death instinct.[4] Here I shall only make a brief comment. In the first place, aggressiveness and the death instinct should not be considered to be the same thing, as is sometimes implied. Freud described the death instinct as a tendency to return to a previous state; as an illustration he mentions the migration of the salmon. Now this book has been stressing that the deepest unconscious – and, 'beyond' it, the indivisible mode of being, where symmetry rules and there is no space–time, no movement, no happening – always makes itself present. There must almost inevitably be a confusion between this mode and death, which we are used to identifying with lack of movement. If Freud's ideas are reformulated in terms of the relationship between the indivisible or symmetrical and the heterogenic or asymmetrical modes of being, we get a clear expression of a deep insight which Freud seems to have had but not expressed in a satisfactory way. Then it would not be the death instinct which we come across with, but a desire for the indivisible mode, which makes itself present in more or less dissimulated ways.

If this is true, then Klein's idea that the death instinct is projected outwards at the beginning of life could be reinterpreted as follows. The new-born baby finds himself disturbed in his 'immobile peace' by the irruption, for the first time, of various sorts of very intense desires and impulses which are highly heterogeneous or asymmetrical, yet full of symmetry, as their intensity shows. He then tries to avoid conflict – creating asymmetry in order to remain at a deep level of symmetry as in the womb. This results, so far as his development already allows him, in a confusion of self and external world and does not rid him of his intense feelings, for he is now in a symmetrical world.

I believe that, if seen from this angle, the problem appears in a new light. One can begin to understand why the Freudian conception of the death instinct would provoke two conflicting sentiments. On the one hand, there is the tendency to reject it as non-biological and, on the other, a feeling that to do this amounts to rejecting a deep and mysterious truth, however strange and disquieting it may appear. It seems too simplistic to think, as some seem to, that the Freudian conception is no more than the mistake of promoting entropy into an instinct.

10 Some examples of the basic matrix of introjection and projection

Example 22
A bi-modal non-bi-logical structure
A patient was becoming bald and was worried lest women should be less attracted to him. One day he arrived rather excited and asked me if I noticed anything about him. He had a wig on, which disguised his baldness but did not hide it completely; it was unnoticeable to a casual observer. The patient felt embarrassed and thought everyone would find out and laugh about it. He attributed to others his own criticisms of himself for wearing the wig.

This attribution does not seem to be describable in terms of disavowing, plundering, or delegating. In fact, the patient had himself recognized, accepted, and acted upon his own desire to correct his lack of hair by means of the wig. On the other hand, he had a spontaneous conviction that others had exactly the same critical attitude which he himself had about the question. Under the pressure of some obscure feeling which had become active in him, he looked at other people, in that respect only, as though they were exactly the same as himself.

We may say that in this very circumscribed stratum of the psyche the limits between the patient and others had disappeared. We are obviously confronted with a manifestation of the basic matrix. One now asks: is this a bi-logical structure? The answer is not easy. In the first place we must remember that we speak of a bi-logical structure when we are confronted with a co-presence of symmetry and asymmetry. I have described this co-presence in terms of different bi-logical structures. That there is asymmetry in the case we are considering, as in all psychical manifestations, is undoubtedly true. Now, is there symmetrical logic? This question could be expressed in this case by asking if there is or is not a distinction between self and others. The patient obviously attributed to others feelings and thoughts which he did not know they had. But they might easily have had them, for, in his human environment, to wear a wig could easily be considered somewhat ridiculous, which is what he felt.

What we can certainly affirm is that, whether bi-logical or not, this is undoubtedly a bi-modal structure. In favour of it being bi-logical is the fact that the person attributes to others feelings and opinions which he has and does not know that all others have. We all make this type of attribution in everyday life, and such a thing appears quite different from attributing, for instance, one's own aggressive

219

desire to another. One would call this latter a projection, whereas our patient would only be making a mistake, but only when there is such a mistake. This leads us to the idea that a mistake of this type of similar to the frequent incorrect generalizations which we all make in everyday life.

In other words, the concept of symmetrical logic seems to entail a reasoning which violates classical logic in the sense that it is incompatible with it: the fundamental antinomy. In the case of the man with the wig, we do not see such antinomy; we see only a non-use of classical logic in the sense that he draws a conclusion which is not warranted but is not incompatible with classical logic in the circumstances in question. So this seems to be bi-modal but not bi-logical reasoning. It is a non-bi-logical bi-modal structure. This is, after abstraction and generalization, another type of non-bi-logical bi-modal structure. It seems to me that it puts important new questions about the frontiers between bi-modality and bi-logic. It looks like a profitable territory to explore.

11 Introjection and projection at intermediate levels

Example 23

A patient dreamt that he was in a sixteenth-century palace whose owner or director was a nun. He felt uneasy in front of her, as he frequently really did in the presence of nuns. She took him through the various rooms of the palace. In one of them she showed him a skeleton wrapped in rugs and said that it was that of a former girlfriend of his. He did not believe her. In another room he found this girl, who shrieked and denied being herself; she was mad.

Important though it is, I shall not dwell upon the meaning of the dream in terms of past and present conflicts. For our present purposes I shall concentrate only on some of its formal characteristics. The following associations are pertinent.

The patient had a terror of nuns because he felt them to be like jailers who limited the liberty of children. Their wimples, with long wing-like appendages, were frightening to him. He also felt that nuns were, in their turn, imprisoned in their respective convents. After telling the dream he remembered some stories about nuns being walled in and buried alive. These also frightened him. On the other hand, as the nuns had their hair cut off, he thought they must look very ugly with their wimples off: not a single hair on their heads. As a child he was afraid that they might carry him away and, when he saw a nun in the street, he would clutch his father and seek his protection from abusive and violent kidnapping. Finally, he also referred to the nuns' loose ample dresses, with so many folds; here so many things could be hidden. Obviously he feared being trapped there.

I want to consider the relation of these associations to the notions of inside and outside, to symbols, and more generally to the question of symmetrical and asymmetrical relations.

The atmosphere of the dream suggests confusion between various things which in ordinary life are clearly distinguished from one another. This confusion is not explicitly stated, only suggested. For instance, from the molecular (detailed) point of view each part of the dream respects classical logic. Yet the elements are arranged in such a way that from the molar (total) point of view the whole dream story suggests an indivision. Note that, if these examples are all taken together, they convey an atmosphere of ambiguity which is difficult to grasp, at first sight, when each is considered separately.

A first example may be seen in the fact that the nun was inside a palace. But, since both nun and palace are mother-symbols, we may translate this by saying that the mother was inside the mother. This said, we may conclude from it, in classical logic, that the palace, being a mother-image, was inside the nun. This, however, is not explicitly said but seems to be implied in the dream.

Next: the nun said that the patient's girlfriend was present inside the mother-palace in the form of a skeleton, i.e. dead. He did not believe her and later saw the girl alive in the palace. The girl, on the other hand, denied her own identity. In other words, we see here three assertions next to one another: (a) the girl is dead; (b) she is alive; (c) she is not the girl. But these assertions are made by three different people: the nun, the dreamer, and the girl. This fact shows or implies a respect for the principles of both identity and contradiction.

But the dream is not likely to be the expression of a controversy regarding these possibilities. We may, instead, follow Freud and say that, in the way things are presented, it is suggested that all three are true for the dreamer. In classical logic this is not acceptable. So we may conclude that the dreamer both respects and does not respect the principles of identity and contradiction. We might also add here that there both is and is not a distinction between being alive and being dead (Simassi structure) and also between being and not being identical to oneself (also Simassi bi-logical structure). What is more, not only are the alternatives of each pair confused, but also both pairs of alternatives are confused. We may call the confusion between the alternatives of each pair a *unification-indivision of the first degree*.

221

Then the confusion between both pairs would be a *unification-indivision of the second degree.* We may call this a *Simassi structure of the second degree.* Such a type of thing does not happen, of course, in every dream. There are dreams in which disrespect for the alternatives 'either/or' is not as visible as here, and other dreams in which it is more so. Viewed from this angle, this dream belongs to an intermediate level of depth.

Something quite similar is seen in the fact that the patient felt at the same time: (a) that the nuns were jailers who limited the liberty of children and were kidnappers of children; (b) that on their part they were jailed in their convents, and were walled in and buried alive there. Strictly speaking this is not a case of treating the asymmetrical relation 'x is a jailer of y' as though it were symmetrical. What is actually affirmed is:

(a) 'the nuns are jailers of children';
(b) 'the nuns are jailers of themselves'.

'To be a jailer' in classical logic is not a symmetrical relation. It is neither reflexive nor irreflexive; it is simply non-reflexive. Here it is treated as such, i.e. in respect of classical logic. In other words, from the 'molecular' point of view classical logic is respected. But from the 'molar' point of view there is a suggestion of indivision; the jailers are jailed by themselves. It looks as though 'putting in jail' had 'struck' the jailers themselves, and in this way, even though classical logic is, strictly speaking, respected, there is an all-pervasive quality about the fact of being jailed: it invades everything. This suggests molar indivision carried out with (molecular) heterogenic components.

Next, you will remember the patient feared he might be sucked into the nuns' garments. This corresponded with his desire to penetrate into and explore his mother's inside. Here, where a desire is expressed by its reverse, we get a suggestion of non-distinction between opposites. Note, furthermore, that here the action 'putting in jail' is the same in both cases, but the person changes from dreamer to nun.

These types of unconscious manifestation which at times seem to defy all attempts at ordination in terms of logic are also, of course, frequently seen in schizophrenics. They may be understood very well if we constantly keep in mind that it is a mixed product, a subtle combination of our two logics which enter into various types of intertwining between themselves: again, the fundamental antinomy!

If we now try to get a synthetic view of what is implicit in the dream, taken together with its associations, we may say that, in contrast to what is seen at the deepest levels, we have the following features at the intermediate levels: the notions of inside and outside, the distinction between persons, and the distinction between a relation and its converse are clearly existent and visible. But they get confused on account of the use, or the irruption, of symmetrical relations in a 'process' which is asymmetrical in the details of its logic. In short, we see bi-logic in an example of an inverted molar structure which we have described before and which corresponds to an intermediate level of depth.

It is at these levels that introjection and projection (which presuppose the distinction between inside and outside) begin to emerge. It is likely that it is at such levels that we observe the phenomenon described by Klein as confusion. This is the expression of a reduced availability of asymmetrical relations.

12 Disavowal does not necessarily entail a complete severance with the self

Example 24
A girl belonging to a family of humble position had a good school record, had entered university, and had obtained a doctor's degree. The educational disparity with her family had become very great. Subsequently she had several psychotic episodes. A prolonged analysis succeeded greatly in modifying her difficulties, and this paved the way to good progress in her career. Her improvement provoked distinctly negative feelings from her relatives.

It looked as though they had felt inferior to the patient on account of her achievements but had denied it. When she became psychotic they were, so to say, compensated by her illness. It seemed here that they had projected their feelings of inferiority on to her and had reached a state of equilibrium in this way. It was as though they said to themselves: '*she* is the one who is inferior, not us'. When she improved they could no longer live this fiction and had to recognize, however unconsciously, that the girl's capacities and education were superior to theirs. Their former feelings were revived.

Assuming this reconstruction to be accurate, we may say that the relatives' reaction to the patient's illness was of a disavowal-denial type of projection. They had freed themselves of something which they did not want to acknowledge as belonging to them. Subsequent developments then forced them to 'take back' what they had expelled. In other words, it seemed that the link between them and the aspects of themselves which they had projected had remained 'there' all the time, however hidden. To understand what had happened to these people we may use the concept of projective identification and say that this was the mechanism they had employed from the beginning, and that now, under the pressure of circumstances, they were forced to undo their projective identification. If we view things from this angle we may then conclude that there is no projection and that the only thing visible here is projective identification.

Further reflection, however, leads to understanding that doing away with the concept of projection and replacing it by projective identification is not quite satisfactory because it blots out the real distinctions which are indicative of real differences.

A third alternative way of looking at things seems more satisfactory. This is to recognize that what may be true for a certain level of the mind is not necessarily true at other levels. The form of projection then depends on the degree of availability of asymmetrical relations, which in this case means availability of time and (correspondingly) space. As we have stated several times, at the level of the mind where spatial and temporal relations (asymmetrical) are unknown, there is not and cannot be a separation between self and not-self. In consequence there cannot be an expulsion or projection, because this entails a distinction between self and the outside. Projective identification or projection-disavowal, therefore, 'happens' only at more superficial levels of the unconscious. At deeper levels, in contrast, something which, if seen from superficial levels, has been expelled still belongs to the self, because, at these levels, everything in the external world belongs to the self. At still deeper levels biological structures get more blurred and finally disappear.

When, as in cases such as the one mentioned, something returns after being disavowed and projected, this must, therefore, be considered from two types of level. At the superficial level the returned thing is felt as being forced into the self; it is received unwillingly as something alien. At a deeper level it has never left the self. *So, if the mind is turned outwards, a happening may be felt as an intrusion; but, when it is turned inwards, it becomes a rediscovery within the self.* Most probably both things happen at the same time, so this may be a source of confusion for the person.

I believe that if we do not consider this dialectic of the unconscious we shall fail to understand many facts regarding introjection and projection. On the other hand, we need further experience along these lines to be able to handle these apparent contradictions so as to be able to let them 'merge themselves in a higher truth that comprehends them'. This is how the Oxford Dictionary puts it when discussing dialectic.

13 The separation or distance between desire or wish and the object of satisfaction

I shall first present the analyses of two examples and then use the results to discuss this subject.

Example 25
A patient with strong oral–cannibalistic desires had various phantasies whose unconscious content was that of eating from or devouring women. Correspondingly, he showed in various ways his fear of being devoured by them. In this connection sexual relations represented a way of eating from the woman and/or eating her. Correspondingly, they also represented the danger of being eaten by her. The psychical processes involved in these phantasies were by no means simple. First, there was a component of projection of the plundering type, which led him to enter the woman and take possession of her contents. There was, however, something else, as was shown in his fear of being devoured by women, in whom he saw his own cannibalism. It is obvious that this view of women did not correspond to the plundering component nor to the delegating one, but was rather nearer to the disavowing–expulsion component. Some further precision is required here. It could not be said that disavowing–denial was present to a marked degree, for the patient acknowledged to a great extent his own desires as well as his voracity towards women. It could even be said that he feared women precisely as a consequence of the awareness of his own voracity. It seemed as though he attributed his own tendencies to them and for this reason he feared them. In other words, the problem was not so much the expulsion of a disavowed–denied desire – this is an exquisitely asymmetrical affair (a happening). On the contrary, he felt women to be exactly as he, almost consciously, felt himself to be. He did not separate self and not–self. In still other words, he had fear of himself in the woman or, still more precisely, fear of himself as a woman. This means that the distinction between self and not–self was not clearly established at the level of this fear. This is a case in which we are confronted with the basic matrix of introjection and projection.

Example 26
Another patient had phantasies of devouring a woman with his

penis; this is clearly an expression of the plundering component: entering inside the woman and devouring her. He also feared castration: that he would be deprived of the instrument with which he plundered. Here we see again that his aggression – which was not necessarily denied-disavowed as belonging to him – was also attributed to women and was expressed in his phantasies of being plundered-robbed-castrated by them, i.e. deprived of his aggressive instrument for plundering. This is equivalent but not identical to the 'plunderer' who was afraid of being trapped (example 21). Both are elements of a wider equivalence class of patients. Note that in these two cases the distinction between 'plunderer' and 'victim', in contrast to the patient in example 23, is maintained. The victim reacts with a defence appropriate to the attack and different from it. Therefore, there is no obvious identification between them.

The same patient had another fantasy. He felt he should always have his penis in erection. To him this meant (unconsciously) having it in a state of readiness to penetrate the woman and accomplish the plundering of her inside. Since he feared being devoured, his erected penis served him, in this context, as a weapon to defend himself from the devouring attcks of women. But also his positive tendencies found expression in this fantasy; his erected penis was an organ which was ready to offer pleasure to the woman.

We may now try to understand *the structure of these (conscious) fantasies* in the light of the two modes. The distinction between the patient himself and the woman was clearly established in both cases. The retaliation which he feared corresponded to the (fantasied) normal asymmetrically structured reaction of a woman who is attacked. In other words, everything seems to develop in terms of the asymmetrical mode. So far I am not able to find any manifestation of bi-modality or bi-logic in the presentational aspects of this case; everything proceeds as it would in the *actions* of everyday life, which obviously must respect classical logic. This, however, does not exclude the possibility of bi-modality or bi-logic at deeper levels.

Note, therefore, a surprising awareness: these circumscribed fantasies can be described and understood at least in their superficial aspects, without making any use of the Freudian notion of unconscious or of bi-logic. It strikes one as a rarity in psychoanalytic work. Perhaps it is not. It would be interesting to study this further.

In general, the cases where we see a mixture of several mechanisms belonging to different levels are also illustrative of another aspect which, in certain cases, must be taken into consideration if we wish to approach an understanding of the complexity of projective mechanisms. I am using the concept of the distinction between the aim, through desire or wish and the object which satisfies it or through which it is satisfied (Freud 1915a, SE 14: 122) in order to show that at times there is a separation or distance between them while at other times there is not. Frequently we may observe that a given object serves to satisfy a certain wish or desire, while another serves to satisfy another wish. In both our cases just mentioned the wish was to devour the woman and was expessed by means of, or resulted in, the fear of being devoured by the woman. The wish was satisfied in the first aspect of the case (devouring with the penis) through the general meaning of sexual intercourse, and in the second aspect through the specific meaning attributed to the erected penis. There is in this latter case an added complication; the unconscious activity of the patient did not lead to attributing to the woman a penis which could attack him but led only to the fear that she might deprive him of his penis, and this meant at the same time a defence and plundering on the part of the woman. In other words, though he and the woman were not distinguishable from one another so far as the desire (plundering) was concerned, the object that was to satisfy this (accepted) desire was not the same, at least initially: the penis in his case, castrating attacks and taking possession of the penis in her case.

In other words, at a very deep level the patient saw the woman, not only as having exactly the same desires as his, but as though she *were* he. At a more superficial level, in contrast, he established the distinction between having and not having a penis, i.e. between himself, a man, and the woman. *So far as the desire was concerned, he was the woman; so far as the object which satisfied this desire was concerned, he was quite different from the woman.* In the first case, instead, the object was the same in both cases: sexual intercourse, to which a devouring meaning was conferred. We may, therefore, conclude that in this case not only did the patient not distinguish himself from the woman with regard to his wishes but neither did he distinguish himself from her with regard to the object with which to satisfy such wishes. The result was that the confusion between himself and the woman was far more radical and, consequently, more frightening than in the second type of projection; he feared his own vividly felt strong desires.

In short the first patient (example 23) saw the woman as he himself was. This corresponds to the deepest levels where the distinction between self and not-self is not yet made. Such deep levels would, in this case, be 'observed' by the more superficial levels where space–time and, therefore, aggression exist, and would be interpreted in the correspondingly terrifying way.

14 The unavoidable dizziness of 'deep' analysis: dissolution of space–time and of the distinction between subject and object

It can be gathered, perhaps, from the panorama of these examples that clinical manifestations and explanations can become extremely complex. Alternative views can be seen to have equal rights to accuracy so that one begins to wonder whether a point may come where psychic life is ineffable.

Here, I think, it is essential to remember that as we go 'deeper' we begin to enter the strata where time and space relations are dissolving, where asymmetrical relations begin to decrease, and we find ourselves confronted with increasing proportions of symmetrical relations. We are then approaching the region of what I have called *symmetrical frenzy* (Chapter 2, section 2, and Part Four). Space–time coordinates become increasingly hazy, so that persons and things begin to fuse with one another until we reach the region described by Freud, where time – and, we must add, space – does not exist. This sort of journey seems to be what happens in the first stages of anaesthesia by the inhalation of gas and in confusional states. It must be kept in mind that this unconscious region is not within direct reach of our intellect because we are unable to think without asymmetrical relations. The unconscious then becomes a reality which belongs to the non-experiential realm, to use the distinction put forward by Sandler and Joffe (1967). Here we are reminded, once more, of Freud's deep intuition when he wrote that 'The Unconscious is the true psychical reality: in its innermost nature it is as much unknown to us . . .' (1900, SE 5: 613).

I think the time is overdue for psychoanalysis to consider systematically the perpetual co-presence and intermingling of time-ness–spaceness and timelessness–spacelessness or, more generally expressed, of heterogeneity and indivision, which constitutes the very essence of human nature: an insight which, though not explicitly formulated by Freud, springs directly from his conception of the unconscious.

Notes

1 I must clear up a point. I have described projective identification (PI) as a symmetrized vector structure which ends up in a Simassi bi-logical structure. In this chapter I am presenting several examples of symmetrized vector structures and I have not named them as PI. The reason is that

there may be some differences of opinion regarding the question whether such structures as mentioned here, while still being symmetrized vector structures, are PI or not. I prefer to leave this question open because, I feel, we are not yet prepared to face it at the present stage of development of our concepts. Note, however, that if these structures were different from PI we would have to establish the differences, and this would lead to distinguishing several varieties of the Simassi.

2 It seems that the delegating component frequently presupposes a disavowal, but not always; for one can entrust (delegate) a protective function to somebody without necessarily disavowing this function. The plundering-robbing component, in contrast, usually seems to be quite naturally associated with disavowal.

3 I am here using words such as 'instinct' and 'tendency' which according to some modern ways of considering the subject would be inaccurate (cf., for instance, Bowlby 1969). Since this is not the moment to discuss this question in full, I will only remark in passing that frequently in psychoanalysis when we speak of 'tendencies', 'drives', 'impulses', or 'instincts' we are in fact making use of possibly more or less sophisticated terms, to refer to the non-sophisticated, more direct concepts of 'wish', 'desire', or 'feeling'. These latter do have a legitimate place in modern instinct theory. I must in all honesty add that the aversion – sometimes it could be called horror – of some 'modern' psychologists for the word 'instinct' seems to me a highly emotional and bi-logical way of being scientific. Also, on my part, I find that the words 'desire', 'wish', and 'feeling' serve as effective and sufficiently eloquent ways of pointing out, in a general manner, the corresponding realities we study in psycho-analysis.

It will be seen, on the other hand, that in the short reflection that follows the word 'instinct' is used in order to be faithful to Freud's writings as translated in the *Standard Edition*; and it is used with the intention of focusing on another, not the 'instinct', aspect of the question. As is known, some people have objected to Strachey's translation of *Trieb* by 'instinct'. I feel that what I have just affirmed in the preceding paragraph probably holds also here. So, following Strachey, I continue to use 'instinct', though 'wish', 'desire', or 'feeling' would do as well.

Symmetrical frenzy, bi-logical frenzy, and bi-modal frenzy

Prologue to Part Four

Two examples of symmetrical frenzy

Some years ago I put forward the concept of symmetrical frenzy (see Chapter 2, section 2, and Chapter 10, section 14). This corresponds to the deeper strata of the stratified structure and can be observed in confusional states. I shall make a brief mention of two examples.

Example 27
This is a personal experience which led me to become aware of the question. Many years ago I was submitted to surgical anaesthesia by gas. I began this experience in perfect consciousness. After a few seconds I saw some things which seemed bright lines and, perhaps, other figures as well. These began to move, something like rotating. The movement became more and more rapid; the visual perceptions began to lose their neat distinction from one another, frantically whirling. Everything was losing its identity and fusing into everything else. My conscious awareness was losing its grip of reality, and I became more and more con-fused until I completely lost consciousness.

This example shows, I think, that our consciousness is intimately linked to or dependent on the perceptual distinction between things. Furthermore, we cannot become aware of the existence of the various perceptible objects if we do not have asymmetrical relations at our disposal, which enable us to distinguish one object from another. On the other hand, our thinking cannot make conceptual distinctions if asymmetrical relations are unavailable. We can conclude, therefore, that our consciousness, in the form of either thinking or perception, needs such relations in order to conceive psychical objects (thoughts) or perceive physical, so-called material objects as different from one another. Pure symmetry is totally incompatible with human consciousness.

Example 28

A man in his seventies was submitted to prostatectomy under general anaesthesia. After the operation he had a mild confusional syndrome. At a certain moment he hit his wife, a small, frail old woman who had been his loving companion throughout decades of married life. I was called for a psychiatric consultation. He received me politely and with a certain suspicion. I suppose he did not understand who I was and why I had come to see him. In order to establish some contact with him I said that I understood he had been operated on, on the prostate gland. He answered that it was his car and not he who had undergone such an operation. A little later I broached, slowly and gradually, the question of his having hit his wife. He flatly denied this.

This case is an example of a mild confusional syndrome in which we see the subject's loss of distinction between himself and his car. Again here we can detect, from a phenomenological point of view, a localized absence of the use of asymmetrical relations and, consequently, a con-fusion, through symmetrization, between two entities, himself and his car, which cannot be recognized as different from one another if certain asymmetrical relations are not available. In contrast with example (27), where the symmetrical frenzy covered the whole field of consciousness, we see it here restricted to only a circumscribed aspect of awareness. We may call it a *localized symmetrical frenzy*.

Note that, in both examples, a physiological alteration in the brain provokes a disturbance of consciousness. This latter, in its turn, could perhaps be satisfactorily and accurately described, even in its details, in terms of the presence or disappearance of *this* or *that* asymmetrical relation, in correlation with the step-by-step physiological changes observed in the brain: a beautiful opportunity for research on the psycho-physical relation!

From all the above we can conclude that *symmetrical frenzy is a more or less intense disappearance of the normal structure of thinking or perception, due to a physiological alteration which provokes a disappearance of asymmetrical relations and their replacement with symmetrical relations. This results in confusion between different things.*

This Part Four deals with something quite distinguishable from symmetrical frenzy, yet belonging to the same realm of the relations between symmetrical and classical logic. I have known examples of it for several years but I did not understand them fully. In fact it is only very recently that I have become aware that these examples are good illustrations of a curious and surprising aspect of the fundamental antinomy which I now propose to call bi-logical frenzy. To put it in a provocative way (I mean provocative of reflection and surprise), I would say that all of us humans live most of our life in an antinomic bi-logical frenzy without even suspecting its existence. I mean to say that *bi-logical frenzy is the surprisingly unnoticed and constant presence of the indivisible mode, in all aspects of our psychical life, ignoring in various ways, at times quite blatantly, the rules of classical logic, yet smuggling its way to acceptance in ordinary life, disguised in the various forms of bi-logical structures.*

A comparison between the definitions enables us to realize that, while bi-logical frenzy is a constant presence in our daily life and is not in itself a pathological manifestation, symmetrical frenzy, instead, is usually found, so far, in abnormal circumstances, except perhaps in some unusual cases of the beginning of the process of natural sleep.

I shall try to show various aspects of this new concept by means of three examples developed in the next three chapters.

11

The multiplication of three-dimensional objects

1 An example of bi-logical frenzy

Example 29

The case I want to discuss concerns a young man of high intelligence who suffered from severe obsessional neurosis, which disturbed his life to a very great degree. He had various sorts of inhibitions which showed the invasion of symmetrical logic into conscious thinking, in spite of the fact that his reasoning capacity was extremely high. He had successfully passed all his examinations for his Ph.D., in the USA, with the exception of one subject which he postponed in-definitely. He constantly brought into the sessions various blatantly bi-logical reasonings worthy of the most severe schizophrenics, which he obviously was not. I shall concentrate here upon one small detail which, however, clearly illustrates some points about the concept of internal world.

Before going to bed he had to empty his bedroom of every object which might cause him anxiety. In particular there was a picture of a landscape which reminded him of his grandmother's native village. In a more or less conscious way he thought that to leave this picture at night in its place would amount to having his grandmother in the room, and this meant sleeping with her, which then meant indulging in impure acts with her. On the other hand, not being psychotic, he realized in some way that things were not as he thought them to be. Here is a strange, but very common, mixture of experiencing two incompatible conceptions.

One day he told me that he had felt the need to take all books with red or blue covers away from his room. He explained that these were the colours of blood and, if they remained there, he would be invaded by thoughts which would disturb his sleep. Several other comments he made are relevant:

(a) 'I have visual representations inside my mind which are copies of the external world.'
(b) 'Each object represents something, and if the object is inside the room then the thing must also be inside the room.'
(c) When he put the objects 'in another room, there must be a safe distance between them. For instance, to put the cigarettes and the clock on the same table is dangerous.'
(d) Arteries and veins were 'symbols of life. The artery is the source of life.' He feared that 'by expanding, it [the artery] may cause some trouble which I must contain inside myself. The vein in particular may be damaged: a passive object which might suffer a sort of flood from the artery and so be damaged.'
(e) He furthermore explained that, when trying to get his mind free from these links between objects or persons, mathematics was very useful to him, because mathematical abstractions did not have such links. For instance, if from experience of the expansion of an artery he passed on to the concept of expansion, he was then relieved. This was because 'expansion is an extremely abstract concept', hence without dangerous associations.

Among his numerous hypochondriacal symptoms there was one which particularly disturbed him. He had some sensations on the left side of his forehead and was convinced that this zone was red, in spite of the fact that nobody else had been able to confirm this assertion. He feared that a dangerous process was taking place in that region and, as a result of it, something might rupture. This argument was discussed at length.

2 Discussion

Having in mind our previous knowledge of the patient I shall now discuss these data. We may say in the first place that the fantasy of the expanding artery which floods the vein and damages it – (d) above – is an expression of the fantasy image of the penis which erects, penetrates the vagina, floods, and damages it. In other words, this is the primal scene. The same fantasy is implicit in the precautions taken to prevent the cigarette, a phallic symbol, from damaging the clock-mother – (c). If this possibility should become a reality, he must then contain it inside himself because his visual representations are a pure copy of the external world. They are material objects.

In other words, it seems that the patient has introjected the primal scene, which he has probably witnessed. As a result, this scene has become both external and internal at the same time. The introjected objects remain independent from him and disturb him to an extreme degree. His fantasies about the primal scene are also expressed by the sensations of his forehead. They correspond to the sexual activity of his parents, which might gravely damage him. This symptom also has other meanings, but I shall not stop to consider them now.

The image of the internal world is seen here in terms of the same type of correspondence existing between external and internal (physical) objects. Both external and internal are three-dimensional worlds. This correspondence is particularly clear in this case, for the patient's own fantasies and fears are expressed in terms of a three-dimensional world. I think that this is also in keeping with the present-day psychoanalytical conception of the internal world. In many other cases things are not as simple, and cannot be understood in their entirety in terms of such a naïve notion of the internal world.

A first complication arises when one considers that internal objects are at the same time present outside; this is seen in the pairs: red books/blue books and cigarettes/clock. Here two aspects of the internal world are seen at the same time. On the one hand, there is that corresponding to emotion; this aspect is felt as inside the subject. On the other, there is that aspect which is represented outside through certain objects and certain actions (i.e. in relations or operations).

Looking into this curious state of affairs it became clear to me that the fantasies of the patient about real objects (the parents) and events played a fundamental role. His internal world reflected his interpretation and elaboration of certain real events. In other words, his internal world, the phantasies and fantasies and feelings which he had developed, started from certain real events. It then existed simultaneously inside and outside him. The changes which he caused outside (for instance, to separate the cigarettes from the clock) had an immediate repercussion; they happened simultaneously in his inside. In one particular case we have mentioned, the internal parents become 'quiet' as a consequence of his having kept apart the pair red books/blue books from the pair cigarettes/clock. It must also be added that the pair cigarettes/clock was not the only external correlate of the relations existing in the internal world. The effects were, however, somewhat different in different cases. For example, the separation of the clock from the cigarettes was necessary to tranquillize the patient's internal objects even if from a distance.

However, in the case of the books, the only thing the patient wanted was that the books should not be near him, and he did not worry about what they could do to each other in the next room.

It seemed as though two factors were at play. On the one hand, there was the importance or weight which the meaning of the objects in question (cigarettes, clock) had for the patient at any given moment. On the other, there was the distance of the books from the patient and, hence, from the objects inside him. The presence of these two factors makes one almost think that a symbolic law of Newton was at work. There was just a suggestion that the interaction between the various internal object inside the patient and the internal objects 'outside' him would be directly proportional to their 'mass'. In this case we would be equating mass with the importance that an object had for the patient. What is more, the force or effect of an object was inversely proportional to its distance from the patient. It would, however, be going too far to pretend that it was directly proportional to the product of their masses and inversely proportional to the square of their distance!

It must be remembered that in this example the so-called external objects, such as books, clocks, and cigarettes, act not as real things but only so far as they represent the internal world. They act in his obsessional world as internal objects placed outside the patient, which still remain inside, however.

3 A geometrical interpretation of the patient's internal world

However much the three-dimensional, material representation of the internal world may initially appear to be satisfactory, as soon as we begin to study things in their intimacy we discover a series of fundamental differences between psychical phenomena and their representation by means of physical things and relations.

We know that in the material world each object is only one object and is in only one place. A particular, individualized chair, for instance, is that chair and not any other. Also, if it is inside a room it is not at the same time outside. In the psychical world, instead, we have seen that the primal scene also happened inside the subject of example 29. This apparent absurdity becomes understandable if we view the unconscious as a set of bi-logical structures. In that case, something which for thinking (classical logic) happens outside may also be seen by thinking as happening inside, because for the sym-metrical aspect of our being there is no distinction between outside and inside. So the primal scene may contemporaneously be seen as outside, inside, and nowhere; and also it may happen and not happen but just be. All depends on the aspect our thinking chooses when it tries to understand the behaviour of the indivisible aspect of unconscious manifestations. In the stratified structure, however, we find all of them. Remember also that the unconscious knows no negation and, hence, treats an assertion as identical to its negation. And so we see that the primal scene took place in three places and *was* not one but three different scenes seen in terms of classical thinking and logic. In fact, it happened first inside the patient, second where the red and blue books were, and third where the clock and cigarettes were: three scenes in three places.

But, if we see the events from the point of view of normal thinking, the primal scene was only *represented* in the mind (or head) of the patient. It is obvious that nothing of this can ever happen with an ordinary physical chair, clock, book, cigarette, or any other three-dimensional object. This makes us acutely conscious of the fact that *the three-dimensional image of the internal world, however much it may have helped in a first approach to the problem, soon reveals itself as utterly insufficient to reflect the enormous complexity of psychical reality.* It must be noticed at the same time that the notion of three-dimensionality implicit in the conception of the internal world has been a fundamental step in our understanding of the mind. For instance, if only the concept of the libido had been employed, the Kleinian approach, which is the starting point of a conception of the internal world, would probably not have got anywhere.

In this book I am contenting myself with presenting some problems as clearly as possible, and making a few suggestions regarding the road to follow for later developments. My comments about this example can be very brief. The primal scene may be represented very well in terms of a three-dimensional image and can also be felt as if it were happening inside 'the mind'. 'The mind', in its turn, can in fantasy be felt as localized inside the head. But, when the primal scene is felt as happening simultaneously in different parts of three-dimensional space, then things become more problematic.

There is, however, a simple possibility which may help understanding. We noted (*Figure 3*, Chapter 3, page 88) that when a mathematician represents a space of n dimensions by means of a space of $n - 1$ dimensions, the spaces of dimensions inferior to $n - 1$ appear repeated in this representation. Now, to consider our case, we have seen that the primal scene was lived by the patient with great emotional intensity. If we follow the conception of representing mathematical spaces, the emotion in question seems to reveal itself as an experience of the primal scene which would be that of a phenomenon corresponding to a region of a space of many more dimensions than three. I say many more dimensions because the objects which represented the primal scene were actually many more than those I have mentioned.

The following idea is also known in mathematics. Given that an n-dimensional space is represented in terms of a lower number of dimensions, then the higher the number is, the greater will be the number of repetitions of parts of that space. We seem to have something like this in this case. The primal scene is repeated over and over in three-dimensional terms. This is what would happen mathematically if a multidimensional figure was expressed by figures in a lower number of dimensions.

I am not yet in a position to establish with precision how many dimensions, in the mental reality of this patient, there were in 'the region of the primal scene'. It seems possible in principle, however, that a more careful clinical observation might succeed in counting all the three-dimensional repetitions of this scene. The resulting number, together with a more detailed application of the geometrical notions just mentioned, may tell us exactly how many volumes a given n-dimensional space 'yields'. This might enable one to assume the number of dimensions of the space represented.

I suggest that, bearing in mind the procedure just mentioned, through the multiple appearances of the same objects, we may begin to understand many problems connected with the notions of outside and inside of the mind, as seen in the light of a more detailed knowledge of geometry and topology. Even in this case, however, we probably would not be able to reach a complete understanding of the reality in question, for there is a third problem I want to mention.

4 Internal world, indivisible reality, and infinite

First, I note that the primal scene was lived by the patient in example 29 in terms of enormous aggressiveness – perhaps related to the fact that he felt his father was extremely dangerous. Second, various objects as well as relations between objects were seen by this patient as intellectual images of a very sadistic primal scene.

From the point of view of the deep unconscious, paternal penis, artery, and cigarette are one and the same thing, and so are also maternal vagina, veins, and clock. The relations (operations) between each of the various couples (penis/vagina, artery/veins, cigarette/clock) are the same as those existing between the elements of each of the other sets. In this way the patient arrived at a complete identification of all three sets and of the relations (operations) between the elements of each of them. In other words, it seems to me that *the isomorphism existing for mathematical thinking between the elements of a certain abstract structure has become in this case absolute identity or non-differentiation between the three structures; all become actual sexual relations.* For a mathematician, these three structures formed by the pairs are all different from one another and only isomorphic between themselves.

We can describe this result in two ways. We can use the help of the principle of symmetry to enable us to follow all the stages of this 'process', or we can simply say that a reality which for rational thinking appears complex and divided into diverse aspects is now 'seen' as though it were one and hence indivisible. All those things which, with our reasoning, we see as symbols of objects or activities are for the indivisible mode the same thing; an isomorphism becomes total identity. For this mode of being, therefore, such things are not distinguishable from one another. There does not exist, for this mode, the distinction between part and whole nor the distinction between anything and anything else, whether they be material objects or persons. But relations do exist in this mode (see Matte-Blanco 1984). I have come to this conclusion only very recently and through the study of the mathematical infinite.[1]

This is, it seems to me, the deepest meaning of the Freudian discoveries about the unconscious. It is obvious that such discoveries would not have been made and even would not have been potentially discoverable if reality were not divisible and if thinking, which divides and separates, did not exist. Deep down the Freudian concept of symbol reflects the simultaneous expression of the separation and at the same time the identity between the symbol and that which it symbolizes. It is a Simassi bi-logical structure.

Exactly the same process would be in action in the internal world as I have tried to show. It seems highly probable that in the case of the internal world we may find correspondences between certain psychical phenomena and *n*-dimensional spaces, i.e. finite-dimensional spaces. As a limit to such spaces we find the infinitely dimensional spaces. Infinitely dimensional spaces would be the image of an indivisible reality. It is here of interest to become aware that this situation would not be different from that existing in mathematics; in fact, it seems clear to me that the paradoxes of the (mathematical) infinite can best be interpreted as being bi-logical structures, i.e. structures in which the indivisible reality is a component (Matte-Blanco 1980, 1984).

5 The bi-logical structures of the material discussed

I want now to compare the variety of repetitions of the same objects and the interrelations between them found in my patient's case (example 29) and what happens in displacement, described as a Tridim bi-logical structure in Chapter 2. In contrast to the usual cases of displacement, the multiplication of volumes found in this case is considerably greater. This suggests that the space which is expressed in terms of three-dimensional sub-spaces may have more dimensions than do the usual Tridim structures considered so far. If this were the case we should conclude that *Tridim structures may be distinguished between themselves in terms of the dimensions of the space which is three-dimensionalized.*

I have a strong impression that the multiplication of objects is an expression of the great intensity of the patient's emotions with regard to the primal scene. If this were so, we would be confronted with a very *new and possibly fertile conception: the more intense an emotion is, the greater the number of dimensions of the geometrical objects which represent it would be.* Note that this would be a geometrization of a concept (intensity) alien to geometry. This is something similar to the theory of relativity's replacement of time by a fourth spatial dimension, which, as such, and unlike our experienced time, does not flow but is just there.

We have noted that the Tridim structure expresses the concept of displacement, a characteristic of the unconscious which we have found to be bi-logical. The possibility of three-dimensionalization may also open up the possibility that, if we represent it as a loss of dimensions, we may describe it all in terms of geometrical classical logic. I feel that this question should be explored. It is not easy to do, and in so doing we encounter puzzling facts. In *Figure 3* (Chapter 3, page 88) we took a triangle (*ABC*) and then expressed it in the form of a line. We found that the same point *C* appeared twice. But in the line, even if we call it *C*, it so happens that each of the two points we call *C* is defined in terms of a distance from the origin which is different from that of the other point *C*. Hence, both points are different, because each point is always uniquely defined in terms of the distance from the origin. Therefore we have at the same time one point *C* in a plane which is two different points *C* in a line. Both are the same point, otherwise the triangle would not be such. Further reflection about this question could lead to a unitary super-logic (see Chapter 3, section 9).

6 A second way of looking at the structure

It is quite clear that the patient in example 29 felt or knew at the same time both the differences between the various objects and situations and their identity. This corresponds to a Simassi bi-logical structure, and a curious one because the patient was not psychotic. It is the same type of thing that one sees in the concept of mathematical infinity. However, emotion plays no role whatsoever in the mathematical infinite, whereas here in the clinical example it is, we may say, a cause of the patient's conception. There is much more to reflect about here.

On the other hand, one asks: how come that there is at the same time, in the same things, a Tridim and a Simassi structure? My answer would be: *this case shows a 'process' of three-dimensionalization or a Tridim structure which results in or expresses itself by means of a complex Simassi structure. I say complex because of the number of pairs of objects.* Let this suffice for the moment.

7 General conclusion

I hope I have succeeded in showing that, if we take all the known clinical facts under consideration and we study all their interrelations with implacable rigour, we find we are led into a jungle of fascinating and even frightening possibilities. I also think that, as we get more used to it, we shall understand more, and fright will give way to admiration and joy.

We may summarize this case (example 29) by saying that it is, first, a beautiful example of the fundamental antinomy. In fact all the strange aspects of the case are the expression or consequences of seeing and living the same things in two incompatible ways, the symmetrical and the asymmetrical. Without their co-presence none of the symptoms mentioned could exist. Bi-logic enables us to reach some understanding of it.

On the other hand, it is most striking to see how fantastic, wild, and incredible the symptoms are. Put otherwise, this is not only a beautiful example of the constitutive antinomy but an equally beautiful example of bi-logical frenzy.

Notes

1 The conclusion just mentioned leads to a correction in all my writings before 1984, where I have affirmed the contrary.

12

Bi-modal frenzy

1 A case of bi-modal frenzy

I shall discuss this with the help of an example which, as will be seen, is quite differently structured from the example in Chapter 11.

Example 30
This case deserves special attention because it proposes various important conceptual questions. Here are some details of a period of an analysis. We had been repeatedly considering the patient's attachment to his mother, which was also connected with deep aggressive feelings towards her. This was intensely lived in the transference situation. The analyst was felt to be a powerful mother who could give him what he wanted; at the same time he did not wish to feel any gratitude towards him, and this led him to deny the obvious progress made in the analysis. His denial was, however, ambivalent, because frequently and almost in spite of himself the patient would comment on the very noticeable improvements both in his behaviour and in his relations with others.

After a particular session where we discussed the patient's difficulty in accepting improvement he dreamt that a friend said to him, 'How changed you are, and how different your face is.' In the dream he denied this and took off his glasses to show that he was the same. His friend looked at him and shook his head.

Among the patient's associations he mentioned his desire to change, and also a distinct feeling of weakness. He interpreted the dream as expressing that he had aged, was finished, and should prepare to die. He added that maturity means ageing, and death would therefore follow. He went on to say that he had never stopped to consider the possibility of death, which was something quite theoretical for him. He never thought of the future but lived only from day to day.

This dream shows a denial of his feelings about his own internal reality and a projection of them on to his friend. His denial was sufficiently strong that in the dream he had rejected his friend's remark that he had changed. The problem, however, was not resolved by the dream, for he actually felt he had not changed for either the worse or the better. His comment that maturity leads to ageing implied that if he were to have the benefit of maturity he would also get the very opposite as well, and against his will.

These feelings were connected with intense fantasies about the patient's mother, which can be better seen in a second dream, reported in the same session. He was inside Saint Peter's, Rome, where his four children had been baptized. Among his associations he mentioned the various architects who had built the cathedral: Bramante, Sangallo, Raphael, Michelangelo, and Bernini. The cupola made him think of an abdomen, and its top of a phallus, an umbilicus, and a nipple, all at the same time. He then spoke of his intense attraction to girls' breasts and buttocks. A moment later he thought about his own car. He always had fine cars, with special distinctive features and powerful engines which could reach very high speeds. Recently he had bought one with which he was particularly pleased; he took great care of it, one might even say it was tender care. He had lent it on one occasion to a friend and had worried lest his friend might get hurt.

From the associations reported in this session and from previous work it could be concluded that the car represented the patient's mother's body as well as his own. In Italian the word for 'car' is feminine. He said, 'I want to possess her, control her, identify myself inside her, share one body with her, something like a centaur. At the same time I am afraid of harming myself. The car goes badly when I feel bad.' If the sparking-plugs were dirty it was as though he had damaged his mother. At the same time he had noticed that he had a tendency to damage the car, by slightly scratching the paint or other similar small actions. He felt that these actions were propitiatory and served the purpose of preventing greater damage. On the other hand, he felt them as self-inflicted damage. He commented at this stage that when he had made some scientific experiments on cats he had had feelings of guilt for having killed the cats. He had noticed that every time he participated in such experiments he inflicted some small damage on his car. 'I have made up for killing the cats by harming my car.' I interpreted this type of behaviour as self-punishment for imaginary attacks on his brothers and sisters, personified in the cats.

2 An attempt at understanding

This material is indicative of many things when taken with other information about the patient. I shall here only focus on those related to our subject. In the first dream we can clearly see a denial of the recognition of his change and a projection of this recognition on to his friend. This may be connected with his fear of and reluctance to experience gratitude. On the other hand, the change was reversed from being better to being worse. It had become a destructive change which spared him from feeling grateful, but at the same time could not be tolerated. So in the dream he projected the recognition of his change on to another person. However, it was his own dream and it was fairly clear that the figure of his friend could be an aspect of himself. We may conclude that this process was in some ways a denial, in others a recognition. He found it difficult to accept that he had changed because of the dangers that this acceptance implied, among others the possibility of ageing and death. But, in spite of these manoeuvres, the knowledge of his change remained in the patient. I am unable to say whether there was a splitting of ego-functions, such that there was a simultaneous acceptance and rejection of the recognition in question, or whether one must invoke another entity in the self, seen as different from its own ego-functions, which took over this recognition. In any case it may be confidently said that there was a process of denial, possibly connected with splitting. We can also say there was what may be described, paradoxically, as an *intrapsychic projection* of the aspect denied, in this case a recognition of an aspect of his internal reality. He looked at his inside as though it belonged to another person but had at the same time a form of awareness that it was his own inside. In other words, he was distanced from himself as well as not distanced: an intrapsychic projection.

We can, I think, say that *from one angle a certain aspect of the patient's internal reality was completely denied but from another it was completely accepted.* In order to coordinate, not combine, these contradictory attitudes there was a certain form of splitting which permitted both the acceptance and rejection by attributing them to different 'parts' of the self. Here, exemplified by the imagery of the dream, it is not a question of a combination or mixture of partial acceptance and delegation, on the one hand, with partial rejection, on the other. It is a coexistence of complete acceptance-delegation with complete disavowal-denial. Both aspects are kept quite apart from each other. This seems a clear example of an attempt at resolving the fundamental antinomy with the help of only the heterogenic mode. As such, it is a failure.

Put in other words, the ego or self, which was originally one, has been divided, with regard to this question, into two aspects, one of which has taken over the denial of the reality in question and the other the acceptance. This can be conceived as an example of the creation of certain asymmetrical relations. It is a new birth of a contiguity and from this point of view it is an intrapsychic projection. From another angle, however, it is only an apparent projection, because this concept implies movement from one 'place' to another. A true projection has an isomorphism with space, but here is a case of something appearing in space (distance between both aspects). But it comes from nowhere, from 'no-space': once more, the fundamental antinomy.

Now let us turn our attention to his second dream. You will remember the patient was inside Saint Peter's Cathedral in Rome. Both from the point of view of general symbolism and from his own associations we may consider this as meaning being inside his mother: the cupola-breast-womb crowned by a nipple-umbilicus-phallus. The architects of the cathedral, all of whom he named, were images of his own father as well as of his mother's father. In particular they can be seen as his mother's husband, his own father, in two different roles, as husband and father. You will remember that the associations led to his own cars, which were, on the one hand, like his mother and, on the other, expressions, in power and speed, of his masculine potency. Inside the church he was with his brothers-sisters-children, but in the car the relationship was exclusive; he and his mother-car were one, like a centaur. This required the excluding-killing of his siblings-cats-children. He paid for it by causing some damage to his self-car-mother.

In other words, the dream shows various condensations, seen in the fact that each element of the dream simultaneously plays several roles. Contiguity seems to be lost here, and we see an extensive use of symmetrical relations which squeeze various elements of a set or situation into each other, so that one stands for, and at the same time *is*, all the others. This occurs, for instance, in the case of the cupola, which stands for and also is the abdomen and the breast. These are different parts of the mother which appear as only one. Moreover, there is an identity between part and the whole which makes the cupola stand for and also be the mother. Likewise the top of the cupola also stands for and is the penis. Note, however, that *PS is not visible*.

The aspect which I would like to consider in most detail is the identification-fusion which the patient made, through his car, between himself and his mother. We have seen that he was inside Saint Peter's. In his previous dream his improvement amounted to his decay and death. This was connected with strong fantasies of robbing his mother and taking hold of her possessions. He would be punished for this by being dispossessed of everything, including his own life.

So we may assume that being inside the church was, from this angle, the expression of a plundering-robbing attack upon his mother. But in his associations we may also surmise that he had taken hold of his mother-car to such an extent that he had become identified with her and, incidentally, had also taken hold of his father's potency. We could, therefore, say that, *by invading her, he had enlarged the limits of his own self, so that he had become 'himself-mother'*. Was this an introjection or a projection? If we consider that he had entered and was inside the church we may say that he had invaded his mother, and entered inside her.

However, if we consider his associations about the car, we can say, equally correctly, either that he had *included* her within himself or even that he had *fused* with her. All three possibilities seem to have equal claim to correspondence with the dream and its associations. Alternatively we could say that all three are equally inaccurate ways of expressing his inner reality by the limited means of pictorial description and association. Note that the word 'pictorial' is used to emphasize that psychical reality is described here in terms of images, which themselves are representations of spatio-temporal phenomena. We can at least conclude that terms either of entering inside another person (projection) or of putting the other person inside (introjection) are both equally inaccurate ways of describing the reality that is being conveyed to us by the dreams and associations. What we really are witnessing is a *dissolution of contiguity relations*, that is, of asymmetrical relations. To insist on describing this state of affairs in terms of these very relations which are disappearing amounts to a falsification of this reality.

3 The insufficiency of present-day conceptions of introjection and projection

Let me repeat that at this level of psychical reality it is equally inaccurate to describe the facts of the dreams and associations in terms of either projection or introjection. At a level higher than this, where there is more availability of asymmetrical relations (inside-outside, first–after), these alternatives would not be identical. On the other hand, at a lower level, where symmetry is more conspicuous, there would no longer be a question of equivalence, identity, or lack of it, between such descriptions, for the simple reason that both would be meaningless to thinking. This is because without asymmetrical relations one cannot conceive space–time; so any description of this level which uses such concepts is out of place.

We must therefore conclude that we are looking here at a reality which is becoming increasingly symmetrical, that is, increasingly spaceless–timeless. But we have eyes which can look only in terms of space–time or of asymmetrical relations. No wonder, then, that our descriptions are inaccurate. This is why it is wrong to try to frame certain clinical facts in terms of introjection or projection. We are forcing a certain aspect of reality into a mould which does not fit it. We end up by giving a false description of it.

To be fair, I must point out that even in the middle of my efforts to 'picture' reality more precisely I cannot avoid employing space–time, as is shown in the use of expressions such as 'picture', 'levels', 'dissolution', and many others which, a careful reader will notice, are redolent of space–time. This also happens when people speak of 'structure', a concept built on the spatio-temporal model. In other words, we are handicapped by the limits imposed by the nature of our thinking. But it can be hoped that familiarity with this problem will lead to a more careful consideration of the nature of reality and thence to a better description of it.

Which structure is appropriate to this example? It looks as if the patient is in some ways at a level where the concept of bi-logical structure begins to dissolve, for the intellect, into nothingness. To explain, we have, in this case, already noticed a series of condensations, and these, obviously, are bi-logical structures. I suspect, however, that they are, so to speak, springboards offered to the patient and to us by our nature, which we can use to make dives into deeper waters of symmetry. So, we can say that, in so far as he is a thinking human being, he experiences himself as different from his mother, his car, Saint Peter's, etc. But this is at a conscious or superficial level. In so far as his deeper feelings are shown in the dreams, he is himself, his mother, father, cathedral, and its dome. So we have both symmetry and asymmetry and we could call this a Simassi structure. However, I hesitate to call it this because the concept of Simassi structure implies two simultaneous ways of seeing the same reality, whereas here the asymmetrical and symmetrical aspects seem to be at vastly distant levels. This case seems different from that of a stratified structure. There we see the exact pertinence of symmetry and asymmetry about the same piece of reality, at the same level. Here I do not feel it is so. I would describe it in the following way: neither in the dream nor in the associations can we find the presence of PS. Put both together and we find a variety of condensations, displacements, etc. In other words, when separated both respect the heterogenic mode; together, we find PS. I propose to call this *bi-modal frenzy*: we arrive at the two modes without violating, in the details, the rules of the heterogenic mode.

I hope this example shows that the approach put forward contributes to a better understanding and a more faithful rendering of the great store of subtlety underlying the clinical facts with which we are in daily contact, while at the same time it poses new problems and leaves us – temporarily, I hope – in the midst of unanswered questions.

4 Conclusion

This is the case of a person who is well within the range of normality. The study of his associations during the sessions, together with his dreams and their corresponding associations, reveals an extreme complexity and poses various difficult problems. The dream about Saint Peter's and the associations to it show that the cupola has various meanings while still being the cupola itself: the fundamental antinomy. The subject is the same as the mother-car, which also is himself alone: again the antinomy. The notions of projection and introjection begin to lose meaning in some of his manifestations: the beginning of the zone preceding total symmetry and symmetrical frenzy in the stratified normal structure.

In summary, if we consider the set of all our findings, we become aware that this is a complex case of bi-modal frenzy. In fact, if we did not see the presence of both modes throughout the material presented, the whole of it would be incomprehensible. Dream and associations, however, are an example of moderate bi-modal frenzy.

13

The upheaval of spatial and temporal structures in the dream world: the spatio-temporal Multidim structure

Foreword. The relation within psychical reality of the duality external–internal, in three or *n* dimensions, is one of the most revealing manifestations of the dream. I shall use one patient's dream as a second example of bi-modal frenzy.

1 A dream

Example 31

A man in analysis dreamt that he was looking at a geographical map of the Molucca Islands. In the lower part the names were written in Spanish whereas in the upper part they appeared in French. He was trying to find Lourdes and did not succeed. He also realized that the map had been marked with pencil by Mrs P, a friend of his mother.

In another scene he was about to take a jumbo jet together with his mother. There were many people waiting, and they knew that not all of them would be able to take the plane. As he wanted to make sure that he would get a place, he began to walk towards the landing area, got lost on the way, and found himself in a place where it was forbidden to enter. He anxiously asked a man working there for permission to pass; this man made him enter the area through a zone forbidden to passengers. He finally succeeded in getting on board the jumbo and found two places in the forward section. He felt happy about this because, he thought, this would facilitate going up, with his mother, to the small upper lounge. The seats were also very comfortable and were arranged in such a way that they could become a bed, where his mother would be able to lie down. At that moment he saw his mother, who had succeeded in getting on board and was coming to join him.

During the preceding sessions in the analysis we had been able to understand some meanings of the patient's smoking which had not been considered before. When he was small, his mother used to speak against the habit; his father was a smoker. He also knew that, when his parents were engaged, his mother had given his father a beautiful cigarette box, which he still used. He therefore felt that his mother was not coherent: forbidding him to smoke, while accepting and in some way participating in his father's indulgence in the habit. Putting the cigarettes inside the box given by his mother, which must have represented her, seems to have constituted a form of symbolic coitus. At one time during his childhood the patient began making some cigarettes out of leaves wrapped in small sheets of paper. With great secrecy he used to put these in a tin box given to him by his mother for some other purpose. In this way he imitated and shared the symbolic coitus of his parents. It could be seen from this that smoking constituted something forbidden, a form of incestuous sexual relation.

Mrs P was one of two sisters, friends of the mother, both of whom had remained spinsters for almost their whole lives. As a young girl, P had been engaged but was abandoned by her fiancé shortly before the wedding. After this she decided never to marry. At a late age, however, she changed her mind. Fairly soon after her wedding she became a widow.

Before the patient made this association, I had commented about the Molucca Islands. Since I did not remember well, I asked the patient whether they were the same as the Celebes. He confirmed this. (When later on I looked at the map I realized that they were not the same but only located near each other. This external fact, however, does not seem important, as can be gathered from what follows.) Now, when speaking of Mrs P and her sister, instead of saying that they were 'spinsters' or 'unmarried', he employed the Italian word *celibi*; this was incorrect because, as he himself pointed out, such a term is used in Italian only to refer to males. The oddity of bringing to the same session a dream where the Celebes, never mentioned before, played a role was too striking not to have a meaning. I wondered whether the fact that I had mentined this name could have caused his association. The patient said, however, that after the dream and before the session he himself had in fact thought of this alternative name for the Molucca Islands. It could, therefore, have a meaning.

Coming now to the aircraft part of the dream – the jumbo, going up into the air, can be seen as the image of an erecting penis. This interpretation might seem rather far-fetched, but it becomes much more plausible when linked to the fact that in the dream the patient was also having a bed prepared for his mother. This amounted to implying that he would have taken his mother to bed. Mrs P, on her side, deprived the geographical map of its 'virginity' by marking it. Various other details, added to these, lead to the conclusion that the dream expressed, among other things, a phantasy of sexual relations with his mother. This was a phantasy about which we had spoken in the preceding sessions, when discussing the meaning of smoking and the cigarette box.

2 A comment about the contents of the dream

It became clear that the dream was a point of convergence between a set of recent events and infantile emotions. These were linked to tender and sexual desires towards the patient's mother. In fact it represented the realization of various aspects of a relationship which until then was felt as extremely forbidden. These aspects were forcefully suggested in the following features:

(a) The romantic air trip to the Molucca Islands, which aroused in the dreamer the possibility of exciting experiences.

(b) The participation and mutual sharing between the patient and his mother: he rushed to find a place in the plane, and she fought against obstacles to join him on board. The obstacles, overcome by both the dreamer and his mother, seemed to represent the various prohibitions upon tenderness and sexuality. Worthy of attention is the fact that Mrs P, who 'deflowered' the map of the Molucca Islands, had been abandoned by her fiancé and only after long years succeeded in getting married. As it happens, this situation is isomorphic to the analysand's long wait into adulthood to find a partner. The same thing also applied to his mother, who had married quite late.

(c) The expectation of beautiful moments in the small lounge of the plane.

(d) The bed which the dreamer had affectionately reserved for his mother meant, if taken literally, to 'take her to bed'.

(e) The fact that the loving embrace should take place in the air, among the clouds, towards the sky, suggested a romantic detachment from everyday life, a loving ecstasy, an enthusiasm.

(f) The big rising jumbo plane was a dithyrambic representation of a most powerful erection.

In short, the dream represented or suggested various aspects of an intense, romantic, tender, and sexual union. The intensity of the emotions is very relevant for what follows, for I suggested in Chapter 12 that the more intense an emotion is, the less does a three-dimensional representation of the situation correspond to it. In other words, *intensity seems to constitute a prerequisite for the upheaval of three-dimensional spatial relations.*

3 The contrast between material or external and oneiric, internal reality

Let us start with observable events. If wishes and feelings, together with the recollections from past life which serve to make them apparent, are expressed by means of material or physical actions, we can then usually observe the development of a sequence of actions. Each act will have one or more meanings and precise spatio–temporal relations with the other actions in the sequence. In other words we are confronted with a spatio–temporal structure. An actual sexual relation, for instance, develops through a certain sequence: lying in bed, showing tenderness, caressing, arousal, erection, penetration, etc. Each of these actions has, in a concrete case of intercourse, a precise spatio–temporal relation with the others.

Turning now to the internal world, when we tackle the study of this structure, we do so by studying its representation by means of conscious images which are culled from memories of the material world. It becomes of primary importance to establish where a faithful image of this internal psychical world diverges from an image which would faithfully describe the sequence of corresponding material events. We frequently find, of course, that a dream completely distorts the normal sequence of material events. It is Freud who, more than anyone, has illuminated these distortions, particularly by pointing up the characteristics of the unconscious described by him. For example, clinical observation frequently shows that what is experienced and named as the 'internal breast' is not only a breast but other things as well; this is condensation. What is more, such a breast may be felt not only as internal but also as external or even as neither internal nor external; this is quite disturbing. Further still, the objects are, true enough, individual objects but at the same time they are not. They can at the same time be sets of objects and also general ideas or propositional functions, such as 'breastness' or 'motherhood'. Moreover, we have noted many times that the part is equivalent to the whole at the very least in number of elements. This implies or means that they are infinite sets if seen in the light of Dedekind's definition (Matte-Blanco 1975a: 33, section 27). Furthermore, we observe that the usual relations between material objects are not at all respected in the relations between these 'psychical' objects.

To illustrate these assertions let us now examine the dream in example 31. A first and most important thing to note is that *the immediate general appearance of this dream is that of something tidy, 'neat and proper', respectful of the reality of objects in space and time* existing when one is awake, with none of the distortions, incongruities, and extravagances found in many other dreams. Some of the dreamer's desires are obviously expressed in a way which corresponded to the relations which would have been found if they had been expressed and acted upon in material reality. First, there is nothing strange in the fact that two people in love want to isolate themselves from ordinary life and choose to make a trip to the Far East. Second, the fight to overcome the difficulties opposing their union is well represented by means of the fight to get into the plane. Third, the jumbo's little lounge offers possibilities corresponding to what is observed in ordinary life. Fourth, the description of the seats is connected with, or evokes, the bed to the patient. This, if taken together with the loving care taken to reserve the seats, serves to convey eloquently a desire to go to bed with the mother.

Having noted this factualness about the dream we look further and 'take off'. The phantasy of a loving embrace in mid-air already begins to show something more than what everyday material reality succeeds in explaining. The material fact of the rise of the plane does look like a symbol of the 'flight into the heights', that is, towards ideals of beauty, towards the heavens. The image in question is a good representation of this desire. It must be added, however, that it already reflects certain more subtle and more general features of psychical life. In fact, in the material world boarding a plane and getting away from the earth constitute only a problem of relations between material objects; the aeroplane is nearer to the sun and farther from the earth. In the present dream image, instead, the sun and the sky can *also* be seen as representing truth and beauty, and the earth representing that which is prosaic, 'terrestrial'. But the relations existing – on the one hand, between what is truth or beauty and what is prosaic and, on the other, between the sky and the earth – are actually the same, or at least isomorphic. It is precisely for this reason that one can employ the comparison with the material flight to refer to the flight of the spirit. This dream seems clearly to be doing this.

Up to now everything is relatively simple. The events of the external world serve to represent events in the psychical world which are isomorphic to them. Said more generally, they belong to the same type of abstract structure, i.e. the set of all the structures which are isomorphic between themselves.

Consider the dream now in terms of the way it represents one material phenomenon by means of another. In the present case, the event of the erection is symbolized or represented by the event of a jumbo jet which rises from the earth. There is no doubt that both phenomena are isomorphic between themselves with regard to certain relations which take place in both: the form of the objects, the fact of rising, and the angle of the rise, etc. Here is a simple question of representing a material phenomenon by means of another material phenomenon. The amplification of the size of the penis seen in the representation by means of the jumbo may help to convey or represent a more subtle fact: the intensity of the desire. But even in this case a moment's reflection leads to the awareness that the isomorphism remains.

4 Some conceptual delimitations: types of structure

From our initial analysis we may conclude that all the aspects of the dream considered so far faithfully represent the psychical relationship of the dreamer with his mother as well as the intrapsychical representation of it, all in the three-dimensional world. In other words, the external, three-dimensional world is, thus far, a faithful image of the psychical world, because the structures which are discernible in both these worlds belong to the same *types of structure*. By this I mean, as in mathematics, that two structures are of the same type if, first, the same number of operations (relations) is defined in both; second, it is possible to establish a one-to-one correspondence between the respective operations; and, third, the system of axioms of the second structure can be obtained by replacing each operation of the first structure by the corresponding operation of the second (cf. Lombardo-Radice 1967: 721).[1]

We may now consider the isomorphisms between psychical and external reality in the other aspects of the dream. First, the trip expresses the desire for isolation in order to be together. Likewise in the external world, if one wants to send a couple of material objects into isolation, one sends them away together. The isomorphism here is obvious. Second, it also may easily be seen that the fight to reach the loving union is isomorphic to the material fight to reach the aeroplane. Third, identical considerations hold for the jumbo's lounge, the description of the seats, and the 'take-off'. The jumbo jet rising from the earth also has a similarity to an erection.

5 The upheaval of spatio-temporal relations observed in this dream

The preceding analysis shows that it is possible to find a correspondence between the relations appearing in a dream and relations observed in the material world. I shall now try to show that this correspondence blatantly disappears when we no longer consider the isolated parts or subsets of the dream but start to look at the spatial relations existing between some of the situations or actions represented.

In sexual intercourse the bed is different from the persons participating in the act and from any of the parts of such persons. Moreover, it is in a quite definite spatial relation with these persons. It is an asymmetrical relation; the persons are over the bed, and the bed is under the persons. The same thing holds in the case of the persons themselves; if one is to the right or over the other, then the other is to the left or under, and so on. Likewise the penis is different from the vagina; the one penetrates the other, and this, in its turn, is penetrated: again an asymmetrical relation.

But in the representation of intercourse in this particular dream (example 31) things stand in a completely different way; the penis (jumbo jet) contains both its possessor (the dreamer) and the woman, and also contains the bed. In other words, the whole (man) is inside a part of itself (penis), and the woman as well as the bed are also inside the penis. Put in more general terms: the (asymmetrical) relation part–whole between the penis and the body is replaced by another relation isomorphic to it and also asymmetrical; this is the relation between contained and container. Once this is done, the new relation is treated as though it were symmetrical. The body contains (includes) the penis, and the penis contains (includes) the body. In classical logic, to affirm this is, of course, equivalent to saying that the part is equal to the whole.

In addition to being the penis of the dreamer, the inside of the jumbo may also be seen as the vagina-womb of the mother. These representations taken together imply that not only does the vagina contain the penis, but also the penis contains the vagina. Here a 'normally' asymmetrical relation is treated as if it were symmetrical. However, the question is far from being fully explored in the preceding remarks. Normally the woman's vagina is part of herself, or inside the woman's body: an asymmetrical relation of course. In the dream, however, the woman is also in the vagina – inside of the jumbo; again an asymmetrical relation is treated as though it were symmetrical. Both, in their turn, are inside the jumbo-penis, which is inside them. What is more, the bed is inside the penis-jumbo-vagina, so that things are still more complicated. There is in the dream a concurrence of asymmetrical relations as seen every day and asymmetrical relations treated as symmetrical. In other words, the dream is a bi-logical structure and, as such, is an expression of the fundamental antinomy.

In short, we are confronted in this case with a remarkable chaos of spatial relations. Probably more than one reader will 'explore' a way out of this muddle by remembering that the psychoanalytical interpretations such as those mentioned attribute several symbolic roles to the jumbo, but that such roles are different from one another, only they appear as components in a process of condensation. This remark is true but misses the point. *The point is that this dream pictures the material reality of plane and persons in a way which is for ever precluded in actual material reality. Such relations as are simultaneously represented by the same objects in the dream cannot ever be expressed simultaneously in physical reality.* This is the problem we are studying. To ignore it or cancel it by replacing simultaneity by succession means rejecting the existence of dream life. To explain: in a real sexual relation the bed, the partners, the penis, the vagina, etc. are at any and all moments different from one another. And so are the actions and the relations. As, in factual reality, they are all present simultaneously in the sexual relation, it is impossible that the jumbo may be at the same time penis, vagina, and aeroplane, that a woman be inside her own vagina, or a man inside the woman's vagina and simultaneously inside his own penis. The reader may complete this reasoning by reviewing, in this light, one by one all the other aspects of the dream we have considered.

It is important to become aware that we psychoanalysts, who know very well the characteristics of the unconscious, sometimes tend to ignore or retouch some aspects of our patients' dreams and in this way manage to live comfortably in a less crazy world. In this present study I am trying to ignore some of these comforts and look at all this confusing and disturbing reality as squarely as possible.

The chaos in question can be described, as just seen, with the help of the principle of symmetry, but our exploration does not finish there. We must try to discover all the implications of this oneiric[2] behaviour.

6 Freud and dreams

The following quotation from Freud is pertinent to our subject. Speaking of the means of representation in dreams, he writes (1900, SE 4: 312, notation added):

'The different portions of this complicated structure stand, of course, in the most manifold logical relations to one another. They can represent [a] foreground and background [b], digressions and illustrations, conditions, chains of evidence and counter-arguments. When the whole mass of these dream-thoughts [c] is brought under the pressure [d] of the dream-work, and its elements are turned about [e], broken into fragments [f] and jammed together [g] – almost like packed ice – the question arises of what happens to the logical connections which have hitherto formed its framework. What presentation do dreams provide for "if", "because", "just as", "although", "either or", and all the other conjunctions without which we cannot understand sentences or speeches?

'In the first resort our answer must be that dreams have no means at their disposal for representing these logical relations between the dream-thoughts. For the most part dreams disregard all these conjunctions, and it is only the substantive content of the dream-thoughts that they take over and manipulate. The restoration of the connections which the dream-work has destroyed is a task which has to be performed by the interpretive process.'[3]

This admirable text concisely contains one of Freud's profound intuitions about the mind. My studies, especially the more recent ones (Matte-Blanco 1975a, 1976a, 1976b, 1978, 1981, 1982, and 1984), all of which in one way or another start from *this* Freud, suggest the following comments. The Freudian discovery expressed in the first phrase of the second paragraph, that is, the absence of means for representing logical relations, can be seen, in its turn, not as a lack but as something positive; there is something in dreams which contains implicitly, though in another way, all the relations that seem to be absent. More explicitly, the symmetrical or indivisible mode of being contains 'everything', but this cannot be immediately visible to thinking, for thinking needs relations. Faced with this, thinking tries to solve it by *translating* the experience of the indivisible into relatable thoughts. This implies that relations must necessarily be defined, otherwise thinking could not distinguish one element from another. I believe this is the task Freud refers to in the last sentence of the quotation.

The expression 'translation' was first used by Freud on several occasions (see, for instance, SE 14: 166). 'Thinking the indivisible mode', however, is, so far as this mode is concerned, not thinking at all. For this mode, as we have already discussed many times, is alien to our thinking. I have proposed to call this attempt at thought by the name of *'thinkating'* (Matte-Blanco 1981: 511–12, sections 46 and 47, and 525, section 75).

The concept of relation requires the (logical) existence of a triad: something, something else, and the relation between these two things (Matte-Blanco 1975a: 330). When the indivisible mode is put in front of one or various triads, it frequently treats them all – so far as thinking can understand this 'procedure' – as though they were only one thing: another way of 'living' or being.

It is at this point that we must clear up a first aspect of this important ambiguity. As Freud has pointed out (1900 SE 4: 313 para. 2; SE 5: 489 paras. 2 and 3, 506 para. 2 fn. 2), the absence of logical relations is not always found in dreams. In fact there are many aspects of dreams in which logical relations are present; they may even be expressed in words in the dream itself. (See also Freud 1900, SE 5: 450, footnote mentioned in note 3 to this chapter.) He distinguishes the 'general behaviour' of dreams – more generally put, of the unconscious. However, it is necessary to add that this characteristic is usually found, either in dreams or in unconscious manifestations, next to or mixed with other aspects which in fact do not employ assymetrical relations in a greater or lesser degree. Put in another way, these other aspects do not follow the laws of thinking. It seems, therefore, more accurate to say that *the dream reveals in a greater or lesser degree of purity a mode which is alien to thinking.* But it also employs thinking. In other words, *the dream is bi-logical.*[4]

The dream is, in short, a mode of being which behaves in front of reality as though reality were indivisible. To explain further, if we take into consideration not only one dream but a set of dreams we see that they reveal the presence of the indivisible mode (symmetrization) mixed with logical thinking in proportions which differ or vary from one dream to another or from one part of a dream to another. These facts make us aware that the term 'unconscious' comprises a great variety of manifestations which are different from one another. It is not free, at all, from ambiguity. Summarizing: the proportion between the two modes of being – indivisible or symmetrical mode and heterogenic or asymmetrical mode (thinking) – and also the type of bi-logical structure vary from one dream manifestation to another.

Before returning to our dream I should like to stop to consider again some aspects of the relation internal–external. It is naturally a spatial relation which is at the foundation of the conception of the internal world. This must be viewed as being either in a real or in a symbolical space,[5] for otherwise there would be neither the need for nor the possibility of speaking of internal reality at all.

Seen in this perspective, the first paragraph of the quotation from Freud on page 260 may represent the starting point for further reflections, because Freud employs a number of spatial comparisons to refer to logical relations. He suggests that parts of the structure 'can represent [a] foreground and background' [b]. It is easily seen that he means that they represent foreground and background at the same time. This is an incompatibility which, anyway, uses the notion of space. He goes on to speak of 'the whole mass of these dream-thoughts' [c], making a comparison with a volume, a three-dimensional space. This mass 'is brought under the pressure' [d], implying a vertical or horizontal dimension and, furthermore, the use of the concept of pressure with regard to thinking: a spatial object to which a force is applied. Next he says that 'its elements are turned about' [e]; this is the mathematical notion of transformation, applied to three-dimensional space and time. Next the elements are 'broken into fragments' [f]; this is reminiscent of breaking the 'object' into pieces, again implying three-dimensional space and time. Finally Freud refers to the elements as 'jammed together' [g], again employing three-dimensional space and force, and to their becoming 'almost like packed ice'. These last two comparisons, if taken together, suggest the concept of putting one part inside the other in such a way that the various elements of each of these parts get mixed up with the various elements of the other parts.

If we consider these seven remarks of Freud as a whole we may legitimately conclude that *they reveal precisely* what the title of this chapter refers to: *an upheaval of spatial structures.* It must be added that the upheaval, as he describes it, refers to three-dimensional spatial structures, for it is obvious that he is speaking only of three-dimensional space in each of the above-mentioned remarks.

We must now ask whether the dream we are considering (example 31) could be described in terms of the notions explicitly employed by Freud. It seems to me that this is possible only in part. These descriptions, with only one exception, refer to things which can occur in a three-dimensional world. The structures are destroyed, but their parts may be treated as masses [c]; they may be subjected to pressure [d], turned about [e], broken into fragments [f], and jammed together almost like packed ice [g]. *Freud is speaking of objects which occupy regions of a three-dimensional space.*

In contrast, when he points out that the same parts form foreground *and* background [a, b], we become aware that this case is different from the others just mentioned. In fact, the foreground is distinguished from the background because they are different zones (regions) of the depth dimension of a three-dimensional space. In such a space it is not possible for the same region to be in the foreground and in the background, because this would be a violation of the laws of three-dimensional space.

In a bi-logical world submitted (partially) to the principle of symmetry the situation in question is, instead, perfectly possible. In fact, if A is before B, then in this world B is before A. In other words, the same thing may at the same time be in the foreground and in the background; the notion of depth is blotted out. *Freud's phrase in question, therefore, implies the principle of symmetry as well as classical logic,* which permits the distinction between foreground and background; *in other words, it implies a Simassi bi-logical structure which, as such, is the expression of the fundamental antinomy.*

We have repeatedly seen that when an n-dimensional space is represented in terms of an $(n - 1)$-dimensional space, the $(n - 2)$-dimensional sub-spaces of this space appear repeated in the representation. In this way three-dimensional volumes may be repeated. Alternatively, if we consider, for instance, a five-dimensional space we can know, for instance, that there are regions in this space in which various volumes or three-dimensional spaces are found. If we now 'look' at such volumes with our three-dimensional eyes, they will seem to us to be one and the same volume; the volumes are catapulted into one another.[6] Perhaps this alternative way of looking at the question leads to a deeper understanding of certain things which are immediately seen with the help of the principle of symmetry. Among other things, this way would enable us to understand better the violation of the principle of non-contradiction which sometimes is observed when the principle of symmetry is applied; in this case one would have to postulate an infinite number of principles of non-contradiction, each linked to one n-dimensional space (Matte-Blanco 1975a: 51–3). It is a difficult problem, and we must still work in a deep and subtle way before we can get to a 'region' where we are sure to have reached a better insight into the question.

7 The spatio-temporal Multidim structure

To return to the dream (example 31) and its structure. One asks: with what type of bi-logical structure are we confronted? A preliminary answer is that it is none of those we have already mentioned. In fact, it is easy to see that it is not of the Alassi type, because there is obviously no alternation whatsoever in it. Neither is it Simassi, because it is not the same reality that is seen simultaneously with 'asymmetrical and symmetrical eyes'. It is also very different from the symmetrized vector structure of projective identifications. Nor is it an epistemological see-saw or the molar structure.

At first sight the structure of the dream seems most like a Tridim structure. The jumbo is a symbol of the penis and of the vagina, and, seen in this light, one can say that it is a condensation of both. But the question is not that simple. First, in the formation of a composite figure we see that a person who appears in the dream has traits of different persons, and none of these traits is necessarily shared by the other persons who are components of the figure, otherwise we would not become aware that it is a composite figure. The present case, instead, is, of course, not about persons but about parts of the body. Here the vagina and the penis can both be considered as having a circular section and both are supposed to have a cavity inside, though the cavity of the urethra is much smaller than that of the vagina. In other words, a hollow cylinder, however forced or far-fetched it may be, would be common to both the penis and the vagina. Second, in a Tridim structure the composite figure does not suggest any violation of the laws which rule happenings in three-dimensional space. Though it is not actual reality, it could be. In this case, in contrast, an ordinary three-dimensional jumbo could not function at the same time as a penis, a vagina, and a jumbo! In the dream it does all three. Third, furthermore, the penis and the vagina as represented by the jumbo can be seen, not so much as the concrete organs, but as the respective classes in which such organs are elements. One of these elements would be the penis of the patient, and the other, the vagina of the mother.[7] I conclude that this is a bi-logical structure – because we witness a variety of expressions of symmetry which appear. But it is not a Tridim structure.

What is it, then? To find an answer to this question I assume, in the first place, that my analysis of the dream was correct and, among other things, that in the unconscious the jumbo did fulfil and represent the various roles mentioned, corresponding to both part and whole objects. In that case the first thing to recall is that we have been struck many times by the fact that the same thing fulfils the functions of jumbo, penis, and vagina at the same instant in time.

Recapitulating some previous conclusions I want to note that for sexual intercourse to take place it is necessary that the penis be different from the vagina, and the latter must contain the first and not vice versa. In this dream both are the same at the same time. An asymmetrical spatial relation is treated as symmetrical. Turn to the idea of time for a moment. It is considered an order structure; in other words, each instant comes before or after any other instant. It can be represented in terms of a line, one-dimensional space. It is usually considered to be isomorphic to one-dimensional space. It 'flows' from the past to the present to the future, and each instant comes before a number of certain instants and after a number of some other instants.

Looking at the dream in this light, we may say that all objects are catapulted into one another, and the same happens to all instants. It is as though vagina is also penis and at the same instant at which it is penetrated by the penis it also penetrates the penis. Put in other words, *all the spatial and temporal relations are catapulted into one another in such a way that each thing and each happening which our intellect grasps are also all other things and all other happenings.* Spatial objects appear (to use Freud's words, just quoted) jammed together; and the same thing happens to portions of time.

Now, I have already mentioned in this chapter that, when an n-dimensional space is represented or defined in terms of an $n - 1$, $n - 2$, etc. space, it is found in this case that lower-dimensional spaces appear repeated. Courant and Robbins (1941: 232) speak in fact of 'inverting our reasoning'. I mentioned how, when a two-dimensional triangle (ABC, say) is represented by a one-dimensional line, then one of the vertices (C, say) of the triangle is repeated. Here, when dimensions are reduced, that which is the something (point C) becomes two things, let's call them points C_1 and C_2, located in different zones of space. The same thing happens in three dimensions, but now lines and not points are repeated. And so on, of course, with higher dimensions.

Let us re-invert this reasoning and, instead of representing with reduced dimensions, increase the number of dimensions. In such a case, things that are portrayed in our three-dimensional world as different may appear in a space of more dimensions as one and the same thing when viewed by our three-dimensional eyes. Psycho-analytical reader, please do not be discouraged. We have just seen that, with our triangle ABC, when represented or defined in one line, we have $CABC$. The point C appears twice. Now when we travel along a line *CABC*, by re-inverting our reasoning we would conclude that the point *C* is only one point when the line is in a plane, hence in triangular form. A cube (three dimensions) expressed in a plane (two dimensions) results in a repetition of lines (one dimension). But go up in the succession of dimensions and you will soon arrive at a situation in which what had appeared as several in an *n*-dimensional space is in fact only one thing in a space of higher dimensions.

With these considerations in mind the dream can be understood better by saying that what we know to be several and different three-dimensional objects are treated as though they were only one. We conclude that these (spatial) objects (penis, jumbo, vagina) are treated as being only one in a space of more dimensions. *What we see is a multidimensionalization of what to us is a number of three-dimensional objects.* I propose to call this a multidimensionalized structure, in short a Multidim structure. *Note that bi-logic is visible in our analysis of the dream plus associations and not in either of them if seen alone.* In other words, neither the dream nor the associations show symmetrical logic, only classical heterogenic logic: the two modes appear together only when 'uni-modal' dream and unimodal associations are considered together. We may call this fact the expression of a *bimodal frenzy*.

At the present time I am unable to say how many dimensions this new space has. I need much more study and reflection before I can advance in this problem. But I think this does not detract from the validity of the conclusion just put forward. I still have another question to consider. We have seen in the dream that the penis-vagina-jumbo would appear to be able to penetrate and to be penetrated and to fly all at the same time. This does not seem possible in one-dimensional time. Considering that time is isomorphic to a one-dimensional space, what if we assume that not only space but also time has been multidimensionalized? This would come in very handy to the penis-vagina-jumbo. For if they are a multidimensional spatial object in a one-dimensional time, which is the normal way we think, then they cannot fulfil all the functions for which they are made. But in a time of higher dimensions it would be possible for the same object to fly, penetrate, and be penetrated at the same time! What is more, these three actions would be the same action yet also remain three different ones; this is a bi-logical structure. For this reason I propose to call the whole structure of the dream a *spatio-temporal Multidim structure*.

I realize that I may be called foolhardy and may be accused of having let myself be carried away by my fantasy. My reply is that I have only been consistent. I have only followed, to their extreme consequences, various aspects of a dream which at first sight appears all tidy and which, in its analysis, carried out by means of the classical analytical technique, turned out to pose very serious problems. The dream was one in which the images and events, which at first sight seem to conform rigorously to what is usually observed in the development of happenings in the material world, turned out to be a rather complex bi-logical structure which we have described as spatio-temporal multidimensionalization. The presence of an ordered appearance in a dream, when seen in the light of the dream and its associations, turns out to be totally incompatible with our present conception of space and time. But it is quite understandable and ordered if seen in terms of an experience by the patient of a space of more than three dimensions and a time of more than one dimension.

Notes

1 Here I should like to point out that it is in fact possible in principle to delimit 'sets that comprise psychical reality' in terms of mathematical logic if one remembers that an n-ary operation is nothing else but a subset of an $(n + 1)$-ary relation. For example, the binary operation of addition, i.e. the operation of adding two numbers – say, $3 + 4$ – can also be described as a 3-ary relation, in this case the 3-ary relation between 3, 4, and 7. If the operation is multiplication, then the relation would be between 3, 4, and 12. With this in mind as a model, the problem of finding the 'psychical operations' becomes that of finding the relations between 'psychical things' or happenings. This problem is within our reach. Once such relations have been discovered, one can go on to find *classes of relation* and *types of structure*. This is for instance what I have already done in one case: I have singled out, say, two elements: the 'rising of the jumbo' and the 'longings of people in love'. These two are elements of the class defined by the set of relations which identify 'the flight into the heights'.

2 From the Greek *oneiros* = 'a dream', pertaining to the subject of dreams.

3 My interpretation of this is as follows. The second paragraph of the quotation refers to the meaning transmitted in normal thinking, which in a footnote in SE 5: 450 he describes as 'general behaviour'. The first paragraph describes the various distortions of this general meaning, brought about by the special characteristics of the unconscious, that is, by its bi-logical structures. Note that this is a way of referring to the fundamental antinomy. We may, therefore, conclude that Freud was, in

some obscure way, aware of the fundamental antinomy, as a result of his awareness of the contrast between classical logic and the symmetrical logic (obviously not expressed in these terms). But he did not bring it to full light.

4 Only since the beginning of 1984 have I become aware that things and relations do exist in the indivisible mode. But they are all 'in the same thing', and, therefore, thinking cannot grasp them as separate, because thinking can attribute relations only to two or more things that *appear* existentially apart or separated. This is not the case with the indivisible mode. Here there is a second ambiguity I have just indirectly alluded to. In the indivisible mode, things and relations do exist but are structured in a way which thrives in the midst of the acceptance of the compatibility of things that appear incompatible to thinking. This is most clearly seen in the mathematical infinite, where each number 'contains' every other number, and this is unacceptable to thinking (see Chapter 2, section 8). I consider what I have just said an important (new and recent) insight but will not dwell upon it here because it is not necessary at the level of the discourse of this book. Whoever wishes to understand better the apparently obscure remarks I have just made may see Matte-Blanco 1984.

5 By real space I mean the space of our daily sensory expression. By symbolic space I intend something whose structure is isomorphic to that of real space, just as an obelisk may be seen as a symbolic penis, or a book as a symbolic breast.

6 For further details see Courant and Robbins 1941: 233, and Matte-Blanco 1975a: 412–14 (taken from Courant and explained a little more).

7 I do not remember a dream representing both a whole person and one of his organs which are at the same time physically separated in space, i.e. in different regions of space. It seems a question worthy of consideration.

Epilogue to Part Four

We have seen two examples of symmetrical frenzy, one of bi-logical frenzy, and two of bi-modal frenzy. In symmetrical frenzy we see the 'invasion' of the indivisible mode which results in a diminution of consciousness which leads to confusion and eventually to loss of consciousness. No consciousness can exist in the absence of the heterogenic mode. In bi-logical frenzy we see various simultaneous appearances of the sexual realtions between the parents. For the indivisible mode they are the same thing. For the thinking (heterogenic) mode they are different things, and are not the parents.

Finally, in the two cases of bi-modal frenzy we can observe a striking incompatibility between the perceptual aspects of the dream, clearly submitted to classical logic, and the multiple meanings of each of the dream images and actions. We have studied the detail of these meanings with the help of the technique of free association. If these two sets of knowledge furnished by the dream are confronted, we become aware of the existence of a Simassi bi-logical structure and hence of the fundamental antinomy between the indivisible and the heterogenic modes of being. And this amounts to saying that the indivisible mode permeates dream.

Dreams such as this are a common occurrence in every person. The important consequence we can draw from this fact is that the indivisible mode is present everywhere in our dream life; it permeates it, and we are not aware of it. We grasp different objects, exept when the dream becomes confused. In the first case we discover the indivisible by means of the interpretative work, in the second by the con-fusion of images. Both cases are witnesses of the indivisible in dreams. After having become aware of this, we soon

269

realize that the psychoanalytical interpretative work also reveals the same thing in waking life. In particular I would like to refer to an important fact I have frequently discussed: the unconscious does not know individuals but only classes. Each individual person or thing is, for our thinking, an element of one or several classes. Unconscious thinking, instead, does see the individual but at the same time treats it as if it were the class: no distinction between individual and class. In other words, the divisible or heterogeneous and the indivisible are always together and always incompatible.

I would like to give another example of the non–distinction between individuals who are, for our consciousness, quite different.

Example 32
After a very long period of analysis one of my patients brought to the session something he had never told before. When he was about nine years old he fell deeply in love with a girl slightly older than him. She was, however, his elder brother's love. So, in one way or another, he was, in his fantasy, 'allotted' her sister. But he remained faithful to his first love. Life separated them, and he had various women, both successively and simultaneously, who were important for him.

In the session in question he told me that, after many years, he had an indirect contact with his first love. His various associations showed that all his successive women were, in some way or another, related to the first one, each in a particular aspect. It became very clear that he had been searching all his life for THE WOMAN, and each one of his women was and was not THE WOMAN – not even the initial girl. In other words, all his life he had searched for the class in each individual, and the result was that the class was there and it was not. The indivisible totality was in each individual and it was not.

It may be objected that these cases show nothing that our previous searches have not already found. Maybe it is so. But what I feel is that the formulation of bi–logical and bi–modal frenzy and the path followed in searching for it makes us vividly aware that we are all the time immersed in the indivisible, without ever realizing it.

Another aspect which seems pregnant of future developments is that the psychoanalytic technique provides a new path towards the discovery of the indivisible. To explain, Zeno's pradoxes lead, in my opinion, to the indivisible through showing the contrast between an approach to space and time in terms of the finite and an approach in terms of the infinite. I shall not develop this argument and shall content myself by saying only that the psychoanalytical method offers a quite different approach. In both cases, however, it is classical logic which leads us to territories which are outside of its kingdom!

PART FIVE

Towards the future

14

The notion of object

Foreword. In the remaining chapters of this book I am going to deal essentially with concepts which can be employed only partially in present-day clinical work but which, I feel, will become important in due time. It will be a challenge to future generations of psychoanalysts to understand how and when these concepts may apply and to create new notions which may serve to modify or complete them. If they respond to this, perhaps not only psychoanalysis but also mathematics and epistemology could be enriched. Perhaps too the aspects, either of knowledge or of being, where there is unity in nature will become more apparent. Psychoanalysis, especially through the study of dreams, offers unique opportunities of discovering recondite aspects of being, some of which may even eventually apply to other subjects.

The aim of this chapter is, in the first place, to study those aspects of the concept of object which are implicitly employed in the conception of the internal world. I shall try to make these more explicit and also to discuss some of the difficulties which the present-day concept of object raises.[1]

1 The Freudian concept of object

I will begin with a definition from Freud:

'The object of an instinct is the thing in regard to which or through which the instinct is able to achieve its aim. It is what is most variable about an instinct and is not originally connected with it,

273

but becomes assigned to it only in consequence of being peculiarly fitted to make satisfaction possible. The object is not necessarily something extraneous: it may equally well be a part of the subject's own body. It may be changed any number of times in the course of the vicissitudes which the instinct undergoes during its existence; and highly important parts are played by this displacement of instinct. It may happen that the same object serves for the satisfaction of several instincts simultaneously, a phenomenon which Adler (1908) has called a "confluence" of instincts.'

(1915a, SE 14: 122–23)

This conception contains notions which clarify various uses of the word 'object' found in writings about the internal world. An early question that arises is about the distinction between objects of an instinct and objects of love and hate. Strachey's translation of Freud tells us: 'Thus we become aware that the attitudes[2] of love and hate cannot be made use of for the relations of instincts to their objects, but are reserved for the relations of the total ego to objects' (SE 14: 137). This acute distinction refers implicitly to the level of what I have termed psychical happenings. Instinctual relations with their objects belong to a more primitive level. Those of the total ego with its objects, which include love and hate, belong to a more developed and organized level. This confronts us immediately with certain questions which the conception of the internal world and psychoanalysis in general must face. How can the experience of the unity of the individual be preserved in the midst of these different levels?

The solution seems to lie in that the ego, and, 'higher up', the self, establishes a relation with its external and internal objects which is not separated from the relation of the instincts with their objects. But the relation of the ego and of the self contains the relation between instincts and object as part of its structure, in such a way that both are not separable in reality from one another. The notion of subordinate space (Chapter 15, page 297) can clarify these interrelations.

A second aspect is that the distinction between inanimate objects and persons is made only at a highly asymmetrical level, that is, at a 'rational' one; at a deeper, more symmetrical level it does not exist. This leads us straight to the fact that at such levels all objects are treated as though they were persons. For example, the breast, either good or bad, has intentions and activities, establishes positive or negative relations, and all these are things which a non-personal object obviously cannot do. We shall presently return to this when we consider the notions of part and whole objects.

Let us now turn to a fundamental, rather puzzling, and paradoxical problem, that raised by Freud in the first quotation above. This is the variability and number of objects to which he refers. Although what he says there is true, it is not the whole truth. For the various objects which satisfy a given instinct must all belong to the same class; this will be that of 'satisfiers of the instinct in question'. But we know from our earlier discussion that in the 'deep unconscious, where the principle of symmetry rules, each element of a class is identical to the whole class, hence is the same as any other element of the class. *In other words, the distinction between various objects which satisfy a given instinct or feeling is in fact made only in terms of classical logic,* which enables us to recognize at the same time both their differences and their belonging to the same class, i.e. their equivalence. Milk, for instance, and a book are quite different things, but both are elements of the class of objects which give oral satisfaction, physical or symbolic. They are identical but only in that aspect. In the so-called deep unconscious, instead, these two objects, owing to the fact that they are felt or treated as elements of the same class, are not at all different; they are the same thing. At the levels of the deep unconscious a class is indivisible. Here it is not true, at this level, that the objects which satisfy a desire or a feeling are many and diverse. They are in fact only one, indivisible, identical to that which the level of thinking calls a class or set.

Two very important aspects of this deep identity between part and whole emerge. First, a part of the body which satisfies an instinct is felt as a part only at a certain level of thinking. At deeper levels the parts and the whole individual are the same thing. This is a fact of daily psychoanalytical observation. Anyone can check on this by introspection. At the moment when satisfaction by means of a part of the body is taking place – when eating, moving, being caressed, or even feeling pain, for instance – there is a 'double recording'. The part of the body is satisfied, but so also is the whole self. The two aspects may occupy the first plane in a different way but they are always 'there'. Second, in a similar way, the external object, for instance a loved or hated person, is not distinguishable at very deep levels from the subject him- or herself. This leads to a better understanding of why the object of love or hate is always, in some way, a reflection of ourselves. At superficial levels one can speak of projection; at deeper levels it seems more precise to speak of non-distinction between self and not-self.

2 The various types of object

The distinction between part and whole objects has played an important role in Kleinian conceptions:

'WHOLE OBJECT: describes the perception of another person as a person. . . . The whole object contrasts both with the part object and with objects split into ideal and persecutory parts.'

(Segal 1964 [1973]: 128)

'PART OBJECTS: are objects characteristic of the paranoid-schizoid position. The first part object experienced by the infant is the breast. Soon other part objects are experienced – first of all the penis.'

(Segal 1964 [1973]: 127)

Note that, whereas the whole object is clearly defined, the part object is not. I shall discuss the ambiguity of the concept later in this chapter.

An object may be split into an idealized or ideal object, which represents the maximum expression of all that is good, and a bad or persecutory object, which represents all that is bad, also conceived in its maximum expression. The concept of *good object* is also employed, and this is something different from that of the ideal object, in the sense that the qualities of the good object are not maximized, either in a positive or in a negative sense. The good object, instead,

'is felt as a source of life, love and goodness, but it is not ideal. Its bad qualities are recognised and it may be experienced as frustrating in contrast to the ideal object; it is felt to be vulnerable to attacks, and therefore it is often experienced as damaged and destroyed. The good breast and the good penis are felt as belonging respectively to the good mother and the good father, but they may be experienced before the whole-object relationship is fully established.'

(Segal 1964 [1973]: 127)

The notion of a *multitude of objects* already appears in Klein's first writings. It seems that in her conception it is possible to distinguish two types of multitude of objects – first, that resulting from a fragmentation of an object. Here Klein quotes her own daughter:

'Melitta Schmideberg regards this multiplicity of persecutors as being a projection of the child's own oral-sadistic attacks on its father's penis, each separate bit of his penis becoming a new object

276

of anxiety (cf. her paper "The Role of Psychotic Mechanisms in Cultural Development", 1930).'

(Klein 1932: 206–07, n. 4)

The same idea is clearly suggested in various parts of the same book. If, instead of considering Klein's various isolated comments on the subject, we draw them together we may then conclude beyond any doubt that she was of the opinion that the experience of multiplicity of the objects could be the result of their destruction.

We have noted earlier that this aspect of Klein's work is more particularly seen in *The Psycho-Analysis of Children* (1932: e.g. 206–07). She has called attention, as nobody else before her, to two fundamental facts of psychical life. These are the enormous intensity of deeper psychical processes (which, we may add, tends to an infinite intensity) and the enormous multiplicity of the inside of the mind, which is isomorphic to and reflected in the child's phantasies about the inside of his or her mother.

It seems that, when the mind utilizes a Tridim structure in imaginatively expressing this multiplicity of objects and intensity of phantasy feeling, this fact indicates that it has no other means at its disposal in consciousness than that of a three-dimensional space. In such a case imagination can convey such multiplicity by increasing the number of dimensions, with the result that Multidim structures emerge. We become aware of this if we carry out a rigorous logical analysis of dreams and associations.

An analysis of the concept of a *bizarre object* leads to the conclusion that it too is a bi-logical structure. It is evident that one aspect of this conception respects the rules of classical logic: it is an object, it is delimited, it moves, etc.; all are asymmetrical properties. In the midst of this conception, however, one can detect obvious symmetrizations – for instance, the fact that an aspect or 'piece' of a personality behaves as a whole personality (part = whole). Likewise the controlled or engulfed object becomes angered and controls the piece of personality; it acquires the characteristics of a personality. In other words, the bizarre object displays a simultaneous co-presence of both modes.

I feel, however, that, even though the conception of a bizarre object shows a simultaneous co-presence of symmetry and asymmetry, there is some difference from a Simassi structure. In fact it does not seem that the co-presence takes place simultaneously, as occurred in the example given in Chapter 2 (example 4, page 47) when an equivalence was noted between a door and the jaws of an animal. When a part of a living being becomes identical to the whole being we certainly must describe this as the 'action of symmetry'. But the participation of a symmetrized aspect in the bizarre object structure does not seem to be the same as seen in the Simassi structure, or in the Alassi, Tridim, Multidim, or all other bi-logical structures found so far. But there is an exception: a distinct similarity with that aspect or that moment of the epistemological see-saw when the anus becomes a whole individual (see Chapter 2 example 5, pages 49–50). But the similarity seems to stop here . . . or maybe not, because a wide 'dialogue' seems to express itself in the relation between object and personality, a dialogue similar to that described in the epistemological see-saw, only in this case it is not quite of a 'see-saw type'. I shall go no further here.

In short, it seems that the bizarre object is a bi-logical structure different from all others so far known, but its distinguishing features are, to me, difficult to define. Further study could clarify matters. The trouble is that Bion himself, in his subsequent evolution, does not seem to have returned to this conception of his, nor do I know of others who employ it habitually, so the opportunities to know more about it are scant.

Internal and external object. As various authors have pointed out, the conception of the internal object and internal world has been built from the model of the introduction of food. Put in a more general way, it has been built from a model of activity in a three-dimensional space. We have stressed many times that psychoanalytical ideas about the inside of the mind or of the self have, so far, always remained linked to this model, and this has resulted in a strong limitation of comprehension and research.

The concepts internal and external should be seen in relation to the number of dimensions of the space considered. This is because that which is internal to a space of a given number of dimensions may be external to a space of a lower number of dimensions. This apparently odd finding will be discussed in the next chapters. It is certainly not easy at present to ascertain in clinical practice the number of dimensions being experienced by a person, but this possibility does not seem barred for ever, if our research is careful.

3 Towards new developments

Reflection about these concepts, made in the light of clinical observations, raises a series of questions which I shall now try to discuss.

First, *what is an object?* I suggest that the person-object is, in some

278

way, always a reproduction of the personality. I have already discussed this question elsewhere (Matte-Blanco 1975a: 125–29); I shall add here that when the object is felt to be inside the self it is a *substructure of the self*. In fact, it has some of the characteristics of the self, except when it is felt as an intruder or a foreign body. It would seem that, even in this latter case, it may nevertheless express some disavowed attitude of the self.

Mathematicians would say that the object is *a structure immersed in the self* and so one of the structures of the self. We might in fact choose the various objects as representants of the various structures of the self.

Types and number of objects. The word 'object' has become stereotyped. It seems to cause great satisfaction to some people. Sometimes it is used in the plural, suggesting that there are many objects; at other times it is used in the singular, as though suggesting something very general. How many types of object are there? The answer seems to be that there are really very few; father and mother are unquestionably whole objects, while breast and penis are part objects. Mention is also made of dangerous faeces and other part objects having qualities which usually are of a destructive kind, for instance the fragmented penis; also the mother reduced to bits. The concept of bizarre object has permitted, perhaps, all these bits to be subsumed under one name. Bion (1967) has pointed out that the particles in question lead an independent life outside the ego. It could be said that, in phantasy, they become persons which either contain or are contained in external objects. We could compare such objects to unicellular beings, similar to the original cell.

I think that bizarre objects are split-off 'parts' of the personality which have come to be experienced as whole 'personalities'. Each of these may 'incarnate' one or a few functions of a personality which itself is conceived as having many functions. They are in their spatial aspects isomorphic with *lying spaces or sub-spaces* of a given *n*-dimensional space. This in turn is isomorphic with the total personality. The bizarre objects would have, therefore, a lesser number of dimensions than the original personality from which they originated. At the same time they have become independent from it. So to speak, they have ceased to be isomorphic to sub-spaces, but become isomorphic to '*independent spaces*' of a smaller number of dimensions.[3]

Apart from those just mentioned, one does not hear of other types of object. It seems strange, for instance, to think of any internal hand or foot or head or fingernail. If such an idea were plausible the object in question could certainly then be felt as a person, distinguishable from other objects-persons by its special function. In the case of the hand this would be grasping; in the foot, stamping; in the head, thinking; in the fingernail, scratching; etc. They would each have, as a spatial object, a smaller number of dimensions than the original personality from which they came. This idea is important, as will be seen later.

At the same time, of course, at deeper levels the breast not only stands for the whole mother but *is* the whole mother. The same thing holds for the penis and the whole father. Thus the various types of object finally converge into two: those which are the father and those which are the mother. These are at times felt, respectively, as penis-father and womb-mother, breast-mother, etc. They are like sub-spaces which have become 'independent spaces'.

A similar principle holds with regard to the number of objects. The enormous multiplicity of objects is connected with and serves to express the infinite power of a given single object, which can be either destructive or beneficial. Note, however, that each of the types of a given part object is connected with a given function of the personality. These functions can be put into correspondence with dimensions. The number of objects which are experienced at any time seems, instead, related to the intensity of these functions; greater number means greater intensity. There is a correspondence here between intensity, which is only theoretically measurable, and the more easily measurable number of objects.[4]

On the other hand, as just mentioned, a greater or lesser number of objects can, in turn, be expressed in terms of a greater or lesser number of dimensions.

The paradoxical bi-logical structure of the object. Clinical observation shows that an object – breast, penis, good or bad mother – is often felt as something quite concrete. Frequently it is experienced as a well-defined three-dimensional object which has the characteristics of a person who is felt as being inside the self and who performs good or bad actions. Sometimes it is expelled in fantasy by means of vomit or diarrhoea. All this corresponds to a characteristic of the unconscious: to treat physical and psychical reality as identical – an expression of the principle of symmetry. At the same time it is absurd, from some points of view, to attribute material qualities to the internal object. It is obviously absurd, for instance, to say that someone has an internal penis which measures so many centimetres in length and so many in diameter; or that somebody has introjected the right breast of his mother, Mrs Maria B, and that, considering that it was congested at the moment of the introjection, it is now a sphere of the size of a small melon. Whoever spoke like this would be thought mad. Yet, in some way not easy to understand, the object *is* felt as concrete or well delimited (even as a person), and is felt as though it were inside, while also being outside at the same time: again the principle of symmetry in action.

By contrast, we frequently hear mention of '*the* breast', which, upon reflection, clearly indicates the class or set of all breasts. In fact, if seen from this angle, the breast is no longer a concrete individual object, but rather a class of objects, and no longer is inside the individual. It would even be nearer to the truth to say that the individual is inside the breast. The breast as a class, breastness, includes every individual breast. In this case the 'concrete' introjected breast, seen as a spatial object, would be isomorphic to a region or sub-space (cf. Chapter 15, page 297) of a wider space isomorphic to breastness. In consequence an individual who has introjected a breast would, in so far as he is the breast, also be isomorphic to a region of the space which is isomorphic to breastness. It must be kept in mind, however, that this individual also has other dimensions as well as breastness. This would mean that, so far as the breast is concerned, he is being isomorphic to either a region or a sub-space inside breastness. But with regard to the other dimensions he is outside breastness. This gives an inkling of the complexity which this question unravels when it is broached with concepts more sophisticated than that of material, three-dimensional space.

It seems to me that there are two problems about the concept of object for usual (so far) psychoanalytical thinking. First, there is the problem that the object is felt as being quite concrete and yet, at the same time, as not having the characteristics of a concrete object. Second, the internal breast, or any other internal object, is felt at the same time as not internal, because it is something more general, like *the* breast or breastness. In fact it is so general as to be no longer internal to the self; rather the self may be said to be in some way internal to the object.

However imperfect these descriptions may be, I believe that with a little reflection many analysts must agree that they describe something that is observed daily in psychoanalytical practice. I think many analysts simply take them for granted. It is surprising to me that they do not become surprised when confronted with such a great number of paradoxes. It is quite impossible to order and understand this type of clinical fact in the light of classical logic only.

Bi-logic, on the other hand, illuminates the issues. Take, for instance, a classical-logical view of the object as something 'concrete' and delimited (the internal breast, say). Suppose that at this moment symmetrical logic slips in one or several of the ways described in bi-logical structures. As a consequence of this, we observe that, in the midst of a classical-logical process of reasoning, the object becomes all the objects. It is then an infinite set. From the point of view of classical logic this is an absurdity or an antinomy, a contradiction between laws. But it is something perfectly coherent in a bi-logical system. One could call this a *bi-logical paradox*, provided it is clear that it is an antinomy in the first logical system and it is neither contradictory nor paradoxical in the second. This would represent, I believe, a new use of the term 'paradox': a bi-logical use, which, however, seems justified in order to be able to describe this curious situation.

I want to try to understand the paradox just mentioned by means of an example. Euclidean three-dimensional space is, of course, conceived as being infinite. Any three-dimensional object in this space – for instance, a house, or a group of houses, a breast, or a penis – can be described as a (finite) region of the (Euclidean) three-dimensional infinite space. More accurately, it is said to occupy a region of it.

The class of all conceivable breasts could be considered as occupying a set of regions; and this would also be an infinite set. When the breast is considered as something concrete (one breast) it will occupy one region. If this breast, concrete or delimited object, is also seen, in conformity with the principle of symmetry, as identical to the set of all breasts (identity between the part and the whole), it will then be also and simultaneously the (infinite) set of all the regions just mentioned. In classical logic it cannot at the same time be both alternatives (element and class). But in bi-logic this is quite possible. It is important to keep in mind that in any of these three possibilities (part, whole, part-and-whole) the dimensionality of the object is the same: three-dimensionality.[5]

Part object: a witness to the birth of thinking. I have often reiterated that in the experience of indivisible unity no distinction is made either between self and not-self or between something and something else. This distinction seems to be 'discovered' with the first frustration. For it is then that the principle of non-contradiction is also discovered.[6] '*x* is good', '*x* is bad' would be among the first propositional functions defined as a consequence of frustration. This must be the splitting of the object into a good and a bad object. With this comes the first glimmer of the idea '*x* is good and not bad' at the same time. This has the beginning of the principle of non-contradiction in it. In adult classical-logical thinking, it is not possible to identify an individual by means of only one propositional function; many of them are needed. For example, Helvi R. is a woman (propositional function: 'x is a woman'), a Finn (propositional function: 'x is a Finn'), twenty-five years old ('x is twenty-five years old' defines the class of all those who are twenty-five years old), born in Helsinki ('x is born in, etc.'), a singer, blonde, and so on. The individual Helvi R. is then defined as 'the element of a one-element class formed by the intersection of a certain number of classes' (Matte-Blanco 1975b: 336).

Let us now consider a bad internal breast. What defines it as bad is the pain it causes (an internal sensation of hunger), which is not clearly defined: unpleasant sensation or, better, *the* unpleasant. This is not quite defined either. What defines it as a breast is only its 'otherness'. This is the fact of it being something different from the self; it would then be the not-self. The bad breast's 'concreteness' or individuality thus rests upon two things: the fact of it being not-self and the fact of it being unpleasant. We say that the small baby identifies it as a bad breast. If the baby could explain this concept he would possibly say that what defines it is constituted by only two propositional functions: 'x is not-self' and 'x is unpleasant'. Perhaps the first is, in its turn, a consequence of the second – though one could, perhaps with equal correctness, say that the second is a consequence of the first.

It is obvious that this analysis is a simplification, because, even if we admit the improbability that only two propositional functions are present in this initial identification of the breast, each of these two propositional functions presupposes other propositional functions. What is more, thinking cannot develop at only one 'point' but it rather requires a 'region' of triads (Matte-Blanco 1975a: 345–49), perhaps an infinite number of them. However this may be, it is obvious that, if we compare *the concept* of bad breast, as we imagine that the child sees it, with that of an individual person we soon realize that in the first case the number of intersecting classes which defines the bad breast is immensely inferior to the number of classes of the second one; to define an individual in a given class we have to employ many more properties than those required to define the class.

We may, therefore, say that the asymmetrical relations which are visible arising *out* of the experience of indivisible unity at the dawn of thinking are very few. It then becomes understandable why the breast is felt as the indivisible unity, 'clad', up to this point, in very scarce clothing of relations. It can easily be simultaneously lived as a (relatively) indivisible unity *and* as a (relatively) concrete object. It may also rather obscurely be considered as an infinite set. All this is already bi-logic. Put in a few words, the so-called part-object breast is found at the first crossing, at the first point of the co-presence of the experience of indivisible unity with dividing heterogenic thinking. Perhaps it is the first example of a bi-logical structure.

I now want to consider *splitting and idealization*. Psychoanalysts speak of idealized and persecutory objects. If the meaning of 'ideal' is intended as that which is conceived of as perfect of its kind, we then may call the process which corresponds to persecution with the name of *negative idealization*. The fundamental relation between both concepts is in this way underlined; the objects are in fact different from one another only with regard to the sign.

Distinction or splitting between a good and a bad object is a prerequisite for positive or negative idealization. This splitting, in its turn, requires the distinction between self and not-self. In other words, it presupposes the moment of development in which the baby obscurely discovers that he is not *the* indivisible unity – which *we* see from the outside as the mother–child unity – i.e. it presupposes the birth of thinking, the discovery of the principle of non-contradiction, as we have already seen.

Once the splitting into a good and bad object has taken place, the child seems to feel that each of the new objects is one indivisible unity. He 'sees' each symmetrically. Yet the child has already begun to think, that is, to establish asymmetrical relations which differentiate each thing from all others. The result is that, unconsciously and from an asymmetrical point of view, he 'sees' this 'symmetrical seeing' of symmetrization as something infinite. The good object is idealized, it is 'seen' as having all goodness: as infinitely good. Likewise the frustrating object is negatively idealized, that is, it is seen as infinitely bad. *We can therefore speak of symmetrization translated (asymmetrical) into infinitization.* This way of looking at things represents a characteristic conjunction of both modes of being: a typical bi-logical structure of the Simassi type. I would like to add that idealization is seen with regard not only to part object but also to whole ones. Correspondingly, symmetrizations 'translated' in terms of infinity are not exclusively part-object phenomena.

Part object: an ambiguous notion. At the present moment of development of psychoanalysis we find that some analysts behave as though the reference to part objects represented for them a guarantee of 'work in depth'. It would seem as though 'the breast' and 'the object' (always or almost always intended as part object) would confer a special prestige to whomever employs the terms. When I come across such attitudes, and this happens frequently, I am reminded of two processes isomorphic to it. First, some years ago there was an attitude in some young priests who felt they were extremely 'progressive' because they wanted to say mass and receive communion not once or twice a day but four or five times. Second, there was also the historical evolution of psychoanalysis from the Oedipus complex or phase to the ('deeper') anal-sadistic complex (or phase), to the still deeper oral phase, thence to foetal psychical life. No doubt this evolution has followed a fertile path, but it also has, in some ways, led to the implicit belief that exploring the earlier stages of development was the only way to 'deepen' our knowledge. One may ask why the process has not gone on to consider the pre-foetal 'stages' and metempsychosis! There seems to be a misunderstanding here; the notion of earlier stages of development is implicitly considered as synonymous to that of deeper levels. What in fact happens seems to be this: the earlier stages usually or always correspond to deeper levels, but the converse is not true, for there can be a deep level which refers to later stages. This imprecision is readily solved if we define the depth of a mental level in terms of the proportion between symmetry and asymmetry observed in it.

In the case of the idea of the part object, the attitude in question has led to an ambiguity. For adult thinking the breast is obviously a part of the feminine body, and its properties, activities, or characteristics are a part of the characteristics of a mother. The same thing holds for the penis with regard to a man. If, instead, we consider the manner in which the unconscious treats these objects, we soon realize that things are not this way. The deeper levels of the mind, and these are the levels where we find part objects, are characterized by two important features. First, the part tends to be confused with the whole; and the deeper the level the more complete this confusion becomes. Secondly, part objects are, at these levels, considered as persons. This is quite clear, for instance when Bion (1967) speaks of the hostility of particles towards the psyche which has expelled them.

If we integrate these two aspects of the 'behaviour' of the unconscious we may say that *the smallest unit which exists for certain levels of the unconscious is the person and not one aspect of it.*[7] However, classical-logical thinking, even though it recognizes that the concept of person entails that of a unit, is capable of seeing various aspects in it; but the deep unconscious sees every unit as indivisible. Furthermore, it sees or knows only one aspect of a person (one at a time, as it were) and treats this aspect as though it were a whole person.

To the deep unconscious, the breast is a person who does not have parts, and for us observers appears too simplified to be describable as part object. In other words, the behaviour of the unconscious with respect to the breast may be considered as the personification of the 'breast property or aspect' of the mother, a property or aspect which

285

the unconscious obscurely perceives, in a simplified way, in terms of very few (implicit) propositional functions. These propositional functions, if there are more than one, become fused in only one: a unifying, not a dividing, tendency.

If one were to put these ideas in terms of space, one would say that, for the visible aspect of an adult's thinking the adult mother is isomorphic with an n-dimensional space, and the concept of breast would be, for an adult, isomorphic to one of its sub-spaces, which has a number of dimensions considerably smaller than n. At the same time the adult sees a mother as a whole object, and the breast as a part object. This would mean, from a certain angle, that a mother is not viewed as isomorphic to a sub-space but as isomorphic to an 'independent space'. At 'deeper' levels of the mind, however (levels which are preponderant in the small baby), the breast is not seen as (isomorphic to) a sub-space, but as (isomorphic to) an independent space.

I think that anyone who has analytical experience would be able to confirm these assertions. They are in fact nothing else but the explicit and more precise formulation of concepts which are inherent in psychoanalytical work with part objects. Once these concepts are clarified, one becomes aware that the term 'part object', together with the concept underlying it, is extremely ambiguous because it tries to describe reality from a point of view which is neither entirely that of the unconscious nor that of scientific thinking. In fact the unconscious knows only 'total' objects, which appear as extremely simplified to scientific thinking. For instance, is a person-mother reduced to a person-breast, or a person-father reduced to a person-penis? On the other hand, in 'scientific' descriptions of the behaviour of the unconscious, the word 'part' is misleading because it points precisely to the opposite of what it means to describe. I have no intention of proposing alternatives but I will say that expressions such as 'breast-mother', 'personified penis', or 'penis-person' seem more accurate to me. I think it is useless to try to go against the stream and I believe, instead, that a greater familiarity with the concepts underlying our present conceptions will end by eliminating their unsatisfactory use without pain.

Notes

1 Consider, for instance, that Freud refers to 'object' and to its connections to other concepts around 250 to 300 times.
2 German *Beziehungen*, literally 'relations'. In the first edition this word is

printed *Bezeichnungen* ('descriptions' or 'terms'), which seems to make better sense. The word 'relations' in the later part of the sentence stands for *Relationen* in the German text.

3 The concept of 'independent space' deserves some explanation. For centuries scientific thinking has viewed three-dimensional, so-called material space as something not related to other spaces, but as something considered in itself. If I am not wrong, it was towards the end of the nineteenth century that the view was developed of 4-, 5- . . . *n*-, up to infinite-dimensional spaces. It then became clear that any *n*-dimensional space could be seen as a sub-space of a space of a higher number of dimensions, or as a 'hyperspace' of a space of a lower number of dimensions. I propose to call 'independent space' a space of any number of dimensions so far as it is considered in itself and not in its relations to other spaces. This happens frequently. We usually view our three-dimensional body without putting it in relation to objects which have a higher or lower number of dimensions. I believe this precision is useful for our study.

4 For the question of measurability of psychical processes, see Matte-Blanco 1975a: part V.

5 As for cardinality, the question is not so clear. We know that the cardinality of the set of points called Euclidean space is that of the continuum or power of the continuum. The cardinality of a set of regions is not clear to me. On the one hand it seems that it can be put in bi-univocal correspondence with the set of integers, for the set is formed of a number *n* of regions, *n* being any natural number. In this case this set may arrive at having the cardinality of the set of all natural numbers or integers. On the other hand, it does not seem impossible but I am not sure that it is possible to put it in one-to-one correspondence with a set of points, in which case it would have the power of the continuum. It would seem that in bi-logic both these alternatives can coexist. The case, however, requires further reflection before drawing a conclusion. It seems that the third possibility, part *and* whole, can also be seen along similar lines to the second. If this were so, the matter should also be further studied.

6 For further details, see Matte-Blanco 1975b: 255–59 and 262–69.

7 The assertion about the person being the smallest unit is true only for a zone of co-presence between both modes, i.e. that zone where the notions of small and big are still amply available, and this is the reason for the reference to certain layers. The 'gymnastics' of co-presence are disturbing and exciting!

15

Some more mathematical concepts of space, dimension, outside, and inside

Foreword. My aim in this chapter is to introduce some further mathematical concepts which I believe will be helpful if we are to try to think further about the internal world.[1] Now, I am aware that many psychoanalysts are inclined to discount the value of mathematical notions for the study of the internal world. They seem to feel that there is no correspondence between psychical objects and mathematical abstractions. I believe that such views are based on a misconception of mathematics and a rather too simple-minded idea about the concepts regularly used by psychoanalysts.

Such critics often think of mathematics in terms of arithmetic. I must confess that if this were true I would be inclined to agree with them. In fact, arithmetical calculations do not have much of a part to play in our understanding of the internal world. The notions of outside, inside, and dimension, however, are matters for detailed study in mathematics and these concepts are quite clearly central to psycho-analytic thinking. Psychoanalytic conceptions about inside and outside are mostly taken without much thought from the more or less naïve notions which are ordinarily employed in our everyday understanding of the physical world. Clear definitions and consider-ations of the spatial notions employed in psychoanalysis are absent. Because ordinary spatial notions can be expressed in mathematical ways, it seems likely that the formal consideration of exactly these concepts by mathematicians might be useful.

1 The concept of space

To understand what I have in mind the reader must allow me to present some rather elementary concepts of geometry and topology which seem indispensable for understanding the complexity of internal psychical reality and its relationship with the material world. To the reader who does not think he or she is a mathematician I would say: do not despair, have some patience, and what follows will be easier than you think. I hope you will forgive some repetition, for it gives greater assurance when considering the internal psychical world and will save getting muddled in problems which appear insoluble when they are formulated in an unsatisfactory manner.

To start with, it is impossible to think properly about the concept of an internal world without having some notion about the concepts of space and time. So we start with a question. Kant is reputed to have asked: 'What are, then, space and time?' Obviously, I have no space in this book to answer fully such fundamental questions, had I the knowledge to do so. I will have to content myself with making some suggestions about how these matters can be considered.[2]

Descartes affirmed that the mind or spirit was intensity and matter was extension. This remark assumes a new meaning in the context of what I have said about emotion in Chapter 14; I have suggested that the expression of the intensity of an emotion seems to be related to the number of dimensions by which it is expressed.

> 'The space of the child, of the primitive man, of the organic patient, perceptual space . . . could all be reunited under the common name of *psychological space* . . .
>
> 'We then have *physical space*. It would be that which we employ in less anthropocentric thinking in order to place external objects and processes.
>
> 'We see them in the visual space, we hear them in the auditory space but we think them as developing in physical space.'
>
> (Hessen 1950: Vol. 3, 99, my italics)

I would also mention *mathematical space* and it is to this I turn. In mathematics the term 'space' is usually employed 'to denote the "ambient" in which the facts of geometry are imagined to be immersed' (Manara 1980: 556). On the other hand, it is possible to go on generalizing and arrive at a concept of space which enables us to give a geometrical interpretation of any set which can be related to common-sense intuition. These generalizations give rise to the concept of abstract space.

Space and perception. The three quotations suggest, in some way, that the concept of space has been developed from a reflection about our perceptual experience. Starting from this, thinking has gone on to more and more abstract conceptions where our perception and imagination are in some way left behind. Yet they are somewhere present, as a component, even in the midst of the most abstract, non-imaginable conception of space. I think that the work of future analysts in this field should never abandon the more primitive conceptions of space, but at the same time they will have to go on to the more abstract mathematical notions that clinical experience suggest (for instance, the Multidim structure). It seems to me that future psychoanalysis can make important contributions to the development of very abstract concepts 'lodged' in the midst of the very concrete perceptual experiences of dream and imagination. I also believe that the concept of multidimensionalization, not only of space, but also of time, is a step in this direction.

2 Numbers, points, and space

Let us remember some elementary notions. We start from the set of natural numbers {1, 2, 3, etc.} which, as is known, is an infinite set. We add 0 and the negative numbers (which also constitute an infinite set) and we then have the set of all integers. We now add *rational numbers*, i.e. those which can be written as a quotient between two integers – for instance, 1/1, 5/1, −2/3, and 55/999. As can be seen from this example, the integers are a subset of the set of rational numbers.

This enumeration does not exhaust the set of numbers. There are others, called *irrational numbers*, which cannot be written as the quotient of two integers – for instance, the square root of 2, π (pi) (= 3·14159 . .), and '*e*' (= 2·71828 . . .). If we wish to express these numbers in terms of decimals, we will find that an infinite number of digits is required in each case and that these digits are not repeated in regular cycles, as happens in the case of some rational numbers (10/3, for example, can be written as 3·33333 . . . up to an infinite number of digits).

The set of rational and irrational numbers is called *the set of real numbers*. To these must be added the imaginary numbers, which we shall not consider here. The set of real numbers can be put in one-to-one correspondence with the set of all the points of *an oriented straight line*, that is, a straight line to which a certain *sense* has been assigned. That sense is called the positive, and the opposite sense is called the negative.

The notion of sense essentially points to the concept of *ordination of the points* of the straight line. By convention we may now choose a point, which we shall call the origin and indicate by the number 0, and *a unit of measurement*. Once this is done, it is possible to establish a one-to–one correspondence between the set of real numbers and the set of the points of this straight line (which is called *the real-number line or real axis*). Thus to each real point there corresponds one and only one real number. The number corresponding to the given point is usually called the abscissa of the point. (For further details see Martinelli 1974: ch. 1.)

3 Dimension

Preliminary notions. Starting from these notions we may now consider what is meant by dimension, which is not without difficulty and certainly cannot be discussed here in all its meanings. I shall try, however, to give some idea of it, because it is essential for the consideration of the so-called internal world; on the other hand, although it has scarcely been mentioned in psychoanalysis so far, it is now perhaps beginning to be used. Dimension is employed in relation to the concept of space (Matte-Blanco 1975a: 409):

'It is common knowledge that the point is said to have no dimensions, that the line has one dimension, the surface two and the volume three. What we call "real space" is three-dimensional.

'There are two ways of considering the problem of space, the analytical and the geometrical. In the analytical method the *number* is considered to be the fundamental object and its geometrical representation is only a way of *visualising* it. In the space of one dimension the number determines the point. When there are two variables, x and y, which determine a given point, we speak of a space of two dimensions. This is frequently represented in a system of co-ordinates, x and y, in which a given value of x and a given value of y determine a point. When the variables are three we speak of a space of three dimensions or volume. It is obvious that for the analytical method there is no limitation in speaking of a space of four, five . . . *n* dimensions, according to the number of variables. Space of three or of fewer than three dimensions may be visualised in a geometrical representation but this is not the case with spaces of more than three dimensions.'

Dimension and structure. I suggest that it is not possible to develop the concept of dimension, and hence that of space, without *the concept of structure*. We have started from the set of real numbers, represented by the oriented straight line or real axis. Now the real axis is an order structure, and the same may be said of the set of real numbers, which is in one-to-one correspondence with it. A set to which one or more relations have been assigned is called a structure.[3] Order is in fact a fundamental type of structure, in which the relation is that of order, i.e. point a precedes or follows point b.

Even the more abstract definitions of dimension make use of the concept of structure. It seems pertinent to mention at this point that Russell (1903 [1948]: ch. 44) develops the concept of dimension from that of sequence which requires that of order and, hence, of structure. Let us now try to see how the concept of dimension is based upon the order structure.

Let A be a set: $A = \{1, 2, 3\}$, i.e. a set formed of three elements. This is a subset of the set of all natural numbers or integers. Starting from it we may now form the so-called Cartesian product, in this case $A \times A$, which may also be written as A^2. This product is the set of all *ordered pairs* – that is, pairs which have a first and second element – that can be formed with the numbers 1, 2, 3. The number of such pairs is $3 \times 3 = 9$. (Note that the product of a set by itself, $A \times A$ or A^2, is not the same as the square of a number.) In order to facilitate the construction of the Cartesian product, the following table may be used.

$A = \{1, 2, 3\}$
Now, $A \times A = \{(1, 1), (1, 2), (1, 3), (2, 1), (2, 2), (2, 3), (3, 1),$
$(3, 2), (3, 3)\}$ (a total of $3 \times 3 = 9$ elements)

Written in another way, $A \times A = A^2$.

$A = \{1, 2, 3\}$

A

	1	2	3
1	1, 1	1, 2	1, 3
2	2, 1	2, 2	2, 3
3	3, 1	3, 2	3, 3

A

Note that in this case each compartment corresponds to one element of the new set, $A \times A$. Each element of this new set is an *ordered pair*; for instance (1, 2) is not the same as (2, 1).

We may now multiply $A^2 \times A = A^3$.

$$A^2 \times A = \left\{ \begin{array}{l} (1,1,1), (1,1,2), (1,1,3), (1,2,1), (1,2,2), (1,2,3), \\ (1,3,1), (1,3,2), (1,3,3), (2,1,1), (2,1,2), (2,1,3), \\ (2,2,1), (2,2,2), (2,2,3), (2,3,1), (2,3,2), (2,3,3), \\ (3,1,1), (3,1,2), (3,1,3), (3,2,1), (3,2,2), (3,2,3), \\ (3,3,1), (3,3,2), (3,3,3) \end{array} \right\}$$

Written in another way, this set is: $A \times A \times A = A^3 = 27$.

A

	1	2	3
1, 1	1, 1, 1	1, 1, 2	1, 1, 3
1, 2	1, 2, 1	1, 2, 2	1, 2, 3
1, 3	1, 3, 1	1, 3, 2	1, 3, 3
2, 1	2, 1, 1	2, 1, 2	2, 1, 3
2, 2	2, 2, 1	2, 2, 2	2, 2, 3
2, 3	2, 3, 1	2, 3, 2	2, 3, 3
3, 1	3, 1, 1	3, 1, 2	3, 1, 3
3, 2	3, 2, 1	3, 2, 2	3, 2, 3
3, 3	3, 3, 1	3, 3, 2	3, 3, 3

$A \times A = A^2$ (left label)

$A \times A \times A = A^3$

(a total of $3 \times 3 \times 3 = 27$ elements)

It can be seen in this case that each compartment of the table contains one element of the new set, and that this element is not formed by an ordered pair but by three numbers put in a certain order. In other words, the elements of A^2 are ordered pairs, that is, sets formed in their turn by two elements each, whereas the elements of A^3 are sets formed each of three elements: ordered triplets. We can continue to form ordered 4-ples, ordered 5-ples . . . ordered n-ples.

Dimension and total order. With these notions in hand, we can now tackle better the concept of dimension. Let us consider the ordered set of all real numbers, which we can identify with the letter R. This is a *totally ordered set*. Each and any of its elements (i.e. any number) is less than that which follows it and greater than that which precedes it. We know already that this set can be put in one-to-one correspondence with the points of a straight line. If we take R we have a space of one dimension, whose elements are the numbers or points. Each element is identified by only one number, i.e. the distance of

293

the point from its origin. If we now form the Cartesian product $R \times R = R^2$ each element is then identified by two numbers, i.e. the distances of the abscissa and of the ordinate from the origin. In a graphical representation this can be done by means of the so-called Cartesian system of abscissae and ordinates, i.e. two perpendicular straight lines. The set of all ordered pairs of $R \times R$ identifies all the points of the plane, which is a space of two dimensions.

We may now proceed to construct R^3. In a graphical representation this is obtained by tracing a perpendicular line to the plane formed by the abscissa and the ordinate of the plane. In this way each point of this new, three-dimensional space is determined by an ordered triplet, whose first number indicates the distance[4] from the origin, that is, from the 0 in the abscissa; the second number indicates the distance from the origin in the ordinate of the plane, and the third the distance from the origin in the ordinate of the volume (depth).

We can, therefore, see that a point is determined in the straight line by only one number, in the plane by two and in the volume or three-dimensional space by three. It is said that in these cases the point has, respectively, *one, two, or three degrees of freedom*. To explain, since we must fix the origin or 0, we may say that a point in a line is determined by two numbers: 0, and the distance of this point from 0. Correspondingly in a plane it is determined by three numbers and in a volume by four. As 0 has 0 degrees of freedom, i.e. it is at 0 distance from itself, this explains why we speak of one, two, and three degrees of freedom as just said.

From the analytical point of view, nothing prevents us from building up to 4, 5, 6 . . . n degrees of freedom. We then speak of a space of four, five . . . n dimensions. It can easily be seen that the number of dimensions of a given space coincides with that of the degrees of freedom of the point in that space, or (said in other words) with the number of elements contained in each of the ordered n-ples of the space in question; and the pairs or the triplets or the n-ples of numbers are nothing else than the set of all the coordinates that determine the point in the set in question. And each of these coordinates is nothing else than the respective distance from the origin, (a) of the abscissa, (b) of the ordinate in the plane, (c) of the ordinate in the volume, (d), (e) . . . (n) of the successive ordinates, according to the dimensions of the space under consideration.

Definition of a point in a given space. I shall try to explain this concept by means of an example – see *Figure 6.* Take a given rectangle of, say, 5 × 10 cm. If this rectangle is a region of a plane, as is represented in this figure, then each of its four vertices is determined by two numbers which are the values of the respective abscissa of $X1$-coordinate and the ordinate of $X2$-coordinate of that point in the plane. In *Figure 6* we see that the point A is defined by the ordered pair (1.5; 3) the first number (1.5) corresponding to the abscissa or $X1$-coordinate, and the second one (3) corresponding to the ordinate of $X2$-coordinate. If the rectangle were a sub-space of a volume we would have to add an $X3$-coordinate, which would locate the point in the dimension depth. In this case the point would be defined by a set of three numbers, a triplet – say, in this case, (1.5; 3; 7). We can to up the scale to 4-, 5- . . . n-ples, according to the number of dimensions of the space. In a space of, say, ten dimensions, each point of a region of it is determined by a set of ten numbers, each of which gives the position of the point in one dimension of the space to which the point belongs.

Domain of definition of each dimension. We know that the cardinality or number of elements of the set of points of the real axis is that of the continuum or, as it is also said, the power of the continuum, which is the same as the cardinality of the set of real numbers. The set of all these points or numbers constitutes what is called the domain of definition (see Spiegel 1974: 20) of the function called dimension, i.e. the set of all possible values that each dimension may

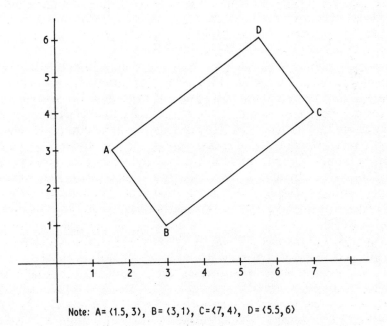

Note: A= ⟨1.5, 3⟩, B= ⟨3, 1⟩, C=⟨7, 4⟩, D=⟨5.5, 6⟩

Figure 6

take. We may, therefore, say that the domain of definition of each dimension has the power of the continuum.

Domain of the set of dimensions. This is a different concept from that of the domain of definition of each dimension. We have already seen that the concept of space of *n* dimensions is built starting from the concepts of sequence and of Cartesian products of the set of real numbers. It is known that the terms of a sequence are identified as (for instance) $s1$, $s2$, $s3$ . . . sn, that is, employing the sequence of the set of integers of natural numbers. The same thing holds for any Cartesian product, in our case R^1, R^2, R^3, . . . R^n. It seems inconceivable, for instance, to speak of a term S_π (pi lowered) of a succession or of a Cartesian product of R^π (pi raised). Put in more general terms, *the set of dimensions may be put in one-to-one correspondence with the set of integers or natural numbers*, that is, it has the cardinality or power of this set. This is called *the power of the denumerable*, which is infinitely smaller than that of the continuum. I do not know any mathematical study on dimension which is not based upon this fact, which seems to be, so far, a fundamental principle in mathematics.

In contrast to this principle, Meltzer (1975: 224) affirms: 'It would seem to us that splitting-and-idealisation would arise as a logical necessity somewhere *between* the establishment of bi-dimensionality and *before the transition* to three-dimensionality' (my italics). If Meltzer means to say that there are psychical phenomena such as those he mentions which happen in a set with the power of the continuum, then he may be putting forward a revolutionary new concept of dimension, such as the very recently developed 'fractal'. In this case it would be most important for him to explain it further. Or he may be using the mathematical concept of dimension in an incorrect way, and then it would be necessary to explain why he does so. I am not saying that Meltzer is wrong, but that, without apparently knowing it, he uses a concept of dimension which by its nature must be mathematical and yet may be incompatible with present-day mathematics. Psychoanalytical experience may arrive at a new conception of space which is richer than the present one. But, in order to be fertile, each new conception must be clearly explained and justified.

Sub-spaces, hyperspaces, lying or subordinate spaces, and regions. The expression that a given point has only one degree of freedom means that this point is defined in a space of one dimension, the line. If the point has two degrees of freedom, it is defined in a plane, if three in a volume, which can be represented with the system of (three) Cartesian coordinates. We may conceive a point with 4, 5 . . . *n* . . . up to an infinite number of degrees of freedom; and the dimensions of the corresponding space are the same as those of the degrees of freedom.

Let us now consider a straight line which is in a given plane. It is said that in this case the straight line lies in this space (Sommerville 1929 [1958]: 4–9). A plane may lie in a volume, and this, in its turn, in a space of four dimensions.[5]

Put by means of examples, the plane (two dimensions) is a hyper-space of the line; the volume (three dimensions) is a hyperspace of a plane, which in its turn is a sub-space of a volume. The volume is a sub-space of a four-dimensional space, and so on. This is a very important concept to consider in a study which aims at developing the idea of internal world so as to make it capable of comprehending clinical realities which hitherto have passed unnoticed on account of lack of notions capable of 'lodging' them.

Lying spaces are also called sub-spaces or subordinate spaces (Martinelli 1974: 346). The concept to be kept in mind for our purposes is that of the relationships existing between spaces of different dimensions. The term 'lying' depicts the situation in an eloquent way which seems useful in the study of the mind, because the internal objects are conceived of as beings, endowed with activity; and the term 'lying' transmits this idea, just as the adjective 'subordinate' points to other aspects of the problem which are also important to our context.

Let us proceed. Starting from the point 0, a straight line extends infinitely in both senses. A subset of this line, for instance that comprised between points 3 and 7 with both endpoints included, is called *a segment of a straight line.* It has the dimension of the line, i.e. one dimension. In the case of subsets of a plane, of a three-dimensional space, or of a space of any other dimensions, we speak of *a region or sub-region of a space* (Sommerville 1929 [1958], and Courant and Robbins 1941 [1969]). A cube, for instance, is a region of three-dimensional space. With three sections perpendicular between themselves, we could obtain from it eight smaller cubes, each of which has, as is obvious, the same number of dimensions as the original cube: again three regions. The distinction between, on the one hand, a sub-space (or subordinate or lying space) of a space, which is always of a lower number of dimensions than its space, and, on the other hand, the region of a space, which is always iso-dimensional to it, seems to be of prime importance for a study of the internal psychical world, as we have already seen in the Tridim structure and in the Multidim structure.

4 The concepts of external and internal

If applied to the mind, these concepts have many similarities with those which hold in so-called material real space and in geometry. But they have many fundamental differences. There is an 'isomorphism' between all three but certainly not an identity. The most important difference, as I see it, is that whereas the principle of symmetry is not normally found in finite geometry, or in the finite spatial sensory world, it has a most important role in psychical life, including, as we have already seen, our notions of internal and external. And this fact creates a colossal difference.

If, however, we wish to build on solid ground our notions of external and internal world we must try to know quite clearly the (asymmetrical) corresponding notions of geometry, mathematical analysis, and topology. We cannot ignore them for the simple reason that we cannot do away with them. So far, they are used in psychoanalysis in a very primitive and vague sense, and this results in obscurity and imprecision. The road I am proposing is to try first to master these notions and, once this is done, to be prepared to use them with freedom and creativity in the exploration of the psychical internal and external. This is a complex jungle with many more things in it than in present-day mathematics.

I now want to try to build the notions of external and internal from some simple and basic mathematical notions. We shall proceed step by step.

(a) Bounded, open and closed, half-open, and half-closed intervals.

'Suppose a and b are two numbers such that $a < b$.[6] The set of all numbers x between a and b is called the *open interval* from a to b and we write[7] as $a < x < b$. The points a and b are called the endpoints of the interval. Note that the open interval does not include its endpoints.

'The open interval $a < x < b$, together with its endpoints a and b, is called the closed interval between a and b and is indicated as $a \leq x \leq b$.'

(Ayres 1965: 2)

The closed interval, for example between a and b, is indicated in the following way: [a, b]; the open interval is written (a, b); when it is closed at one extreme and open at the other it is called half-open or half-closed and is indicated respectively as (a, b] or [a, b) (see Spiegel 1974: 4, and Cecconi and Stampacchia 1974: 36). As can be seen, all intervals we have so far considered have endpoints. These endpoints act as bounds so that intervals are automatically *bounded intervals*.

(b) Unbounded intervals. Let us take any number, for instance *a*. The set of all numbers *x* less than *a* is called an unbounded or infinite interval. It is sufficient to compare this concept with that of a bounded interval to understand why it is so called. Other examples of unbounded intervals would be all numbers equal to or less than any number, *a*; all numbers greater than *a*; all numbers equal to or greater than *a*.

(c) Neighbourhood. Let *a* be any number, for instance 100, and let δ be any other positive number, for instance 3. The set of all real numbers between *a* − δ and *a* + δ (in our case the numbers between 97 and 103) is called a δ neighbourhood of *a*. The concept of neighbourhood is, therefore, that of an open interval.

Let us now give a more difficult definition which says exactly the same but in a more concise way: 'The set of all points *x* such that | *x* − *a* | < δ[8] where δ > 0 is called a δ neighbourhood of the point *a*' (Spiegel 1974: 5).

When the number *a* (in our example: 100) is not a member of the neighbourhood, this latter is called a *deleted* δ *neighbourhood of* a. In our example it would be constituted by all numbers greater than 97 and less than 103, with the exception of 100.

(d) Interior, exterior, and boundary. Let us consider the already mentioned interval *a* < *x* < *b*. Any point *x* which is greater than *a* and less than *b* is called an interior point of the interval. As can be seen, the numbers *a* and *b* are not interior points of the interval just mentioned.

This definition is simple and understandable, but it is necessary to render it more explicit in order to understand better the concepts of interior, exterior, and boundary in the case of sets which do not refer to points in the straight line, for instance subsets of the plane or of the three-dimensional space, and so on. To explain further, take a set, *S*, of real numbers, and a point *P* which belongs to the set *S*. If there exists a δ neighbourhood of *P* such that all the elements of this neighbourhood belong to the set *S*, then it is said that *P* is an interior point of *S*. (As can be seen, if this condition is met, then the definition of interior point given a moment ago is a particular case of this more general definition.)

We may give an example. If the set *S* is the closed interval [90, 110], the point 100 is an interior point of this set, because if we take, for instance, the number 6 as δ, then the 6 neighbourhood of 100 would be all the numbers which are greater than 94 and less than 106; and, as can be seen, all such points belong to [90, 110]. 100 is, therefore, an interior point of *S*, because all the elements of the 6 neighbourhood of 100 (that is, all the numbers greater than 94 and less than 106) belong to S. In other words, there is at least one δ neighbourhood of P such that all its elements or points belong to S. It will also be seen that, if instead of 6 we choose 3, 5, 8, or 9·9999 as δ, then the points corresponding, respectively, to the 3, 5, etc. neighbourhoods of 100 are all included in S. From this fact the reader will realize that, if the condition that there is one such δ is met, it then follows that there are an infinite number of δ neighbourhoods all of whose points are interior points of S.

I have employed the concept of neighbourhood in order better to explain that of interior point, and I have done it because this concept enables us to give the most general definition of the concept of interior point, one particular case of which may be that of an open interval in a straight line. In the particular case of the straight line we may say that the concept of interior point requires that the point in consideration should belong to an open interval contained in the set. This precision enables us better to define the concept of exterior point and boundary point. Let us study the first of these two.

Consider a point P', and let it be, for instance, 80, and consider a 4 neighbourhood of 80, that is, the set of all numbers x such that $76 < x < 84$. Now we can say that the point P' belonging to the neighbourhood or open interval in question is an exterior point of the set S already mentioned [90, 110]. In other words, a point P' which does not belong to a certain set S is an exterior point of S if there exists at least a δ neighbourhood of P', such that all the points of this neighbourhood do not belong to S.

If, instead, it so happens that for every possible neighbourhood of a point P some of these points belong to the set S and others do not, then the point P is called a boundary point of S. As an example of boundary points of the already mentioned set S, we could mention the points 90 and 110, because every neighbourhood of these points, whatever the δ chosen, must necessarily contain points wich are in S and points which do not belong to S (see also Lipschutz 1965: 47).

We are now in a position to define the interior of a set as the set of all its interior points. Correspondingly the exterior of a set is the set of all its exterior points. The boundary of a set is the set of all its boundary points.

Until now and for greater simplicity we have considered only real-number sets, which are sets of points of the straight line. The same type of definition holds for the sets of points of a plane and for those of a volume, only in this case the point is identified, not with one number, but respectively with two and three (the Cartesian systems of coordinates). From this we can generalize to a space of any number, n, of dimensions.[9] This generalization is summarized in the following quotation, which makes use of intuitive understanding:

'We point out, though, that in the elementary cases we shall consider, the notion of neighbourhood will be spontaneously visible. For example, as neighbourhood of a point in the straight line one can assume a segment containing this point as an interior point; as a neighbourhood of a point in the plane a parallelogram (or a rectangle or a circle) containing the point as an interior point, and so on.'

(Martinelli 1974: 37)

The fact that, according to these definitions, the boundary of a set does not belong to the interior of the set coincides with the concept employed in ordinary life; for example, the surface of the human body is not its interior. It will be seen, however, that the more precise definition given will enable us to understand certain things which otherwise we would not be able to understand. So whoever becomes familiar with these notions will find that the problem of psychical internal reality can be better discovered, understood, and formulated with their help.

Further problems. I have presented certain elementary notions which start from the set of real numbers and from so-called Euclidean spaces. As is easily understandable, a number of problems connected with our subject have not been discussed here. The concept of dimension, for instance, can be further studied, even in the aspects already discussed (see Courant and Robbins 1941: 248–51); and the same can be said of the notion of interior and exterior. One could, furthermore, consider various particular characteristics of each of the various types of space described in mathematics, among which one might mention, in particular, the spaces built from complex numbers.

All this belongs to a further stage of the development of the conception of the internal psychical world, which is still very distant from our present possibilities. I hope we have made a start in this direction.

Imagination and thinking. It seems clear that imagination can consider only spaces of three dimensions. When we try to imagine a space of four or more dimensions we do it 'seeing' as if it had three and then we make use of certain 'tricks' which facilitate the correction of the errors resulting from our limitation. This also holds for spaces of two dimensions: who can imagine a plane without imagining it as a surface of a volume? And the same can be said of the space of one dimension: who can imagine a line and 'see it' with no width (because it would then be a plane) and with no thickness (because it would then be a volume)? The answer is that the line cannot be imagined.

But a space which is not of three dimensions may be thought of. We may make an abstraction of the volume on which, in our vision or imagination, it lies, and conceive a plane. We can do the same thing with a line. Correspondingly, once the concepts are clear, and once we know well what we mean by them, nothing prevents us from conceiving a space of three, four . . . or infinite dimensions. But these spaces are for ever alien, in themselves, to our imagination. Note, therefore, this very important fact: although thinking leans, so to speak, on imagination, it can go beyond it and explore regions which seem to be barred – structurally and for ever – to imagination. This, however, is not the only possibility or 'merit' of thinking, for we must add that, thanks to its translating function, however imperfect this is, thinking 'attracts' or tries to bring the indivisible reality into its own territory. It brings into the realm of human thinking something which is completely alien to it – i.e. something which, owing to the structure of human thinking, is for ever and irretrievably alien to it. So thinking 'moves' in a territory which is beyond the reach of imagination but in which imagination is comprised, as being in a lying space. At the same time, thinking dares to think something which is beyond its own realm, beyond its reach: the 'daring feat of a sub-space' trying to 'bring' into itself the space in which it lies.

I have the impression that psychoanalysts do not make sufficient use of the distinction between thinking and imagination in the construction of a theory about the internal world, and tend to treat the first as though it were the second. The practical result is a conception of the world which is based, quite unconsciously, on the data furnished by imagination. This leads to a lack of awareness and to error.

Whoever is interested in getting further insights into the contrast between thinking and imagination could read the amusing *Flatland, a Romance of Many Dimensions*, written by 'A. Square', in real life the English mathematician E. Abbott (see Abbott: 1962). Abbott has given us a way to help us to see how an object may be either interior or exterior, according to the dimensions of the spaces considered. Think of a cube made with a piece of paper, whose faces are, let us say, 20 × 20 cm each. Suppose that in the interior of one of these faces a square is drawn, *ABCD*, of 5 × 5 cm, and that one of its sides, *AB*, extends in both directions further than the points *A* and *B*. The drawing would be as *Figure 7*.

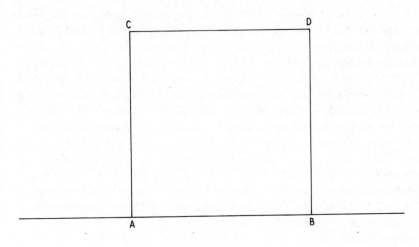

Figure 7

Suppose now that on this square and exactly coinciding with it we put a cube whose faces are also 5 × 5 cm. In this case the cube is in the interior of the greater cube; one of its faces (a square) coincides with the above-mentioned square; and one of the sides (straight line) of this square face coincides with (a part of) the line which extends further than the points *A* and *B*.

In summary, the small cube is, for a three-dimensional being, a region of the bigger cube, i.e. it is inside the three-dimensional space and outside the square or two-dimensional space. For a two-dimensional being, the cube is only a region of a plane and is in the interior of its own space and outside one-dimensional space; whereas for a one-dimensional being, the cube is a segment of a line and is inside its own space. And all three are right. *In other words, the concepts of internal and external must be defined in relation to the dimensions of space.*

It must be noted, however, that in this case the amount of information about the cube varies enormously according to the number of dimensions which are used by thinking beings. The one-dimensional beings we have imagined can develop a whole mathematical theory about the straight line, which could be applied to the side of the square belonging to the boundary of the cube. They could get to know the real-number system but would know nothing about the plane. The same would hold, *mutatis mutandis*, for two-dimensional beings and for us, three-dimensional beings.

But, if our thinking capacity for abstraction, whatever our dimensionality may be, frees itself from concrete imagination, we

303

can then make discoveries about worlds which cannot be imagined. (*Flatland* describes the adventure of such discoveries.) This is *precisely what is necessary in order to arrive at a deeper knowledge of the internal psychical world.*[10]

Therefore, if, instead of imagining, we think, we can then define a four-dimensional object, i.e. a region of a four-dimensional space, which is outside a three-dimensional cube. For instance, if we put a 'four-dimensional book' inside a drawer of our desk (that is, a three-dimensional drawer), it will seem to our eyes, which can see only three dimensions, that this book is all inside the drawer. The book is really outside the drawer (except for its three-dimensional boundary, in a similar way to the game above), *but our eyes do not perceive this fact.* We can apply the same type of reasoning with a higher number, and up to an infinite number, of dimensions.

This example makes us aware of how limited our habitual notions of interior and exterior are. Paraphrasing a common expression, we cannot really say, 'How flat they are'. We can, however, affirm, quite correctly, if with a certain delusion, 'How cubic or how "volumetric" our ordinary conceptions of interior and exterior are!'[11]

Here is a further example which illustrates what I am driving at. Let us now imagine that there exist two one-dimensional beings – for instance, two small beings who are isomorphic but not identical to two segments of a straight line. They are capable of thinking, and they are placed along the straight line which extends to either side of *AB*, in our last illustration. One of these beings is placed on the left side of *A* and the other on the right side of *B*; and they can communicate between themselves by some contraption, also unidimensional. We may posit as a condition of our 'experiment' that these beings have not even the slightest suspicion of the existence, not even of the possibility, of spaces of more than one dimension. Once they have established communication between themselves and have combined their respective observations, they can affirm that between the points *A* and *B* of their straight line there is precisely the segment *AB* of this straight line. We know that this something is a side of the square *ABCD*, but they do not know it, because they know only the side *AB* of this square and do not, and cannot, know that there 'exist' other sides. For these beings the segment *AB*, all of it, is inside the straight line which they 'inhabit'. We know, furthermore, that the square itself is outside the straight line, and that only one part of its boundary coincides with the straight line.

Let us now go on and suppose that there are some two-dimensional beings who inhabit the surface of this big square, who know the dimensions 0, 1, and 2 and do not have the slightest suspicion of the existence of a three-dimensional space. In this case such beings know only the surface of the cube which coincides with the square *ABCD*. For them this cube has no height; it is only the square *ABCD*. They can go around the square but they cannot guess that it is the face of a cube.

We ourselves may be the next set of beings, three-dimensional ones, who have no conception of, nor can guess, what lies outside the dimensions of our own awareness.

Notes

1 I would like to express my gratitude to Professor Flavio Donati, of the Mathematical Institute of the University of Rome, for his suggestions for improving the precision of the text of this chapter. I must add, however, that the responsibility for whatever deficiencies of this text remain is entirely mine.

2 For more details cf. Matte-Blanco 1975a: ch. 32.

3 In cases of this type the concept of operation and not that of relation is generally employed, but we can also use this last notion because an n-ary operation is a subset of an $(n + 1)$-ary relation.

4 I employ here, without defining it, the intuitive concept of distance.

5 In this latter case (Sommerville 1929 [1958]: 6–8):

'The three-dimensional region is not now the whole of space, but will be called a *hyperplane* lying in hyperspace. A hyperplane is thus determined by four points. . . . We may now extend these ideas straight away to n dimensions, and at the same time acquire both greater generality and greater succinctness in expression. The series: point, line, plane, hyperplane (or as it is more explicitly termed, *three-flat*), . . . n flat are regions determined by one, two, three, four . . . $n + 1$ points, and having zero, one, two three . . . n dimensions, i.e. an r-flat is determined by $r + 1$ points, and every p-flat ($p < r$) which is determined by $p + 1$ of these points lies entirely in the r-flat. We shall suppose that the n-flat, or space of n dimensions, contains all the points.'

6 $<$ = less than; $>$ = greater than; $\leq$ = equal to or less than, etc.

7 That is, defined as.

8 Read: absolute value of $x - a$ is less than δ.

9 A general study of dimension is that of Nagami (1970).

10 One cannot exclude a priori the possibility that thinking is, among other things, a function of the number of dimensions that imagination can use.

Put more concretely, with our 'three-dimensional imagination' in hand we have been able to *think* of infinitely dimensional spaces and develop our conception of them, and of the world in general, along certain lines. What would the result have been if we had been able to 'see' a (region of a) space, say, of ten dimensions? Perhaps very different indeed.

Correspondingly, it seems possible that beings having 'one- or two-dimensional imagination' may have fewer possibilities of thinking than us. Things become still more complex if we remember that human beings are, if seen from a certain angle, adimensional, or alternatively, infinitely dimensional.

11 I believe that a deeper analysis of the game that I have put forward *might* show (though I am not sure) that this game uses the concepts of three-dimensional space all the time. In fact, how would it be possible for unidimensional beings to be in communication between themselves? How is it possible for them *to be* in unidimensional space or line, and 'occupy' a segment of this line? To take our case, as three-dimensional beings, if we *are* a region of space *and also are* thinking beings, this latter fact is connected with the fact that *we are beings with more than three dimensions*. Perhaps (I am not sure) in the game I have put forward, the thinking beings considered have at least one dimension more than does the space they inhabit. However, even if this supposition is right, the example of these various one-, two-, and three-dimensional beings would still hold good as illustrations.

306

16

The concept of internal world: past, present, and future

1 Dimensionality of objects and of the internal world

I now want to investigate what I mean by *psychic dimensionality*. Although I have introduced some ideas in the introductory chapters I want to repeat them here but to add greater detail and depth.

Both the experience of the body and the external world appear to us spatially three-dimensionally with the addition of the time dimension. They constitute the substratum whence psychical processes develop. We, therefore, start from the hypothesis which is almost a certainty, that *everything which is psychical in us expresses itself at some time by means of three-dimensional space plus time*. Note that this assertion does not say that psychical phenomena develop in space–time but only that they are expressed by means of space–time. In fact, following Freud, we have repeatedly suggested that some psychical manifestations are both atemporal and aspatial. Others can be understood in terms of correspondence with a space of a number of dimensions higher than three, perhaps up to an infinite number of dimensions in certain cases. The latter space would be a mathematical way, asymmetrical or heterogenic, of course, of expressing an experience of indivisible unity, which is atemporal and aspatial. This would be similar to the notion of mathematical infinite, which is an asymmetrical way of expressing indivisibility.

Said in a slightly different way: psychical phenomena can be understood in terms of a space of dimensions higher than three; but they are expressed by three-dimensional means. How can this be done? We have already developed this argument several times in the book. I will repeat it again in the light of the mathematical discourse of the previous chapter.

If there is a space of dimensions higher than three, imagination cannot 'perceive it' directly, but is able to register its existence through a three-dimensional grasp. When such 'grasping' takes place, then the three-dimensional world appears as though it were altered. Sometimes volumes are multiplied; in other cases there takes place an apparent disorganization, and the observer becomes aware of certain incompatibilities and contradictions.

These problems can be made clear, as we have noted many times already in this book, with the help of geometry. If a mathematician wishes to represent a region of a space of n dimensions by means of a space of $n - 1$ dimensions, then the spaces of $n - 2$ dimensions or of dimensions inferior to $n - 2$ are repeated in such a representation. For example, if we take a region of a space of two dimensions, for instance the triangle ABC, and if we try to represent it in a straight line, space of one dimension, we must then 'open' the triangle – for instance, at the point C, and make the sides AC and BC rotate until they are in the same straight line with the side AB. We shall then have the triangle represented by the straight line $CABC$. Observe that in this case the point C appears twice.

The same thing can be done if we wish to represent a volume, for instance a cube in a plane. In this case each straight line which represents the point of convergence between the planes (imagine a cube made of paper which we unfold until it becomes a sheet of paper) will appear repeated twice, and each point of intersection of three non-complanar straight lines will appear three times. If we now go up in the sequence of dimensions, we shall find that, in a representation of, say, a four-dimensional figure in terms of fewer dimensions, volumes are repeated. To mention the most simple example, we start from a segment of a straight line, for instance AB. We now consider the most simple two-dimensional figure, the triangle, and let this be ABC. The most simple three-dimensional figure is the tetrahedron, in our case $ABCD$. In a four-dimensional space we have the corresponding four-dimensional tetrahedron, in our case $ABCDE$. This contains five vertices and also five three-dimensional tetrahedra. (For further details see Courant and Robbins 1941: 227–34, and Matte-Blanco 1975a: 408–14.)[1]

. If we wish to represent a four-dimensional tetrahedron in a three-dimensional space, we may do it by means of five tetrahedra, which in our case would be $ABCD$, $ABCE$, $ABDE$, $ACDE$, and $BCDE$. If we draw this representation, we then shall find that these five three-dimensional tetrahedra have a central zone in common which, in order to make the representation in question, has been taken five times from the four-dimensional tetrahedron. Put in another way: just as the points and the lines are repeated in a representation, respectively of a plane in a line and of the volume in the plane, so we also see that volumes are repeated in the representation of a region of, say, a six- or seven-dimensional space in terms of a lower-dimensional space. Or again we may choose to express the same idea by saying paradoxically that, for example, in a four-dimensional tetrahedron there is, in its central zone, a volume which (if seen in terms of a three-dimensional space) is 'there', in the four-dimensional space, five times.

Let us now consider a five-dimensional tetrahedron. It contains six vertices and fifteen three-dimensional tetrahedra. These tetrahedra also have a central zone in common which in a representation of the five-dimensional tetrahedra must appear repeated a greater number of times than in the preceding case. In the case of a six-dimensional tetrahedron we find that it contains seven vertices and thirty-five three-dimensional tetrahedra! In this case, *in* the six-dimensional tetrahedron certain volumes (spaces of three dimensions) are, so to say, repeated in a certain region of this tetrahedron a much greater number of times; that is, the volumes *fill, 'one inside the other', so many times the same six-dimensional region!* This is a way of expressing the reality of six-dimensional space by means of lower-dimensional spaces.

The return of the indivisible. Recently, I have become aware of an antinomy caused by the definition of a space in another space of a lesser number of dimensions. To take the simplest case just seen, that of a triangle *ABC* defined as the line *CABC*. The point *C* becomes two points *C*, located in 'different points' of the line in question. Now, each point in a line is unique and different from all other points, and is defined in this line by the distance from the origin of 0. Suppose now that the first point *C* is 5 cm from the origin and the second, say, 15 cm. Let us agree that $C = 5$ is, like all other points, unique. It follows from this that the second $C = 15$ either is not $C = 5$, in which case the definition put forward by Courant is not permitted; or, inevitably $C (= 5) = C (= 15)$, i.e. $5 = 15$, which, as a simple reasoning shows, leads to $1 = 2$. This leads to $1 = 2 = 3 = \dots$ *n*, as already seen.

In other words, the multiplication of spaces leads to the antinomy of something (a point, a volume, etc.) which is always the same unique something and also a number of other somethings. It is one *and* many; so even in geometry we cannot escape from the co-presence of both modes! We might say that when an indivisible (in this case, the point *C*) finds that the intellect tries to divide it, then it creates a Babel in the intellect: 5 = 15. It kicks back and in this way makes its presence felt.

A future generation of psychoanalysts thoroughly familiar with mathematics may make great progress in psychoanalysis. This in turn, if taken into consideration in mathematics, could result in important progress in mathematics and physics. The reason seems to be that nature, indivisible and at the same time divisible, reveals some of its faces better in a given subject of its study, for instance in psychoanalysis, and some other faces better in another subject, such as mathematics. We may, paradoxically, see better in psychoanalysis with the help of mathematics and also see better in mathematics with what we have learnt in psychoanalysis with the help of mathematics.

To summarize, some psychical objects and experiences are lived as though they were three-dimensional, while others are lived as though they had more than three dimensions. The internal world – that is, the (structured) set of objects, feelings, and experiences – would probably frequently have a number of dimensions higher than three. There is a great deal of clinical evidence which suggests that there are aspects of the internal world which are alien to the notions of inside, outside, and dimension.

2 The spaces of introjection

In the light of the considerations just mentioned it becomes evident that an object can be introjected into and become internal to a certain spatial 'thing' while remaining external to spatial 'things' of fewer dimensions. The relation between the concept of object and that of space, however, needs some explanation. No human thing, either mental or physical, can be said to be a geometrical space, for the concept of geometrical space deals with points, lines, volumes, etc., and dimensions. All of them are abstract concepts quite different from the sensory quality of material objects and also from the properties of mental objects. But physical or mental objects can be said to have dimension as one of their properties and, in this sense, be isomorphic to spaces of 1, 2 . . . *n* dimensions. For simplicity's sake we may use the incorrect expression 'an object is introjected into a space'. But this expression must be used in the sense that it is introjected into the self or an aspect or substructure of it which is isomorphic but not identical to a given space of *n* dimensions. *The isomorphism refers, in this case, only to the dimensions.* Please keep this in mind in case an incorrect use of these concepts slips in, in this rather early stage of the study of this subject.

I imagine the reader may consider the following reflections rather abstruse and difficult to follow. My hope is that, by working on them, he or she will eventually find them quite clear and also find that they increase the understanding of the process of introjection.

First, the object may be isodimensional with the aspect or substructure of the self into which it is introjected. In such a case the object would be a region of this aspect of the self. That is, it would be included in its space but would not be all of it. For instance, a table has three dimensions, the same number as the room where it is, but is not the whole room: only (it occupies) a region of it. When the object is isodimensional with an n-dimensional aspect of being where it is introjected, it will then be external to any aspect of a lower number of dimensions. Example: a book (three dimensions) which is on a table is external to the two-dimensional surface of it, on which it rests. It may on the other hand be inside a drawer. Inversely, when the object is treated as internal to an n-dimensional substructure of the self, this means that it is, implicitly, one of two things. Either it is a region of the n-dimensional substructure, or it is inside a sub-space of that n-dimensional substructure and will, therefore, have a still lower number of dimensions. We may then choose to say, taking the cue from geometry, that the object is a region of a lying or sub-aspect of that aspect or substructure of the self, and, as such, it will have a lower number of dimensions than the substructure.

Second, the object may be 'seen' as if it had only the dimensions of the sub- or lying aspect, when in reality it has a greater number. I suspect that this happens in cases where a parental image which has multiple meanings has been introjected. Each of such meanings – for instance, love, protection, aggression, subtlety, authority, and so on – may be put in correspondence with one of the dimensions of a given space, five in the example just given. Perhaps it is useful to give an example. Take a temperature chart as used in hospitals, where time is represented in the horizontal and temperature in the vertical dimension of the surface of the sheet, which is two-dimensional. The same type of thing can be done with spaces of 2, 3 . . . n dimensions. Similarly the object-parent may be introjected *in toto*, say, as a five-dimensional object, but at a certain period only one or two of its aspects may be felt or experienced. I have seen, for example, cases in which a parent was seen for a long time as only hostile or distant. After several years of analysis the patient discovers that there were other aspects of the object which were in fact present in him, active and important, but not considered. It then becomes a

311

source of great satisfaction to discover how many hidden, yet introjected, good qualities a parent had given him as a present.

Third, the object may have a number of dimensions lower than that of the aspect of the self into which it is introjected. It will then be in a region or sub-aspect or lying aspect of this latter, and this implies different conditions from the previous case.

Fourth, the object can have a dimensionality superior to that of the aspect of the self into which it is intended to be introjected. In this case only an aspect of the object, an aspect which has a lower number of dimensions and, therefore, can lie in something with a lower number of dimensions, will be introjected. This case is similar but not identical to the second case just described. The difference lies in the fact that, whereas in the first case the whole n-dimensional (spatial) object was introjected but only a sub-space of it was considered or used at the time, in this case it is only a lower-dimensional component of it that is introjected. To give an example: a parent's attitude may be too complex for a small child to grasp, and in consequence the child's attention will be (unconsciously) focused on only some aspects of it, and those aspects but not others will be introjected. A concrete case of this may help. We are told that, when walking daily from his home to the Center of Advanced Studies in Princeton, Einstein became friendly with a little girl who followed, also daily, the same route. At a certain point he began to help her in her studies of mathematics. Now, it is highly probable that, when explaining the elements of mathematics, Einstein used a language which, to an expert, contained deep intuitions about the subject. It is equally likely that at least some of these non-expressed intuitions were not grasped by the girl, who probably 'took in' the more elementary notions, even if these were absorbed in a way which was probably different from how she would have absorbed them from a less profound teacher.

My guess is that most of the introjections refer only to such aspects of the objects which have a number of dimensions lower than what can be found in the object itself. This is probably a new meaning of the expression 'part object'. To explain further, a penis – the same discourse may be developed in connection with the breast, as described by Klein (1957: 3–4, 5–6, 15–16, 39, etc.) – if seen according to what is now the classical Kleinian notion of part object, would be one example of it. Suppose we accept that it is a part object. As is well known, the class to which a penis is an element (remember that the unconscious treats the individual as identical to the class of which it is an element, but conscious thinking does not), if viewed from this angle, may be found to have various real or fantasied properties, such

312

as creativity, capacity for giving pleasure, protection, capacity for violent penetration, cutting, and tearing, and so on. Now, it is almost certain that a given introjection of the penis may concern only certain aspects of the penis and not all. If we conceive or describe each of the aspects as being isomorphic to a one-dimensional object, then the penis will be isomorphic to an n-dimensional object in an n-dimensional space. And it is certain that unconscious phantasy may be concerned with one or several but not all the properties mentioned. *The introjection will then be that of a part of a part object.* This is a rough hint, and possibly not a completely accurate one, concerning a question which deserves to be greatly developed.

Fifth, an object may be simultaneously introjected in structures of the self which have different dimensions. According to the dimensionality of the object there would be various possibilities. I am afraid we cannot go into this now.

To summarize, I believe that this short analysis is sufficient to show how a more precise use of the concept of interior and dimension leads to the possibility of an enormous increase in our understanding of introjective processes. *So far the only possibility that has been considered in the analytical literature is that of introjection of a three-dimensional object into a three-dimensional space.* Clinical experience suggests that there are other possibilities. Introjection may be better understood and delimited in the light of these concepts. I have no doubt that in the future we shall be able to speak of various types of introjection, according to the dimensions involved in the process. In order to progress along the path of these possibilities it is necessary to consider in the first place the problem of dimensionality of the objects and of the internal world, and then the possibilities of ascertaining dimensionality. In particular it is useful to reflect about the distinction just made between two possibilities. On the one hand, we can perhaps introject an n-dimensional object *in toto* and initially using only some of its properties; these correspond to only some of its dimensions, while the others remain as a reserve to be used at a later time. On the other hand, the introjection could be of a substructure of the object. This distinction, I feel, *may turn out to be a light which illuminates clinical material and opens up new possibilities in therapy.*

3 The internal world: a retrospective and prospective view

In the light of all the subjects dealt with in this book we can now try to single out some notions which may help to delimit and subsequently develop a conception of the internal world which aims at being more faithful to its true reality than the rather naïve or too simple conceptions so far in circulation.

It seems that we may describe at least three meanings of the concept of internal world, as follows.

The first meaning of internal world. This would be the set of the internal objects. These may be conceived as being isomorphic to isodimensional regions of the space corresponding to the self. Alternatively they may be isomorphic to lying spaces or sub-spaces of the complete space where the self lies. My suspicion is that all objects are 'sub-spaces of the self' because, if they were considered as regions, the unity of the self, which always exists (even in splitting) would, perhaps, appear as impossible. This is, however, a matter for further study. There is a vast programme of research to develop in order to discover the various existing possibilities, also in relation to the dimensionality of the spaces under consideration.

The second meaning of internal world. This refers to the self as a structure, seen as an n-dimensional space. This is independent from the conscious or unconscious phantasies that can arise about the self.

Hanna Segal (1964 [1973]: 16–17) has studied the relation between unconscious phantasy and defence mechanisms and has pointed out that the distinction between both

> 'lies in the difference between the actual process and its specific, detailed mental representation. For instance, it is possible to say that an individual at a given moment is using the processes of projection and introjection as mechanisms of defence. But the processes themselves will be experienced by him in terms of phantasies which express what he feels himself to be taking in or putting out, the way in which he does this and the results which he feels these actions to have.'

(p. 16)

One could say that there is a correspondence between the unconscious phantasies and the structure of the particular defence mechanisms or the general structure of the self. Perhaps it is an isomorphism. Whatever it may be, it seems that the structure of the self and its substructures (defence mechanisms, and so on) can be put in correspondence with a space. The second meaning of internal world would, therefore, refer to this space.

It seems necessary to become aware that *the concept of internal structure is not entirely coincident with that of internal object*. This latter may be an internal structure or part of another internal structure which may have other parts or aspects which are not objects but *non-*

objectual interrelations of the self. In order better to clarify this important concept we can give the example of nutrition. Food has a certain chemical structure. The digestive process reduces it to more elementary components, and with these the organism synthesizes the substances which constitute the tissues. Abraham (1924) spoke of the metabolism of the introjected object. At this moment it is sufficient to note that the internal world is organized and that this organization cannot be seen exclusively in terms of internal objects. *The objects are metabolized and give way to traits which the objects may or may not possess and which themselves are not objects.* Just as we do not have a physical internal milk, cheese, meat, or fruit, but do have their primitive component elements used for entirely new syntheses not existing in the 'objects' called milk, cheese, meat, or fruit, so the same thing happens with the objects. The individual 'psychical' human being, while having many things in common with other fellow beings, is a unique synthesis of the most varied components.

This is an essential subject, which requires further exploration. We can understand the structure of the internal world by studying the interrelations of its various aspects, represented at times by phantasy but also seen by interrelations between actions, thoughts, attitudes, or contrasting desires. We may, for instance, choose to restrict our study and bring into focus only the apparent distortions of external reality resulting from unconscious phantasies, where certain new structures are revealed, as a result of projection.

In other words, this is an opportunity to study the internal world as seen in such projections. Though such an approach would furnish information about only one aspect of the internal world, it is sometimes convenient, from a practical point of view, to consider this aspect as a thing in itself. This leads us to:

The third meaning of internal world. We have already seen that in the dream as well as in waking life the external world is treated in a way which does not correspond to what appears to be its real structure. This itself seems at first sight to be three-dimensional. What happens in cases of this type is that the external world is seen in such a way as to make it usable for the representation of the internal world. The apparent distortions[2] of the external world observed in dream or in waking life are in this case the expression of the internal world by means of the external world.

I would like to insist that this third meaning is an aspect or particular case of the second, as already explained. It, however, deserves sometimes to be studied in isolation because such a study may enable us to understand some subtle and complex structures of the internal world and of the self, whose complexity might

315

otherwise escape us. The following comparison may help. One may consider a space of five dimensions in itself and discover a number of conceptual facts about it, which cannot be imagined. If we try to represent these concepts and facts in a three-dimensional space, we will then be able to understand or imagine better the structure of the space in question. This is the type of thing that may be obtained from a detailed study of the third meaning of internal world.

The collapse of the antithesis internal–external. It seems that this is the right moment to speak about certain notions which are frequently linked, especially by Kleinian analysts, to the concepts of external and internal world. These are, as we have repeatedly seen, implicitly thought of as being three-dimensional. Some people seem to make the assumption that when they reach an understanding of the relationship between the individual and his internal objects they have reached something final. And so they speak of the relation to the internal breast, internal mother, and so on as the *summum* of understanding. This is a pious illusion. There are essential facts about the mind and the 'relations' between the individual and other individuals (breast, mother, father, world) which simply cannot be grasped in terms of the antithesis external–internal. These facts refer to the non-three-dimensional aspects which are essential to human beings and which are the expression of the experience of indivisibility which itself is part of human nature. Thinking frequently tries to conceive such aspects in terms of space, but when it does so, the best it can achieve is to use the concept of infinite and infinite-dimensional space. Frequently these concepts are introduced in various implicit ways, which may lead to confusion. The concept of the infinite, for instance, underlies but is not explicit in some of the Kleinian formulations, as already suggested in Chapter 7, and also in some of the views of other authors, such as Bion and Meltzer. The attempt to translate the non-spatial and timeless aspects of human nature into space–time is essential to thinking but it is always a form of 'thinkating' (Matte-Blanco 1981) even if from some points of view it is very subtle thinking.

The fact that we cannot escape from our own indivisible mode of being or experience of unity is visible, very naturally, in the effort to express such aspects of ourselves by means of bi-logical structures. By this means we succeed, somehow, in 'imprisoning' the ungraspable indivisibility in some structures which we know but are not able to express fully.

I consider the awareness of the indivisible, and its search in human manifestations, to be of primary importance for the understanding of human beings. We must resign ourselves to the fact that some aspects of ourselves do not refer to the external or internal world nor to an intermediate 'area'; they are, as Meltzer (1975) puts it, 'located nowhere'. It is precisely when we are studying the internal world that we must keep this in mind, in order to avoid pitfalls and falsifying the formulation of facts.

Notes

1 In another work (Matte-Blanco 1975a: 415–56) I have already studied this problem and I cannot go into the details here. I shall confine myself to quoting only one of its conclusions (p. 423):

'As a conclusion we may say that numerous facts which at first sight appear completely chaotic become perfectly well-ordered if we apply the concept of space of more than three dimensions. The dreamer (and the unconscious) behave like a geometrician who handles a number of variables superior to three and who is forced to use in his representation a space of dimensions not higher than three.'

We have already seen that this conclusion is very useful for understanding clinical reality.

2 I say 'apparent distortions' to imply that they are seen as distortions in terms of simple everyday views. In fact they may, at least at times, be the expression or unravelling of more recondite aspects of the external world which are isomorphic to some aspect of the internal world.

An account of Melanie Klein's conception of projective identification
by *Luciana Bon de Matte*

Note: In order to facilitate references made earlier in the book to quotations appearing in this Appendix, the quotations on the following pages have been numbered.

Definition of the concept; its beginning and development. Melanie Klein proposed the name 'projective identification' (we shall abbreviate it as PI) to refer to a psychological mechanism which: (1) 'is based on the splitting of the ego and the projection of parts of the self, into other people' (Klein 1963: 103). At various times she devotes long paragraphs to its description, while at other times she adds a new element to it, almost in passing, in phrases which, though short in themselves, have gradually accumulated and made it possible to understand the process more clearly.

As Klein herself points out, the origin of the concept goes back to the beginning of her studies:

(2) 'Already in my paper "An Obsessional Neurosis in a Six Year Old Girl", which was read in 1924 but not published until it appeared in *The Psycho-Analysis of Children*, envy bound up with oral-, urethral- and anal-sadistic attacks on her mother's body played a prominent role. But I had not related this envy specifically to the desire to take away and to spoil the mother's breasts, although I had come very near to these conclusions. In my paper "On Identification" (*New Directions in Psycho-Analysis*), I discussed envy as a very important factor in projective identification.'

(Klein 1957: 6, n. 1)

319

In 1932 in *The Psycho-Analysis of Children*, Klein devotes much time to the description of aggressive fantasies against the inside of the mother's body and of sadistic intrusion against it; but it was only in December 1946 that she gave a comprehensive description of and named the phenomenon (Klein 1946 [1952]: 300):

(3) 'The phantasied onslaughts on the mother follow two main lines: one is the predominantly oral impulse to suck dry, bite up, scoop out and rob the mother's body of its good contents. . . . The other line of attack derives from the anal and urethral impulses and implies expelling dangerous substances (excrements) out of the self and into the mother. Together with these harmful excrements, expelled in hatred, split-off parts of the ego are also projected onto the mother or, as I would rather call it, *into* the mother. These excrements and bad parts of the self are meant not only to injure but also to control and to take possession of the object. In so far as the mother comes to contain the bad parts of the self, she is not felt to be a separate individual but is felt to be *the* bad self.

'Much of the hatred against parts of the self is now directed towards the mother. This leads to a particular form of identification which establishes the prototype of an aggressive object-relation. I suggest for these processes the term "projective identification".'

In 'On identification' (1955: 313, n. 3) Melanie Klein refers the foundations of her discovery back to Freud, noting that the concept of PI was present in Freud's work, although he did not give it that name. In fact, she quotes the following paragraph from *Group Psychology and the Analysis of the Ego*, when Freud is discussing identification by introjection and also says (Freud 1921, SE 18: 112–13):

(4) '(We see that) the object is being treated in the same way as our own ego, so that when we are in love a considerable amount of narcissistic libido overflows on to the object. (It is even obvious, in many forms of love-choice, that the object serves as a substitute for some unattained ego ideal of our own.) We love it on account of the perfections which we have striven to reach for our own ego (and which we should now like to procure in this roundabout way as a means of satisfying our narcissism).'

(The brackets enclose words from Freud which were not quoted by Klein and were not between brackets in Freud's text.)

It is pertinent to add here that in the same work, a little further on (p. 113), Freud says: (5) 'the ego becomes more and more unassuming and modest, and the object more and more sublime and precious until at last it gets possession of the entire self-love of the ego, whose self-sacrifice thus follows as a natural consequence. The object has, so to speak, consumed the ego.'

In another passage Melanie Klein makes reference to the work of M. G. Evans:

(6) 'M. G. Evans, in a short unpublished communication (read to the British Psycho-Analytical Society, January 1946), gave some instances of patients in whom the following phenomena were marked: lack of sense of reality, a feeling of being divided and parts of the personality having entered the mother's body in order to rob and control her; as a consequence the mother and other people similarly attacked came to represent the patient. M. G. Evans related these processes to a very primitive stage of development.'

(Klein 1946 [1952]: 300, n. 2)

From the various occasions on which Melanie Klein describes PI and its connections, I have chosen the following rather extensive quotation (Klein 1952: 206–08), because it conveys various important aspects of her conception of PI:

(7) 'I have described elsewhere [see *The Psycho-Analysis of Children*, 1932: 185] how the oral-sadistic impulses to devour and scoop out the mother's breast become elaborated into the phantasies of devouring and scooping out the mother's body. Attacks derived from all other sources of sadism soon become linked with these oral attacks and two main lines of sadistic phantasies develop. One form – mainly oral-sadistic and bound up with greed – is to empty the mother's body of everything good and desirable. The other form of phantasied attack – predominantly anal – is to fill her body with the bad substances and parts of the self which are split off and projected into her. These are mainly represented by excrements which become the means of damaging, destroying or controlling the attacked object. Or the whole self – felt to be the "bad" self – enters the mother's body and takes control of it. In these various phantasies, the ego takes possession by projection of an external object – first of all the mother – and makes it into an extension of the self. The object becomes to some extent a representative of the ego and these processes are in my view the basis for identification by projection or "projective identification". Identification by introjection and identification by projection appear to be complementary processes. It seems that the processes underlying projective identification operate already in the earliest relation to the breast.

The "vampire-like" sucking, the scooping out of the breast, develop in the infant's phantasy into making his way into the breast and further into the mother's body. Accordingly, projective identification would start simultaneously with the greedy oral-sadistic introjection of the breast. This hypothesis is in keeping with the view often expressed by the writer that introjection and projection interact from the beginning of life. The introjection of a persecutory object is, as we have seen, to some extent determined by the projection of destructive impulses onto the object. The drive to project (expel) badness is increased by fear of internal persecutors. When projection is dominated by persecutory fear, the object into whom badness (the bad self) has been projected becomes the persecutor *par excellence*, because it has been endowed with all the bad qualities of the subject. The re-introjection of this object reinforces acutely the fear of internal and external persecutors. (The death instinct, or rather, the dangers attaching to it, has again been turned inwards.) There is thus a constant interaction between persecutory fear relating to the internal and external worlds, an interaction in which the processes involved in projective identification play a vital part.

'The projection of love-feelings – underlying the process of attaching libido to the object – is, as I suggested, a precondition for finding a good object. The introjection of a good object stimulates the projection of good feelings outwards and this in turn by re-introjection strengthens the feeling of possessing a good internal object. To the projection of the bad self into the object and the external world corresponds the projection of good parts of the self, or of the whole good self. Re-introjection of the good object and of the good self reduces persecutory anxiety. Thus the relation to both the internal and external world improves simultaneously and the ego gains in strength and in integration.'

In later references to the concept (Klein 1955), the author uses expressions which lead to a clearer understanding:

(8) 'products of the body and parts of the self are felt to have been split off, projected into the mother, and to be continuing their existence within her.'

(p. 310)

(9) 'entering other people and actually stealing their lives.'

(p. 331)

(10) 'to scoop out the breast and to enter the mother's body in order *to obtain by force the gratification she withholds.*'

(p. 329, my italics)

(11) 'intrude into his mother in order to rob her and thus get more food and satisfaction.'

(p. 329)

(12) 'I conclude that Fabian has always been searching for his ideal father and that this is a strong stimulus towards his projective identifications.'

(p. 333)

Aims of PI. The purposes or aims of the process were suggested by Melanie Klein, and Hanna Segal (1964 [1973]: 27) presents them as follows:

(13) 'Projective identification has manifold aims: it may be directed towards the ideal object to avoid separation, or it may be directed towards the ideal object to gain control of the source of danger. Various parts of the self may be projected with various aims: bad parts of the self may be projected in order to get rid of them as well as to attack and destroy the object, good parts may be projected to avoid separation or to keep them safe from bad things inside or to improve the external object through a kind of primitive projective reparation.'

PI's connection with developmental-physiological processes. Melanie Klein points out that (14) 'Projective identification is bound up with developmental processes arising during the first three or four months of life (the paranoid-schizoid position) when splitting is at its height and persecutory anxiety dominates' (1955: 311).

On the other hand, envy, greed, and frustration are an important stimulus to PI. In particular:

(15) 'Projective processes dominated by greed are, as I have repeatedly remarked, part of the baby's relation to the mother, but they are particularly strong where frustration is frequent. (As I have pointed out in various connections, the urge for projective identification derives not only from greed but from a variety of causes.)[2] Frustration reinforces both the greedy wish for unlimited gratification and the desire to scoop out the breast and to enter the mother's body in order to obtain by force the gratification she withholds.'

(1955: 328–29)

Furthermore (Klein 1957: 7):

(16) 'At the unconscious level, greed aims primarily at completely scooping out, sucking dry, and devouring the breast: that is to say,

323

its aim is destructive introjection; whereas envy not only seeks to rob in this way, but also to put badness, primarily bad excrements and bad parts of the self, into the mother, and first of all into her breast, in order to spoil and destroy her. In the deepest sense this means destroying her creativeness. This process, which derives from urethral- and anal-sadistic impulses, I have elsewhere defined as a destructive aspect of projective identification starting from the beginning of life. One essential difference between greed and envy, although no rigid dividing line can be drawn since they are so closely associated, would accordingly be that greed is mainly bound up with introjection and envy with projection.'

Joan Riviere (1936 [1952]: 40) has suggested that introjective processes are modelled on the function of taking in 'good' nourishment and projective processes on that of excretion.

So the physical corollary of PI in its oral aspect is to suck the breast rabidly, and this corresponds to greedy, envious introjection; on the other hand, the physical corollary of PI in its urethral-anal aspect is to evacuate excrements.

Aggressive and loving object relations in PI. The excrements which are expelled with hatred cause the mother to be felt as dangerous and hostile. The phantasy, accompanied by anger and anxiety, of introducing inside the mother badly digested faeces, which contain harmful elements but at the same time take out from the body essential or vital substances, is the source of great persecution anxieties.

Nevertheless, PI is not always concerned with the bad parts. It also includes the projection of positive aspects. The physical corollary in this case is, as before, also the expelling of excrements, now felt as presents. The healthy excreta expelled without suffering are a visible proof of the good use made of food, and a sign that all is well inside the child. The mother is now felt as friendly and receptive. In his phantasy the child must imagine that he arouses pleasant reactions in his mother: peacefulness, satisfaction, feeling that her efforts have been appreciated, and renewed feelings of love, unity, and under-standing for the child and his needs. The mother, on her part, may experience a tender gratitude for the co-operation of the child in his own process of growth, and in laying the bases of his first tender, responsible, and appreciative relationship: the prototype of the love object relation. The child's phantasy is, therefore, tied to a sort of primitive projective reparation:

(17) 'A happy relation to the first object and a successful internalisation of it means that love can be given and received. . . .

Introjective and projective identification, when not excessive, play an important part in this feeling of closeness, for they underlie the capacity to understand and contribute to the experience of being understood.'

(Klein 1963: 112)

Development of personality, projection, introjection, and relations with the external world.

(18) 'By projecting oneself or part of one's impulses and feelings into another person, an identifiction with that person is achieved, though it will differ from the identification arising from introjection. For if an object is taken into the self (introjection), the emphasis lies on acquiring some of the characteristics of this object and on being influenced by them. On the other hand, in putting part of oneself into the other person (projecting), the identification is based on attributing to the other person some of ones own qualities.'

(Klein 1963: 8)

If the child is a prey to anger, his reaction may be different; instead of projecting what is harmful, in his desire to keep safe his good internal object about which he is concerned, he searches outside himself for a safe place, which he will find in the objects which have given him gratification and positive experiences: the breast, the mother, the father, or other people. This in turn tightens the bonds and, owing to the relief given him, increases his love and his gratitude (Klein 1946 [1952]: 301): (19) 'The identification based on this type of projection again vitally influences object-relations. The projection of good feelings and good parts of the self into the mother is essential for the infant's ability to develop good object-relations and to integrate his ego.'

The return of objects with re-introjection is also very important, and equally so is, therefore, the character of projection. Furthermore (Klein 1946 [1952]: 303): (20) 'As regards normal personality, it may be said that the course of ego-development and object-relations depends on the degree to which an optimal balance between introjection and projection in the early stages of development can be achieved.' And also (Klein 1963: 8): (21) 'If the interplay between introjection and projection is not dominated by hostility or over-dependence, and is well-balanced, the inner world is enriched and the relations with the external world are improved.'

If re-introjection refers instead to an object penetrated by force, the

325

feeling of internal persecution becomes stronger, considering that the object contains the dangerous parts of the self, and that

> (22) 'the process of re-introjecting a projected part of the self includes internalising a part of the object into whom the projection has taken place, a part which the patient may feel to be hostile, dangerous, and most undesirable to re-introject. In addition, since the projection of a part of the self includes the projection of internal objects, these too are re-introjected. All this has a bearing on how far in the individual's mind the projected parts of the self are able to retain their strength within the object into which they have intruded.'

> (Klein 1955: 341)

Violent projection induces the feeling that the corresponding introjection is itself violent; this gives rise to various feelings of depersonalization and to anxieties of being persecuted, as a retaliation; for instance:

- fears that may range all the way from fears of having lost parts of the self to a complete loss of identity;
- fears which may range all the way from fears of being physically harmed to the fear of annihilation;
- fears of being controlled in body and mind in a hostile way by other people;
- fears that the penis may be attacked inside the mother, with resulting sexual impotence or disturbances of potency in general;
- various phobias, including those of robbers, spiders, and others. Klein (1963: 110) writes that (23) 'Claustrophobia, as I have elsewhere suggested, derives from two main sources: projective identification into the mother leading to an anxiety of imprisonment inside her; and re-introjection resulting in a feeling that inside oneself one is hemmed in by resentful internal objects.'

If the excessive projection is of the good parts, the mother becomes the ideal ego, the good parts are felt to be lost and therefore idealized, and the ego becomes weak and impoverished. The source of security is felt to be no longer internal but in others, giving place to an exaggerated dependence on those external representatives of an individual's own good parts. This dependence disturbs a good love relationship and also results in fears of having lost the capacity to love, due to the fact that the object is felt to be loved primarily as the representative of the self.

Hanna Segal (1964 [1973]: 36) points out that PI represents the earliest form of empathy, of the possibility of identifying with

326

somebody else, and also provides the basis of the earliest formation of symbols. Therefore, the mechanisms of defence of the paranoid-schizoid position, according to this author, not only fulfil a defensive function but must also actually be considered to be steps in development. Similar considerations are also made by Joan Riviere (1936 [1952]: 40). It is, therefore, important to consider as Segal does (1964 [1973]: 55) that a normal process, which in itself leads to positive consequences, may be disturbed by internal and external causes which result in the bad experience predominating over the good one. Furthermore:

> (24) 'In normal development, the infant projects parts of the self and internal objects into the breast and the mother. These projected parts are relatively unaltered in the process of projection, and when subsequent re-introjection takes place, they can be reintegrated into the ego.'
>
> (Segal 1964 [1973]: 55)

Under unfavourable conditions PI acquires pathological features which Bion was the first to describe.

Disintegration and integration. It is important to keep in mind that even in highly pathological circumstances, as Klein (1955: 342, n. 1) has eloquently remarked:

> (25) 'I would say that however strongly splitting and projection operate, the disintegration of the ego is never complete as long as life exists. For I believe that the urge towards integration, however disturbed – even at the root – is in some degree inherent in the ego.'

On the other hand, with the elaboration of persecutory anxieties the violence of PI lessens, and this (26) 'implies a diminution in the strength of the paranoid and schizoid mechanisms and defences and a greater capacity to work through the depressive position' (Klein 1961: 250).

Further insights about the mechanism: Fabian and Richard. It is interesting to observe that in two of her latest published works Klein describes a variety of fresh insights about projective identification, which enable one to grasp better the complexity and richness of her conception of it. In her work 'On identification' (1955, also republished in 1963) Klein makes a fine analysis of the novel *If I Were You* by Julien Green, which is a rich quarry for the study of PI.

Fabian, a young clerk, discontented with his life, acquires the magic power of changing places with other people as a result of a pact with the devil. In the analysis of the underlying motives for the choices of the objects on to which the protagonist projects himself, we can gain some insight into other aspects of the problem.

The fundamental condition is one of having common characteristics with the object.

> (27) 'For the individual to feel that he has a good deal in common with another person is concurrent with projecting himself into that person (and the same applies to introjecting him). These processes vary in intensity and duration and on these variations depend the strength and importance of such identifications and their vicissitudes.'
>
> (Klein 1955: 341)

This sharing of one's own aspects with those of the chosen person is shown to be very important in:

(a) giving an opportunity to realize or satisfy one's own frustrated or denied tendencies;
(b) recuperating the projected parts of the conflict and being able to reunite them with the parts in contrast which remained in one's own person;
(c) repeating the experience and relationships which one had as a child, this time with a prospective value or meaning of the (repeated) experiences and relationships.

In the novel all the people chosen by Fabian represent and put him in contact with different infantile situations and relations: desired breast or mother, father, brothers. And all this offers him the chance to face various frustrating situations and either get satisfaction from them or overcome them: desire of power, aggressive desires, desires of sublimation, reparation phantasies. In this way he relives infantile phantasies: hatred of his mother who frustrates him orally and genitally, rivalry with his father, jealousy and resentment with regard to the primal scene, oral and Oedipal desires towards his mother, homosexual submission to the feared father, desire to fertilize his mother and give life to brothers who are not born, gratitude to the good father who created him, and so on.

Klein draws our attention, among the other characteristics, to the concrete character of the phenomenon.

Apart from Fabian, who gets out of his own self and puts himself literally inside his victims, Melanie Klein illustrates the same fact with the case of Richard, whose PIs were expressed materially by a drawing of an aeroplane which represented himself entering inside his mother-analyst (Klein 1961: 266). At other times, his PIs were expressed by drawing sharp geometrical figures in such a way that they intruded into one another or were contained one inside the other. Later on, as the analysis progressed, the violence of PIs decreased, and this change was expressed by a change in the drawings, which lost their sharp penetrating and invading characteristics (Klein 1961: 217, drawing 33, n. II).

Another characteristic is the depth to which the part separated from the self becomes submerged in the chosen objects. The degree of depth is very important for the development. If the depth is excessive, the patient feels that parts of his self are far off and he does not know where they have gone to, and this is a source of great anxiety and insecurity (Klein 1955: 336–37). If, instead, the individual maintains some of his own characteristics, and especially if he keeps a critical attitude to the person into whom he has entered, he will be able to abandon this particular PI and eventually choose others, maintaining or increasing his interest in reuniting himself with his own primitive self.

Types of projective identification. PIs can be successive or simultaneous. Successive PIs give a chance to acquire greater maturity by putting the individual in a condition to choose objects which are more adequate each time and therefore lead him to a greater integration. Simultaneous PIs are sometimes in conflict with one another. For example, when Fabian identifies with the devil, who represents his evil parts, he identifies simultaneously with Esmenard, in whom he finds a part of himself which is potentially an assassin. The devil momentarily assumes the role of a protective super-ego which liberates him and moves him away from his identification with Esmenard, whom he momentarily makes the receptacle for all his evilness. This identification with Esmenard is a clear example of an inadequate use of the process, because it does not take account of the entire personality but only offers the indiscriminate satisfaction of an aspect of the phantasy which is both feared and resisted; it has a very primitive and suffocating character and creates the danger of not being able to escape from it. Identifications which are too intense and suffocating often push the patient towards other identifications with objects which show opposite characteristics; this has the consequence of 'an indiscriminate flight to a multitude of further identifications and fluctuations between them' (Klein 1955: 339), leading to instability and weakening of the ego.

Mutual projective identification. This is the name which Klein gives to a phenomenon which she analyses in the case of Richard, in drawing 20, where it can be seen that everyone – Richard himself, his father, his mother, his brother – each has parts in the territory of the others (Klein 1961: 144).

Projective identification can be *direct*, when it has the aim of using and appropriating specific contents of the chosen person. But it can also be *indirect* and in this way arrive at a third person through the medium of the person who has been chosen for identifying with. The individual who identifies in this way overpasses the chosen object or goes beyond it, taking advantage of every aspect of its situation. The object (individual) is chosen because, to paraphrase Ortega y Gasset, it is he and his circumstances which are also made use of. In Fabian, the identification with Camille suggests that he not only appropriates the person of Camille but, through him, arrives at Elise, who represents his feminine part, and also arrives at all his relations, benefiting in this way from a more mature and integrated situation; he is married and lives in a family group. In this passage, through his victims, Fabian overcomes his anxieties, recovers his good objects, and develops his capacity to love.

Notes

1 This is a slightly modified version of a paper read at the Institute of Psychoanalysis of Rome on 27 February 1970 and published in *Psyche* (1970).
2 The comment in brackets appears as a footnote in Klein (1955).

Bibliography

Abbott, E. (1884) *Flatland, a Romance of Many Dimensions*. Oxford: Blackwell, 1962.

Abraham, K. (1924) A short study of the development of the libido. In *Selected Papers of Karl Abraham*. London: Hogarth Press, 1942.

Aquinas, St Thomas (1880) *Summa Theologiae*, Q LIII Art. II.

Ayres, Jr, F. (1965) *Modern Algebra*. New York: McGraw-Hill.

Bergson, H. (1906) *L'Evolution Créatrice*. Paris: Librairie Felix Alcan, 1934. In *Oeuvres*. Paris: Presses Universitaires de France, 1970.

Bion, W. R. (1957) Development of schizophrenic thought. *International Journal of Psycho-Analysis* 38: 266–75.

—— (1957) Differentiation of the psychotic from the non-psychotic personality. In *Second Thoughts: Selected Papers on Psycho-Analysis*. London: Heinemann, 1967.

—— (1963) *Elements of Psycho-Analysis*. London: Heinemann.

—— (1967) *Second Thoughts: Selected Papers on Psycho-Analysis*. London: Heinemann.

—— (1975) *A Memoir of the Future, Book One: The Dream*. Brazil: Imago Editora.

Bon de Matte, L. (1970) Introduzione allo studio della identificazione proiettiva. *Psyche* 7, 1: 37–48.

Boole, G. (1954) *An Investigation of the Laws of Thought*. New York: Dover Publications.

Bowlby, J. (1969) *Attachment and Loss, I: Attachment*. London: Hogarth Press/Institute of Psycho-Analysis.

—— (1973) *Attachment and Loss, II: Separation, Anxiety and Anger*. London: Hogarth Press/Institute of Psycho-Analysis.

Bria, P. (1981) Introduction to the Italian translation of I. Matte-Blanco *The Unconscious as Infinite Sets*. Torino: Einaudi.

Brierley, M. (1951) *Trends in Psycho-Analysis*. London: Hogarth Press.

Cecconi, J. P. and Stampacchia, G. (1966) (1974) *Analisi matematica*. Napoli: Liguori.

Courant, R. and Robbins, A. (1941) *What Is Mathematics?* Oxford: Oxford University Press, 1969.

De Bianchedi, Tabac, E., Antar, R., De Podetti, M. R., De Piccolo, G., Miravent, I., De Cortiñas, L., De Boschan, L.T., and Waserman, M. (1984) Beyond Freudian metapsychology. *International Journal of Psycho-Analysis* 65, 4: 389–98.

Ellenberger, H. F. (1970) *The Discovery of the Unconscious*. New York: Basic Books.

Evans, M. G. (1946) Unpublished communication read to the British Psycho-Analytical Society. Quoted by Melanie Klein in 'Notes on some schizoid, mechanisms' in M. Klein, P. Heimann, S. Isaacs and J. Riviere *Developments in Psycho-analysis*, London: Hogarth Press, 1952.

Ferenczi, S. (1909) Introjection and transference. In *First Contributions to Psycho-Analysis*. London: Hogarth Press, 1952.

—— (1915) The analysis of comparisons. In *Further Contributions to the Theory and Technique of Psycho-Analysis*. London: Hogarth Press, 1950.

—— (1926) The problem of acceptance of unpleasant ideas – advances in the knowledge of the sense of reality. In *Further Contributions to the Theory and Technique of Psycho-Analysis*. London: Hogarth Press, 1950.

Fraenkel, A. A., Bar-Hillel, Y., and Levy, A. (1973) *Foundations of Set Theory*. Amsterdam and London: North-Holland Publishing.

Freud, A. (1969) *Normality and Pathology in Childhood*. London: Hogarth Press/Institute of Psycho-Analysis.

Freud, S.: all quotations are from *The Standard Edition of the Complete Psychological Works of Sigmund Freud*, 24 vols. London: Hogarth Press/Institute of Psycho-Analysis.

—— (1892–99) Extracts from the Fliess papers: Draft H; Draft K. In SE 1.

—— (1894) The neuro-psychoses of defence. In SE 3.

—— (1896) Further remarks on the neuro-psychoses of defence. In SE 3.

—— (1900) *The Interpretation of Dreams*. SE 4, 5.

—— (1905) *Jokes and Their Relation to the Unconscious*. SE 8.

—— (1909) Notes upon a case of obsessional neurosis [the Rat-Man]. In SE 10.

—— (1910a) *Leonardo da Vinci and a Memory of His Childhood*. In SE 11.

—— (1910b) 'Wild' psycho-analysis. In SE 11.

—— (1911) Psycho-analytic notes on an autobiographical account of a case of paranoia (dementia paranoides) [the Schreber case]. In SE 12.

—— (1913a) The claims of psycho-analysis to scientific interest. In SE 13.

—— (1913b) *Totem and Taboo*. In SE 13.

—— (1915a) Instincts and their vicissitudes. In SE 14.

—— (1915b) The unconscious. In SE 14.

—— (1917a) Mourning and melancholia. In SE 14.

—— (1917b) A metapsychological supplement to the theory of dreams. In SE 14.

—— (1916–17) *Introductory Lectures on Psycho-Analysis*. SE 15, 16.

—— (1921) *Group Psychology and the Analysis of the Ego*. In SE 18.

—— (1923) *The Ego and the Id*. In SE 19.

—— (1924) The dissolution of the Oedipus complex. In SE 19.

—— (1925a) Negation. In SE 19.

—— (1925b) *An Autobiographical Study*. In SE 20.

—— (1933) *New Introductory Lectures on Psycho-Analysis*. In SE 22.

—— (1938a) *An Outline of Psycho-Analysis*. In SE 23.

—— (1938b) Some elementary lessons in psycho-analysis. In SE 23.

Fuchs, S. H. (1937) On introjection. *International Journal of Psycho-Analysis* 18: 268–93.

Grinberg, L. (1962) On a specific aspect of counter-transference due to the patient's projective identification. *International Journal of Psycho-Analysis* 43: 436–40.

—— (1963) Psicopatologia de la identificación y contraidentificación proyectivas y de la contratransferencia. *Revista de Psicoanálisis* 20, 2: 112–23.

Guntrip, H. (1968) *Schizoid Phenomena, Object-Relations and the Self*. London: Hogarth Press/Institute of Psycho-Analysis.

Hadamard, J. (1945) *The Psychology of Invention in the Mathematical Field*. Princeton NJ: Princeton University Press.

Hartmann, H. (1964) *Essays on Ego Psychology*. London: Hogarth Press.

Heimann, P. (1952) Certain functions of introjection and projection in early infancy. In M. Klein, P. Heimann, S. Isaacs, and J. Riviere *Developments in Psycho-Analysis*. London: Hogarth Press.

Hessen, J. (1950) *Lehrbuch der Philosophie*, 3 vols. Munich: E. Reinhardt.

Jaques, E. (1955) Social systems as a defence against persecutory and depressive anxiety. In M. Klein, P. Heimann, and R. E. Money-Kyrle *New Directions in Psycho-Analysis*, London: Tavistock.

Jammer, M. (1987) Zeno's paradoxes today. In Giuliano Toralto di Francia (ed.) *Infinity in Science*. Rome: Instituto della Enciclopedia Italiana.

Jones, E. (1938) *Papers on Psycho-Analysis*. London: Baillière, Tindall & Cox, 4th edn.

Kant, I. (1781) *Kritik der reinen Vernunft*. In *Sämtliche Werke*, Vol. 2. Frankfurt: Insel, 1956.

Kernberg, O. F. (1980) Some implications of object relations theory for psycho-analytic technique. In H. P. Blum (ed.) *Psycho-Analytic Explor-*

ations of Technique. New York: International Universities Press.

Klein, M., (1932) *The Psycho-Analysis of Children.* London: Hogarth Press.

—— (1935) A contribution to the psychogenesis of manic-depressive states. *International Journal of Psycho-Analysis* 16: 145–74.

—— (1946) Notes on some schizoid mechanisms. In M. Klein, P. Heimann, S. Isaacs, and J. Riviere *Developments in Psycho-Analysis.* London: Hogarth Press, 1952.

—— (1948) *Contributions to Psycho-Analysis 1921–45.* London: Hogarth Press.

—— Heiman, P., Isaacs, S., and Riviere, J. (1952) *Developments in Psychoanalysis.* London: Hogarth Press.

—— (1955) On identification. In M. Klein, P. Heimann, and R. E. Money-Kyrle *New Directions in Psycho-Analysis.* London: Tavistock.

—— (1957) *Envy and Gratitude.* London: Tavistock.

—— (1961) *Narrative of a Child Analysis.* London: Hogarth Press.

—— (1963) *Our Adult World and Other Essays.* London: Heinemann Medical.

Kline, M. (1953) *Mathematics in Western Culture.* Oxford: Oxford University Press.

Lampl-de-Groot, J. A. (1954) Problems of psycho-analytic training. *International Journal of Psycho-Analysis* 35: 184–87.

Laplanche, J. and Pontalis, J.-B. (1973) *The Language of Psycho-Analysis.* London: Hogarth Press/Institute of Psycho-Analysis.

Lipschutz, S. (1965) *Theory and Problems of Set Theory and Related Topics.* New York: McGraw-Hill.

Lombardo-Radice (1967) *Instituzioni de Algebra Astratta.* Milan: Feltrinelli.

Lotze, H. (1856) *Mikrokosmus.* Leipzig: S. Hirzel, 5th edn, Vol. 3, 1909.

Manara, C. F. (1980) Spazio. *Enciclopedia della Scienza e della Tecnica* 11: 556.

Martinelli, E. (1974) *Il Metodo delle Coordinate.* Rome: V. Veschi.

Matte-Blanco, I. (1940) Some reflections on psycho-dynamics. *International Journal of Psycho-Analysis* 21: 253–79.

—— (1943) An approach to the problems of spatial extension in the mind. *International Journal of Psycho-Analysis* 25: 180.

—— (1954) *Lo psiquico y la naturaleza humana.* Santiago: Ediciones de la Universidad de Chile.

—— (1955) *Estudios de Psicologia dinámica.* Santiago: Ediciones de la Universidad de Chile.

—— (1959) Expression in symbolic logic of the characteristics of the system unconscious or the logic of the system unconscious. *International Journal of Psycho-Analysis* 40: 1–5.

—— (1973) Le quattro antinomie dell'instinto di morte. In *Enciclopedia 1973* Instituto della Enciclopedia Italiana.

—— (1975a) *The Unconscious as Infinite Sets: An Essay in Bi-Logic.* London:

Duckworth.

—— (1975b) Creatività ed ortodossia. *Rivista Psicoanalitica* 21.

—— (1976a) *God unknowable* (unpublished).

—— (1976b) Basic logico-mathematical structures in schizophrenia. In D. Richter (ed.) *Schizophrenia Today*. Oxford: Pergamon Press.

—— (1978) Un contributo psicoanalitico al pensiero logico e matematico. In *Psicoanalisi e Instituzioni* the Proceedings of the International Congress at the University of Milan, 1976. Florence: Le Monnier.

—— (1980) Infinito matematico: struttura bi-logica (da una riflessione psicoanalitica ad una riflessione matematica). In *Scienza, Linguaggio e Metafisica*. Naples: Guida.

—— (1981) Reflecting with Bion. In J. S. Grotstein (ed.) *Do I Dare Disturb the Universe?* Beverly Hills: Caesura Press.

—— (1982) Scoperte freudiane, limiti e sviluppi della formalizzazione. In Mario Pissacroia (ed.) *Delle Psicoanalisi possibili: Bion, Lacan, Matte Blanco*. Rome: Borla.

—— (1984) Reply to Ross Skelton's paper 'Understanding Matte-Blanco'. *International Journal of Psycho-Analysis* 65, 4: 445–60.

Meltzer, D. (1967) *The Psychoanalytic Process*. London: Heinemann Medical.

—— (1975) *Explorations in Autism*. Perthshire: Clunie Press.

Mire y Lopez, E. (1946) *Psiquiatria*. Buenos Aires: 'El Ateneo'.

Nagami, K. (1970) *Dimension Theory*. London: Academic Press.

Nelkon, M. (1981) *Principles of Physics*. St Albans: Hart–Davis Educational, 8th edn.

Niederland, W. G. (1959) Schreber: father and son. *Psychoanalytic Quarterly* 28: 151–69.

Olivetti Belardinelli, M. (1971) *Identificazione e Projezione: Naturale Caratteristiche*. Bologna: Cappelli.

Piaget, J. (1947) *The Psychology of Intelligence*. London: Routledge & Kegan Paul.

Rascovsky, A. (1960) *El Psiquismo Fetal*. Buenos Aires: Paidos.

Rayner, E. (1981) Infinite experiences, affects and the characteristics of the unconscious. *International Journal of Psycho-Analysis* 62: 403–12.

Riviere, J. (1936) On the genesis of psychical conflict in earliest infancy. In *Developments in Psycho-Analysis*. London: Hogarth Press.

Russell, B. (1903) *Principles of Mathematics*. London: Allen & Unwin, 1937. Spanish translation, Buenos Aires: Espasa-Calpe, 1948.

Rycroft, C. W. (1968) *A Critical Dictionary of Psycho-Analysis*. London: Nelson.

Sandler, J. and Joffe, W. G. (1967) The tendency to persistence in psychological function and development. *Bulletin of the Menninger Clinic* 31: 257–71.

Schafer, R. (1968) *Aspects of Internalization*. New York: International

Universities Press.

Schatzman, M. (1971) Paranoia or persecution: the case of Schreber. *Family Process* 10, 2: 177–207.

Segal, H. (1964) *Introduction to the Work of Melanie Klein*. London: Hogarth Press, 1973.

Sheldon, W. H. (1940) *The Varieties of Human Physique*. New York and London: Harper Brothers.

—— (1942) *The Varieties of Temperament*. New York and London: Harper Brothers.

Sommerville, D. M. Y. (1929) *An Introduction to the Geometry of n Dimensions*. New York: Dover, 1958.

Spiegel, M. R. (1974) *Advanced Calculus* (Schaum's Outline). New York: McGraw-Hill.

Storch, A. (1924) *The Primitive Archaic Forms of Inner Experiences and Thought in Schizophrenia*. New York and Washington: Nervous and Mental Disease Publishing Co. (trans. from the German).

Strachey, A. (1941) A note on the use of the word 'internal'. *International Journal of Psycho-Analysis* 22: 37–43.

Strachey, J. In SE 3: 184, n.; SE 14: 24; SE 15: 6, editor's introduction; SE 20: 174.

Toynbee, A. (1948) *A Study of History*. London: Oxford University Press.

Van der Leeuw, P. J. (1969) On Freud's theory formation. *International Journal of Psycho-Analysis* 50, 4: 573–81.

Viola, T. (1974) *Introduzione alla teoria degli insiemi*. Turin: Boringhieri.

Index

Abbott, E. 302
Abraham, K. 102, 110, 177–8, 184, 315
absence: of mutual contradiction and
   negation 8, 9, 16, 24–5, 60; and
   presence of temporal succession,
   alternation between 9, 12, 16, 26, 61
abstract space 289–90
abstraction cancelled by principle of
   symmetry 78–9
affects, see emotions
aggression: 193, 195; and asymmetry 54,
   170; Klein on 140–1, 148, 162; level of
   169–70; of traumatized people 162–4
aircraft, dream about 252–9, 264–7
Alassi (alternating asymmetrical-
   symmetrical structure) 33, 37, 46–7,
   50, 109, 204
alephs 64
alteration of ego 103–5
alternating asymmetrical-symmetrical
   structure, see Alassi
alternation: between absence and
   presence of temporal succession 9, 12,
   16, 26, 61; equivalence-identity and
   conjunction of 9, 13, 16, 26, 61
anabolism 178
anaesthetics, effect of 233–4
animism 182, 198
antinomic bi-logical structures,
   numbered examples of: (1) 44–5; (2)
   45; (3) 47; (4) 47–8; (5) 49–50; (6) 72;
   (7) 72–3; (8) 73–5; (9) 96; (10) 98;

(11) 187; (12) 87; (13) 201–2; (14) 202;
   (15) 202–3; (16) 203–4; (17) 205–7;
   (18) 207–8; (19) 208–9; (20) 210–14;
   (21) 214–17; (22) 219–20; (23) 220–3;
   (24) 223–4; (25) 225; (26) 225–7; (27)
   233–4; (28) 234–5; (29) 236–7, 243,
   244; (30) 245–51; (31) 252–9, 264–7;
   (32) 270
antinomy, fundamental, of human
   beings and world: 43, 44, 70–99, 185;
   concept, example of 70–6; emotion
   and unconscious, relation between
   83–5; examples of, see antinomic bi-
   logical structures, numbered
   examples of; introjection and
   projection and 133; modes and logics
   73, 77–81, 82–3; symmetry as
   expression of falsehood 85–7;
   unconsciousness of Freudian
   unconscious 87–92; unitary super-
   logic 92–6
anxiety: 193; castration 197; and Klein's
   work 140, 143, 144–5, 154
Aquinas, St Thomas 137n.
Archimedes' principle 7
Aristotelian logic 63, 105
assertion and negation treated as
   identical 13
assimilation 179, 181–2
assimilatory delusions 103, 104–5
asymmetrical-symmetrical structures, see
   Alassi and Simassi; see also asymmetry

dizziness of deep unconscious 141, 217, 228

dreams: bi-modal frenzy and 245–51 (*see also* Tridim); of books by Freud 210, 211, 213; clinical examples of 208–9, 210–17, 220–2, 252–9, 264–7; Freud on 4, 13–17, 27, 156, 217, 255, 260–3, 265; symmetry in 25, 36; *see also* bi-modal frenzy; phantasy

eating 131–2, 225–7

Edison, T. A. 99

ego: alteration of 103–5; and id and super-ego 135; identification with object, *see* identification by introjection; impoverishment of 153, 192; multiplicity in 134–5; object and 274; weakened 104–5, 192; *see also* ego-ideal

ego-ideal: 152, 191; delegation to 205–7; object as substitute for 152; replaced by object 120, 122, 123; *see also* ego

Einstein, A. 96–7, 98–9, 151, 183, 312

emotions/feelings: and antinomy, fundamental 76, 96, 97–8; awareness of 91; bi-logical structures and 62, 76, 91; conscious zone of 53; haziness and 96, 97; infinity and 39–41; intensity of 141–2, 255; Klein and 139, 140–5, 154; 'memories' in 74, 162–4; as mother of thinking 98; prejudice and 58; principle of symmetry and 20–1, 62; schizophrenia and 54; scientific discoveries and 97, 183; unconscious and 83–5; *see also* anxiety; fear; love

enrichment 153

epistemological see-saw 49–52

epistemology 60

equinumerosity 69, 140

equivalence-identity and conjunction of alternation 9, 13, 16, 26, 61

ethology and symmetrization 180–2

Evans, M. G. 193, 321

examples, *see* antinomic bi-logical structures, numbered examples of

expulsion, disavowal-denial 187–8, 191, 193, 201–2, 206

exterior 299–300

external and internal: described 127–8; mathematical concepts of 298–305;

realities contrasted 255–7; reasons for 124–7

external object 278

external reality replaced by internal reality 9, 11, 16, 26, 61

external world 130–1; different from internal 127

externalization, *see* projection

falsehood, symmetry as expression of 85–7

fantasy: 129, 137, 151; about primal scene 236–41; *see also* phantasy

fathers, sets of 53, 55; *see also* penis

fear 140, 141, 142

feeling, *see* emotions

'fending off', *see* splitting

Ferenczi, S. 102, 121, 184

finality of inductive projective identification 189

finite quantities, *see* mathematical

fixation, points of 106

Fliess papers 103–6

food, *see* eating

formalization 64

Franklin, B. 146

Frege, G. 64

frenzy, *see* bi-logical frenzy; bi-modal frenzy; symmetrical frenzy

Freud, A. 172–3, 177, 211

Freud, S./Freudians: on death instinct 181, 218; on disavowal-denial 187, 188, 203–4, 206; dream of books by 210, 211, 213; on dreams 4, 13–17, 27, 156, 217, 255, 260–3, 265; on ego, id and super-ego 135, 152, 191; on identification and projection 120–3, 152, 161, 320–1; on internal world 27–41; on introjection 37–8, 131–4, 171–2, 184; on libido 171–2; masculine mode of thinking of 162; on negation 203–4; on object 273–5; on repression 118, 172; on symbol 242; *see also* bi-logical structures, Freudian; projection, Freudian; unconscious, Freudian

fusion and separation 140

Galileo, G. 66, 93

Galton, Sir F. 10

generalization/s: principles of (PG) 45;